The first forty years of p[...] by the Nehru-Gandhi family: a phenomenon unique [...] of modern democracies. It is unique not only because three generations of the same family produced prime ministers in succession, but also as the challenges they faced were unparalleled.

The Dynasty covers this era in all its bewildering diversity. It is a book of interpretation and analysis, yet anecdotal and lively, bringing to life the critical period in which the Dynasty made a decisive contribution towards the shaping of modern India.

As a career civil servant S. S. Gill was directly associated with the framing and implementation of government policies for almost the entire duration of the Dynasty's rule. He also had the opportunity of working closely with Indira Gandhi and Rajiv Gandhi. While writing this book he interviewed scores of politicans and bureaucrats who had served the three prime ministers for years. This gives the narrative the intimacy and directness of an insider's account.

Some readers may feel that, at times, the author has been irreverent to the illustrious members of the Dynasty. But any such impression would be based on the writer's inability to bend inconvenient facts to pay homage to celebrity.

S. S. Gill, a career civil servant, retired as Secretary, Ministry of Information and Broadcasting in 1985. The same year he was awarded the Padma Bhushan.

Since his retirement he has been regularly contributing articles to leading English dailies and magazines.

THE DYNASTY

*A Political Biography of the
Premier Ruling Family
of Modern India*

HarperCollins *Publishers* India

HarperCollins Publishers India Pvt Ltd
7/16 Ansari Road, Daryaganj, New Delhi 110 002

First published by HarperCollins Publishers India 1996
First published in Paperback 1997

ISBN 81-7223-265-9

Typeset in Palatino by
Megatechnics
19A Ansari Road
New Delhi 110 002

Printed in India by
Gopsons Papers Ltd
A-28 Sector IX
Noida 201 301

To

SATYA

— Our little Mother Teresa

One owes respect to the living.
To the dead one owes nothing
but the truth.
— *VOLTAIRE*

Acknowledgements

While writing this book I interviewed scores of politicians, civil servants and scholars. This not only gave me a better understanding of the forces that shaped the Nehru-Gandhi era, it also provided deeper insights into the character of the three members of the Dynasty. It is my privilege to acknowledge my debt of gratitude to the following persons in this connection.

I had several sessions with Shri I.K. Gujral and I learnt a great deal from him. Shri Chandrajit Yadav, Smt. Subhadra Joshi and Dr. Karan Singh liberally shared with me impressions of their close association with Mrs. Indira Gandhi.

For the Rajiv era I had the opportunity to extensively interview Sarva Shri Arun Nehru, Arun Singh, Arif Mohammad Khan, Natwar Singh and Mani Shankar Aiyar.

I am particularly thankful to Profs. Rajni Kothari, Bipan Chandra, Ajit Mozoomdar, Shri John Lal and S. Patwant Singh for having agreed to go through some portions of my book, and their highly perceptive comments.

My discussions with Sarva Shri Nikhil Chakravartty, Jaipal Reddy, George Verghese, Rajmohan Gandhi and Sharada Prasad were extremely useful.

I profited much by my wide-ranging talks with Profs. Ravinder Kumar, Yogendra Singh, D.L. Sheth, G.S. Bhalla and Dipankar Gupta.

It was highly informative to talk to a number of civil servants who had worked closely with Mrs. Gandhi and Rajiv Gandhi. They spoke to me very freely, but on condition of anonymity. The only person who did not impose this restriction was Shri N.K. Mukarji, ICS, and I am much indebted to him for his candid comments.

In the end I must also thank my daughter-in-law, Kamini Gill, who helped me in punching the manuscript on my PC.

Whereas I am highly indebted to the persons mentioned above in the writing of this book, the responsibility for the views expressed in it is entirely mine.

S.S. Gill

Contents

INDIRA GANDHI

RAJIV GANDHI

Preface

When a friend learnt that I was writing a book on the Nehru-Gandhi dynasty, he asked as to how will it be different from scores of tomes already written on the subject. Then I also recalled a publisher's lament that most of the people who have half a mind to write a book, write it. And in this age of rapidly vanishing forests, one should go easy on the use of paper to save trees.

Yet, despite these forbidding reasons I have gone ahead with my project. For one thing, like all authors, I am convinced that mine is a different book. I am not aware of any other publication which covers the four decades of the Nehru-Gandhi era as a specific period in the history of post-Independence India. Secondly, my narration is confined only to the years of power of Jawaharlal Nehru, Indira Gandhi and Rajiv Gandhi. It is essentially a political biography, with particulars of personal life touched upon only so far as they illuminate political actions.

In one respect I may claim a special association with the period covered in this book. I was selected to the IAS in 1952 and retired from service in 1985. So, I joined government service when the First Five Year Plan was launched. I was closely associated with land reforms and community development as a district collector, served as Personnel Manager, Bhilai Steel Plant, and as Home Secretary to the government of Madhya Pradesh. I was working in the Central Secretariat, New Delhi, during the Emergency. I drafted the Report of the Mandal Commission as its Secretary, and was appointed Secretary General for organizing the IX Asian Games. I was Secretary, Ministry of Information and Broadcasting during Operation Blue Star, Indira Gandhi's assassination and Rajiv Gandhi's installation as prime minister.

My only purpose in giving these tedious details is to make the point that for almost the entire period under review, I was directly associated with programme implementation and policy formulation in both the state and Central governments. This, I presume, gives immediacy and directness of an insider to my account.

Most biographies narrate events in a chronological order. I have, instead, adopted a thematic approach. I feel that this lends sharper focus to various aspects of my subject's regime as compared to a sequential description cluttered with a multitude of on-going activities. For instance, separate chapters on 'Democracy' and 'Socialism' in the Nehru section gave me a better opportunity to discuss his political credo, than I could in a chronological narrative.

I had the good fortune of personally knowing several politicians and civil servants who served Indira Gandhi, and most of those who worked closely with Rajiv Gandhi. I had detailed discussions with these persons which gave me valuable insights into the Nehru-Gandhi era. Whereas several politicians agreed to be identified, most civil servants preferred anonymity. Thus, many of my observations will have to be accepted on trust. This is particularly so about the Rajiv period. But I have tried to be very careful in handling unrecorded facts, as I realize that my book stands or falls with its credibility. My sources are mostly primary, and all facts likely to raise controversy have been cross-checked from at least two sources.

Some readers may feel that I have not been sufficiently respectful to members of the greatest political dynasty of modern times. My only defence is that I had no personal axe to grind, and carried no chip on my shoulder. Nehru was a hero to me in my youth. I received nothing but kindness from Indira Gandhi and Rajiv. I got good postings and two Presidential awards, including the Padma Bhushan.

This is essentially a book of interpretation and analysis; I have tried to critically appraise the performance of the three members of the dynasty during the four decades of their prime ministership. Somebody said that history is a jury which can neither be packed nor bribed. As I was too small a fry to load the dice of history, I chose to be its humble scribe.

I may also mention a serious handicap from which every

biographer of an Indian prime minister is bound to suffer. Owing to its obsessive concern with secrecy, the government does not allow private persons to see official records. Even in the case of Jawaharlal Nehru, the published collected works cover only the first *four* years of his prime ministership. And the Nehru Memorial Museum and Library does not allow public access to the Nehru papers for the post-Independence period. Sonia Gandhi is the sole custodian of all records relating to the Indira and Rajiv eras. So far, no researcher has been allowed to consult them.

This denial of access to his source material proves a crippling constraint for a biographer. Inevitably, it forces him to rely either on secondary sources or personal interviews. In several cases, it becomes impossible to trace even documented references to the original source. I would request my readers to keep this limitation in mind while wanting me to quote chapter and verse in support of some of my observations.

S.S. Gill

Jawaharlal Nehru

1

The Grey Dawn

At the stroke of the midnight hour on 15 August 1947, when Jawaharlal Nehru was celebrating India's tryst with destiny and the nation stepped out from the old to the new, for millions it was a day of deep mourning. Countless innocents on both sides of the divide were being butchered, and the communal frenzy that had seized the masses was raging like a mad bull. Carrying their meagre belongings and heavy loads of woe, torrents of refugees were continuously pouring into Punjab and West Bengal, over-straining the limited civic amenities and slender resources of these truncated states. Soon this deluge of human misery was to over-flow into adjoining states and set them ablaze with fires of vengeance. Delhi itself became a scene of unprecedented violence and Nehru had to personally jump amidst frenzied crowds to save some victims of mob fury.

The Indian people had waged a most heroic struggle to gain freedom. But its finale had left the national leaders downcast and vanquished. While accepting the Mountbatten Plan Nehru had said, "It is with no joy in my heart that I commend these proposals..." Mahatma Gandhi's agony was more intense. In January, 1946, he had told Maulana Azad,"If the Congress wishes to accept partition, it will be over my dead body."[1]

But the most deeply shaken were the great Muslim patriots like Maulana Azad and Khan Abdul Ghaffar Khan. The Maulana said, "India gained her freedom, but lost her unity."[2] And when the lion-hearted Khan learnt that the Congress had accepted Partition, he "was completely stunned" and repeatedly said, "the Frontier would regard it as a treachery if the Congress now threw the Khudai Khidmatgars to the wolves."[3]

This blood-splattered backdrop to India's freedom was not the best augury for her future. Other countries have also paid heavily in human lives to win independence. But that blood was shed in a noble cause and the sacrifice fired the imagination of their people for generations. The carnage accompanying the Partition had no connection with shaking off the colonial yoke. An act of sheer barbarism, it only brutalized the surviving populace and left behind a trail of bitterness, hatred and vengeance.

It is an irony of history that the most benign act of the colonial rulers was largely responsible for the Partition holocaust which saddled Nehru with a back-breaking burden. The Labour government of Prime Minister Clement Attlee suddenly announced on 20 February 1947 that the British would leave India on 30 June 1948. Lord Mountbatten, the new Viceroy appointed in March 1947 to oversee the transfer of power, advanced the date of withdrawal to 15 August 1947. So, the entire business of partitioning a subcontinent, dividing its civil services and the armed forces, apportioning respective shares of all assets down to the office equipment, had to be completed in just 72 days. And within this period a new administrative set-up had to materialize to take over the governance of the newly-born country.

The British government and their Viceroy had, of course, their own reasons for this hasty retreat. With a rapidly deteriorating law and order situation and communal riots erupting all over, the colonial rulers wanted to escape the blame for the country slipping into anarchy. It served their interests to quit India at the earliest.

The first Prime Minister of India thus found himself engulfed by a plethora of problems and crises even before he had taken the oath of office. Nehru was not a man to mope or moan, indulge in self-pity, or seek alibis. From the start he set himself a gruelling work-schedule of 18 hours a day, and kept it up for the seventeen years of his prime ministership.

His most pressing problem was that of containing the flood of refugees gushing into the country from both East and West Pakistan. The dimensions of this catastrophe can be visualized from the tally of half a million dead and 5-6 million rendered homeless. It was a gigantic task to help these displaced people get over the trauma of Partition, piece together the broken bits of their lives, and revive their hopes in a meaningful future. Thousands of refugee camps were improvised to give them temporary shelter. Besides providing the bare necessities of life, arrangements were made for the schooling of children, health care and sanitation. A Ministry of Relief and Rehabilitation was created to settle the homeless, find jobs for the unemployed, arrange exchange of property between the Indian and Pakistani refugees, advance educational and business loans, and attend to such other matters.

Even more urgent was the question of preventing a retaliatory backlash against the Muslim population of India. Nehru had before him the evidence of rapidly escalating communal reprisals in the Capital, and alarming reports of similar happenings were coming in from several parts of the country. He fought this menace on a war footing and, ignoring some dissenting voices in his cabinet, ordered firm punitive action against the rampaging mobs.

Anyway, these were one-time problems; they were not integral to the process of the transfer of power, and they were resolved in due course. Nehru's real challenges lay elsewhere. India had become independent after suffering the ravages of colonial exploitation for two centuries. The country's industry was decimated, the famed urban handicrafts ruined and rural artisans thrown out of work, "thus resulting in the progressive decline and disruption of centuries-old union between agriculture and manufacturing industry."[4]

The challenge to repair, reconstruct and reshape the country was a task of mind-boggling complexity. Several factors combined to define Nehru's nation-building agenda. Foremost, obviously, were the values embodied in the National Movement inculcated under the influence of Mahatma Gandhi. These were: an abiding concern for the poor; national unity through mass mobilization;

communal harmony; culture of consensus; abhorrence of violence; sanctity of means; and total commitment to democratic norms. These values were enshrined in the Indian Constitution, and served as the mandate for Jawaharlal. Within the broad framework of this mandate there was the task of formulating concrete policies and programmes, and creating suitable institutions and instrumentalities for the realization of national goals. It was in this arena of action and implementation that Nehru's real battle lay.

Unlike Gandhi, it was an article of faith with Nehru that India's salvation lay in modernization through industrialization and cultivation of a scientific temper. This, to him, was the surest way for the traditional Indian society to pull out of the mire of conservatism, superstition and obscurantism, and imbibe the mores and values of a progressive, modern, industrial society.

There were no models available to Nehru in 1947-48 as to how a backward country with a long history of colonial abuse could modernize through whatever means. However, Nehru not only had a clear idea of his goals, but also the means by which to achieve them. For him growth and social justice had to be achieved with the 'willing cooperation' of the people and without resort to coercion or violence.

Never before had a leader undertaken such a formidable enterprise. The agenda itself had immense dimensions and bristled with contradictions. It is a measure of the man that these daunting obstacles did not deter Nehru, nor deflect him from his chosen path. The stabilization of democracy and normal governance of such a problem-ridden country were stupendous tasks in themselves. But Nehru constantly kept enlarging the domain of his role as a prime minister and left hardly any area untouched which concerned the welfare and development of his country. It is the cosmic scale of his canvas and the all-embracing sweep of his global vision which make the Nehruvian saga so fascinating. It is packed with titanic activity, a ceaseless quest for new avenues, grand designs, glorious achievements, heartbreaking failures and Himalayan blunders.

An attempt has been made in the following pages to capture the essence of Nehru's vast agenda, and to appraise its lasting impact on the Indian polity. But before surveying his work, it may be useful to see Nehru as he saw himself, for his capacity for introspection is matched by few men of action.

2

Nehru on Nehru

*O*n completion of *The Discovery of India* Nehru wrote, "It is mine and not wholly mine, as I am constituted today; it represents rather some past self of mine which has already joined that long procession of other selves that existed for a while and faded away, leaving only memory behind."[1]

The fascination of Nehru-watching lies as much in the complexity of his multi-layered personality as in its variegated richness and emotional splendour. And you find him ever so ready to provide glimpses into the workings of his mind. But his introspection was essentially a cerebral activity. Though he wrote millions of words, nowhere do you find the veil lift on his private life. With the hurly-burly of public life claiming all his time, it became an emotional necessity for him to be all by himself to recharge his mental batteries:

"In the midst of activity, I could separate myself from it (the crowd) and look at it as a thing apart. Sometimes, I would steal an hour or two, and forgetting my usual preoccupations, retire into that cloistered chamber of my mind and live, for a while, another life."[2]

It is in this 'cloistered chamber' that Nehru mused on life and its vagaries, nursing his loneliness, watching the flux of time and the changes wrought by it and, occasionally, making some delightfully candid confessions. Perhaps no other mass leader has analysed his relationship to the crowds with such candour, or shown such a keen awareness of the predicament of being a product of two opposite cultures.

Nehru was Anglicized before he left for his schooling in England at the age of fifteen. His father, Motilal, the strongest childhood influence on him, was an ardent admirer of the British. Nehru's seven years spent in England left a deep imprint on his mind. "I had imbibed most of the prejudices of Harrow and Cambridge. And in my likes and dislikes I was perhaps more an Englishman than an Indian."

Even in later life he repeatedly acknowledged the profound impact of Western thought on him. "... I approached her (India) almost as an alien critic, full of dislike for the present as well as for many of the relics of the past that I saw. To some extent I came to her via the West, and looked at her as a friendly Westerner might have done."[3]

But this cultural alienation caused him considerable discomfort and made him a spiritual exile. It could be one reason why he delved deep into India's past to discover the mainsprings of her civilization:

> I have become a queer mixture of the East and West, out of place everywhere, at home nowhere. Perhaps my thoughts and approach to life are more akin to what is called Western than Eastern, but India clings to me, as she does to all her children, in innumerable ways; and behind me lie, somewhere in the subconscious, racial memories of a hundred ... generations of Brahmins. I cannot get rid of either that past inheritance or my recent acquisitions. They are both a part of me, and, though they help me in both the East and the West, they also create in me a feeling of spiritual loneliness....[4]

This feeling of loneliness would stay with him all his life. It was much aggravated by the near denial of a normal family life owing to circumstances beyond his control. The postscript to his autobiography shows how utterly forlorn he felt at times:

> My wife's death in Switzerland ended a chapter of my existence and took away much from my life that had been a part of my being... My mother's death later broke a final link with the past. My daughter was away studying at Oxford. I would return to my home from my wanderings almost unwillingly, and sit in that deserted house all by myself...[5]

But more than his personal tragedies, Nehru's loneliness arose out of an existential predicament. In a letter to his wife Kamala he wrote:

> After these long years of inner turmoil, struggle and deep
> reflection, I gradually reached certain conclusions. But as I went
> on untying the knots of my mind, I felt that I was getting further
> and further away from others.... The gulf between them and me
> went on widening... After seeing the attitudes of my colleagues,
> I started feeling day by day that I will have to travel alone on
> my journey.[6]

Nehru frequently looked at the passing cavalcade of humanity
through the window of his 'cloistered chamber' and wistfully
observed life changing and moulding all that it touched. Even
more acutely was he aware of the changes within. From his prison
cell he wrote to his sister Vijaylakshmi Pandit:

> I have become introspective in jail and I see a long procession of
> strangers calling themselves by my name, rather like me and yet
> different, with something about them that attracts and something
> that repels. And this long procession of past selves gradually
> merges into the present ever-changing self. Which of these
> innumerable shadow selves is me?[7]

Recalling the interval between the writing of *Autobiography* and
The Discovery of India he observes:

> I suppose I have changed a good deal in these twelve years. I
> have grown more contemplative. There is perhaps a little more
> poise and equilibrium, some sense of detachment, a greater
> calmness of spirit.[8]

Nehru spent nine years of his adult life in jail and this gave him
time not only for writing books, but for nostalgic reminiscences:

> The years I have spent in prison!... How many yesterdays of my
> youth lie buried here; and sometimes I see the ghosts of these
> dead yesterdays rise up, bringing poignant memories, and
> whispering to me: "Was it worthwhile?" There is no hesitation
> about the answer — If I were given the chance to go through my
> life again... my major decisions in public affairs would remain
> untouched.[9]

Public affairs: that is where Nehru sought refuge from his
haunting loneliness. And that was also the way to his *nirvana*. For
an intellectual who loved books and the life of the mind, the

changeover to a life of action was total:

> Long long ago I tried to learn from books and perhaps I learnt
> something from them. But all my later lessons have been learnt
> from men and women—humanity in the mass. It is a hard school
> but an efficient one, and it has little place in it for the graces.[10]

Now the hard school of life and its tumultuous action absorbed
him completely. However, for Nehru, action could never quite be
severed from intellection:

> The call for action has long been with me; not action divorced
> from thought, but rather flowing from it in continuous sequence.
> And when, rarely, there has been full harmony between the two,
> thought leading to action and finding its fulfillment in it... then I
> have sensed a certain fullness of life and a vivid intensity in that
> moment of existence.[11]

And there is no getting away from action in any case:

> Everywhere there is what is called the strength of life... All action
> is really a challenge to life.[12]

But whereas action exhilarated him and dulled the pain of
loneliness, it was the resolution of inner conflict which posed the
basic problem. "The real battlefield is in every person's body and
mind and decisions are made there only. Only their shadow falls
outside."[13]

Elaborating further, he writes:

> I became a battleground, where various forces struggled for
> mastery. I sought an escape from this; I tried to find harmony
> and equilibrium, and in this attempt I rushed into action. That
> gave me some peace; outer conflict relieved the strain of the inner
> struggle.[14]

A sensitive, cultured and private person, sucked into the vortex
of public life: that was the paradox of Nehru. If the cause was not
as great as the liberation of his country, he would have avoided
joining a mass movement. Politics was not his vocation, but circumstances made it his destiny.

His preference for privacy notwithstanding, he had a tremendous
zest for life and boundless energy to live it to the full. A life of
action certainly provided him the much-needed escape from the
tensions and conflicts of the 'battleground' within. Having landed

in the arena of the national struggle, he became its most active and itinerant torch-bearer. Even after Independence, his pace would have broken down persons half his age. His success in changing his persona made most of his countrymen think of him primarily as a man of action.

Nehru's first intimate contact with the masses came through his involvement with the problems of the peasants of Pratapgarh. "Since his university days he had a horror of speaking in public."[15] It was during this phase of his political life that he acquired confidence in public speaking. This also started his lifelong affair with the 'crowds', which shows an interesting facet of his personality. Whereas he had a deep affection for the people of India, his relationship with them was quite complex: "I have great faith in the masses of India, illiterate as most of them are. In spite of this illiteracy, which will, of course, rapidly disappear, they have a basic culture and a tenderness which makes life worthwhile for them and for others."[16]

And, "I do not idealise the conception of the masses and, as far as possible, I try to avoid thinking of them as a theoretical abstraction."[17]

Crowds fascinated him. "I am never tired of watching a crowd and playing upon its moods and a strange sense of kinship with it comes over me."[18] Also, the crowd invigorated him. "Whenever I feel stale and tired, I go among the people and I come back refreshed."

But despite his great rapport with the masses, he realized that the basis of the relationship was rather brittle:

> I took to the crowd and the crowd took to me, and yet I never lost myself in it; always I felt apart from it. From my separate mental perch I looked at it critically, and I never ceased to wonder how I, who was so different in every way from those thousands who surrounded me, different in habit, in desires, in mental and spiritual outlook, how I had managed to gain goodwill and a measure of confidence from these people.[19]

There was, no doubt, an element of illusion and make-believe in the hero-worship of Nehru. To the deprived masses, he was an idealized, fairy tale prince charming — an answer to their romantic fantasies. This scion of a wealthy family, so handsome

had renounced all worldly comforts for the sake
as a natural object for their veneration. But could
vds for granted? "Always I went straight to the
ed it, and so far I have always had courtesy and
m it, even though there was no agreement. But
crowds are fickle, and the future may have different experiences
in store for me."[20]

He was not only beset by such doubts, his patrician exclusive-
ness was not the stuff mass leaders are made of:

> The question that my friend had asked me still remained
> unanswered: did I not feel proud of this hero-worship of the
> crowd? I disliked it and wanted to run away from it, and yet I
> had got used to it, and when it was wholly absent, I rather missed
> it. Neither way brought satisfaction, but, on the whole, the crowd
> filled some inner need of mine. The notion that I could influence
> them and move them to action gave me a sense of authority over
> their minds and hearts; and this satisfied, to some extent, my will
> to power.[21]

Despite being a very private person, Nehru could be surprisingly
open about his failings and foibles. "I do not think I am a secretive
individual; I am probably franker about myself than the average
man," wrote Nehru in a letter to Padmaja Naidu. This trait was
essentially born of the deep personal integrity of the man, and
the absence in him of any cant and hypocrisy, but with, perhaps,
a dash of bravado.

After studying in England for 7 years, "... as I landed in Bombay, I was a bit of a prig with little to commend me."[22] Despite
being impressed by Fabian socialists in England, he admits, "My
politics had been those of the middle class, the bourgeois."[23]

Talking of Gandhi's influence on him in his early days, he says,
"I gave up smoking. I did not smoke for five or six years... this
was not just to make myself 'better' ... if I dislike smoking in
public, why should I do it in private? That is, if I did not want to
smoke in public, in a crowd, so it was untruthful to do something
in secret that I did not want to do in public..."[24]

Nehru was elected Congress President in 1929. His election
came about entirely because of Gandhi's pressure, as only 3 of

the 18 Provincial Committees had supported his candidature.[25]
Though he was elated at holding this prestigious post at 40, the
manner of his getting it made him very uncomfortable. "I have
seldom felt so annoyed and humiliated as I did at that election...
I did not come to it by the main entrance or even the side entrance;
I appeared suddenly by a trap door and bewildered the audience
into acceptance... My pride was hurt, and almost I felt like handing back the honour."[26]

In 1939 the election of Subhash Chandra Bose led to bickerings
within the Congress party. Even otherwise things were not going
well:

> I was disgusted with myself and in a press article I wrote: 'I fear
> I give little satisfaction to them (my colleagues), and yet that is
> not surprising, for I give even less satisfaction to myself. It is not
> out of this stuff that leadership comes and the sooner my colleagues
> realized this the better for them and me.'[27]

But it is in a personal letter to Padmaja Naidu that one by one
he peels off layers of pretence, sham and fakery with Dostoevsk-
yan rigour and takes almost a sadistic delight in self-flagellation:

> Many things are wrong with me... The first thing you must
> remember about me is that I have a knack of imposing on people...
> and I produce in their minds exaggerated notions about myself...
> Again you are wholly right in saying that I have been a failure
> in my individual relationships. I suppose the reason for this failure
> is my incapacity to give... I have been and am one of those who
> take from individuals without giving much in return...[28]

But his introspective *tour de force* is his celebrated article "The
Rashtrapati", published anonymously in *Modern Review* (Nov.
1937). It is hilariously puckish, bold and provocative. Perhaps no
mass leader has dissected his public image with such directness
and clinical detachment. Nehru had been elected Congress President twice, and there was talk of giving him a third term. He
describes the Rashtrapati moving through adoring crowds, his
face lit up by a smile:

> The smile passes away and yet again the face becomes stern and
> set, impassive in the midst of the emotion that it had roused in
> the multitude. Almost it seemed that the smile and the gesture

accompanying it had little reality behind them; they were just tricks of the trade to gain the goodwill of the crowds whose darling he had become. Was it so?

... Is all this natural or the carefully thought-out trickery of the public man? ... Whither is this going to lead him and the country? What lies behind this mask of his, what desires, what will to power, what insatiate longings?

... From the far north to Cape Comorin he has gone like some triumphant Caesar passing by, leaving a trail of glory and legend behind him. Is all this for him just a passing fancy which amuses him, or some deep design, or the play of some force which he himself does not know?

... Men like Jawaharlal Nehru, with all their capacity for great and good work, are unsafe in a democracy. He calls himself a democrat and a socialist... (but the) mind is ultimately a slave to the heart... A little twist and Jawaharlal might turn a dictator sweeping aside the paraphernalia of a slow-moving democracy.

The intensity of this introspection leaves you breathless! But is it also an exercise in self-catharsis, an attempt to exorcise the ghosts within by exposing them to the glare of daylight?

3

Nehru on Gandhi

When Nehru returned from England in 1912 after completing his studies, he had no clear idea as to what he wanted to do. He was vaguely interested in the national movement and attended the Bankipore Congress session the same year. "It was very much an English-knowing upper-class affair...," he observed. After joining the Allahabad High Court Bar he had a feeling of "being engulfed by routine of a pointless existence." "Politics, which to me meant the aggressive nationalist activity against foreign rule, offered no scope for this." Then came World War I and he followed its course with keen interest. He got married to Kamala in 1916.

It was with the anti-Rowlatt Act agitation that Gandhi really arrived on the Indian political scene. The call for action stirred Nehru and he wanted to join the Satyagraha Sabha. Motilal was appalled at his son's impulsive decision, and Gandhi advised Jawaharlal not to do anything which may upset his father. The agitation led to the massacre at Jallianwallah Bagh, causing countrywide revulsion against colonial rule. With a view to mobilizing the masses, Gandhi launched his Non-Cooperation Movement on 1 August 1920. This started not only the most active phase of the freedom struggle, it also commenced a deep, productive and lasting relationship between him and Jawaharlal.

Temperamentally and culturally there was nothing in common between them. One was the product of the Western liberal tradition, the other soaked in the Indian ethos. No wonder, being men of great integrity, they differed frequently and clashed once in a while. Nehru devotes large portions of his *Autobiography* to debunking various 'fads', 'backwardness' and the 'revivalism' of Gandhi, and its longest chapter deals with his 'Paradoxes'. It would be incorrect to say that Nehru had a love-hate relationship with Gandhi, yet it was not a very easy association either.

Of the two, Gandhi's was a much stronger personality. His means and ends were clearly defined, and he was not easily swayed by emotion. He influenced Nehru much more than Nehru influenced Gandhi. But it was an indirect sort of influence in several ways. To a large extent, Nehru imbibed Gandhian values in the very process of opposing him. This conflict also helped him to clarify and refine his own concepts and approaches.

Nehru was a rationalist; reason to him was the key to understanding and action. Gandhi, a deeply religious man, often relied on his instinct, intuition and mystical insight to reach his conclusions. This created problems for Nehru.

"As for Gandhi," wrote Nehru, "he was a very difficult person to understand, sometimes his language was almost incomprehensible to an average modern..."[1]

When Gandhi decided to 'fast unto death' in September 1932 on the issue of Communal awards, "I felt angry with him at his religious and sentimental approach to a political question, and his frequent references to God in connection with it. He even seemed to suggest that God had indicated the very date of the fast. What a terrible example to set."[2]

Later, when Gandhi began his 21-day fast in Yeravda prison in May 1933, Nehru wrote:

For me the fast was an incomprehensible thing... I wondered more and more if this was the right method in politics. It seemed to be sheer revivalism and clear thinking had not a ghost of a chance against it.[3]

Nehru was very unhappy at the signing of the Gandhi-Irwin pact resulting in the withdrawal of the Civil Disobedience Movement, and "I told him that his way of springing surprises upon us frightened me; there was something unknown about him which, in spite of the closest association for fourteen years, I could not understand at all and which filled me with apprehension. He admitted the presence of this unknown element in him, and said that he himself could not answer for it or foretell what it might lead to."[4]

No wonder once Nehru complained, "... a leader must have a rational grasp of the situation, and is expected to give adequate reasons for his political decisions, especially when he wants others to follow him."

Politically Gandhi was a great revolutionary, but socially he was a traditionalist. Nehru prided himself on being a modernist with a scientific outlook. It is this gulf which explains the differences in their outlook. Whereas they give an idea of Nehru's reaction to some traditional Indian attitudes and prejudices, they had little relevance to the national effort in which the two leaders were engaged. Their differences on ideology and political perspectives were more significant and, at times, led to serious clashes between the two.

Nehru had not only a logical mind, he had a definite, long-term view of the country's future:

"But about our goals there was an entire absence of clear thinking... Gandhiji was delightfully vague on the subject, and he did not encourage clear thinking about it either."[5]

Nehru, dejected after the collapse of the Civil Disobedience Movement, wrote in Alipore jail:

What after all was he aiming at? In spite of the closest association with him for many years I am not clear in my own mind about his objective. I doubt if he is clear himself. One step is enough for me, he says, and he does not try to peep into the future...[6]

In the larger context of social and economic justice, Jawaharlal was exasperated by Gandhi's refusal to differentiate between the exploited and exploiters:

With all his keen intellect and passion for bettering the downtrodden and the oppressed, why does he support a system, and a system which is obviously decaying, which creates this misery and waste? He seeks a way out, it is true, but is not the way to the past barred and bolted? And meanwhile he blesses all the relics of the old order which stand as obstacles in the way of advance — the feudal States, the big zamindaris and taluqdaris, the present capitalist system. Is it reasonable to believe in the theory of trusteeship to give unchecked power and wealth to an individual and to expect him to use it entirely for the public good?[7]

In fact this blurring of the class issue worried Nehru continually and in *Whither India?* (1933) he wrote:

> Congress cannot escape having to answer the question now or later of which class or classes in India are we especially striving for? Do we place the masses, the peasantry first, or some small class at the head of our list?... History shows us that there is no instance of a privileged class or group or nation giving up its special privileges willingly.[8]

The two leaders had irreconcilable differences over the shape of the Indian polity after Independence. Gandhi outlined his vision in *Hind Swaraj* written in 1908 and, except for some clarifications, he stuck to it all his life. As the goal of freedom came in sight, Gandhi wrote a long letter to Nehru in 1945 to reiterate his position:

> I believe that if India is to attain true freedom...then sooner or later we will have to live in villages in huts, not in palaces... The essence of what I say is that the things required for human life must be individually controlled by every person; the individual cannot be saved without this control.[9]

In reply to this letter Nehru stated:

> It is many years ago that I read *Hind Swaraj* and I have only a vague picture in my mind. But even when I read it 20 or more years ago it seemed to me completely unreal...It is 38 years since *Hind Swaraj* was written. The world has completely changed since then, possibly in a wrong direction... A village, normally speaking, is backward intellectually and culturally and no progress can be made from a backward environment. Narrow-minded people are much more likely to be untruthful and violent.

Emphasizing the need to provide the basic amenities of a decent life to the people, he added:

> ... It seems to be inevitable that modern means of transport as well as many other modern developments must continue and be developed. There is no way out except to have them. If this is so, inevitably a measure of heavy industry exists. How far will that fit in with a purely village society?

And as a clincher he added, "As you know, the Congress has

never considered that picture, much less adopted it. You yourself have never asked to adopt it except for some relatively minor aspects."

Not only is the tone of this letter more terse than any other Nehru wrote to his master, it is also written from a position of strength by a person who knows that now it is he who is calling the shots.

Both Gandhi and Nehru were deeply concerned about the plight of the have-nots, and it was their ultimate objective to improve it. But they not only looked at the matter differently, but had different solutions to prescribe. For Gandhi it was essentially an ethical issue: change of heart of the individual was the key to it. Nehru held that socialism was the only rational solution to the problem. As Nehru wrote:

> Gandhi is not ignorant of the subject, for he has read many books on economics and socialism and even Marxism... But I am becoming more and more convinced that in vital matters the mind by itself does not carry us far... The emotions govern the general outlook and control the mind... Gandhiji underwent a tremendous conversion during his earlier days in South Africa... Since then he has had a fixed basis for all his ideas... He listens with great patience and attention to people who make new suggestions to him, but behind all his courteous interest one has the impression that one is addressing a closed door.[10]

As to Gandhi's view of socialism, 'Sometimes he calls himself a socialist, but he uses the word in a sense peculiar to himself which has little or nothing to do with the economic framework of society which usually goes by the name of socialism. Following his lead, a number of prominent Congressmen have taken to use that word, meaning thereby a kind of muddled humanitarianism.'[11]

Non-violence for Gandhi was a moral imperative; Satygraha, its practical expression. For Nehru these were just useful strategies in the freedom struggle, especially, pitched as the Congress was against a much superior physical force:

... for the National Congress as a whole the non-violent method was not, and could not be, a religion or an unchallengeable creed or dogma. It could only be a policy and a method promising certain results, and by those results it would have to be finally judged.[12]

In his Presidential address at the Lahore Congress Session (1929) he declared: "... if this Congress or the nation at any future time comes to the conclusion that methods of violence would rid us of slavery then I have no doubt that it will adopt them."[13]

Nehru rejected non-violence as a moral imperative, and his views on the subject were openly pragmatic. He believed, "Violence itself though bad, cannot be considered intrinsically immoral." Further, "Violence is the very lifeblood of the modern State and social system. Without the coercive apparatus of the State taxes would not be realized, landlords would not get their rents and property would disappear."[14] And to top it all, "Democracy indeed means the coercion of the minority by the majority."[15]

For Gandhiji, even the most desirable ends could not justify wrong means. But his 'spiritual heir' said, "I am convinced that Gandhiji has done a great service to us by stressing the importance of the means. And yet I feel sure that the final emphasis must necessarily be on the end and the goal in view."[16]

With his rationalist approach to life, it is not surprising that Nehru could not empathize with Gandhi's view of religion, who maintained:

No man can live without religion. There are some who in the egotism of their reason declare that they have nothing to do with religion... My devotion to truth has drawn me into the field of politics... those who say that religion has nothing to do with politics do not know what religion means.[17]

But Nehru argued:

Often in history we see that religion, which was meant to raise us and make us better and nobler, has made people behave like beasts. Instead of bringing enlightenment to them, it has often tried to keep them in the dark; instead of broadening their minds, it has frequently made them narrow-minded and intolerant of others.[18]

An offshoot of Gandhi's religious outlook was his aversion to the values of Western civilization. Nehru considered these essential to modernity and wrote to his mentor:

> You misjudge greatly, I think, the civilization of the West and attach too great an importance to its many failings. You have stated somewhere that India has nothing to learn from the West and that she has reached a pinnacle of wisdom in the past. I entirely disagree with this viewpoint and I neither think that the so-called Ram Rajya was very good in the past, nor do I want it back. I think the Western or rather industrial civilization is bound to conquer India...[19]

With his socialist leanings, Nehru was committed to planning as he considered it the surest and safest course for the balanced growth of a backward economy. But Gandhi thought, "In my opinion his planning is a waste of effort. But he cannot be satisfied with anything that is not big."

With such divergence of views it is not surprising that there were occasional clashes between the two Titans. Nehru's protestations were more frequent, but Gandhi's rejoinders more incisive.

After a longish sojourn in Europe Nehru returned to India in 1927, with his socialism updated and politics radicalized. He carried through the Madras Congress a number of "aggressively anti-imperialist and pro-socialist" resolutions. This impatience and stridency was not to Gandhi's liking, who wrote to him in January 1928, "You are going too fast, you should have taken time to think and become acclimatized." Nehru wrote two letters to Gandhi explaining his stand. These irritated Gandhi further and he sent him a sharp rejoinder:

> The differences between you and me are so vast and radical that there seems to be no meeting ground between us. I cannot conceal from you my grief that I should lose a comrade so valiant, so faithful, so able and so honest as you have always been; but in serving a cause comradeships have to be sacrificed.[20]

Upset over the Mahatma's withdrawal of the Civil Disobedience

Movement, Nehru recorded in his prison diary in July 1933, "I am getting more and more certain that there can be no further political cooperation between Bapu and me. At least not of the kind that has existed. We had better go our different ways."[21]

On his side Gandhi wrote to Agatha Harrison on 30 April 1936, "But Jawaharlal's way is not my way. I accept his ideal about land, etc. But I do not accept practically any of his methods."[22]

From the above account it may appear that Nehru and Gandhi were at loggerheads most of the time, and spent a lot of energy in exchanging acrimonious letters. Far from it. Significant as their mutual differences were, much more vital was the deep respect and affection that they had for each other. Gandhi once said:

> Somebody suggested that Pandit Jawaharlal and I were estranged. It will require much more than differences of opinion to estrange us. We had differences from the moment we became co-workers, and I have said for some years and say now that not Rajaji but Jawaharlal will be my successor.[23]

Once, when Gandhi chided him, Nehru complained, "No one has moved or inspired me more than you and I can never forget your exceeding kindness to me. There can be no question of our personal relations suffering. But even in the wider sphere am I not your child in politics, though perhaps a truant and errant child?"[24]

Nehru's fretting and fuming aside, Gandhi's imprint on him was decisive and indelible. He confessed, "... there was only one major change in my life, one which came almost like a bolt: it was Gandhi. One could consider it a break in my life, in my inner and outer life."[25]

Nehru first saw Gandhi in action during the martial-law days in Punjab in 1919. And he wrote:

> We all worked together... Repeatedly I was astonished at his appraisal of the situation, of what should be done. First most of us reacted against it... and, a little later, we found that it was the right policy.[26]

Despite all the differences Nehru had with Gandhi regarding his religious and mystical approach to politics and reliance on his inner voice, Nehru realized, "Though many people in India may disagree with him on hundreds of matters,... at a time of action and struggle when India's freedom is at stake they flock to him again and look up to him as their inevitable leader."[27]

It is possible that at certain critical moments when sharp differences arose between the two, Nehru may have parted company with his leader. But, "It became apparent that his methods were not silly; they brought results."[28]

That was the bottom line for Nehru. There is no escaping the conclusion that one major reason why he stuck to Gandhi despite a lot of inner turmoil was the acute awareness of his preceptor's unmatched hold over the Indian masses:

> Always we had a feeling that while we might be more logical, Gandhiji knew India far better than we did, and a man who could command such tremendous devotion and loyalty must have something in him that corresponded to the needs and aspirations of the masses.[29]

Nehru, too, was a great crowd-puller. But at a deeper, cultural level, he could not relate to them. And he was fully aware of this fact. As to Gandhi, "He came to represent India to an amazing degree and to express the very spirit of that ancient and tortured land. Almost, he was India, and his very failings were Indian failings."[30]

Accordingly, "In any policy that might be framed he cannot be ignored. In any national struggle his full association and guidance are essential. India cannot do without him."

A remarkable aspect of the disagreements between Gandhi and Nehru is the moral courage and intellectual integrity displayed by both. They unhesitatingly aired their serious differences through correspondence and writings in a frank and forthright manner. Being Gandhi's junior and a disciple, it required much greater courage for Nehru to clash openly with the master. Gandhi, on his part, never took offence at his apostle's outbursts. And two of his observations about Nehru show rare perspicacity and have stood the test of time. Nehru's radical rhetoric worried many conservative leaders. Gandhi assured them, "He is undoubtedly an extremist, thinking far ahead of his surroundings.

But he is humble enough not to force the pace to breaking point...
The nation is safe in his hands."

As to their differences, "He says that he does not understand
my language, that he speaks a language foreign to me. This may
or may not be true. But language is no bar to union of hearts. And
I know this — that when I am gone he will speak my language."[31]

"Years bring the philosophic mind." Cares of office and setbacks
mellow the most intrepid of radicals. After he became prime
minister, Nehru shed his revolutionary rhetoric, preferred compromise to confrontation, and was more tolerant of the imperfec-
tions of the system he worked. In his conversations with Tibor
Mende, recorded nearly a decade after he became prime minister,
a long section is devoted to his relations with Gandhi. There is
not a single instance where he criticizes his guru and in several
places even defends Gandhi's so-called 'backward outlook.'
Partly it may be owing to respect for the departed leader, but it
largely stemmed from changes in Nehru's perceptions.

Earlier he had complained that talking to Gandhi was like
addressing a closed door. Now he explains that Gandhi had an
"amazing capacity to tone down opposition by his friendly
approach. There was no aggression in it and yet it was a hard
approach. He did not give up any essentials, but he would compromise on the non-essentials only."[32]

There was a time when Nehru disapproved of Gandhi's references to Ram Rajya and said that it was neither "a very good thing
in the past, nor do I want it back." But he tells Tibor Mende,

> He always referred to Ram Rajya. To a person like me this sounded
> like going back to some primitive state, but that was a phrase
> which was understood by every villager... The point is that Gandhi
> was always thinking of the masses and of the mind of India and
> he was trying to lift it in the right direction.[33]

When asked specifically about his disagreements with Gandhi,
Nehru replied, "... in spite of my difference with Gandhi, more
and more I came to believe in him as a tremendous revolutionary
force in the right direction."[34]

Agreeing that Gandhi 'spiritualized' him in a broad sense,

Nehru explained, "This is the kind of influence Gandhi had on vast numbers of people. It changed the whole manner of our living."[35]

This process of spiritualization was abruptly snapped when an assassin's bullet silenced the voice that millions had come to love and live by. India lost her moral compass, and Nehru his emotional and spiritual anchor. "... the light has gone out of our lives and there is darkness everywhere," he said in his impromptu homage to Gandhi. But he paid the most enduring tribute to his master by fulfilling his prophecy: he increasingly spoke his language and ensured that the nation was safe in his hands.

4

Nehru's Political Credo-I

Rooting of Democracy

𝒪f everything else about Nehru is forgotten, his rooting of democracy in India alone will ensure his grateful remembrance by his people. A comparison with the fate of the democratic enterprise in other third-world countries should give some idea of the magnitude of this achievement.

Jawaharlal did not have to make a special effort to be a democrat. His innate decency, respect for others and sense of fair play were the mainsprings of his humanism. Democracy was the basic political impulse of such an individual. Even his socialism and secularism were derived from it.

Of course, there were important contributory factors, like his seven-year stint in England, the environment of liberal democracy there, and the intellectual climate at Cambridge which helped him shape his political philosophy.

But it was the anti-colonial struggle which ultimately gave body to his abstract concepts of democracy and socialism. And here, his chance encounter with the peasants of Pratapgarh district in 1920 was a watershed. Urged by a group of *kisans* (peasants) who had come to Allahabad from the interior, Nehru saw in the raw the condition of the peasantry:

> I listened to their innumerable tales of sorrow, their crushing and ever-growing burden of rent, illegal extractions, ejectments from land and mud-huts, beatings... A new picture of India seemed to rise before me, naked, starving, crushed and utterly miserable.[1]

For the city-bred Nehru, brought up in luxury, educated abroad, this revelation came as a thunderclap. This led to Nehru's much more intimate involvement with the freedom movement, and brought him into close contact with Gandhi. For the next quarter of a century he was wholly consumed by this struggle, as without freedom neither his peasants could get justice nor the country make any progress.

Leaders of the national movement differed on a number of issues, but there was total agreement as to the form of government that India should have after liberation: it was to be a democracy. From the days of Dadabhoy Naoroji, Gokhale and Tilak, the oft-declared goal was a free, democratic India. Gandhi lived democracy in all his actions. Nehru, therefore, did not have to start from scratch in laying the foundations of a democratic polity. And the Constituent Assembly had no problems in declaring India a Sovereign Democratic Republic.

India's history and culture also provided a fertile soil for the growth of democracy. Her ethos is essentially pluralistic: tolerance and accommodation lie at its core. Her extreme ethnic, social, linguistic and religious diversities require that group conflicts are settled through adjustment, adaptation and compromise. This is obviously best provided by a popular, representative form of government.

Even the colonial rule, in one sense, gave the Indians some experience in building and operating the basic institutions of democracy. Most importantly, the British created an elaborate legal framework based on equality before law. Then, the shadow-boxing in the Viceroy's Council, introduction of Dyarchy in 1921, holding of elections to the Central Legislative Assembly in 1934 and the provincial legislatures in 1937 and, above all, the valuable experience gained in running provincial governments from 1937-39, all these provided important lessons in operating the democratic machine. At a lower level were the useful skills learnt in managing organs of local government. But it must also be remembered that owing to stringent qualifications, on the eve of Independence only 11 percent of the adult population was eligible to vote.

Nehru was keenly aware that the democratization of a traditional society with a low level of literacy required the raising of the political awareness of the people. Therefore, throughout his active political life he acted as a tireless educator of the masses. Constantly on the move, and addressing vast multitudes, he spoke at length on the major issues before the country and the manner in which they should be tackled. As Prime Minister, he wrote long, fortnightly letters to all the chief ministers, giving his views on various national and international problems.

He always defended freedom of speech and, indeed, invited criticism of his government. He told the Constituent Assembly, "... there is always a possible tendency for those in authority to become a little complacent. ... I welcome the vigilance of the Honourable Members of this House in drawing our attention to our failings or any error or delinquency on the part of the administration."[2]

And while addressing the All India Newspaper Editor's Conference (1950) he said:

> To my mind, the freedom of the press is not just a slogan... it is an essential attribute of the democratic process. ...even if the government dislikes the liberties taken by the press and considers them dangerous, it is wrong to interfere with the freedom of the press... I would rather have a completely free press with all the dangers involved in the wrong use of that freedom than a suppressed press or a regulated press.

Nehru was particular to take everybody along in the governance of the country. It is, perhaps, unique in the history of democracy that five of the fourteen ministers of his first cabinet were non-congressmen. And some of them like Shyama Prasad Mookerji and B.R. Ambedkar had been staunch critics of his party.

For almost a generation, from 1947 to 1964, Nehru remained the helmsman of independent India. It was fortunate for the country, as it gave him enough time to nurse the tender plant of democracy into a sturdy tree. Some critics have complained that this long dominance of the Indian polity by such a towering personality perpetuated single-party rule, and this hampered the growth of a robust opposition. This is a very academic sort of objection. The fact of the matter is that it was this unbroken single-party rule for three decades which provided the necessary continuity for democracy to take root in Indian soil.

India won freedom after a prolonged and valiant struggle, and with freedom came democracy. But in the very manner of their arrival, the two great achievements were flawed to some extent. The actual transfer of power was a tame and legalistic affair. And as if to emphasize the point, Nehru adopted the colonial system of administration in its entirety. The Constitution of India cannibalized the much maligned Government of India Act of 1935 to the extent of incorporating 235 of its sections. The entire judicial and administrative framework of old rules, regulations and procedures was also adopted wholesale. No wonder that this mode of transfer of power did not bring about the sort of radical transformation that the national leaders had been talking about.

Modern democracy rose as a result of a slow, evolutionary process in response to a particular set of historical developments. It is essentially a child of the Industrial Revolution. Industrialization creates the opportunities for the emergence of an urban, entrepreneurial, capitalist class. With progressive control over means of production it acquires more and more say in the government's decision-making processes. This leads to a dispersal of state power, which is a necessary prerequisite in the growth of the democratic environment. In India, owing to the constraints of colonial suppression, normal growth of industry was stifled and the capitalist mode of production remained stunted. Thus, on the eve of Independence, India did not have a robust national bourgeoisie which could play its traditional role.

Moreover, India's historical experience was based on the rule of absolute monarchies. There was no precedent of popular agitations or movements for protecting the masses from excesses or inequities of their rulers, or conferring any legal rights on them vis-a-vis the state. India borrowed the British model of parliamentary democracy without having to pay the price which Britain did. Magna Carta was signed in 1215. King Charles I was beheaded in 1649. Then came the Civil War. The Bill of Rights, limiting the monarch's arbitrary powers, was passed in 1688. Thereafter followed a series of Reform Bills from 1832-1884, which gradually enfranchized various sections of the people. And women had to wait till 1928 to get full voting rights.

In India, the fruits of this prolonged struggle for human rights spanning seven centuries were gathered in a much shorter span of time. Moreover, the Constitution and the social agenda that the lawmakers gave the country were the most liberal and progressive. Universal adult franchise was accompanied by full freedom of speech, movement and assembly. Radical labour laws were enacted and public servants were given complete security of service. The blueprint for a welfare state was comparable to that of the most mature and affluent democracies of the West. And all this was done without first creating an environment of social discipline and civic responsibility.

Nehru showed great courage in taking this giant step towards making India a full-fledged, liberal, democratic, welfare state. It was also an act of faith in his people:

> I am a convinced believer in adult franchise, for men and women, and though I realise the difficulties in the way, I am sure that the objections raised to its adoption in India have no great force and are based on the fears of privileged classes and interests.[3]

Nehru's difficulties arose from two sources. First, the traditional mores which governed the social universe of the people. Second, the inadequacies of the legal fabric itself.

The linchpin of democracy is the principle of equality before law. Though all the national leaders strongly advocated this precept, they derived their inspiration from the Western model. Culturally this concept is not only alien but abhorrent to a caste-ridden, socially differentiated society. "For Englishmen, the law, if it is to be universal, impersonal and impartial, ought to be blind, an idea graphically illustrated by the representation of justice as... a blind-folded woman holding balanced scales... For the Hindu, the reverse was true; the differences among men in society were central to their legal identity, rights and obligations."[4]

This basic contradiction has drained democratic institutions of their content and given rise to a host of paradoxes. The judicial system, instead of protecting the weak, actually favours the strong. The legislators — the makers of law — strive to operate above the law. The electoral system, designed to give a voice to the downtrodden, is manipulated to exclude them from the electoral arena. The police, instead of controlling crime, patronizes the big-time criminal. In all important spheres of national activity, it is the law which adjusts to the individual, instead of the individual adjusting to the law.

Nehru very much wanted to establish an egalitarian and just social order. But, to some extent, the Indian Constitution is itself tilted towards the strong. The fundamental rights confer specific rights on the individual which can be enforced in a court of law. These cover such diverse areas as equality before law; right to protection of life and personal liberty; right to property; freedom of speech, association and movement; right to freedom of conscience and propagation of religion. All these rights, with the exception of right to property, are fundamental to the existence of a civilized and open society. But the Directive Principles of State Policy, which constitute the social conscience of a humane and compassionate welfare state, are just a litany of lofty ideals and pious sentiments as none of them can be enforced through a judicial forum. For instance Article 38 desires that "the state shall *strive to promote* the welfare of the people by securing and protecting *as effectively as it may* a social order in which justice, social and economic and political shall inform all the institutions of national life" (emphasis added). Article 39 says that the State shall "direct its policy towards securing" the right of the citizens "to an adequate means of livelihood," and prevent "concentration of wealth and means of production to the common detriment." Free and compulsory education for all children upto the age of 14 is another objective towards which the State 'shall strive'. It is ironic that whereas millions of able-bodied persons starve as they have no right of employment, the millionaires were given a fundamental right to their wealth — not unoften ill-gotten.

What tilted the scales here was the primacy of class interest. The ruling class, including Nehru's cabinet colleagues, was not prepared to replicate even the Meiji Restoration in India through an enlightened act of voluntary renunciation of some of their possessions and privileges. And Nehru, on his part, was not the person to fight to the bitter end any battle which threatened the stability of the state.

But there is a danger of overstretching this point and drawing the facile inference that behind the facade of egalitarian professions, India is ruled by the capitalist class. This view is not only unfair to Nehru and many of his colleagues who honestly strove to establish liberal democracy and a just social order, but also ignores the extremely complex structure of the Indian polity. In fact even neo-Marxist scholars like Althusser, Habermas and Poulantzas concede that "the modern industrial non-Communist state is not simply a product of class struggle but is a relatively autonomous force."[5] The Rudolphs, specifically examining the case of the "marginality of class politics of India," have described the state as a "third actor" vis-a-vis the two historic adversaries of class politics, that is, capital and labour.[6]

In the Indian context this 'third actor' is all-pervasive. Two-thirds of the industrial labour works in the public sector. And the state sector which controls the commanding heights of the economy, also owns the entire infrastructure for the growth of industry. As to the business and industrial class, it has always looked to the state for protection and patronage. The much maligned 'quota-permit-licence-Raj' has actually served to create a protected business environment for the local entrepreneur, and the nationalized financial institutions have generously met his needs for easy credit.

Politically, rural India is much more important than the urban sector, as 80 percent of the population live there (in the forties). The Scheduled Castes and the Scheduled Tribes, though occupying the lowest rung of the social order, constitute one-fifth of the electorate. Such large constituencies, obviously, cannot be ignored by any party.

Thus, India's socio-political reality does not allow the emergence of clear-cut class differentiation or conflict. There are so many powerful interest groups in this diverse and heterogeneous society, and their allegiance is so essential to any political outfit aspiring for power, that every party tries to cast its net far and wide to maximize its catch. During the freedom struggle the Indian National Congress had evolved electoral mechanisms of adjustment, conciliation, and consensus for resolving group differences and conflicts. This system provided adequate protection against any powerful group acquiring a position of complete dominance. Nehru was one of the creators of these devices and, naturally, he used them effectively as Prime Minister. He always wanted to take everybody along, and when an interviewer complained about his not being sufficiently tough in implementing radical reforms, he replied:

> They criticise me for my weaknesses, but this is too large a country with too many legitimate diversities to permit any so-called 'strong man' to trample over people and their ideas. The 'strong man' concept itself is undemocratic and something repugnant to the spirit of our country as well as our times.[7]

The elements which contributed to the diffusion of class politics also gave Indian democracy a broad centrist orientation. While leading the National Movement, Gandhi took care that the Congress followed the middle path and refused to alienate any important section of the people.

Another factor which contributed to making the polity centrist was the shrinkage of the ideological spread of the Congress. During the freedom struggle it was a kangaroo party carrying all sorts of formations in its pouch. But, after independence, with perspectives narrowing in the pursuit of power, the parties of the left and the right dropped out. The Socialists left the Congress in 1948 and, later, in alliance with the Kisan Mazdoor parties, formed the Praja Socialist Party in 1952. On the other hand, Congress stalwarts like C. Rajagopalachari and K.M. Munshi formed the Swatantra Party representing the propertied classes.

Even as a matter of policy, Nehru mostly preferred to plough the centrist furrow. His concept of a mixed economy was basically centrist, and so was the doctrine of non-alignment. Both were based on avoidance of extremist, radical or blatantly partisan politics. Secularism in operation has to be centrist, as it is based on a sort of religious non-alignment and willing tolerance of diverse orthodoxies. And as to democracy, it can flourish only in a culture of consensus, fostered by following the middle course in such a diverse society.

The primary test of a functioning democracy is the manner in which elections are conducted. Three general elections were conducted during Nehru's tenure. All of them were held on time; there were no charges of malpractice, and the results carried credibility with the people. Preparing for a countrywide poll in the world's largest democracy is a colossal task at the best of times. For the first general election, held from October 1951 to February 1952, the entire groundwork had to be done from scratch. There was house to house enumeration to register 172 million voters for the first time. There were 77 political parties, contesting 472 parliament and 3,205 state assembly seats.

Certain aspects of these elections have special relevance for the growth of democracy in India. Firstly, the turn-out normally hovered around 60 percent of the registered electorate. Secondly, Congress's share of the vote was around 45 percent, and never touched the 50 percent mark. Thus, as a result of the multiplicity of political parties, Congress retained power without ever securing a majority of the votes cast. Third, owing to fragmentation of the non-Congress vote, no opposition party was able to register much of a presence at the national level. This has virtually turned India into a single-party democracy. But whereas opposition parties remained on the periphery in these elections, they did manage to secure among themselves more than half the votes cast. Obviously, democracy in India was vigorously alive.

For Nehru the results of these elections could not have been very gratifying, as the Congress could garner only 45 percent of the vote. In 1957 the Communist vote went up from 3.3 to 8.9 percent, and that of Jan Sangh from 3 to 6 percent. In the state assemblies the Congress suffered a decline. In Orissa, Bihar, Uttar Pradesh and Bombay, Congress failed to win majorities and formed coalition governments with the help of independents. But the real shock came with the formation of the first non-Congress government in Kerala by the Communists. They also registered handsome gains in West Bengal, raising their share of votes from 10 to 18 percent. Similarly, they doubled their vote in Punjab.

The last election of the Nehru era, held in 1962, saw the emergence of various types of sub-nationalisms and regional parties. Dravida Munnetra Kazhagam (DMK) demanded the formation of Dravidastan by separation of the four southern states from the Indian Union. Hill Leaders Conference in Assam raised its demand for regional autonomy, and the Akalis wanted a Punjabi Suba. Whereas the Communists strengthened their position in the Parliament, a matter of greater significance was the rapid rise of Jan Sangh, which increased its seats from 3 in 1952 to 14 in 1962. No less important was the rise of the Swatantra Party, which secured 8 percent of the votes and 18 seats in its very first election.

The electoral setback was accompanied by certain developments which weakened party democracy. Temperamentally, Nehru was not a party man, and organizational affairs did not interest him much. Except as an instrument for fighting elections, Nehru did not have much use for the Congress in the governance of the country. J.B. Kriplani was Congress President during the critical period of country's Partition. After Independence the Nehru government did not consult him or associate him in the framing of the official policy. When his repeated protests against this neglect were ignored, he resigned.

Much more important in this context is the Nehru-Tandon clash. It resulted from a conflict of ideologies. Sardar Patel and the formidable group of his followers in the party were strongly opposed to Nehru's socialist policies. Purushottam Das Tandon, a firm opponent of the Nehruvian line, was put up by the right as its candidate. His antagonist, J.B. Kriplani, was supposed to enjoy Nehru's covert support. Tandon got elected and this created a crisis in the party. Nehru not only felt rebuffed, he realized that the persistence of this trend would pose a threat to his political future. Matters came to a head with the constitution of the Central Election Committee in 1951. The death of the redoubtable Sardar in 1950 had weakened Tandon's position. Yet, when Nehru tried to put pressure on him to reconstitute the Congress Working Committee and the Central Election Committee, Tandon refused to oblige.

At this provocation even Nehru was goaded into action. Before the scheduled Working Committee meeting, he resigned both from the Central Election Committee and the Working Committee. Maulana Azad followed suit the next day. The Tandon faction was aware of the approaching general election and Nehru's importance for a Congress victory. Thus cornered, Tandon resigned, bringing the crisis to an end.

In this confrontation, technically and constitutionally, Tandon was more in the right than Nehru. This conflict did damage the party democracy, and here Nehru must carry a large share of the blame.

To make matters worse, Nehru permitted himself to be persuaded to take over as Party President. Without realizing the implications, he set a very harmful precedent for which the Congress had to pay dearly. When he relinquished the post in 1954, the mild and pliable U.N. Dhebar was installed in his place. And in the fullness of time, in 1959, Dhebar dutifully canvassed for the induction of Nehru's daughter, Indira Gandhi, as his successor. This assured that there was no clash between the legislative and organizational heads of the party. It is unlikely that a perceptive leader like Nehru did not realize that his position had been strengthened by weakening party democracy.

There is no clinching evidence that Indira Gandhi's unopposed election was influenced by her father. But Caesar's wife has to be extra cautious in her public conduct. The elevation of Mrs. Gandhi did send out the wrong institutional signals and under less scrupulous leaders it encouraged the cult of nepotism. Nehru must have felt a little uncomfortable on this occasion, as he told a press conference, "Normally speaking, it is not a good idea for my daughter to come in as Congress President when I am Prime Minister."[8]

But later he made amends for this deviation from paternal loyalty when he said before the Congress Parliamentary Party, "It is superfluous for me to say that Indira is my daughter and I have love for her. I am proud of her good nature, proud of her energy and work, and proud of her integrity and truthfulness."[9]

During his radical phase Nehru would have been more restrained in promoting his daughter. Later, bent under the cares of office and engulfed by problems, his idealism had waned and vision dimmed. Once he wrote to Rafi Ahmed Kidwai, "It is impossible in this complicated and crooked world to get everything straightened out easily or quickly. One has to take one step at a time. A right step taken leads necessarily to right results."[10]

How perfectly the apostle mimics his master! There was a time when Nehru was so critical of Gandhi's approach of 'one step at a time'.

5

Nehru's Political Credo-II

Socialism: Scientific and Otherwise

*O*f all the items on Nehru's political agenda, socialism had the highest profile. And it caused the maximum controversy.

Jawaharlal was never a dogmatic socialist, nor did he join any socialist organization. As to his brush with socialism during his student days, he told an interviewer, "... it was really at Cambridge that, broadly speaking, certain socialistic ideas — partly Fabian Socialism, partly some slightly more aggressive socialistic — ideas developed. But it was all very academic."[1]

What gave Nehru a deeper socialist orientation was his landmark visit to Europe in 1926-27 after a break of 13 years. During this period he travelled extensively, read a lot and came in contact with a number of radical thinkers and activists. Of particular importance was his close association with the Congress of Oppressed Nationalities and the League Against Imperialism. Both were dominated by the leftists and supported the anti-colonial movements. This exposure helped him to a clearer understanding of Marxism, and strengthened his commitment to the socialist ideals: "I turned inevitably towards Communism ... (though) it was not a doctrinal adherence ... (I was also) attracted (by) the tremendous changes taking place in Russia."[2] But even in the midst of his ideological fervour, he was perceptive enough to observe, "The Russians have an extraordinary capacity for propaganda," and, "Personally I have the strongest objection to being led by the nose by the Russians or anybody else."[3]

As a socialist he really arrived with his presidential address to Lahore Congress in 1929. He declared:

I must frankly confess that I am a socialist and a republican, and am no believer in kings and princes, or the order which produces the modern kings of industry, who have greater power over the lives and fortunes of men than even the kings of old, and whose methods are as predatory as those of the feudal aristocracy.[4]

Never before had such heresies been uttered from a Congress pulpit. The ideas, the words, the idiom were all unfamiliar to the audience of the twenties. It scandalized the elders and electrified the youth.

Nehru's presidential address at Lucknow in April 1936 contains, perhaps, the most radical and comprehensive assertion of his socialist credo:

I am convinced that the only key to the solution of the world's problems and of India's problems lies in socialism, and when I use this word I do not do so in a vague humanitarian way but in a scientific, economic sense... I see no way of ending the poverty, the vast unemployment, the degradation and the subjection of the Indian people except through socialism. That involves vast and revolutionary changes in our political and social structure, the ending of vested interests in land and industry. ...This means the ending of private property, except in a restricted sense, ... I should like the Congress to become a socialist organization.[5]

But, frankly, "How does socialism fit in with the present ideology of the Congress? I do not think it does."[6]
And half-hearted measures would not do:

Reformism was an impossible solution to any vital problem at a critical moment when the basic structure has to be changed, and however slow the progress might be later on, the initial step must be a complete break with the existing order which had fulfilled its purpose and was now only a drag on the future progress.[7]

Thus, looking at the objective conditions in India, he could not escape the conclusion that, "A clash of interests seems inevitable. There is no middle path. Each one will have to choose his side."[8] Consequently, "Everything that comes in the way will have to be removed, gently if possible, forcibly if necessary. And there seems little doubt that coercion will often be necessary."[9]

But he also appreciated that India could not import a prefabricated, foreign revolutionary model. "If socialism is to be built up in India, it will have to grow out of Indian conditions, and the closest study of these conditions is essential."[10]

These reflections represent the farthest reaches of Nehru's revolutionary ideas. And they go pretty far. Conceptually his radicalism was clearly anchored in Marxism:

> ... the theory and philosophy of Marxism lightened up many dark corners of my mind. History came to have a new meaning for me. ... It was the essential freedom from dogma and the scientific outlook of Marxism that appealed to me.[11]

He looked at private property from a Marxist angle and wrote:

> There is a great deal of loose talk ... about confiscation and the like. Confiscation, persistent and continual, is the basis of the existing system. There is the daily confiscation of part of the labour product of the worker.[12]

But despite the expression of such deep faith in Marxism, Nehru was sufficiently realistic to admit:

> I am very far from being a Communist. My roots are still perhaps in the nineteenth century, and I am too much influenced by the humanist-liberal tradition to get out of it completely.[13]

Nehru was too eclectic and liberal to be completely won over by any single orthodoxy. He did not join even the Congress Socialist Party which was formed with his blessing. For the same reason he could never empathize with the Indian Communists:

> Their basic error seems to be that they judge the Indian national movement from European labour standards ... (It) is obviously not a labour or proletarian movement. It is a bourgeois movement, as its very name implies, and its objective so far has been, not a change of the social order, but political independence ...[14]

Even during his radical phase in the twenties and thirties, he was usually "moderate in action" whenever a situation of confrontation developed. His presidential address at the Lucknow session in 1936 is the apogee of his radical views. But in the same address, immediately after asserting "Socialism ... is a vital creed which I hold with all my head and heart," he said, "Much as I wish for the advancement of socialism in the country, I have no

desire to force the issue in the Congress and thereby create difficulties in the way of our struggle for independence. I shall cooperate gladly and with all ... even though they do not agree with
the socialist solution."[15]

Soon after this session there was a delightful exchange of letters
between the two leading industrialists of the country, G.D. Birla
and P. Thakurdas, which shows what a clear perception the capitalists had of Nehru's radicalism. On 23 April 1936, Birla wrote
to his peer, "Mahatmaji kept his promise... he saw that no commitments were made. Jawaharlalji's speech was thrown into the
wastepaper basket... Jawaharlalji seems to be like a typical English
democrat... Out for giving expression to his ideology, but he re-
alizes that action is impossible and so does not press for it... things
are moving in the right direction." Thakurdas replied, "I never
had any doubt about the bonafides of J... only I feel that a good
deal of nursing will have to be done to keep him on the right rails
all through."[16]

Nehru had learnt from Gandhi that no cracks should be allowed to develop in the national movement, and controversial
social and economic issues could be taken up after Independence.
But even when India became free, the compulsions of national
unity prevailed. This approach did, however, perpetuate the
status quo, and the agenda for structural changes had to be
shelved.

The basic problem with Nehru was that, as Subhash Chandra Bose
observed, he lacked a 'revolutionary perspective.' "Without revolutionary theory," says Lenin, "there can be no revolutionary
movement." Revolutions do not happen just because their time
has come. The sort of changes that Nehru visualized in the polity
were certainly revolutionary in nature. But one cannot conceive
of circumstances when a revolutionary situation arose without
giving rise to strong counter-revolutionary forces. And unless the
leadership is prepared to join battle, the status quo prevails.

After Independence, Nehru's emphasis was much more on
consensual politics than on radical transformation. The adoption
of the Objectives Resolution in January 1947 by the Constituent

Assembly clearly shows the shift in Nehru's position. In the Assembly, B.R. Ambedkar asserted that if the Objectives Resolution "has a reality behind it and a sincerity... I should have expected a provision (for making) economic, social and political justice a reality (and, consequently, that) there would be nationalization of industry and nationalization of land."[17] Nehru, wanting to avoid controversies on such matters stated, "... we have laid down, not theoretical words and formulae, but rather the content of the thing we desire."[18]

How wary Nehru had become of upsetting the vested interests is shown by the composition of his first cabinet. Five of its fourteen members were non-Congressmen. They were: Dr. John Mathai and C.H. Bhabha, both Directors of Tatas; Sir S.K. Shanmukhan Chetty, an eminent merchant banker; Dr. S.P. Mookerji, leader of Hindu Mahasabha; and Dr. B.R. Ambedkar. Except for Ambedkar, all of them were deeply entrenched in the capitalist culture, or had strong rightist orientation. Baldev Singh was the son of a big industrialist, and Raj Kumari Amrit Kaur belonged to a princely family. Sardar Vallabhbhai Patel and Dr. Rajendra Prasad were wholly opposed to socialism. Only Maulana Abul Kalam Azad, Jagjivan Ram, N.V. Gadgil and Rafi Ahmed Kidwai had any ideological affinity with Nehru. But except for Maulana Azad, all others were political lightweights at that time. This being the complexion of Independent India's first cabinet, it was futile to expect it to become an instrument of revolutionary change.

Looking to the direction in which Nehru was moving, the Congress Socialist Party headed by Jayaprakash Narayan walked out of the Congress in April 1948. In its resolution it warned, "The Congress is in danger... of being overwhelmed by anti-secular, anti-democratic forces of the Right." Later, in December 1948, J.P. Narayan wrote to Nehru, "You want to build socialism with the help of capitalism. You are bound to fail in that."

Nehru was faced with a real dilemma. By nature he was incapable of endorsing violence. India had managed to overthrow a mighty empire by non-violent means. Was it not possible to adopt the same approach to dislodge the propertied classes? Secondly, he was fully aware of the fragile basis of Indian unity. It could be nursed only by a culture of concensus and compromise.

To escape his predicament, Nehru started moving on four tracks simultaneously. Firstly, he increasingly expressed the view that Marxism had become outdated and, in any case, it was not applicable to the Indian situation. In a speech in 1955 he said:

"Socialism and Communism might help you to divide your existing wealth, if you like, but in India, there is no existing wealth for you to divide; there is only poverty to divide..."[19]

By inference, socialism suited the rich countries only!

Secondly, he took a number of steps to democratize the polity, injected it with a modest dose of socialism, and created that vast infrastructure which is basic to a self-sustaining economy. He introduced planning for balanced growth. The state was assigned a primary role for laying the foundations of a modern industrial society and ensuring both accumulation and distribution. Nehru also enacted a series of ameliorative and 'empowering' laws for land reforms and labour welfare. Special schemes were framed under the Five Year Plans to promote village, small-scale and cottage industries for generating rural employment. Community Development, Panchayati Raj and credit co-operatives were designed to transfer resources to the countryside and introduce democratic decentralization. Special stress was laid on economic and technological self-reliance to reduce dependence on foreign agencies.

Thirdly, he promoted the concept of 'mixed economy' by combining the positive features of capitalism and socialism. In an interview he spoke of a "third way which takes the best from all existing systems — the Russian, the American and others — and seeks to create something suited to one's own history and philosophy."[20] Economic co-existence was essential if ruinous ideological conflicts were to be avoided. "While public sector must obviously grow and even now it has grown ... the private sector is not something unimportant. It will play an important role, though gradually and ultimately it will fade out."[21] How this vanishing trick would occur in such an accommodative climate, Nehru did not elaborate.

Fourthly, from time to time, he harked back to his radical past in an attempt to renew and strengthen the socialist agenda. In 1953, he invited Jayaprakash Narayan to join his cabinet along with some of his colleagues to strengthen the left. J.P. Narayan was agreeable only if his 14-point agenda was accepted. Nehru did not find this feasible.

Then, in 1955, at the Congress session at Avadi, it was resolved that "Planning should take place with a view to establishing a socialistic pattern of society." This was the first time that the Congress officially adopted socialism as its goal, though what a 'socialist pattern of society' meant was anybody's guess.

The extent to which Nehru's egalitarian agenda was implemented, as also its successes and failures, will be examined in later chapters. But at a conceptual level, Nehru the socialist sang his swansong at the Bhubaneshwar session of the Congress in January 1964. The Resolution on Democracy and Socialism, drafted under his guidance, declared that the Congress wanted to promote democratic socialism by peaceful means. But this time fate intervened and the smooth flow of benign words was cut off by a stroke that Nehru suffered at the session. And four months later the voice which had expressed such noble thoughts and lofty sentiments was stilled forever.

It would be wrong to blame temperamental factors alone for Nehru's inability or reluctance to give body to his socialist vision. Top leadership of the Congress party has been mostly dominated by conservative elements. From the day Nehru started toeing the socialist line, there was opposition from within the party, and even Gandhi did not support him. Reacting strongly to this attitude he conveyed his irritation to Gandhi in 1934:

> I feel that time is over-due for the Congress to think clearly on economic and social issues... But it appears that whether the Working Committee knows anything about the subject or not, it is perfectly willing to denounce and excommunicate people who happen to have made a special study of the subject and hold certain views... The resolution of the Working Committee shows astounding ignorance of the elements of socialism...[22]

Nehru's famous address at the Lucknow session asking for the abolition of private property created a crisis in the party. Seven members of the Working Committee, including stalwarts like Vallabhbhai Patel, Rajendra Prasad and J.B. Kriplani tendered their resignations. They also wrote to Nehru that as the Congress had not adopted socialism, its preaching by the organization's president was "prejudicial to the best interests of the country and to the success of the national struggle for freedom."[23] When Nehru protested, he was nicely rebuked by Gandhi.[24]

Nehru gave high priority to planning, but the creation of a planning apparatus proved to be a painful exercise. Moving slowly, in August 1948 Nehru suggested the appointment of a minister for social and economic affairs to attend exclusively to economic problems. But the proposal was rejected by the cabinet. Later, in 1949, an American expert, Dr. Solomon Trone, reported to Nehru "... conditions in India were alarmingly similar to those of China at the end of Second World War" and drastic action was required to evolve a unified national plan. A specially appointed sub-committee of civil servants described Dr. Trone's conception of planning as 'fundamentally totalitarian' and thus inapplicable to Indian conditions.[25]

The Congress Working Committee finally approved the proposal to set up a planning commission on 25 January 1950. But Sardar Patel ensured the deletion of the following passage from its mandate : "the progressive elimination of a social, political and economic exploitation and inequality, the motive of private gain in economic activity or organization of society and the anti-social concentration of wealth and means of production."[26]

P.D. Tandon was elected Congress president as a result of the ganging up of the old guard. A letter written by K. Hanumanthaiya to Tandon provides a glimpse into the pre-election manipulations. "So far as Mysore votes are concerned, almost to a man, they will stand by you... I also had (a) discussion with Sardar Patel. I expect you and the Sardar to work unitedly... and lead us out of the chaos and confusion that Pandit Nehru's leadership has landed us in."[27] Another insight into the alignment of forces in this contest is provided by Kochanek, the eminent historian of the

Congress, when he reveals that G.D. Birla, the doyen of Indian industrialists, had financed Tandon's election campaign.[28]

So determined were right-wing elements to frustrate any assault on privilege that when the Bihar Land Bill was referred to Rajendra Prasad, President of India, for his assent, he sat over it for months. It was only when Nehru sent him a letter in September 1950, threatening to resign on this issue, that the Bill was approved.[29] In September 1951, Nehru again threatened to resign when Rajendra Prasad "wished to act unconstitutionally and send a message to the parliament stating his fundamental objections to the Hindu Code Bill."[30]

The extent to which Nehru had lost support for his egalitarian measures within his own party is, perhaps, best illustrated by the defeat of the Constitution (17th Amendment) Bill in 1963. The Supreme Court had declared void a crucial provision of the land-ceiling legislation. When the Bill was introduced in the parliament to rectify this lacuna, it was defeated as some 125 Congress MPs absented themselves.

While judging Nehru's socialist credentials, note should also be taken of how the left forces unwittingly pushed him into a corner. The Indian communists, who had become Stalinists, denigrated Gandhi and declared war on the state to force a proletarian revolution. The Socialists had walked out of the Congress in 1948 and gone into opposition. Whereas on the one hand these moves proved suicidal for the Indian left, on the other they greatly weakened Nehru's position against the rightist elements within the Congress.

The basic task facing India after Independence "was whether there could be any method of transforming the established pattern of wealth, status and power other than a frontal assault on the beliefs and structures that had institutionalized and sanctified a rigid social hierarchy."[31]

In his earlier years Nehru thought that a 'frontal attack' was the only course open to India. Gradually, he came round to the view that change should be effected through Gandhian methods of persuasion and co-operative effort, as the cost of a violent class conflict was unacceptable. But even the second option implied radical changes in society. And Nehru did not have the grit and toughness to undertake that task. The odds he had to face were colossal. But on several occasions he made his task unnecessarily difficult by an overzealous pursuit of consensus. For instance, the cabinet he formed on taking over as Prime Minister was weighted too much in favour of the privileged classes. Whereas the inclusion of Sardar Patel and Rajendra Prasad was unavoidable, there was no justification for his not inducting some leftists in his team. Again, when he reconstituted the Congress Working Committee after P.D. Tandon's resignation in 1950, he did not include in it any of his staunch supporters, and most of the members of the previous committee were retained. Similarly, when the Planning Commission was formed in 1950, none of its six members was a prominent socialist. And its chairmanship was first offered to Rajendra Prasad!

Opposition to Nehru's policies was certainly formidable. But this situation arose primarily from his refusal to assert his authority sufficiently. After the death of Sardar Patel and exit of P.D. Tandon as the Congress president, there was nobody left in the party to challenge him. Yet he allowed himself to be pushed aside owing to his reluctance to join battle and offend propertied interests. It may, therefore, not be too uncharitable to conclude that his commitment to socialist ideals was not as deep as he would have us believe. Gandhi, Birla and Thakurdas had correctly appraised him when they concluded that his actions would be 'moderate'.

Nehru's public image as a crusader for socialism rests on his introduction of planning, creation of the public sector, enactment of land reforms legislation, and laying the groundwork of a welfare state. In fact none of these measures are essentially socialist. Most advanced capitalist democracies have implemented them much more effectively, and with much less fanfare. Nehru himself wrote in 1958, "I do not myself see where socialism comes in the present policies we are pursuing. It is true that we have some major industries in the public sector. That is hardly socialism."[32]

It is also a fact that during Nehru's tenure monopoly capitalism grew unchecked, income disparities widened, nearly half the population subsisted below the poverty line, and social justice remained a distant goal. Nehru was himself quite aware of these facts and his well-known essay, "The Basic Approach" (1958), shows how desperately he tried to rationalize the ideological compromises he had to make. After arguing that the gap between socialism and capitalism was closing, he stated, "If socialism is introduced in a backward and underdeveloped country it does not make it any less backward. In fact we then have backward and poverty-stricken socialism."

Further, he emphasized, "The only way is through hard work and increasing productivity of the nation and equitable distribution of its products." And, "It is clear that in the final analysis it is quality of human beings that counts... Final remedy for bringing in socialism is education and health of the individual, *never mind who controls the state and means of production*"[33] (emphasis added).

Ultimately, "In considering these economic aspects of our problems we have always to remember the basic approach of peaceful means; and perhaps we might also keep in view the old Vedantic ideal of the life force which is the inner base of everything that exists."[34]

The position stated in the above excerpts may be fully defensible from a particular standpoint. But it was pathetic for Nehru to pen them, the 'dark corners' of whose mind had been earlier 'lightened up' by the 'theory and philosophy of Marxism.'

Does it mean, then, that Nehruvian socialism was just hot air and did not leave any impact on the Indian polity? Far from it. For one thing, his incessant campaigning for the socialist agenda for four decades created a mass awareness about the relevance of socialism to the Indian situation. Continuing the Gandhian tradition of genuine concern for the downtrodden, he sensitized the Indian conscience to their plight and problems. His state-welfarism, though practised in most capitalist democracies, had a socialistic slant. He was far more successful in rooting parliamentary democracy, and the dynamics of adult franchise in a vast, poverty-stricken country is itself a check on the ruthlessness of capitalism. But as to 'scientific socialism', the record is uninspiring. And, as shadows lengthened and the vision clouded, Nehru began replacing his revolutionary idealism with the solace of Vedantic metaphysics.

It is not unoften that intrepid iconoclasts end up worshipping their broken idols.

6

Three Critical Errors-I

Neglect of Mass Education

"Let it be remembered," wrote J.K. Galbraith, "that there is no literate population on this planet that is poor, no illiterate population that is otherwise than poor."[1] Nehru himself observed, "In the final analysis no subject is of greater importance than that of education. It is men and women in a country that make and build a nation, and it is education that is supposed to build those men and women."[2] And the Indian Constitution requires the state to provide, within a period of ten years from its commencement "free and compulsory education for all children until they complete the age of fourteen years" (Article 45).

When India became independent, her literacy rate was 14 percent. During the seventeen years of Nehru's office it grew at less than one percent per year. According to the 1991 census, it stood at 52 percent. In other words, in the 44 years since Independence, the literacy rate has gone up by 38 percentage points.

No other head of government in the third world was more enlightened and cultured than Nehru. None was more deeply committed to development with social equity. It is, therefore, surprising that he failed to give the highest priority to universal literacy, as the success of every plan for economic growth or social justice was contingent on the support of a literate population. This neglect becomes all the more difficult to explain in view of his ceaseless efforts to politically educate the Indian masses and the Congress Party through his speeches and writings.

"We want to spend large sums of money on education," Nehru told Tibor Mende. "On the other hand we want to spend money on wealth-producing activities too, so that we may have money to spend on education."[3] He firmly believed in planning, and planning is basically an exercise in determining priorities between competing demands. Whenever there was a financial crunch, it was the allocation for education and social welfare that was reduced. Obviously, mass education was not considered an overriding priority.

Nehru swore by socialism, and his aim was to establish an egalitarian social order in India. Yet countries which never proclaimed such noble ambitions, quietly went ahead and effectively introduced some radically equalitarian policies. During the Meiji period in Japan a regulation was introduced in 1872, saying, "Henceforth throughout the land without distinction of class and sex in no village shall there be a house without learning, in no house an ignorant individual. Every guardian, acting in accordance with this, shall bring up his children with tender care, never failing to have them attend school."

Most capitalist countries, which shunned the shadow of socialism had opted for compulsory mass literacy by the beginning of the 20th century. And with the communist states it was an article of faith. Even small Asian countries like Sri Lanka, Thailand, Singapore, Malaysia, and the two Koreas required all children to attend school.

Two aspects of the government policies in promoting universal education merit attention. First, the provision of funds for expanding the educational facilities and second, the pattern of this funding.

During the first three Five Year Plans framed under Nehru, the allocation for education ranged between 7.8 to 5.9 percent of the Plan budget (subsequently this figure declined by about 50 percent). This provision was about half to one-third of the funds provided for other important sectors like industry, agriculture and communications. In other words, programmes of immediate growth were given much higher priority. More importantly, India has been spending around 3 percent of her GNP on education, which is abysmally low, especially in view of the leeway to be made. Even developing countries like Algeria, Egypt, Indonesia, Kenya, Malaysia, Philippines, Sri Lanka, Thailand and Vietnam spend two to three times the share of their GNP on education as compared to India. Their literacy rates range anywhere from 80 to 90 percent.

And what is the quality of this primary education? According to the Ministry of Education's own publication, *Challenge of Education (1985)*:

> Where (primary) schools exist, 40 percent have no pucca buildings, 39.72 percent have no blackboards, and 59.50 percent have no drinking water. Thirty-five percent schools have a single teacher to teach 3 or 4 different classes... many schools remain without any teacher for varying periods of time and some teachers are not above subcontracting teaching work to others...[4]

If these official statistics sound a bit alarming, then here is a nugget from the same report to put things in proper perspective:

> Education is not a ritual. It cannot be taken as having been delivered till a child has reached the level of attainment envisaged as a norm for a 14-year-old boy or girl. *With dropout rates ranging around 77 percent*, enrolment, by itself, loses its meaning except as a frame of reference[5] (emphasis added).

What an anomalous situation! On the one hand there is severe shortage of funds to expand primary educational facilities; on the other the bulk of the expenditure incurred goes waste as three-fourths of enrolled students drop out half-way through.

Perhaps more disconcerting than the state of primary education is the elitist bias built into the pattern of its funding. As a share of the total plan allocation for education, 58 percent of the funds were earmarked for primary education in the First Plan. This provision sharply dropped by 40 percent for the Second Plan, and again slipped further for the Third. On the other hand, resources given to Higher Secondary, University and Technical Education were 35 percent of the total provision in the First Plan, and jumped to 63 percent in the Second Plan. In the Third Plan there was a slight drop of 3 percentage points.

What was the impact of these allocations on the growth of primary and university education? Whereas the former grew by an average of 6.2 percent during the fifties and 5.0 percent in the sixties, the latter registered a growth rate of 12.4 percent and 13.4 percent respectively over the same two decades.[6] In other words, in a poor country with a literacy rate of 14 percent in 1947, higher education grew 200-250 percent faster than primary education during the regime of a prime minister who was an ardent advocate of social justice.

The main reason for this inverted growth of the educational system is its elitist bias. It is reflective of a caste-ridden, hierarchical society, where education has always been an exclusive pursuit. Those who talk nostalgically of India's great scholastic traditions and love of learning, should also remember that the doors to even basic literacy were closed to three-fourths of her people. When India became independent, her political and ruling class mostly came from the upper castes. Despite the most altruistic motives, they were burdened by the baggage of tradition. To a high caste Hindu, the spectacle of a university campus littered with Shudras and Mlechhas (Untouchables) was violative of the natural order of things. And it was unnatural for him to strive towards such a goal.

Nehru was totally free of any caste bias. Yet, with his Tripos from Cambridge and strong commitment to modernization, his instinctive preference was for higher education, research and other high visibility aspects of learning.

An important objective of mass education was to reduce social distances and promote an equalitarian culture. But in the process of implementation, it further split the society in two unequal segments. One, which studied in the English medium in prestigious private schools, and the other which went to ill-equipped village or municipal schools. The former, comprising upper caste, upper class students, were trained to become administrators, professionals and captains of industry. The latter continued to slog as "hewers of wood and drawers of water" in the tradition of their sires and grand-sires. Here again Manu was reincarnated through a highly divisive education system, directly under the nose of the socialist Nehru.

Some 'well-meaning' and 'pragmatic' educators have argued that the present system of education does not meet the needs of the village children; that a villager hardly ever makes use of his literacy; that in the absence of constant reinforcement, the children lapse back into illiteracy and even if a poor peasant manages to send his children to university at great cost to the family, he does not get a job even after graduation. If these arguments are accepted at face value, India should drop all plans for mass literacy. Yet there is a clincher based on objective facts which contradicts this view. Of the major states of India, the four with the lowest literacy levels are Bihar, Uttar Pradesh, Rajasthan and Madhya Pradesh.[7] And, both economically and socially, they happen to be at the bottom of the national ladder. On the other hand, the four states with the highest literacy rates are Kerala, Maharashtra, Tamil Nadu and Gujarat.[8] And undoubtedly, in terms of income levels and quality of life, they come in the top bracket of well-to-do states. Significantly, Kerala, which is far ahead of other states in literacy levels, also has the most impressive record in family planning. And this depite the fact that more than 40 percent of its population consists of Muslims and Catholics, who are traditionally against contraception.

In a survey of Bombay city conducted by T.D. Lakdawala in 1963, it was found that whereas the monthly income of an illiterate was Rs.103/-, that of a literate was Rs.145/-. Further, a matriculate earned Rs.327/-, a graduate Rs.650/-, and a technician Rs.1,000/- plus per month.[9]

The Education Ministry's report referred to earlier says, "Many studies have shown that in the field of education, investments in elementary education yield the highest rate of return and have a significant impact on productivity and the general well-being of the masses.[10] Yet the country's planners were seeking these returns from heavy industry and mega dams, treating mass education primarily as a dispensable frill.

The only way to universalize education is to make it compulsory.

It has been argued that whereas the authoritarian regimes of Japan, Korea or the communist countries had no problem enforcing this provision, the case of a democracy like India was very different. But the London county made primary education compulsory in the 1870s, and 31 states of the USA had done it by 1900. It is the same with most other Western democracies.

One serious disincentive to compulsory primary education is supposed to be the loss of income from child labour. This view is wholly fallacious. Child labour only displaces adult labour and depresses wage rates all around. As pointed out by Myron Weiner, "In pottery industry... children are employed in spite of high levels of local adult unemployment. Adults are displaced by children who are paid less with the result that the poor are made worse off by child labour. Adult unemployment is widespread in areas in which children are at work."[11]

Millions of children in India who should be normally attending school are employed in cottage industries, road-side eateries and as domestic servants. Offical agencies look indulgently at the employment of children in small-scale industries producing gems, carpets, brassware, etc., as their export earns the country valuable foreign exchange. It is argued that the low wages of children not only keep the cost of production down, their 'tiny deft fingers' are better suited to carpet weaving and such other fine crafts. Even if one ignores the barbaric implications of bartering the poor children's childhood for the sake of earning a few extra dollars, the logic itself is flawed. Iran and Turkey manufacture much finer carpets for export without employing child labour. Moreover, the labour component in the price of an export quality carpet is marginal.

In fact, argues Wiener, Indian goverment policy promotes the employment of children. "Small scale industries are legally permitted to use child labour directly or to sub-contract with so-called family owned workshops... The government policy of supporting cottage industries and the small-scale sector promotes the employment of children in unregulated hazardous work. And through its centres for training chidren as weavers for the carpet industry, government competes with the schools to attract children."[12]

Scarcity of resources is often cited as a reason for the slow expansion of primary education. But this scarcity has not inhibited the fast growth of higher education in which the elite have a personal stake. The fact is that if the children of poor parents start attending schools, factories will lose cheap labour, upper class housewives will lose low paid and docile domestic servants, and the government will have to divert funds from higher to primary education. As Gandhi very aptly said, the heart of India's problem lay in the heartlessness of its educated people.

The British, "adopted the traditional model of the public education system which was obviously meant for the upper social classes and was too costly to admit of any large-scale expansion. Its content was also mainly book-oriented rather than life-oriented, and it cultivated white-collar attitudes rather than the dignity of manual labour."[13]

After Independence, Nehru had no reservation in retaining this system in its entirety. And why not? Was it not this system which had produced the great national leaders and the mighty bureaucracy?

Paulo Freire says, "... the school, whatever its level, finds itself playing a most important role, that of an instrument of social control."[14] "All over the world," writes Ivan Illich, "schools are organized enterprises designed to reproduce the established order, whether this order is called revolutionary, conservative, or evolutionary... In poor countries schools retionalize economic lag."[15] Friere has repeatedly stressed that education is a value-loaded, political activity. "There is no such thing as a neutral educational process. Education either functions as an instrument which is used to facilitate the integration of the younger generation into the logic of the present system and bring about conformity to it, or it becomes the practice of freedom, the means by which men and women deal critically and creatively with the reality and discover how to participate in the transformation of their world."[16]

The Indian model of education is, of course, entirely integrative. It is designed to produce docile, receptive, conformist students. But the ruling classes which have designed this model, and Paulo Friere who describes its attributes, underestimate the subversive potential of the written word. Mass education, irrespective of its content, quickens the mind, tempts it to dream forbidden dreams and stray into mine fields.

The Total Literacy Campaign was started by the National Literacy Mission in the late eighties to give a push to mass literacy. Though there was nothing revolutionary in these official campaigns, the mild awakening they produced in the countryside threatened the political establishment. For instance, a lesson in a textbook for neo-literates in Nellore district described how a woman became indignant at the sight of the youth of her village squandering away all on *arrack* (alcohol) and mobilized the rest of the women to force the closure of the *arrack* shop in the village. The women learners of Nellore decided to translate the message into real life by forcibly closing down the *arrack* shops in their villages and by preventing liquor auction. As a large part of the state's revenues accrued from this source, and some of the biggest *arrack* contractors were Congressmen, this was greatly resented by the chief minister of the state. At a meeting of the district collectors "he fulminated against 'some of the material in the publications brought out by the literacy missions' which he felt was 'not in conformity with the policies of the goverment,' and warned that such lessons would be expunged."[17]

The association of some voluntary organizations with literacy campaigns made them special targets of official ire. The Kerala Shastra Sahitya Parishad, which had taken a leading part in the literacy movement, was disbanded immediately by the Congress chief minister when his party came to power.[18] In Pondicherry, another organization was accused by the goverment of being anti-patriotic. The chief minister was greatly incensed by a song in a post-literacy primer which asked: "freedom for the country but why poverty for us?"[19]

In Madhya Pradesh, "the Raigarh collector was suddenly transferred in spite of the fact that he was doing really good work in motivating people to attend the literacy classes ...." "The Durg collector... had started a vigorous literacy campaign ... He too was abruptly transferred." A local public man remarked, "... big-time farmers of the district have been discouraging the literacy campaign for fear of losing the illiterate cheap labour."[20]

Though the above instances belong to the post-Nehru era, their message is equally relevant for the earlier period as well. 'Pedagogy of the oppressed', even in the conventional and conformist mode, carries seditious messages. After all, the rulers of the princely states were more straightforward in their approach when they discouraged the opening of new schools.

Nehru often showed impatience at the slow progress of various development schemes. But as to education he stated, "Education is spreading fairly well and today we have some fifty million boys and girls in our schools and colleges."[21] And he was still more elated about the state of women's education. He wrote, "Already I see major changes taking place which are not perhaps so evident to outsiders ... Probably the biggest revolution that is taking place in India is through women's education which affects directly the home."[22]

What was the basis of this optimism? Female literacy crawled from 8 to 16 percent between the census of 1951 and 1961: a measly rise of 8 percentage points in ten years — and that too from such a low base. Yet, somehow, Nehru appears to have convinced himself that this was the "biggest revolution that is taking place in India."

Nehru spoke and wrote millions of words on matters of national concern. But his utterances on mass education are relatively few. He set up numerous commissions and committees to examine important issues of public policy. But no high-level agency was created to advise the goverment on universalization of literacy. The Education Commission was established in the year of his death, and a National Education Policy framed four years later. It is a pity that no serious effort was made to construct a model for mass literacy specifically suited to India's needs.

A wholly indigenous, holistic model was available to Nehru on tap. But Gandhi's concept of Basic Education appeared too rustic to the Western educated elite. His scheme for free and self-financing, compulsory education for seven years in the children's mother tongue, with manual and socially productive work at its core, seemed too pedestrian for the smart children of the urban elite. No wonder, then, that Basic Education was criticized by the Congress Party's National Planning Committee under Nehru. "They objected to the emphasis on vocation and child labour, and offered instead a broad curriculum for elementary education, and expansion of facilities for technical education. Financial responsibility for compulsory education was assigned to be that of the State."[23]

In fact Gandhi's was a remarkable scheme for a poor, over-populated and developing country. But it was only a conceptual outline, and had to be fleshed out through trial and experimentation. Owing to his great prestige, it was adopted by several states. But their whole approach was ad-hocish. "We started Basic Education and instead of making corresponding changes at the secondary stage, made modifications in the basic education itself to fit into the secondary stage."[24]

Basic Education was adopted by a large number of village schools. In the city schools where children do even clay modeling with clean and synthetic plasticine, how could parents agree to their darlings soiling their hands with lowly earth and mud. Right from the beginning, it was perceived as a poor man's scheme — a second-class and cheap method designed for the village children. It was totally rejected by the urban, educated classes. With this sort of stigma attached to it, Basic Education died an unnatural death.

When Nehru introduced land reforms, he aimed at changing property relations in the countryside. The public sector was created to enable the state to control the commanding heights of the economy. Community development and Panchayati Raj were meant to promote participatory democracy and thus empower the masses. What did he expect education to do? For one thing, he wanted the country to have a vast reservoir of trained manpower to modernize the economy through rapid industrialization. Then, in a general sort of way, he hoped that mass education would break the shackles of superstition and obscurantism, and help people to become enlightened citizens of a progressive democracy. But he did not treat mass education as the prime mover for the success of all his other reforms. Nor was he worried that without basic reforms the colonial education system would only help consolidate the hegemony of the existing ruling class, and thereby frustrate his egalitarian agenda.

The Education Commission observed, "A major reason for our failure to bring about radical reconstruction of the educational system in the past has been the fact that we have ignored the close relationship between social and educational transformation and the consequent need for a simultaneous effort on both fronts."[25] On the other hand the Commission said, "... while it is comparatively easy to introduce educational reforms that support the existing social structure, it is extremely difficult, if not impossible, to implement radical educational reforms which threaten the existing social structure or run counter to its imperatives."[26]

Radical reforms are difficult to implement in any vital sector of the national activity where the elite classes have vested interests. But in the case of universal education, Nehru had no concrete policy of reform before him, nor did he try to speed up the existing system. Even some very obvious reforms, like delinking of degrees from employment, or making special efforts to accelerate female literacy were ignored. Consequently, India kept wasting scarce resources on producing armies of unemployable graduates and her female literacy rate remained among the lowest in the world.

No area of reform was more important for a resurgent India than mass education, and in none was Nehru's failure more pronounced. And if Nehru did not perceive the seminal value of mass education, none of his successors could. This neglect would give India the distinction of entering the 21st century with more than half the illiterates of the world living within her borders.

7

Three Critical Errors-II

Land Reforms Derailed

"*The* heart of power, prestige, and standing in the village," said Daniel Thorner, "lies in land. Put land in the hands of those who are working it and you crack the existing concentration of power."[1]

Once Gandhi started mobilizing the peasantry to give a mass base to the freedom movement, the question of land reforms received continuous attention from the Congress. After Independence it was a high priority item for the Nehru government. The First Five Year Plan recognized:

> The future of land ownership and cultivation constitutes perhaps the most fundamental issue in national development. To a large extent, the pattern of economic and social organization will depend upon the manner in which the land problem is resolved.[2]

Though the question of modernization through industrial growth was at the centre of Nehru's agenda, he fully realized that social transformation in rural India will occur only if the parasite class of zamindars (landlords) is eliminated, and the tiller of the land given ownership rights in his land. And this was the thrust of the entire land reforms programme. But the end result of this massive effort shows how the class interest of the land owners ultimately prevailed, and how Nehru's honest and earnest attempts were partially frustrated.

Briefly, land reforms were implemented in two phases. During the first phase the zamindari system of intermediaries was abolished and the tenants were given proprietary rights to the land they cultivated. In the second phase, a ceiling was placed on the size of land holdings of individual owners to ensure a more equitable distribution of land.

But land reforms was a state subject and the relevant legislation had to be passed and implemented by the state governments. And that is where the shadow fell between the concept and the act. To begin with, the legislation itself was full of loopholes. For instance, the zamindars were allowed to retain self-cultivated land in the form of *Khud Kasht, Sir,* or home farm. The nature of self-cultivation did not mean use of manual labour; mere supervision of agricultural operations was considered good enough. The size of home farm was also not clearly defined, and it was mostly exempted from land ceilings. Then there was a provision for the 'resumption' of land by a landlord. This enabled the zamindar to take away from a tenant the land he had never cultivated in the past but wanted to cultivate now. "This was a concession to landowners almost unparalleled in the history of land reforms."[3] Lakhs of cultivators lost their tenancy as a result of this provision. Then, under the scheme of voluntary surrender, a tenant could relinquish his holding in favour of the landlord. This was only a cover for forcing the defenceless cultivators to give up their tenancy right in favour of the zamindars. Also, even though the zamindari abolition laws entitled tenants to proprietary rights, they could do so only by paying the stipulated compensation. Several cultivators did not have the means to do so and, thus, the original proprietors continued to be the owners.

Similar was the case with the imposition of land ceilings. The ceiling laws were under discussion for nearly a decade. During this interval big landowners parcelled out their excess land in the form of fictitious transfers, bogus sale deeds and partitions. Several categories of land like orchards and plantations were exempted from the operation of this law. Taking advantage of this provision, large tracts of land were listed under exempted categories in collusion with the revenue officials. The proprietors naturally saw to it that if land became surplus with them, it was the least fertile piece they parted with.

At a more basic level, there were two prerequisites for the success
of land reforms. One, the accuracy of the revenue records and,
two, the ability of the newly empowered categories to enforce
their rights. For centuries, the landlord-tenant relationship was
governed by oral understanding, and the formal status of the
cultivator was not generally shown in official records. It was,
therefore, not possible for a large number of tenants to establish
their tenancy for lack of documentary evidence. As to the second
requirement, most of the tenants were poor and illiterate. They
were not even aware of their rights. And, they did not have the
resources to seek legal remedies.

Top leadership of the Congress was generally opposed to radical
agrarian reforms. Whereas the party bosses never expressed their
opposition openly, they were adept at sabotaging or diluting any
substantive move to take land away from the zamindars and give
it to the tillers. Political expediency also worked against the landless. Most of the state chief ministers continuously put pressure
on the Central government to go slow on agrarian reforms so as
not to antagonize the landed interests which controlled vote
banks. Even if they had no personal stake in land, they were
apprehensive of the rightist parties gaining ground against the
Congress in the next election.

In concrete terms, what was the outcome of various land-reform
measures adopted by the state governments? On the plus side,
the institution of absentee landlords was eliminated. These intermediaries between the cultivator and the state, in addition to
collecting revenue, also used to impose a number of inequitous
cesses of their own. These too were swept away along with the
zamindars. This naturally reduced considerably the semi-feudal
exploitation of the peasantry. So far as tenants of zamindari
estates were concerned, nearly 20 million of them acquired
ownership rights in the land they had cultivated for generations.[4]
Also the rate of rent payable by share-croppers and tenants was

substantially lowered. An incidental benefit was the accrual of large areas of zamindari grazing and forest lands to the state.

The debit side of land reforms is equally significant. If they hit the big landlords, they harmed the small cultivator much more. Owing to various loopholes in the land reform laws, millions were deprived of their tenancy rights. Ironically, even the absentee landlords claimed large areas as their 'home-farm', thus robbing their tenants of the opportunity to become proprietors. On the other hand, the number of large landowners increased as a result of eviction and resumption. For instance, "In Bombay, between 1948 and 1951, the number of protected tenants declined from 1.7 million to 1.3 million; in Hyderabad (State), between 1951 and 1955, the number declined by 57 percent and the area held by them by 59 percent... of every 100 protected tenants in 1951, only 45 still held the same status by 1954 ..."[5]

In Nehru's scheme of social transformation, the constraints imposed by caste structures did not figure anywhere. Having studied Marx, he realized that in an agrarian society land was power, and the entrenched power structures could be altered only by changing the existing patterns of land ownership. But he did not appreciate that in India the economic hierarchy of feudalism was greatly reinforced by the rural hierarchy of caste. Big landowners belonged to the upper castes and agricultural workers to the lower castes. And caste structures were far more durable than the patterns of land ownership.

Gandhi himself believed in the caste system, and Congress never mounted a frontal attack on this pernicious institution. Incomplete land reforms not only left the high caste big landowners on top of the economic pyramid, they also, thereby, left intact their social dominance. In later years this unfinished agenda of land reforms was to create serious problems for Nehru's successors and keep caste in the forefront of Indian politics.

Moving away from the immediate impact of agrarian reforms, in what manner did they alter overall land ownership patterns and the class character of the peasantry? In the first place, whereas landlords as intermediaries vanished, 'landlordism' remained. The zamindars managed to become owners of large farms and employed hired labour to cultivate them. As upper castes are ritually debarred from engaging in manual work, they did not cultivate their own farms. The law also protected their so-called self-cultivated land, *Sir* or the homestead from the ambit of the tenancy laws.

Most importantly, as stated earlier, nearly 20 million tenants acquired ownership rights in the land cultivated by them. This considerably enlarged the size of the proprietary class and, to some extent, shifted the base of rural power in favour of the intermediate peasantry. Having ceased to be employees of landlords, a large number of them became employers of labour. Thus, they lost their radical character after their co-option by the propertied classes. These beneficiaries mostly belonged to the Shudra castes, and with their newly acquired respectability, they became ardent exploiters of labour, which largely comprised the Scheduled Castes.

The real losers in this game were those tenants who either could not establish their tenancy or did not have the money to pay compensation. Further, lakhs of them were evicted and they joined the ranks of the landless workers. Even owners of small farms met the same fate after their fields were purchased by the newly empowered landowners. For the landless, the ceiling law on holdings was a cruel joke. Only about 0.6 percent of the total agricultural land in the country was declared surplus, and even this was not distributed to them in its entirety.[6] Moreover, the land surrendered under these laws was of the poorest quality and of little use to the allottees.

A wholly unintended and far-reaching impact of agrarian reforms was the emergence of capitalist agriculture. Zamindars, who became owners of large farms, also got substantial compensation for their alienated estates. The newly empowered intermediate peasantry was ambitious and enterprising. As the acquisition of additional land became risky, the "enactment of ceiling legislation became, as it were, a means of extra-economic pressure on the landlord class, who thereby were forced to step up the process of the shift to capitalist farming."[7] This was a significant move towards the modernization of agriculture, increase in productivity and switch-over to commercial crops. However, "It effectively disrupted whatever was left of the 'feudal' coherence of the backward societies. It substituted market contracts for such paternalistic relationships as still survived from century to century."[8]

Land reforms could have been effectively used to raise the political and social consciousness of the peasantry. But Nehru restricted the formulation and implementation of this programme to his advisers and administrators only. Also, the new agrarian legislation was framed without any pressures or participation from below. Actually, after attaining Independence Nehru never used the vast party apparatus of the Congress to prime social reform or propel the process of democratic revolution. If Party cadres had been used to educate the timid and illiterate peasants about their new rights, and to assist them in enforcing those rights, it would have not only given a new dimension to land reforms, but rejuvenated the Congress party. In the absence of public participation and a mass upsurge, the agrarian agenda ended up as an administrative fiat with limited impact on the consciousness of the peasantry.

Even if land reforms did not result in restructuring the patterns of land ownership and the base of rural power as visualized by Nehru, what was their impact on national politics?

The big landholders were the mainstay of the Congress as they controlled the vote bank. Despite the introduction of adult franchise and the rising anger of the landless at being cheated by land reforms, rural politics did not get aligned along class lines. For one, rural society was too fragmented on the caste basis for any such polarization. Secondly, the landlords had too strong a hold on the dependent lower peasantry to permit any independent mobilization. As A.R. Desai observed, "Their (Indian peasants') helplessness lies in the objective conditions of their dependence and not the subjective conditions of their backwardness."

For Nehru, industrialization was the engine of change. He had a limited understanding of the multi-layered, integrated nature of the agrarian system which made it a composite whole. He perceived the peasantry primarily as an economic category and did not pay attention to its social dynamics. He, therefore, did not try to raise the social awareness of the lower peasantry through political action to make it a potent tool in his campaign for social transformation. Consequently the rural poor in India continued to be voiceless.

With increasing self-assurance and expanding political constituency, the newly empowered intermediate peasantry became one of the most powerful demand groups in the country. Cutting across class affinities it was able to mobilize horizontally the loyalty of fellow Shudra castes, which constitute more than 50 percent of the country's population. And vertically, it had a strong hold over the landless, the majority of whom belonged to the Scheduled Castes. The assertion of its rights and interests were, in certain spheres, opposed to those of the urban bourgeoisie, and this conflict widened the rural-urban cleavage which subsequently came to be known as the Bharat versus India divide. Ideologically, the politics of this class was clearly centrist: the only change it wanted in the system was more and more concessions to further consolidate its existing privileges. As the agenda of radical land reforms threatened the vested interests of the proprietary class, and the Centre could not satisfy its rising aspirations, the peasantry gradually drifted out of the Congress fold.

As to the ideological dimension of the agrarian reforms, they were not even remotely socialistic. They did bring to an end the semi-feudal mode of agricultural production, but this only gave rise to the emergence of capitalist agriculture. The saddest part of the incomplete land reforms is that Nehru's hope of reshaping agrarian relations by giving land to the tiller seems to have been lost for good.

Nehru himself had no illusions about the souring of his dream of a transformed, socially equitable rural India. He wrote in a letter, "Indeed it has become rather a joke in some foreign countries when they refer to land reforms in India. We have talked tall and done nothing."[9]

Basically, the inadequacies of land reforms resulted from lack of political will, and Nehru has to carry a major share of the blame. Without any commitment to egalitarianism, Japan enacted a law in 1946 to give land to the landless, and in three years flat the job was completed 100 percent. So did several other East Asian countries. And India kept discussing the land ceilings legislation for a decade before enacting the necessary laws! By then the horse had bolted from the stable.

8

Three Critical Errors-III

Colonial Bureaucracy Preserved

Nehru was in his mid-forties when he wrote his autobiography. During the previous two decades of political activity he was closely associated with the Non-Cooperation and Civil Disobedience movements. He had already served his first term as the Congress President and four terms in prison. With all this exposure, he had obviously acquired an intimate knowledge of the colonial administration and the ways of the bureaucracy. Thus, when he wrote, "But of one thing I am quite sure, that no new order can be built up in India as long as the spirit of the ICS pervades our administration and our public services" it was a remark anchored in practical knowledge and conviction. He further observed, "Therefore, it seems to me quite essential that the ICS and similar services must disappear completely, as such, before we can start real work on a new order."[1]

After becoming prime minister in the Interim Central Government in 1946, he said at the Meerut Session of the Congress, '... the Civil Services were fossilized in their mental outlook and wedded to the bygone and obsolete methods. They refused to move with the times and their conduct and attitude have not changed...'

In a letter to Patel he wrote:

> ... our troubles may be due to lack of system or policy apart from individuals ... decisions taken are not given effect to and are hung up inordinately. It is difficult to catch the culprit for some suitable excuse is always forthcoming. I am shocked at the slowness of our work and the delays that continuously occur. I felt, therefore, and feel still that it is necessary to overhaul this entire system.[2]

In view of this awareness Nehru gave high priority to reorganizing the civil administration. He set up the Secretariat Reorganization Committee in July 1947. Thereafter he appointed several committees and commissioned experts to examine this issue. A whole chapter on 'Reform in Administration' was included in the First Five Year Plan. Later, he invited Paul Appleby, an American expert on public administration, to examine how India's administrative system could be improved. Nehru circulated his report to all the chief ministers, referred to it repeatedly and urged early action on it.

At the macro level Nehru created new structures for a host of developmental and welfare activities. The setting up of the Planning Commission in 1950 was a landmark decision. Community Project Administration was also set up at the same time. No less important was the creation of a vast public sector to accelerate industrial growth and control the commanding heights of the economy. Then there was the formation of a number of economic ministries to look after the rapidly expanding industrial and commercial activities of the state.

Nehru was quite clear as to what he expected from a revamped administration. The First Five Year Plan stressed, "From the maintenance of law and order and collection of revenue, the major emphasis now shifts to development of human and material resources and the elimination of poverty and want... (there is also) need for structural changes to raise the level of administration..."

But at the operational level, what was the actual outcome of his efforts to reorganize the administration? The labels of ICS and IP were replaced by IAS and IPS; bureaucracy multiplied at an unprecedented scale; systems and procedures remained wholly intact; the Kafkaesque labyrinths of the government departments got ever more tortuous; red tape multiplied and corruption galloped.

The extent to which colonial rules and procedures were preserved is aptly illustrated by the observation of a former Cabinet

Secretary. Rules of Business of the Central Government provide the frame within which the ministries transact their business. After independence, these rules "were respected almost *in toto*, the only change being the substitution of Minister for Executive Councillor, and the Prime Minister for Governor General. The states were also advised to follow suit."[3]

The Fundamental Rules and Supplementary Rules are the financial Bible for every government office. They were framed in the twenties and, except for periodic amendments, regulate the transaction of all financial business even today. The *Indian Police Act*, which determines the character and structure of the police force, was enacted in 1861. The *Indian Penal Code* and the *Criminal Procedure Code*, which govern the administration of criminal law, were passed in 1860 and 1898. The pivotal *Indian Evidence Act* came into force in 1872. The *Indian Telegraph Act* was passed in 1885, when even the wireless had not been invented. In this age of satellite television and E-mail, it still governs the licensing and operation of communication systems, creating no end of problems.

Laws, rules, and procedures not only give shape to the institutional framework, they also fashion the outlook of the bureaucracy which administers them. They reflect the temper and values of the age in which they are framed. The fact that India is still governed by a legal system conceived and formulated in the colonial era, and most of it in the 19th century, shows that this country is even today ruled by the colonial ethos of that period.

How is it that Nehru did not follow through his resolve to restructure the bureaucracy? He, no doubt, had his reasons to go slow on reforms. The partition of India caused a revolutionary upheaval without creating a revolutionary upsurge. Even a normal, efficient and well-staffed administration would have caved in under its pressures. But India's administrative set-up after Partition was in a state of disrepair. One half of the 1200 ICS officers were British, and they left India after Independence. Another hundred or so went to Pakistan. The same was the case with other services. Thus it was with greatly depleted cadres of the higher civil services that Nehru had to tackle the immediate problems of settling refugees, controlling communal frenzy and restoring a semblance of normality. No less urgent was the challenge of holding the country together.

Whereas these factors were valid reasons for not forcing the pace of reforms, they cannot serve as alibis for inaction. Despite his repeated assertions for a radical overhaul of the system, Nehru did not initiate any significant move for reforming the civil administration. How does one explain this?

Nehru was approaching sixty and he was battling on too many fronts. He wrote to his sister a few months after assuming office, "It is difficult for me to explain to you the situation here, and the difficulties we have to face all around. It has been impossible in these circumstances to do many of the things we wanted to do. All planning has been postponed. We live here from crisis to crisis and almost all work is suspended."[4] And a little earlier he had written to K.P.S. Menon, "I am so tired of second rate work that sheer efficiency appeals to me."[5] His zeal for reform was soon encrusted with the patina of custom and habit. The virtues of immediate peace, stability and continuity obscured the distant advantages of turbulent change. He told the Lok Sabha in 1954, "We had, fortunately, a peaceful transfer of power in this country, with a running machine. A running machine has its advantages and disadvantages."[6] Five years later, in an interview to a journalist, Nehru said, "I think the services, by and large, are very good... what is really wrong is not the human material, but the procedures inherited by us from the past." But he did not explain as to why these procedures could not be changed, or whose job was it to change them.

It is surprising that the same bureaucracy he had berated earlier for its conservatism, he later used as a delivery system for radical change. Though Nehru showed early awareness of the fact that 'no new order can be built up in India so long as the spirit of the ICS pervades our administration,' it is doubtful if he fully realized the basic character of modern bureaucracy and its unsuitability for the task of social transformation. The colonial administration was designed by the British to give stability and respectability to the imperial order. The mainstay of the system was the Indian Civil Service, modelled on the scheme conceived by Macaulay. The recruits to this elite corps were selected on the basis of a competitive examination; they had security of tenure and a definite career plan. The service was hierarchical, professionally trained, and each officer had clearly defined functions. Objectivity and anonymity were prized virtues. Impersonal rules and procedures governed the transaction of official business. This is obviously the Weberian model of a legal rational bureaucracy, and the same system governed the other services. With suitable modifications, this is the pattern adopted by most Western democracies.

Weber's concept of bureaucracy grew out of the soil of mature capitalistic economies of the West. The ruling classes there wanted stability, efficiency and continuity. This was also the primary concern of the colonial rulers of India.

But after Independence, the basic theme of the country's polity was change, transformation and reform. This required an entirely different type of administrative set-up and outlook. By retaining the colonial bureaucracy, Nehru inadvertently adopted a system which placed a heavy premium on status quo. Not only that. Certain regressive features of India's social order reinforced some reactionary aspects of the Weberian model. For instance, the rigid caste differentiation in India fits the bureaucratic hierarchal structure like a glove, and provides it with a durable social basis. The Brahamanical love of ritualism exalts the adherence to elaborate rules and procedures to the level of religious veneration.

Forms and structures create their own inner dynamics and impose their own pattern on the work environment. Hierarchical formations inculcate a deep concern for status and protocol. In its working, bureaucracy manifests the power of the state. But pursuit of power becomes a goal in itself. Though it continuously interacts with the people and deals with their problems, its elitist character inhibits the fostering of warmth and empathy towards them. Cultivation of an impersonal and detached approach turns the administrative act into a clinical exercise instead of a human encounter. It keeps proliferating not in response to demand, but as a means to self-aggrandizement.

These traits of bureaucracy pose a threat to the very spirit of democracy and smack of authoritarianism. The Secretary of State was considered the father figure of the ICS. Yet one of them observed, "No bureaucracy in the world will ever transform itself into self-government. The motive power must come from outside. Their very virtues are inimical to a parliamentary system, and it is inevitable that they should magnify the difficulty and dangers of any change."[7] Nehru himself remarked, "The way government organizations and departments multiply leads us nowhere but to waste... If it is not stopped, I tell you the head will remain small and the body will go on increasing in size. Such maldevelopment of organizations is dangerous to our country."[8]

Despite these clear warnings and forebodings, bureaucracy has steadily grown in size and power. How come? For one thing, bureaucracy performs a useful function as the maintenance mechanic of society. Further, both in policy formulation and its execution its role is indispensable. In a developing society in transition, its contribution to holding the social fabric together is particularly important. Its permanent cadres with their rule-bound, impersonal approach, lend continuity and stability to civil administration. As these are also the goals of the ruling class, this creates no dissonance in the management of public affairs.

Secondly, with continuous increase in the functions of the state, the process of governance has become more and more complex. This not only results in a corresponding expansion of bureaucracy, but also in the need for progressively specialized cadres. Though the Indian civil servants are supposed to be generalists, in fact they are specialists in general administration. Their vast and varied experience sharpens their skills as systems coordinators. This gives the bureaucracy great power over the decision-making processes of the government.

After Independence, the two imperative needs of the country were stability and change. To some extent these are conflicting goals, as change is normally unsettling. The colonial bureaucracy was well-equipped to provide stability, but wholly unsuited to initiate change. In fact the shift from a limited government to an

all-pervasive welfare state was quite disconcerting for the bureaucracy, as it implied a change from a ruling to a serving civil
service. Both in terms of its tradition and structure, it was unrealistic to expect it to establish a direct rapport with the masses,
to educate them in the values of democracy and socialism, and
thereby to whittle down an ancient society's resistance to change.
'Keepers of the past' says Paul A. Baran, 'cannot be the builders
of the future.'

Despite Nehru's realization that 'no new order can be built up in
India so long as the spirit of the ICS pervades our administration',
he not only preserved that spirit, but also handed over a good
part of his political agenda to the bureaucracy. No Western country which has adopted the Weberian model, has used it for social
reform. This was a misapplication of tools.

Any programme of social change or reform is an ideology-
driven activity; it is essentially a political act. The Nehruvian plan
for transformation of the Indian society meant churning up the
social cauldron and surfacing of latent conflicts and contradictions. The management of the resultant social ferment and discords was a political and not an administrative issue. Yet the
bureaucracy was entrusted with the job. Predictably, the project
for change collapsed. But here it is not the bureaucracy which
failed its political masters; it is the masters who failed themselves.

Nehrus' own social background has something to do with this
failure. He was basically an aristocrat who did not feel at home
with the *hoi polloi*. The common run of Indian politicians —
grubby, greedy and grimy — did not inspire Nehru's affection or
confidence. He was, therefore, reluctant to associate these 'rab-
ble-rousers' with the implementation of his political agenda.

But Nehru made a major mistake in not risking the association
of the party workers with his programmes. It is quite likely that
their induction would have spurred corruption, promoted disre-
spect for law and weakened the institutional authority. But all
these things have happened in any case. And if this price had to
be paid, it would have been worthwhile to mobilize party cadres
to infuse new life into various projects for reform and growth.

As legitimate outlets to party workers were not provided, they devised illegitimate routes to power, prestige and patronage. During the colonial period, the administrators and politicians sat on opposite sides of the fence, and kept each other in check. This situation continued for some time after Independence also. But both the parties soon realized that co-operation would serve their interests better than confrontation. The officials themselves welcomed this collusion, as it helped in insulating them from public pressures. In the past, if a police inspector misbehaved, the people mounted an agitation, and the politicians took up their cause with the higher authorities. This placed a healthy curb on the arbitrary actions of field officials. Now, the same politicians mediated on behalf of the errant officials to earn their gratitude, and the people's tribunes became their censors. This was a peculiar inversion of the process of participatory democracy: earlier, the bureaucracy had acted as a wall between the people and their representatives; now the politicians became a parallel barrier between the masses and the state. This dual isolation of the electorate from their elected government warped the growth of the Indian polity and had a baneful influence on the evolution of democratic institutions.

But if one accepts that the Weberian model of bureaucracy was unsuited to the needs of a developing country trying to pursue the twin objectives of democracy and economic growth, what was the solution? When Mao Zedong realized that the 'new class' which had risen in China after the revolution was still elitist in outlook and did not relate to the people on an equal footing, he launched the Cultural Revolution. Of course, the experiment proved to be a disaster. But one should not throw away the baby with the bath water. Where Mao went wrong was not in his perception, but his prescription. His objective to send bureaucrats, university dons and other pen-pushers to fields and factories to engage in manual work was well conceived. Savants like Tolstoy and Gandhi have tried to propagate dignity of labour in their own ways. Of course all such experiments have failed as deeply entrenched vested interests cannot be dislodged with a single push. But this does not mean that one should accept the invincibility of bureaucracy as integral to the human situation and not try to create a more humane, free and participatory society.

The British have sedulously cultivated the myth of an apolitical and neutral bureaucracy. India adopted this view without questioning its relevance to the local situation. It has two obvious lacunae. First, at the higher levels of governance, politics and administration overlap. How can a secretary to the government give useful advice to his minister on issues like nationalization, abolition of zamindari, or creation of an egalitarian society unless he has political vision? There are numerous instances of Labour and Social Democratic governments having failed to implement their policies owing to the ideological antipathy of the permanent civil service.

And how can you be neutral between the exploiter and the exploited? If a bureaucrat has to serve governments of all hues with equal zeal and loyalty, then he would operate a gas-chamber and a public health service with equal detachment and efficiency. Could any humane and just society accept this proposition? If this criterion is to be applied, then most of the Nazi convicts at the Nuremberg trials should have been decorated for dedicated service.

Secondly, whatever the agenda of the government it serves, no bureaucracy has ever betrayed its social class. The fiction of neutrality is a cover for not upsetting the existing order. Otherwise, how does one explain that contrary to Nehru's policy formulations, the rich in India kept growing richer, income disparities kept increasing, and political freedom did not lead to economic freedom?

'Commitment' has always been considered a dirty word by the norms of bureaucracy. It offends and violates the holy spirit of 'neutrality'. But in a developing country like India with millions living below the poverty line, how can one hand over the programme of social and economic reforms to a bureaucracy which is not emotionally and intellectually committed to the goals of the polity? In the Indian situation neutrality verges on insensitivity and immorality. A service class which serves a communal regime with as much devotion as a secular one, or a fascist rule with the same loyalty as a democracy, is suffering from moral blindness. In fact there are democracies, most notably the USA, where the chief political executive has the option to fill the top posts with officials of his way of thinking. This may not be the best alternative for India, especially in view of the prevalence of nepotism. Yet the so-called neutral bureaucracy is no remedy either.

One great merit of democracy is that you cannot wrong too large a section of the people too long. A privileged bureaucracy, derived from upper castes and the upper middle class cannot rule the roost indefinitely, especially when its class bias causes deep resentment among the deprived masses. If the polity recoils from radical social surgery, then the next best thing is to broaden the base of the ruling class and democratize it by making it more representative. A bureaucracy in which the balance of class loyalties shifts in favour of the depressed classes would be definitely more sympathetic towards egalitarian policies than the elitist civil servants. The first move in this direction was made when job reservations for the Scheduled Castes and Scheduled Tribes were introduced in 1950. And it was four decades later when the rule of the 'dynasty' had already ended, that this provision was extended to the other backward classes with the acceptance of the Mandal Commision Report in 1990. With this concession, nearly half the posts under the Central government now stand reserved for the oppressed and backward classes.

In short, if India is not to petrify into a bureaucratic state, two things must happen. First, suitable political structures and mechanisms should be created at various levels to give the people and local politicians a stake in running the country. Obviously, these formations will be in addition to the state legislatures and the parliament. Secondly, the bureaucracy's social complexion will have to be changed to reflect the class composition of the Indian society.

When a foreign correspondent asked Nehru in 1961 as to what he thought was his 'greatest failure', he replied, "I failed to change the administration. It is still a colonial administration."[9] By this time Nehru had shot all his bolts and was fully aware that he did not have many miles to go before he could sleep. And he regarded his failure to reform the bureaucracy as the main reason for his unfinished tasks. If not *the* main reason, it certainly was one of the most important.

9

Planning for Economic Justice

*O*ne way to modernize a traditional and under-developed society is to demolish the old formations and replace them with new ones. Nehru's agenda for socialism and land reforms belonged to this category. The other, less unsettling approach is to create altogether new institutions so as to alter the existing balance of power and promote a more equitable sharing of national resources. The introduction of Planning, Community Development and Public Sector aimed at this objective.

Next to the rooting of democracy, the initiation of the planning process was the most important contribution Nehru made to the making of a new India. During his brief visit to the U.S.S.R. in 1927 he saw the fruits of planning and it left a deep impression on him. Owing to the publicity received by the Soviet precedent, planning seemed to have caught the country's imagination in the forties, and a group of leading industrialists prepared the Bombay Plan in 1944.

Nehru had already succeeded in creating wide public awareness about socialism and planning through his speeches and writings by the time India became Independent. He considered planning the linchpin of a welfare state and, at least in the initial stages, he devoted more time to it than to any other subject. Yet it is not certain that the Planning Commission would have been set up when it was, had extraneous circumstances not forced his hand.

Despite the favourable Industrial Policy Resolution of 1948, private industry's response was lukewarm and investment in new enterprises meagre. Agriculture was stagnant and industrial production had not picked up either. Inevitably, prices were rising. As there was no significant improvement on any front, the people felt let down. It was the urgency of this situation which impelled

Nehru to expedite the introduction of planning which he had been talking about all along. He set up a six-member Planning Commission in March 1950. There was nothing radical in its mandate, and its approach was gradualist. Its composition again highlighted Nehru's genius for ambiguity and his desire to avoid ruffling the feathers of the monied classes. Of its five members V.T. Krishnamachari, C.D. Deshmukh and R.K. Patil were former ICS officers. G.L. Mehta was a businessman. Gulzarilal Nanda, a labour leader, was appointed Vice Chairman (he was not a minister then). He and Nehru, its Chairman, were the only two members with socialist leanings. This was hardly the sort of team to shake up the system with its revolutionary ideas.

In fact it seems unbelievable that in the beginning Nehru offered the chairmanship of the Commission to Rajendra Prasad, a diehard conservative, who had no sympathy with any of Nehru's socialistic goals. Luckily, Prasad preferred to continue as Speaker of Lok Sabha. Otherwise, one can imagine the fate of planning if he had accepted Nehru's offer.

The Prime Minister's chairmanship of the Planning Commission greatly enhanced its status and authority. Whereas originally conceived as a purely advisory body, the imprint of the Prime Minister raised its advice to the level of a decree. It is rather anomalous that whereas the Planning Commission had neither any constitutional sanction nor a statutory basis, and was established only by an administrative fiat, under Nehru it became a 'super cabinet' in the sphere of economic policy.

Published in December 1952, the First Five Year Plan (1951-56) emphasized two important approaches for structural reforms. First, it stressed the role of the state as the prime mover of change. Second, it moved away from the facile assumption of raising agricultural production through the adoption of modern techniques and better utilization of resources. The First Plan pointed out that every new advance, while raising production, created new vested interests which, beyond a certain point, "hamper innovation and change.... For development to proceed further a re-adaptation of social institutions and social relationships thus becomes necessary... The problem, therefore, is not one of merely rechannelling economic activity within the existing framework; that framework itself has to be changed."[1]

The focus of the plan was the rural sector and, especially, production of foodgrains, as the food situation was becoming precarious. The Commission recommended the elimination of the unproductive intermediaries so as to ensure more efficient land use. Small landowners were asked to organize themselves into farming cooperatives to overcome the limitations of meagre holdings. Another important recommendation was the launching of Community Development Programmes based on a holistic approach to the development of village communities.

The First Five Year Plan, Nehru himself remarked, "was not a plan in the real sense of the term. It merely brought together various projects already started and contained the essential minimum of measures necessary to get some movement into a badly stagnant economy."[2] Yet this plan was a path-breaking effort and laid the groundwork for much bigger initiatives to follow. On the policy front, clear enunciation of the primacy of the state initiative, its dominance in the economic field, and the exigency of social change as an adjunct of economic growth were notable formulations. Even in quantitative terms its achievements were impressive. At the end of the plan, the national income had gone up by 18 percent and per capita income by nearly 11 percent. Foodgrains production was 5 million tonnes higher than the projected target, thus obviating the need for costly imports.

In several ways the Second Five Year Plan (1956-61) was a landmark document. It provided the conceptual basis for Indian planning and left a deep mark on the course of the country's future development. Its ideological underpinning was provided by the resolution on the Socialist Pattern of Society passed at the Avadi Session of the Congress in 1954. Its framework and priorities were defined by P.C. Mahalanobis, planning adviser to Nehru and Director, Indian Statistical Institute. And its impetus was supplied by the success of the First Plan.

In his Plan Frame Mahalanobis argued that self-sustaining

growth was best achieved by 'increasing the scope and importance of the public sector,' and 'development of heavy industries
was necessary to strengthen the foundations of economic independence.' But as setting up of heavy industry has a long gestation
period, it was considered necessary to promote labour-intensive
small-scale and cottage industries to generate employment. To set
the tone for achieving these objectives, the government came up
with a new Industrial Policy Resolution on 30 April 1956. It reaffirmed the national goal of creating a socialist pattern of society
and outlined a strategy for the state to assume a dominant and
direct responsibility for setting up new industrial undertakings.
It was the foundation laid during this period that led to the growth
of a massive public sector designed to dominate the commanding
heights of the economy.

The Second Plan had several notable features. While giving
high priority to the public sector, it also underscored some of the
basic constraints from which the future Five Year Plans were to
suffer. These were: problems of resource mobilization, generation
of inflationary pressures owing to excessive deficit financing, and
balance of payment difficulties. Then, there was the central importance of agriculture to the Indian economy.

As to plan performance targets for agricultural production and
capital goods were almost fulfilled, though there was a slippage
of 19 percent in power generation. The maximum shortfall occurred in respect of steel and fertilizers.

Regarding the Third Five Year Plan (1961-66), Nehru told a
journalist, "This plan is crucial to our take-off to an independent,
self-generating economy, and all efforts must be mobilized and
intensified to make it succeed. For, remember, the next five years
are going to be a decisive period, perhaps the most decisive period
of our freedom. Either we make the grade, or we break."[3]

This Plan suffered from three severe jolts. The Chinese incursion in 1962 not only forced the government to steeply raise its
defense budget, it also badly shattered the country's morale. In
1964, with the passing away of Nehru, the Planning Commission
itself was robbed of its father figure. And in 1965 came the war
with Pakistan, raising defence to the top of the national priorities.

As the Plan had run only half its course when Nehru died, its final balance sheet would be examined in a later section.

Though Nehru's preference for planning is attributed to his socialist leanings, it is doubtful if he had much choice in the matter. If India was to industrialize rapidly, massive investments in heavy industry and industrial infrastructure were imperative. The Indian capitalist class had neither the financial nor entrepreneurial means to undertake this task. The Indian economy was too weak and defenseless to be handed over to the vagaries of the market forces. As the state itself had only meagre resources, these had to be used frugally and to the best advantage of the country. In view of her mass poverty, it was necessary to marry growth with social equity. Nehru, therefore, opted for planning not so much as a matter of personal preference, but owing to the compulsions of objective reality. In fact it has been the worldwide experience that all late comers to modernization through industrial growth have been able to do so only with massive state intervention and creation of a vigorous public sector.

The question here is not whether planning was the right choice for the country at that time, but as to how well was Nehru equipped for the job? His general concept of planning was quite fuzzy. He told Lok Sabha in 1952, "... the method of working out a plan is ultimately the method of trial and error." But seven years later he told a journalist that subject to the factors of climatic and human conditions, "planning and development have become a sort of mathematical problem which may be worked out scientifically, that is, it is now laid down that if you do this, this is bound to follow and this is going to be the next step and that the third."[4]

The success of the Soviet planning model largely depended upon the authoritarian character of the state. The Indian plans, conceived within the democratic frame, were a mix of command economy and indicative components. Nehru was aware of these limitations and observed, "In India the question before us is how

to combine democracy with socialism through peaceful and legitimate methods ... We cannot achieve (this goal) by any compulsion
or coercion. We have to win the goodwill and cooperation of the
people."[5]

It must have been an eye-opener for Nehru to see that opposition to his radical institutional reforms came not only from outside, but from within the Congress and his cabinet. His pet
projects for co-operative farming and state trading in foodgrains
were undermined by the Congress chief ministers and his own
food ministers. It was these setbacks which dampened his earlier
zeal for radical measures and made him a votary of 'mixed economy'. He opted for this concept both out of practical as also
ideological considerations. The country did not have the men or
means to switch over to a state-controlled economy. The private
sector had a fair amount of capital and expertise, and its nationalization would have eaten up scarce resources without any
corresponding gain. The main problem before the country was
'production', and there was no point in incurring frictional losses
in pursuit of ideological chimeras. Nehru stated before the Lok
Sabha:

> While the public sector must obviously grow and even now it
> has grown, both absolutely and relatively, the private sector is
> not something unimportant. It will play an important role, though
> gradually and ultimately it will fade away.[6]

Of course, this 'fade away' bit was thrown in as a concession
to his Marxian past.

On the ideological plane, Nehru believed that one could not
have a fully state controlled economy without introducing a measure of coercion. His quest all along was to work out a system
suited to "realize economic and social justice without the sacrifice
of freedom and democratic rights of the citizen."[7]

The concept of mixed economy, evolved to reconcile the contradictions inherent in democratic socialist planning, typifies the
Indian genius for compromise. But there should be no doubt as
to whose advantage this arrangement worked. "Planning had led
to the growth of a state sector, whose role to a large extent has

been to build up a cost-free infrastructure for the Indian bourgeoisie by undertaking risky and expensive investments."[8]

The key to the success of the plans was undoubtedly agriculture.
This was inescapable in an agricultural economy. Higher production during the First Plan resulted mainly from the additional area
brought under cultivation. But this was a self-limiting resource
and its potential was soon exhausted. Secondly, the planners'
reliance on higher production owing to agrarian reforms also
proved illusory. Thirdly, it was hoped that with improved and
more intensive methods of cultivation, output would rise. This
again turned out to be a strategy of limited value. Ultimately the
lesson was driven home that food production was directly linked
to investment in the agricultural infrastructure, and optimism was
no substitute for allocation.

Despite considerable complementarity between the two sectors, industry is regarded as a rival of agriculture for the allocation
of resources. In Nehru's scheme of things industrial growth was
imperative to the emergence of modern India and he got an able
supporter in Mahalanobis to give shape to this view. In placing
basic industry at the core of the Second Plan, it was expected not
only to accelerate capital formation, but also reduce the country's
dependence on imports.. The consumer goods' sector was left to
the labour intensive small-scale and village industries in the hope
that this would contain inflationary pressures by generating more
employment. But employment generation was quite low and the
small-scale sector was beset by numerous constraints. Further,
owing to time and cost overruns, heavy industry did not yield
the anticipated returns.

Some critics have also questioned the wisdom of India opting
for capital-intensive, long-gestation, basic industry in preference
to the consumer goods industry with a much higher potential for
employment generation. The poor masses of India, suffering from
long periods of deprivation, needed 'jam today', instead of slog-
ging hard for the benefit of posterity. This is the classic argument
of 'textiles first' exponents, and there is merit in it. But a country
of India's size with its geopolitical compulsions and security

requirements, had to create a solid industrial base to safeguard her freedom.

It is widely held 'that Indian plans though well formulated, suffer owing to poor implementation.' Mega-projects like irrigation dams, power plants and steel complexes could never be completed on time. This not only raised their costs but also delayed the downstream benefits dependent on their commissioning. A faulty information base, snags of implementation, and the distortion of the planning process owing to political pressures ensured that plan targets were not fulfilled. Projections of agricultural growth, resource mobilization, availability of foreign aid, etc., all turned out to be mere guesstimates. States seldom exerted to raise adequate resources or to enforce even mildly radical measures. As the foreign exchange component of the plans was not based on firm commitments made by the international donors or lending agencies, the plan execution was invariably plagued by balance of payments crunch. On the other hand, the planners could not foresee the spurt in population growth resulting from improved public health facilities, nor could they anticipate the erratic behaviour of the monsoons.

Then, self-reliance was an important objective and promoted better utilization of domestic enterprise and production capabilities. For instance, in respect of non-electrical machinery, the import-availability ratio declined from 66 percent in 1959-60 to 31 percent in 1979-80. For electrical machinery and chemical products, imports declined from 38 and 30 percent to 10 and 19 percent over the same period. But self-reliance as an ongoing activity could be sustained only with steadily rising levels of imports and exports. Instead, self-reliance was narrowed down to import substitution, which itself became a sacred doctrine. Not only was the cost of substitution ignored, it became a serious check on growth. As an economist observed in 1964, "Indian export had been constrained by supply bottlenecks and not by demand."[9]

In the final reckoning it was in respect of the welfare objectives that the plans failed to make any significant dent. Social equity and distributive justice did receive occasional attention, but mostly of a ritualistic nature. In any conflict between social and economic goals, it was the former that was generally sacrificed. "A redistributive programme is unlikely to work in isolation from the pattern of growth that India is able to generate."[10] Increasing distortion in income distribution and employment was largely a consequence of skewed investment policies. Further, "... the very pattern and organization of production itself dictates a pattern of consumption and distribution which is politically very difficult to change."[11] In the Indian case the pattern of investment was primarily geared to the growth of GNP, and distributive strategies were not built into it.

Nehru himself had no illusions in this matter. He told Lok Sabha on 11 December 1963, "One thing that distresses me very greatly is that... there is a good number of people who have not profited by planning, and whose poverty is abysmal and most painful."

Nehru's planning, undoubtedly, was the offspring of his socialist thinking. Despite that, there was very little of socialism in the plans. Actually, there is nothing inherently socialistic about planning. Though this concept arose in the socialist countries, after the Great Depression of the thirties, it caught on in the capitalist world also. In fact multinational corporations plan their operations much more scientifically than any socialist country ever did.

The area where the plan made the least impact was in the most vital sector of unemployment and under-employment. At the end of the First Plan 5.3 million persons were unemployed. The Second Plan further added 10 million to this number. As this plan generated only about 6.5 million new jobs, it left a backlog of 8.8 million. And this figure jumped to 12 million at the end of the Third Plan. Thus, on the employment front the country kept slipping back all the time. Its paramount importance notwithstanding, employment generation was never considered central to planning. It was treated as an incidental fallout of economic growth. But the growth strategies could not generate employment to the desired extent. Capital intensive industries cannot be labour intensive at the same time. Rationalization and automation in the private sector industry could not be employment oriented.

Increasing mechanization of agriculture by capitalist farmers actually reduced even the existing employment opportunities. Thus the anticipated shift from agriculture to industry did not take place. And the exodus from villages to cities occurred not owing to the 'pull effect' of industrial growth but the 'push effect' of rural unemployment. Its natural outcome was the growth of huge slums in major urban centres.

Despite all the failings and slippages, planning has served the country well. It yanked the stagnant colonial economy out of old ruts and marked a structural break with the past. During Nehru's time the national income grew at an average of 3.5 to 4 percent, per capita income by over one percent and agricultural production exceeded 3 percent per year. And industrial growth averaged 7 percent per annum. The plans also led to "a great deal of diversification within the industrial structure, a significant upgrading of the skill-base of India's population and a turn-around in the long-standing stagnation of Indian agriculture because of large-scale step-up in irrigation investment."[12] Large allocations for the creation of industrial infrastructure and basic industry laid firm foundations for India's future industrial development and put her on the road to self-sustaining growth.

In quantitative terms these achievements may not appear very spectacular. But to place them in proper perspective, one has to remember that all this progress was made in a purely democratic frame, and without delivering any traumatic shocks to the system by making a radical break with the past.

Nehru's death gave a serious setback to plan performance. For the first three plans the rate of industrial growth averaged 8 percent, and the highest achieved during the next three plans was 6.4 percent. As to capacity utilization, in all sectors from basic to consumer goods, there was a drop of 4 to 20 percentage points after the Third Plan.

10

Public Sector's Commanding Heights

$\mathcal{O}$f planning gave form to Nehru's socialism, public sector gave it content. But looking to the state of the Indian economy and the tasks ahead, it is doubtful if there were any viable alternatives to either planning or public sector available to Nehru. Though the Second World War had given some impetus to Indian industry, it was the contractors and traders who were its main beneficiaries. The entrepreneurial class was still weak and the industrial activity was mainly confined to textiles, sugar and jute.

If the country was to be industrialized, two thrust areas required speedy development. First, the creation of an adequate infrastructure like transportation, power and communications. Second, the setting up of basic and heavy industries. Having taken a deliberate decision to develop infrastructure as a promotional activity, it was not expected to earn much profit. Heavy industry is not only capital intensive, it has a long gestation period. It was, therefore, obvious that private capital would not be attracted to either of these sectors. Moreover, the quantum of funds required was so huge and the returns so uncertain, that only the state could carry this burden.

Though a public sector with a definite ideological slant was launched only during the Second Five Year Plan, its origins lie in the initiatives taken before Independence. Here we are not referring to the establishment of Post and Telegraph facilities, Railways or the Ordnance factories. The colonial government had set up Planning and Development Department in 1944, and the following year Lord Wavell produced a White Paper outlining the government's post-war industrial policy. It was a surprisingly bold and radical document for those times. It stated, "... free enterprise abroad or no free enterprise abroad, *laissez faire* abroad or no *laissez faire* abroad, in India if progress is to be achieved, the development of industry must be planned by government, and planned by government in cooperation with industry."[1] It stressed the importance of socially equitable distribution of wealth, formation of an industrial development corporation, licensing of industry, and nationalization of its vital sectors.

The main reason for referring to this document of purely archival interest is to show its remarkable similarity to the Second Industrial Policy Resolution adopted under Nehru's inspiration a decade later. And the real significance of this correspondence is that in view of India's objective conditions, both an exploitative colonial administration and a benign welfare state came to the same conclusion regarding the country's industrial development: there was no option to the creation of a public sector, with the state acquiring regulatory powers to guide the pattern of investment and the direction of industrial growth.

Whereas Nehru had been talking of the importance of public sector much before Independence, the main features of his approach were stated in the First and Second Industrial Policy Resolutions. The First Resolution, adopted in 1948 was too feeble to merit comment. It was with the Second Industrial Policy Resolution, 1956, that the state gave a mandate for the creation of a strong public sector which would dominate the commanding heights of the economy. In specific terms, the Resolution classified the industrial sector into three categories and specified the respective roles of the public and the private sectors.

Nehru was firmly in favour of heavy industry and considered it as the prime mover of growth and modernization. Consequently, he went in for big dams, big steel plants, heavy engineering complexes, etc. And in this venture he got a very able advocate in P.C. Mahalanobis.

While Nehru's approach to industrialization can be faulted on several counts, it was a stunning feat by any standard. At the commencement of the First Five Year Plan, there were five public enterprises (excluding departmental undertakings) with a total investment of Rs. 29 crores. When it ended, the number of enterprises had quadrupled and investment tripled. On the completion of the Second Plan this tally was raised to 47, with a total investment of Rs.1,948 crores. After the completion of the Third Plan there were 75 enterprises with an outlay of Rs.2,416 crores. Much more impressive was the diversity and the size of these projects. By 1964 the three integrated steel plants, Heavy Engineering Corporation, Bharat Heavy Electricals, Oil and Natural Gas Commission, Air India, Shipping Corporation of India, Fertilizer Corporation of India, Bharat Electronics, Hindustan Machine Tools, State Trading Corporation, Metals and Minerals Corporation, Hindustan Aeronautics and dozens of other mega-projects had been incorporated. In two areas the initiative was particularly path-breaking: establishment of wholly indigenous petroleum industry with Soviet help, and creation of research and development facilities to harness atomic power.

What a breathtaking performance it was, and how well it developed the sinews of India's industrial growth! No other strategy except the one adopted by Nehru could have done the job so well and in such a short time.

Of all the major projects of Nehru, the public sector has attracted the maximum controversy. The socialists felt that it primarily helped the capitalists by providing them with cheap infrastructure and intermediate products. The capitalists treated it as a mortal rival. And their control of the national press ensured continuous denigration of the public enterprises. Consequently, in the public mind it has come to be associated with inefficiency, waste and corruption.

The most serious charge against the public sector is the huge losses piled up by several undertakings and low return on investment. Whereas this is largely true, it has to be qualified on several counts. For instance, it is a fallacy to treat the entire public sector as a single undertaking and then compare its performance selectively with the better-run companies from the private sector.

There are tens of thousands of private enterprises which are managed very badly, have accumulated heavy losses, reneged on their debts, and gone into liquidation. But while discussing the performance of the private sector, this area of darkness is ignored. Though it is a fact that even the aggregate profitability of the private enterprises is higher than that of the public sector, this manner of presentation ignores both the objectives and the constraints of the public sector.

It is taken for granted that an industrial plant is put up to make profits. This is the primary impulse of all entrepreneurs. And it is a very legitimate purpose. But the public sector was created to meet the basic requirements of the national economy, and to fill the critical gaps in its growth. Profit was never the decisive factor. Creation of infrastructure, production of intermediate goods and building of dams were certainly not the most profitable of ventures. But they were crucial for the country's progress. And the greatest beneficiary of these facilities was the private sector itself.

Excessive emphasis on the promotional and social objectives of the public undertakings however itself fostered an attitude which ignored the imperatives of profitability. At least in the earlier stages, it was widely believed that public sector was not expected to make profits. This mind-set promoted a style of management where some nebulous notions of social good obscured the importance of generating surpluses for reinvestment.

With such indifference to profitability, coupled with an excessive zeal to be 'model employers', the public undertakings assumed a host of responsibilities which became a heavy drag on their finances. As most of the projects were established in out of the way places, it became necessary to build large housing colonies for the employees. Along with that came schools, transport, hospitals, recreation centres and shopping areas. No wonder, then, that with such expensive social overheads, and mindless spending on creating in-house facilities which could be hired much more cheaply, commercial goals became a matter of low priority.

The government's pricing policies also loaded the dice against the public enterprises. The infrastructural facilities and intermediate inputs for the production of finished goods were made available at low prices to private units. This was ostensibly done to keep the price of finished products low, and to ensure adequate margins to the private producers.

Public sector's 'model employer' syndrome also had serious implications for productivity, as it was not accompanied by a corresponding 'model employee' obligation. Whereas on one hand the workers enjoyed the best of emoluments and fringe benefits, they were not motivated by any sense of belonging to the organization to which they should give their best. This has resulted in the creation of a 'workers' aristocracy', continuously pampered by the management with a view to avoiding the inconvenience of facing agitations and strikes.

Bureaucratization of the public sector, back-seat driving by the administrative ministries and lack of expertise in setting up large industrial complexes constitute another set of factors for poor performance. Time and cost overruns have been the most persistent features of the execution of public enterprises. Thus most of the public undertakings are excessively capitalized and this naturally affects their profitability.

Grand projects were conceived without the back-up of adequate market research or demand projections. Demand was generally overestimated during this period, as the plans projected a continuous growth of 7 percent, which was double of what was actually achieved. For instance, Heavy Engineering Corporation was designed to fabricate equipment for setting up a one million tonne capacity steel plant every year. As this bore no relation to actuality, the capacity utilization of this magnificent factory has been very low and it has accumulated heavy losses.

Employment generation was an important goal of the public sector. But it was turned into a sacred cow. So much so that after the completion of a project, the absorption of its casual construction labour in the plant was considered almost mandatory. This saddled the enterprise with a large contingent of untrained surplus workers.

As an extension of this philosophy, in the post-Nehru period the government has been continuously taking over sick industries from the private sector. More than a hundred textile mills and several other firms were taken over, and these constitute a large part of the public sector losses. These units comprise outmoded, run-down plants with a heavy debt burden and hordes of workers. There is no way to turn around these units without extensive modernization at a high cost. No private entrepreneur would have gone anywhere near them. But the government has only too readily offered to string this albatross around its neck.

At the operational level, the most serious problems of the public sector arise from the clash of two cultures: the government donning the mantle of an entrepreneur. When it was decided to set up public enterprises, the only organizational model familiar to the government was that of ministries and departments. It was, therefore, natural to copy this model for managing the public industries also.

Internally, no area of public sector working has generated as much heat and acrimony as the management-ministry relationship. The reason for incorporating public enterprises as companies was to ensure a fair degree of autonomy in their working. But this clashed with the administrative ministry's perception of its role vis-a-vis the enterprises under its charge. Historically, the ministries had looked upon themselves as the rulers, the policy makers, the decision takers, the givers of funds, licences and sanctions. Therefore, it did not lie within their zone of experience and thinking to treat public sector managers as their colleagues; it had to be a patron-client relationship.

Despite all the deficiencies of project formulation, execution and operation, the public sector would have done much better if adequate emphasis had been laid on productivity, efficiency and capacity utilization. Whereas great efforts were made to mobilize resources, little heed was paid to exploit the full potential of the existing undertakings.

Most of the factors which resulted in the inefficient working of the public undertakings are, in the ultimate analysis, of a secondary nature. The basic question is: can we have a public (state) sector which is more efficient than the state?[2] This issue has to be answered at two levels. First is the class interest of the ruling elite, which has no socialistic pretensions and no real sympathy with the concept of the public sector.

Secondly, one has to take note of the character of our political class and its highly interventionist role at the ground level. For the local politician, a public enterprise presents a great opportunity for nursing his constituency by securing jobs for his camp followers; cornering lucrative contracts for his cronies who will consequently finance his election campaigns; establishing his hold over the labour unions by espousing their demands, and making money by all manner of jiggery-pokery.

Such a coveted pork-barrel has the public sector become for the politicians that every state government has considered it profitable to create a string of its own enterprises. Whereas Nehru wanted the public sector to dominate the commanding heights of the economy — and it did serve a very useful purpose — the state governments had no such lofty objective in mind. They use the chairmanships of the public sector units as peace offerings to disgruntled politicians who could not be made ministers. Thousands of crores in the states have been spent on setting up all sorts of irrelevant industrial corporations. They neither make profits, nor serve any social purpose. But they do manage to earn a lot of odium for the public sector.

"In the context of economic growth," says Pranab Bardhan, "it is rather the capacity of the system to insulate economic management from political processes of distributive demands, rent-seeking and patronage disbursement that makes the crucial difference."[3] In India, not only has this insulation not taken place, the political processes have wormed their way into every facet of the country's economic life to the detriment of the national economy.

The Nehruvian agenda for the public sector drew its inspiration from socialism. The inefficiency of the public sector is, by association, ascribed to the inherent shortcomings of socialism. But where does socialism prescribe time and cost overruns in the execution of projects? That there should be overstaffing, nepotism and labour indiscipline? That contracts should be awarded to favourites? Enterprises should remain headless? And the politicians allowed to interfere with the management? None of these ills have anything to do with socialism; yet the malfunctioning of the public sector is attributed to it.

The public sector in itself does not lead to re-distribution of incomes, nor has it any poverty alleviation agenda built into it. The multiplier effect of the public enterprises has also been quite limited. "The evidence of income distribution trends, the progress or the lack of it in lifting people above the poverty line, and the peripheral impact of the enterprises outside of the immediate location point to the fact that the social functions have not had a spread and proliferating effect, and have been limited in their scope and have benefited individual groups and immediate neighbourhoods."[4]

One reason why the public sector did not perform better is that its concept and role did not grow and evolve with the fast-changing times. The objective conditions and demands of the sixties were not the same as those of the forties, and in the eighties the situation was radically different. Once the private sector had matured and established a significant presence in the industrial field, the government should have adopted a dynamic policy of shedding off non-essential undertakings and confining its activities to the core sector only. The funds thus raised could have been more gainfully employed for the modernization and expansion of the remaining enterprises, or nursing some critical sectors neglected earlier. Instead, the government turned every undertaking into a fixed destiny, even though many had outlived their utility and were making heavy recurring losses. This observation is, of course, more relevant to the post- Nehru period and is made here to round off this account.

People grow and change with experience. Nehru being an eclectic, changed more than most others. Towards the later years of his prime ministership, he started entertaining doubts about the wisdom of having gone in for mega projects. Earlier he was fascinated by gigantic dams, integrated steel plants, etc. In fact Gandhi had remarked that nothing appeals to him unless it is big. But gradually, Nehru was not only speaking Gandhi's language, but thinking his thoughts also. While addressing the Board of Irrigation and Power on 17 November 1958 he said:

> For sometime past, however, I have been beginning to think that we are beginning to suffer from what we call 'disease of gigantism'... This is a dangerous outlook developing in India... It is... the small irrigation projects, the small industries, and the small plants for electric power, which will change the face of the country far more than half a dozen big projects in half a dozen places.

In 1956 he had described projects like the Bhakra-Nangal dam as the 'new temples of India where I worship.' Two years later he confessed in a letter to S. Saxena that he "doubted very much if the government would have initiated such a project if it came before them at this time. Such a dam was exceedingly expensive, involved considerable amount of foreign exchange and took a long time to be completed. All that India had gained from it was electric power and a little irrigation."[5]

One wonders what course India's industrial development would have taken if these doubts about the relevance of 'gigantism' to the Indian situation had assailed Nehru's mind a decade earlier.

11

Community Development and Panchayati Raj

Democracy, socialism, agrarian reforms, planning, public sector — and then community development, Panchayati Raj and cooperatives — what a burst of titanic activity and initiatives! Nehru just could not do enough to relieve the masses of their age-old deprivation.

The public sector was meant not only to provide a base for industrial growth, but also to make that growth self-sustaining. Similarly, community development and Panchayati Raj were launched to improve the life of the villagers, as also to make that process self-propelling by directly involving the people in programmes of self-help.

Of course, the concept of community development was not new to the country. All communities engage in some form of collective effort for mutual benefit. But the government's involvement in such activities was first stressed by the Royal Commission on Agriculture as early as 1928. After the Second World War, officially sponsored schemes were introduced in several states. But a countrywide beginning was made with Ford Foundation's offer to help start fifteen pilot projects in 1951. The same year, Chester Bowles, the American ambassador to India, offered the assistance of US $ 50 million for launching rural development programmes. So, in 1952 India signed a Technical Cooperation Agreement with the U.S. Government for setting up 55 community projects. The U.S. agreed to supply essential equipment like jeeps, cinema projectors, tractors, road-rollers, etc. Douglas Ensminger, a specialist from Ford Foundation, got closely associated with the programme and became a friend of both Nehru and S.K. Dey.

The Community Development Programme (CDP) was inaugurated on 2 October (Gandhi's birthday), 1952. On this occasion Nehru said, "The work we are about to start today is in the service of the motherland ... If necessary we shall shed our blood, so that millions of our countrymen may go forward and that there may be an end to their trials and tribulations."[1] This throwback to the rhetoric of the freedom struggle is further excelled by a later observation: "I think nothing has happened in any country or in the world during the last few years so big in content and so revolutionary in design as the community development projects in India."[2]

CDP was placed under the charge of the Planning Commission for laying broad policy guidelines and monitoring. S.K. Dey, an America-trained engineer whose stewardship of the Nilokheri Project had much impressed Nehru, was made the Administrator of Community Projects. It was an integrated scheme for the development of man as a whole, and it impinged upon all important aspects of village life. Continuous mass participation was supposed to make it a people's movement.

Community Development Programme introduced three innovations for its proper implementation. First was the concept of a compact 'block', serviced by extension staff under the charge of a Block Development Officer. Second, a state-level coordinator, the Development Commissioner, who was the linchpin of the Programme. And third, the village-level worker or Gram Sewak. He was a multipurpose functionary who served as the delivery point of all the block schemes for about 10 villages placed under his charge. At the district level, it was again the ubiquitous, overworked Collector who functioned as the administrative head of all the blocks within his jurisdiction. He also coordinated the activities of the subject-matter specialists posted in his district.

The Programme was conceptualized at the level of the Central Government and its operational modalities were worked out by the Planning Commission. In 1956, the Community Projects Administration was raised to the level of a ministry and its Administrator, S.K. Dey, was made a minister.

CDP was the first nationwide venture started by Nehru to promote the culture of self-help and participatory democracy. He
described it as 'revolutionary in design.' Till then, the 'paternal'
concept of colonial administration implied that the all-knowing
state was the sole custodian of the people's welfare. Community
Development sought to treat the people as responsible adults who
understood very well their best interests. But owing to centuries-
old deprivation, they needed outside assistance to become self-
reliant. That is where the state came in as a catalytic agent. And
that is why it was made mandatory that in the execution of any
scheme for the welfare of the villagers, they should contribute
half the cost in terms of labour (*shram dan*), material or cash.
Without such a contribution, it was argued, the people will not
have a sense of participation in the creation of new assets.

Nehru earnestly hoped that the programme will become a people's movement. But how could this happen? Right from top to
bottom, both in conception and execution, it was an official programme. It was conceived by governmental agencies, it was
mostly funded by the government, and it relied on collectors and
block development officers for its implementation. So tight was
the official control that the schematic budget for the blocks was
formulated by the Planning Commission and, for quite sometime,
even the state governments could not alter it to suit the local
conditions. Of course, non-officials and people's representatives
were associated at all levels. But that was only for deliberation
and advice. The people knew from where the power and money
flowed.

Nehru was quite aware of the top to bottom syndrome of the
CDP and repeatedly expressed his concern about it. Soon after
the programme commenced, he stated at the Community Project
Conference:

> Sometimes, I begin to suspect and become a little afraid of these
> leads from the top that we, including myself, are giving... I think
> the people themselves should be given the opportunity to think
> about it (CD) and they will affect our thinking... Sitting in big

buildings and offices we might begin to think it is we who are doing the job. We are doing nothing of the kind.

But no definite steps were taken to rectify this flaw. It was, therefore, not surprising if the CDP did not enthuse the masses or secure their full participation. As 50 percent contribution from the people was seldom forthcoming and there was pressure from above to meet the targets, officials devised all sorts of tricks to show results. Works were deliberately overvalued to obtain higher government grant, and then the value of voluntary effort was inflated to comply with the official norms. Local contractors, under obligation to official agencies, were made to execute a part of the work and it was shown as *shram dan*. In several cases the villagers were forced to contribute their labour by the local bigwigs.

There were good reasons for most of the villagers not to contribute even their labour to execute schemes which were supposed to benefit the village. What motivation did a poor landless worker have in donating his labour to dig field channels, do contour bunding, or work on minor irrigation projects when he did not possess an inch of land? Why should he take interest in the construction of a school building or a Panchayat Ghar when his children were not to attend school or he become a member of the village Panchayat. Laying of roads was, no doubt, useful. But not for a person who never left his village, nor had any produce to take to the grain market.

Owing to the enthusiasm and publicity with which the CDP was launched, in the beginning the people's contribution reached the desired levels. For instance, for the First Plan it averaged 54 percent. But then it steadily declined. By 1961-62 it had dropped to 20 percent, and next year declined to 18.[3] These are official figures, and furnish clear evidence of the government's failure to turn community development into a mass movement.

In fact the CDP was flawed at the core, as it tried to ride two horses simultaneously. It owed its conception and initial push to the US government and Ford Foundation. The model familiar to them was that of their own extension service, which was mainly oriented to increasing agricultural production. Their extension staff made the literate farmers aware of a package of improved agricultural practices and new inputs, laid demonstration plots to show the efficacy of their approach and furnished such information as the cultivators required.

After signing the Technical Cooperation Agreement, the US government supplied jeeps, tractors and magic lanterns to India, and Ford Foundation contributed a high-flying adviser. In other words, the US gave India what it was capable of giving. Her approach to the domestic problem of modernizing agriculture was essentially technocratic. And this became the focus of the Indian community programmes also, though it was accompanied by a lot of rhetoric about people's participation and 'shedding blood for the motherland'.

On the other hand, Nehru, Mahalanobis and several official teams visiting China had come back with glowing accounts of the wonderful things happening there. The Chinese masses had been mobilized to build big dams and dig irrigation tanks with manual labour and without the use of modern machinery. Manpower was the most valuable resource of China and she was using it to great effect. The situation in India was very similar. It was, therefore, planned to involve the Indian masses in the construction of community projects and doing other things which will rid them of their poverty and change their social outlook. Elaborate blueprints were prepared, battalions of extension workers recruited and hundreds of crores allotted for this purpose. But to the dismay of the Indian planners and leaders, the programme did not follow the Chinese trajectory. Why ?

There were two basic differences between the Chinese and the Indian approach to people's participation. First, China started its mass mobilization after she had implemented the most thorough-going land reforms. This completely changed property relations in the villages and for the first time there were no large owners to exploit the landless. This created a great upsurge and euphoria in the countryside. In India, agrarian reforms left a vast number of the landless and marginal farmers untouched. Thus the reforms generated no fervour. Secondly, China deployed ideologically motivated party cadres to create a popular ground swell for undertaking community works and social reforms. Nehru did nothing of the sort. The Indian National Congress had organized gigantic mass movements during the freedom struggle, sustained them for long periods, and inspired the people to make tremendous sacrifices without having any immediate gain in sight. This mighty party could have been most profitably used for nation-building tasks after Independence. But Nehru let it rust and rot. And instead, he opted for the colonial bureaucracy to serve as the delivery system for his agenda of development.

In his address to the Community Project Conference referred to earlier, he asked, "How to invest them with that sense of purpose, that eagerness to do things... (the programme) will have to be undertaken with something fiery and with the spirit that moves a nation to high endeavour." And he looked for a spark of that fire in the bosom of career bureaucrats to set the countryside ablaze with a new vision!

In looking for 'something fiery' to move the nation, Nehru was entering the domain of ideology, and of political action. Development Commissioners, District Collectors and Block Development Officers operate in the area of mundane routine. But the mobilization of the masses for evolving new patterns of social and economic behaviour lie completely outside their ken. It is both sad and surprising that despite full awareness of the limitations of bureaucracy, Nehru still preferred to employ it as the agent for development and social transformation.

Of all the great projects of Nehru, the achievements of CDP were the most modest. As the food situation worsened, the programme laid more and more emphasis on agriculture. Yet, ironically, not much success could be achieved in this field either, and ever increasing quantities of foodgrains had to be imported. Equally unimpressive was its record in improving the lot of the poor, in raising their social status, or in generating additional employment.

All the same, CDP was a unique experiment conceived on a grand scale. For the bureaucracy it was the first experience to be cast in the role of a service agency. The fact that hordes of block employees swarmed the countryside as 'agents of change' did animate the masses. In the past, the government was mostly a distant abstraction for the villagers. Now they saw it in action amidst them, trying to solve their problems and attend to their needs. The construction of roads, tanks, school buildings, etc., and the propagation of improved agricultural practices stirred the countryside and stimulated economic activity. Primary health centres spread greater awareness about health problems and gave relief to the sick.

But these gains were incidental to the main purpose of the CDP. The programme failed in its basic objective to create a momentum for self-sustaining growth through self-help and cooperation. Had it been a more narrowly targeted programme, concentrating on fewer items and confining itself to relatively backward areas only, the outcome may have been more rewarding.

Panchayati Raj

The lacklustre performance of the Community Development Programme and, particularly, the failure to arouse mass involvement, led to a landmark experiment in participatory democracy. In 1957, the government appointed a study team to examine the working of Community Development Programme and National Extension Service. The team, known as Balvantrai Mehta Committee, made 'democratic decentralisation' the hub of its report, and recommended the creation of a three-tier system of local government. These tiers were to be created at the village level (Gram Panchayat), intermediate block level (Block Panchayat Samiti) and the district level (Zila Parishad). There were to be direct elections at the lowest, that is, the village level only. The upper two tiers were to be constituted by the chairmen of Gram Panchyats and Block Samitis. The block-level panchayat was supposed to be the nodal point for planning and organization. To give teeth to these committees it was desired to give them substantial administrative and financial powers.

An important aspect of the Panchayati institutions was their autonomous character. Good care was taken that no bureaucrat overlords these bodies at any level. Village Panchayats had paid secretaries to do office work. In the case of Block Samitis, the BDO acted as their secretary. At the district level, the Chief Executive Officer, mostly from the IAS, worked under the control of the Zila Parishad Pradhan.

Of all the projects conceived by Nehru, this one required the least funds, and only meagre back-up from the state. It was mainly people-based. But that proved to be its most vulnerable spot. People's representatives who wield power are extremely reluctant to share it with other representatives of the people. The elected members of the three Panchayati tiers, and especially their chairmen, were immediately perceived as rivals by the members of state legislatures and MPs. Whereas these worthies were scared of the emergence of rural foci of power and patronage, the chief ministers abhorred the prospect of hordes of Panchayati bigwigs joining the ranks of their MLAs seeking all sorts of favours.

The case of Maharashtra is illustrative. The state took Panchayati Raj seriously, speedily created the three tiers and invested them with substantial administrative and financial powers. In due course, the Panchayati leaders, who had more direct interaction with their constituents and personally dispensed patronage, acquired an edge over the local MLAs. This sent these MLAs scurrying to the chief minister and pressure was built up to restore the balance in their favour. Consequently, the state government clipped the wings of Zila Parishads by creating a parallel tier of District Planning Boards and transferred the work of planning and allocation of resources to them. Further, on the plea of raising the status of these Boards, state ministers were nominated as their chairmen.

Whereas Maharashtra learnt its lesson the hard way, the other state governments took care not to burn their fingers and made certain that the Panchayats were not delegated any substantive functions, powers or funds. The block and district-level plans had no real meat in them. Even otherwise, preparation of paper plans is too abstract and sophisticated an exercise for the villagers. Thus, democratic decentralization in the sense of giving people the freedom to manage their own affairs at the local level remained a distant dream.

The argument for not empowering the Panchayats with greater autonomy and authority is the same which the British advanced for not giving freedom to India. At both the higher political and bureaucratic levels it was felt that subjective factors of kinship network, caste loyalties, personal greed and lack of training in administrative procedures would turn Panchayats into hotbeds of corruption, nepotism and factionalism. This is a very specious argument in the most stable democracy in the third world where the masses have been repeatedly complimented for their sagacity and political maturity. More importantly, it ignores the basic character of local administration which, in any case, is highly corrupt and insensitive to the needs of the common man. Even if the Panchayats manage to be equally corrupt, they will be at least a little more receptive to the opinion of their fellow villagers. It is sad but true that the politicians who rule on behalf of the masses and call them their masters, have actually little faith in them.

Though meant to benefit the have-nots, neither the CDP nor Panchayati Raj, or the cooperatives were specifically targeted at the poor. They were all based on the rural sector as a whole and not on class. In the absence of any specific targeting, the main benefits of all these schemes were cornered by the upper caste propertied classes. In Community Development it was the bigger landowners who cooperated with the extension staff in executing various community projects; it was they who made available their fields for laying demonstration plots; it was they who offered land and funds for building schools and Panchayat Ghars. Consequently, a close alliance emerged between the extension staff and the dominant propertied classes.

In the Panchayati Raj institutions the dominance of the village elite was total. It was only they who enjoyed social prestige and controlled the vote banks of the landless employed by them. Nehru himself admitted, "There is no doubt in my mind that our whole system of cooperatives helps only the bigger people; in fact it discourages the poor people."⁴

CD and Panchayati Raj actually aggravated social stratification in the countryside. The association of governmental agencies with the rural elite enhanced their prestige in the eyes of their fellow villagers and tightened their hold over the poorer sections.

In view of the above, it is hardly necessary to stress that there was no trace of socialism in any of these programmes. Actually, by treating the village community and the peasantry as homogeneous aggregates, the class issue got obfuscated to the detriment of the have-nots.

In his younger days Nehru held:

> Reformism was an impossible solution of any vital problem at a critical moment when the basic structure had to be changed, and however slow the progress might be later on, the initial step must be a complete break with the existing order, which had fulfilled its purpose and was now only a drag on the future progress.

But when the hour of reckoning came, it was reformism all the way.

12

Nation in the Making

$\mathcal{I}$ndia is unlike any other nation state. Its diversity, plurality, contradictions and conflicts make it an unmanageable enterprise. In daily commerce, there is little in common between the Tamilians, Punjabis or Bengalis. Their language, dress, food, literature, social habits are disparate, as are their historical and tribal memories, folk heroes and role models. In what sense, then, are they Indians? And, how can they be imbued with an overarching feeling of Indianness which transcends all other identities?

Nehru was much troubled by this question. Unless he could discover the mainsprings of the Indian identity, how could the Indian nation state acquire substance and a personality? So, he delved deep into India's history and went on a great voyage of discovery through the labyrinths of her prehistory.

In the Epilogue to *The Discovery of India* Nehru asks himself, "What have I discovered?" And replies, "It was presumptuous of me to imagine that I could unveil her and find out what she is today and what she was in the long past."

Then, referring to India's millions, "each living in a private universe of thought and feeling," he says:

> Yet something has bound them together and binds them still. India is a geographical and economic entity, a cultural unity amidst diversity, a bundle of contradictions held together by strong but invisible threads. Overwhelmed again and again, her spirit was never conquered...[1]

This vision of pan-Indian civilizational unity was not confined to the educated elite. Nehru found during his travels:

> If my mind was full of pictures from recorded history and more or less ascertained fact, I realised that even the illiterate peasant had a picture gallery in his mind, though this was largely drawn

from myth and tradition and epic heroes and heroines, and only very little from history.[2]

The most telling illustration of this pan-Indian consciousness is furnished by Shankaracharya's continuous travels in the eighth century AD:

> There is a significance about these long journeys of Shankaracharya throughout this vast land at a time when travel was difficult and the means of transport very slow and primitive. The very conception of these journeys, and his meeting kindred souls everywhere and speaking to them in Sanskrit, the common language of the learned throughout India, brings out the essential unity of India even in those far-off days.[3]

Whereas this pervasive consciousness of cultural affinities gave the country a sort of loose bonding, it could never fuse its diverse regions and communities into a nation. But absence of firm political structures gave India great resilience and absorptive capacity. She became a commonwealth of ethnicities, sub-nationalities, sub-cultures and other pluralities, which never got welded into a monolithic political formation. The assimilative capacity of its loose organization imbued India with the faculty of constant self-renewal, as ingestion of foreign influences resulted in cultural cross-fertilization. This ability of the Indian civilization, fostered primarily by absence of dogma, explains its continuity over three millennia.

The skein of Indian national consciousness is woven with three strands: culture, history and politics. India had a cultural cohesiveness which has endured for thousands of years. Though it could not by itself integrate her manifold identities into a composite political formation, it did provide a congenial soil for its emergence.

The historical strand represents an evolutionary process which gradually leads the Indian people towards political unification. The Mauryas for the first time brought the country under the sway of a single ruler three centuries before Christ. Then, in the 13th century AD Allauddin Khilji once again unified the country under his rule. But it was the Mughals in the 16th and 17th centuries AD who furthered the process of Indian unification the most.

There were several noteworthy features of these great empires. First, the rulers were, in effect, suzerains of vast territories with the local satraps possessing considerable internal autonomy. Second, at the local level, the people enjoyed a good measure of self-government. Third, except during the later phase of Aurangzeb's rule, there was ample religious freedom and tolerance. Fourth, all foreign conquerors who entered from the north made India their home and snapped all ties with the mother countries, thus greatly enriching the pluralist ethos of India. Lastly, nationalism was just an incidental by-product of the political organization of these regimes. It was only with the freedom movement that it became a specific, clearly articulated goal.

The colonial rule marks a definite stage in the growth of national sentiment. Young Indians, educated in English universities, returned as torch bearers of liberal democracy, individual freedom and human rights.

British rule is supposed to have effectively united India politically for the first time in history. This is only partially correct. Nearly six hundred princely states, comprising a third of the country's area, were not a part of British India. It was only after Independence that these states were integrated into the country.

In the process of integration British influence was primarily a catalyst. The prime mover was the objective conditions resulting from systematic colonial exploitation of the country. Even the early national leaders like Dadabhoi Naoroji, Justice Ranade, B.G. Tilak and others had a clear perception of the nature of the colonial rule and the urgent need to overthrow it. The freedom struggle for the first time brought all Indians on a common platform and gave them a feeling of shared nationhood. Gandhi, Nehru and other eminent national leaders went out to the peasants and workers, explaining to them the exploitative character of the colonial regime and the value of becoming an independent nation. Gandhi also took good care to keep the movement wholly secular, and above sectarian, regional or linguistic pulls. This gave a truly pan-Indian character to the struggle and won the allegiance of all sections and classes.

When India won freedom, these cultural and historical factors had already laid fairly elaborate groundwork for the emergence of the Indian nation. It was put to a severe test by the partition of the country and the communal carnage that accompanied it. Yet, despite all the problems attendant on the birth of a new nation, the work of blending the Indian people into a national entity went apace.

The two greatest contributions of the Nehru era which helped foster national unity were the framing of Indian Constitution and the integration of the princely states. The Constitution declared India a union of states and provided legal framework for administering a democratic polity. By giving equality before law and guaranteeing fundamental rights, it gave every Indian a stake in the preservation of national unity.

"The troubled history of Third World countries since independence following World War II has revealed that state building must precede and parallel nation building. Contrary to prevailing assumptions... states create nations and economies more than nations and economies create states."[4] The creation of the Indian state, no doubt, provided great impetus to the making of the Indian nation. It was the state which launched various plans for the secularization of the polity, economic growth and social reform. In the absence of these initiatives the state would have lacked the glue which has held the nation together.

But growth in itself is not an integral part of a nation state. It is to the credit of Nehru that he included progressive programmes for development and reform in the agenda of state formation. Although he made the task much more difficult for himself, it enhanced the allegiance of the nation to the state.

The actual process of nation-cum-state formation was far more bumpy than this broad, impressionistic treatment may suggest. "National integration involves a radical shift in the focus of loyalties of the people. The value of a tribal, feudal and parochial ethos should be superseded by the ideals and ends of a democratic, egalitarian and an evolving national identity."[5]

Nehru was fully sensitive to the nature of this culture shock. He wrote in *Discovery of India*, "Old established traditions cannot be easily scrapped or dispensed with... Traditions have to be accepted to a large extent and adapted and transformed to meet new conditions and ways of thought, and at the same time new traditions have to be built up."

By the time he left the scene, Nehru had given the Indian state a fairly cohesive personality and the people were reasonably well integrated. But the state also suffered from certain handicaps which have hampered its growth. The most serious failure of the Nehruvian agenda was that nearly half the population of India hardly benefited from state welfarism. These people, consequently, have no stake in preserving the existing order. This is the most vulnerable area of the Indian state.

Wide disparities in a democratic society lead to conflicts and instability. In India there are too many of them, and they are getting worse with time. There are wide regional disparities, ever widening income inequalities, iniquitous social differentiations, and uneven access to the state's resources. All such imbalances denote the fault lines of the Indian polity.

In post-independence India, the centre-state relations and federal content of the polity have been critical to the formation of the Indian state and making of the nation. There are three major elements which have governed this process. First, the burden of history. India is haunted by too many ghosts from the past. It is a stereotype of the Indian history that the increasing power of provincial satraps has invariably led to the disintegration of the Central authority. This is a major reason for the centralist bias of the Indian Constitution.

Second, at Independence India inherited an overgrown, authoritarian and a highly centralized administration. On top of that she decided to continue with the same apparatus of governance which had been evolved by the earlier, colonial regime. Thus, the new government started with a strong, built-in centrist tilt.

Third, the Constituent Assembly was indirectly elected by the state legislatures. These, in turn, were elected under the Government of India Act, 1935, which laid such stiff property and educational qualifications for the voters that only 11 percent of the adults could be enfranchised. This shows how narrow was the social base of its members. The majority of them came from the upper strata of society and many of them represented propertied interests. Their thinking was coloured by Western models of democracy and they did not represent the Indian mainstream, or its ethos. Nor was this reflected in the document they produced.

In one sense there was something phony about the Indian Constitution. Here was an elitist group laying down the rules of the game which suited it the most. Then, with a great flourish the common man was made to believe that it was his game, and the rules were his rules. The optical illusion designed to give credibility to this ploy was the institution of periodic elections at which he was supposed to decide the fate of his country. Given these circumstances it is not surprising that the Constitution-makers preferred to keep the locus of political power at the top.

Against this background it was natural that the Indian Constitution, though federal in form, contained strong unitary elements. For instance, whereas both the Centre and the states have co-extensive jurisdiction over 47 items of the Concurrent List, the Centre alone has the authority to initiate legislation in this area. All residuary powers are vested in the parliament. Even where the states have the right to legislate, the President (i.e., the Centre) has the power to veto such legislation. Above all, there are emergency provisions under which the Centre can dismiss duly elected state governments, suspend the operation of any law and do away even with the fundamental rights of the citizen. As if these provisions were not draconian enough, the Centre has greatly accentuated their rigour by the manner in which they have been interpreted and implemented.

Centralization did play a vital role in the earlier stages of state formation. Only a centralized polity could have introduced national level planning, created a massive public sector, or promoted a more balanced regional gowth. But this trend runs against the grain of India's historical tradition, as also her extreme social heterogeneity. "What sets India apart from other federal political systems is that in our case, society itself is federal and therefore, federalism in the political sphere has to be seen as no more than a reflection of its basic nature."[6] Thus a progressive devoluton of powers should have accompanied the consolidaton of the Indian state and the accumulation of greater administrative experience by the states.

In India, language-based regionalism represents the most pervasive social identity. Every Indian perceives himself as a Bengali, a Tamilian, a Gujarati or a Punjabi. In terms of language, dress, food, culture, social habits, each regional type evokes a very distinct image. But what is the warp and woof of national identity? There is no such thing as Indian food, Indian dress, Indian language, Indian folk-art, or even Indian literature. The Indian, composed as he is of extremely diverse elements, is a fuzzy and nebulous construct.

This does not necessarily mean that the Indian identity is weak or unstable. But it does imply that it cannot replace the regional identity. And it does not have to. The apprehension that strong states would weaken the Centre is misplaced in the modern context. The rapid means of transport and communication, and the awesome power of the state's armed forces make it highly improbable. As K.M. Panikkar says, "In the present times regionalism in India has generally not been against the Centre, but vis-a-vis other regions. So, it does not weaken the Centre. On the other hand, muzzling of regionalism creates opposition. Actually, regionalism tends to strengthen the Centre as each region looks to it for support."[7]

Besides the Constitutional scheme and the predilections of the Central authority, there are two other factors which have strengthened the centralizing tendencies in the polity. And in both cases Nehru's contribution, even if indirect or unintended, is considerable. It was the Nehru factor which enabled the Congress party to exercise unchallenged sway over both the Centre and the states for 17 long years. This, of course, helped to stabilize various institutions of democracy. But it also turned the state chief ministers into mere surrogates of the prime minister. Secondly, owing to his unmatched popularity with the masses, Nehru did not need the Congress party's support to remain in power. In fact, the Congress was dependent on him to have the privilege of being the ruling party. This situation weakened party democracy considerably, and the Congress became a handmaiden of the PM. The spirit of federalism, obviously, could not flourish in such a climate.

But there is no getting away from the logic of federalism either. Indians live in the states, and it is the state administration that they interact with. Further, it is the state or regional issues that are the stuff of politics. It is members of the legislative assemblies and ministers in the states who represent the masses, and the people approach them with their problems. For most of them the Central government is a distant abstraction. Further, all the revenues are collected from people living in the states and industries too are located there. So it is imperative that the state governments have a major say in the allocation of resources, framing of policies, and administering their territories.

The over-centralized Indian state has naturally created serious problems for the Indian polity. In view of Nehru's stature and the fact that the Congress ruled almost all the states during his tenure, confrontation between the states and the Centre did not occur. But this arrangement was fraught with conflicts. Subsequently, the rise of influential regional parties and even some secessionist movements were a reaction to this phenomenon.

A see-saw tussle between the Centre and the states will remain a permanent feature of the Indian polity. The art of governance at the Centre will lie in maintaining a fine equilibrium between the regional aspirations and the imperatives of national unity. "The great dilemma for a centralizing leader or party in India is that stable power at the Centre can be built up only through control over the states and districts of the country. That kind of power, however, is inherently regional and local in character."[8]

The North-Eastern states occupy a special place in the history of national consolidation. Though British rule ensured internal stability, the North-Eastern states received three severe shocks from the outside world. The first of these was the Japanese incursion during World War II. The second shock was the Partition of the country, which almost severed the region from the rest of India. The third trauma was the Chinese invasion in 1962.

But the greatest commotion in this region resulted from internal developments. The unabated influx of foreign nationals from Bangladesh and Nepal changed the demographic profile of Assam. More serious were the demands made by its Hill tribes for separate states. Their aspirations and struggles ultimately led to the formation of Nagaland, Mizoram, Meghalaya and Arunachal Pradesh. Manipur and Tripura being princely states, merged with India, and were placed under chief commissioners.

The process of integration of the North-Eastern region with India may be examined from three angles. First the official approach as formulated by the Centre. Second, the operational modalities for the implementation of that approach. And third, the response of the tribals themselves to these administrative and political processes.

Special protection provided by the British to the tribals of this region was elaborated under the Sixth Schedule of the Indian Constitution. Further, special constitutional privileges were extended to Nagaland, Manipur and the tribal areas of Assam.

Being a person of deep understanding, Nehru's attitude towards the tribals was humane and accommodating. In an address he outlined his policy of administering the tribal areas: "I am alarmed when I see... how anxious people are to shape others according to their own image or likeness or to impose on them their particular way of living. We are welcome to our way of living but why impose it on others?"[9]

But the administrators and professionals who had to implement his policies lacked his sensitivity and vision. Educated in the country's leading universities, selected in an open competition, and used to the amenities of urban life, they found the unlettered tribals not only primitive, but wholly deficient in culture and refinement. So, they could not resist the impulse to reform and upgrade the tribal way of life. They built roads and airstrips, offices, housing colonies, dams and power stations; and they brought jeeps, lorries and tractors to quicken the pace of development work. In short, they tried to introduce the concepts of speed and efficiency in a slow-moving, leisurely society which lived graciously and saw no reason to accelerate the tempo of its life. This well-meant and misconceived fervour upset the rhythm of tribal life, as it created a mismatch between the rate of change of material and mental environment.

But the greatest damage to the culture of the North-East was done by the wholesale introduction of the political culture and institutions of the plains into the tribal region of the North-East. The tribal communities had managed their affairs for centuries according to established customs. The organic life of the community imposed certain norms of behaviour and conformity for resolving disputes and differences. The authority of the tribal chiefs, elders or panchayats acted as a wholesome restraining influence. Then, without any preparatory work, these areas were suddenly thrown open to full-fledged democracy, adult franchise and electoral politics. It played havoc with their traditional structures by exposing them to the turbulence of competitive party politics. In a highly egalitarian society, some individuals suddenly became ministers, started living in opulence, moved about in a convoy of cars and had a large retinue of hangers-on in attendance. They were simple people, easily misled. Huge amounts of government funds that flowed into their areas for development works were pocketed by politicians, bureaucrats and contractors, and corruption became a way of life.

The sudden import of alien political culture and induction of outside administrators created two cleavages in the tribal society. First, the better paid, better qualified, better housed outsiders created envy and hostility among the tribal communities. The superior airs and arrogance of these 'agents of change' widened the gulf between them and the local population. Secondly, the tribal ministers, legislators and their minions became an elite group within their own community. This was severely resented by the fellow tribals who were used to an egalitarian style of communal life. This internal split within the tribal society was much more injurious and unfortunate.

The last chapter on the merger of the North-Eastern states in the national mainstream has not been written even half a century after Independence. Besides Kashmir and Punjab, this section in the chronicle of India's national integration is replete with turbulence and turmoil. And this poses a continuing challenge to the process of 'nation in the making.'

13

Communalism

Nehru was not a complete socialist. He may not have been a complete democrat either. But he was completely secular down to his fingertips. One of his staunchest critics conceded that his secularism "is almost an instinct with him."[1] So piqued was N.B. Khare of the Hindu Mahasabha at his secular approach that he described him as "English by education, Muslim by culture, and Hindu by accident of birth."

No other national issue did Nehru tackle with as much courage as he did communalism. He repeatedly risked his life to save Muslims during the post-Partition riots, and asserted time and again that India would not become a Hindu state so long as he was the Prime Minister. If the Indian polity did not get communalized after Gandhi's death, much of the credit must go to him. He told the AICC in July 1951, "Let us be clear about it without a shadow of doubt in any Congressman's mind that we stand till death for a secular state." And elsewhere, "In a country like India, which has many faiths and religions, no real nationalism can be built except on the basis of secularity."

Nehru strongly believed that the greatest threat to the Union was posed by majority communalism. In a letter to his Home Minister he said, "The fate of India is largely tied up with the Hindu outlook. If the present Hindu outlook does not change radically, I am quite sure that India is doomed."[2]

As the communalists professed to derive their sustenance from religion, Nehru acquired a strong antipathy to it: "The spectacle of what is called religion, or at any rate organised religion, in India and elsewhere has filled me with horror, and I have frequently condemned it and wished to make a clean sweep of it."[3]

Despite his abhorrence of communalism and the acuteness of his perceptions, Nehru underestimated its disruptive potential. For one thing, as he got over the Partition trauma and the chores of governance occupied most of his time, concern about communalism diminished. Even earlier, in a letter to Lord Lothian he wrote:

> The communalism of today is essentially political, economic and middle class... in India (it) is a latter day phenomenon which has grown up before our eyes... I think it is over-rated and overemphasised ... with the coming of social issues to the forefront it is bound to recede into the background.[4]

To Nehru secularism was the antidote to communalism. For him secularism in operation meant, "first, separation of religion from the political, economic, social and cultural aspects of life, religion being treated as a personal matter; second, dissociation of the state from religion; third, full freedom to all religions and tolerance of all religions; and fourth, equal opportunities for followers of all religions, and no discrimination or partiality on the grounds of religion."[5]

He remained convinced that the government's concentration on social and economic programmes would counteract communalism. So remote was his own experience from ascriptive identities that he never realized how deep-rooted and pernicious the institution of caste was. He said: "Conditions of life have changed and the thought-patterns are changing so much that it seems impossible for the caste system to endure."[6]

"Secularism, among other things, is an ideology of the minorities."[7] Also, a minority is not merely a numerical concept: it emerges as a result of specific socio-historical factors. Unless the less numerous community perceives itself as a minority, it does not become a minority. When the Mughals ruled India, the Muslims never considered themselves as a minority. The Sikhs became an authentic minority only after the armed forces stormed the Golden Temple in 1984 and thousands of Sikhs were butchered all over the country following Indira Gandhi's assassination.

But, for practical purposes, it is the Muslims who constitute the real minority in India. And unless one gets into the shoes of the Indian Muslims, it will be difficult to have a correct idea of communalism in India and assess the efficacy of Nehru's approach to it.

Like most minorities, the Muslims suffer from numerous handicaps. They are the poorest, the least literate, and the most backward section of the Indian population. Their share in civil and military services is far below their numerical ratio. In no sphere of economic activity are they anywhere near the top. Some of the reasons for this sorry state are objective and historical; others flow from their minority status.

India's partition delivered them some staggering blows. Whilst most upper class Muslims migrated to Pakistan, their poor compatriots in India were left leaderless and rudderless. The Muslims who stayed behind were considered crypto-Pakistanis and their loyalty to India was suspect. And the educated, well-to-do section of the Muslims left behind shied away from providing leadership to the community. Owing to their anxiety to establish their nationalist and secular credentials, they preferred to keep aloof from the affairs of their co-religionists. The Congress also unwittingly aggravated the situation. With a view to enlarging its base, it opened its doors to the nationalist Muslim leaders and offered them organizational posts. The resultant departure of secular leadership from within the Muslim community left the field open to the communal elements

These setbacks left the community floundering and alienated, facing a serious identity crisis. But what has made recovery even more difficult is the existential reality of an Indian Muslim, placed as he is in a sea of Hindus which outnumbers him in the ratio of one to seven. Well-wishers keep advising Muslims to join the national mainstream. But communities are not streams of water which can intermix when brought together.

The predicament faced by Indian Muslims is very real and must be duly recognized. Aside from their all-round deprivation, they continually face discrimination in daily life. It is understandable when many Muslims do not qualify for higher posts. But when they are denied jobs even as peons and constables in fair proportion, it hurts. When in communal riots they are not only the worst sufferers but even the local police and administration play a partisan role, it hurts. When these riots occur mostly in areas where the Muslims have been able to improve their economic status and when whole communities of Muslim craftsmen are wiped out, it hurts. All these hurts convey a clear and distinct message: you are the target and the victim because you are a Muslim. This not only tends to reinforce their religious identity, but communalizes it to some extent. Against this background, when Muslims are asked to join the national mainstream, they find it a cruel joke.

There are certain doctrinal aspects of Islam which do not facilitate the process of adjustment and accommodation with other faiths. "It is not generally realized" wrote Rasheeduddin Khan, "that the formulation of essential unity of all religion is an eclectic vedantic perception, a peculiarly Hindu view of the religious phenomenon. For the votaries of semitic religions Judaism, Christianity and Islam, on the other hand, with their defined dogmas and doctrines... any deviation therefrom or accretion and modification to it tantamounts to an interference in the divine will and order, which is impermissible, blasphemous and heretical."[8]

Hamid Dalwai feels that the basic problem of Muslim society lies in the fact that it has never had' a renaissance in its entire history of more than thirteen hundred years.[9] "So great has been the hold of orthodoxy on the Muslim mind that nowhere has Muslim society so far been able to throw up an articulate class of liberal Muslims committed to modern values..."[10]

The pursuit of such orthodoxy can make the community oblivious of its own self-interest. For instance when Sir Syed Ahmed Khan urged the Muslims to accept modern Western education, the Ulema of Deoband came out with the *fatwa* that Sir Syed was a Kafir.[11] Indian Muslims could not have had a greater friend than Nehru. Yet when he died, the Muslim clergy "objected to the recitation of the Koran... on the ground that such a recitation is not permitted by the side of the dead body of a Kafir."[12]

It is easy to criticize Indian Muslims, as they are vulnerable on many fronts. Living in an environment which they perceive to be hostile, they withdraw into the shell of religiosity. Being on the defensive all the time, they have developed a siege mentality. Their vulnerability impels them to strengthen the fortifications within.

"Honest communalism is fear; false communalism is political reaction," said Nehru in a press interview. Living in a climate of fear and discrimination, the Muslims had some reason to be communal. But what about the majority communalism, when the Hindus form more than four-fifth of the population and control every aspect of the country's economic and political life?

In fact Hindu bigotry has a pretty ancient lineage. From the earlier times — when the Brahmanical onslaught overcame the challenge of Buddhism, destroyed Buddhist monasteries and killed monks — to the destruction of Babri Masjid, Hinduism has been occasionally seized by bouts of intolerance. The modern phase of Hindu communalism starts with the creation of the Rashtriya Swayamsevak Sangh. Its ideologue, Golwalkar, said: "Non-Hindu people in Hindustan must either adopt the Hindu culture... or may stay in the country as wholly subordinate to the Hindus."[13]

What helped the Hindu communalists to stoke the fires of hatred were certain emotive issues of high visibility. In the face of the monolithic doctrinal solidarity of Islam, Hindu pluralism appeared weak. Therefore, some Hindu zealots embarked on a campaign of imparting to Hinduism also a greater cohesion of dogma and practice. The most powerful argument with the Hindu communalists was the Islamic injunction of converting followers of other faiths to Islam. Exaggerated accounts of forcible conversion of Hindus by the Muslims rulers were already a cause of deep offence to the Hindus. When this practice of conversion continued even after Independence, it touched a raw nerve and became a provocative communal issue.

Nehru had once observed, "the communalism of a majority community must of necessity bear a closer resemblance to nationalism than the communalism of the minority."[14] Not surprisingly, the incisive and catchy slogan of the RSS is: Hinduism is Nationalism. All Hindu communalists speak in the name of Hindu Rashtra. Whereas all Hindus are supposed to be nationalists by right, the non-Hindus have to prove their patriotic bonafides. These attitudes confront the Muslims with a peculiar dilemma: on the one hand they are accused of not joining the national mainstream; on the other they are found ineligible to join it.

Secularism as a credo was formulated and propagated by leaders of the national movement. But for the lead given by Gandhi and Nehru, India might have gone the Pakistan way. Yet, within the Congress organization, and even at senior levels, there were persons with strong communal bias. "Many a Congressman was a communalist under his national cloak," said Nehru.[15]

Nehru was firmly opposed to any official association with the restoration of the Somnath temple. Yet, Dr. Rajendra Prasad, the then President of India, accepted the invitation to inaugurate it against Nehru's advice.

In the selection of candidates for election and appointment of ministers, the Congress invariably took the religious factor into account. Even a leader of the calibre of Maulana Azad was shifted from the Burdwan Hindu-majority constituency in West Bengal to Rampur in UP where the Nawab's writ still ran. After the dismissal of the communist ministry in Kerala in 1959, the Congress made an alliance with the Muslim League to form the successor government. There could not be a more demeaning trade-off between secularism and opportunism.

Nehru was against any truck with communal organizations on principle. He even opposed Gandhi's meeting with Jinnah in 1937. Yet, "... too many times Nehru fell prey to the strategy of dealing with the communal problem through top-level negotiations with the Muslim communal leaders. This he did in 1938-9, 1941-2 and 1946-7. And by doing so, he ... accorded Jinnah and other communal leaders the much-needed respectability and the status they desired of being the spokespersons of Muslims."[16]

Secularisation is "the process in modern societies in which religious ideas and organisations tend to lose influence when faced with science and other modern forms of knowledge."[17] Except for the recent, half-baked modernization of Indian society, most of the factors which contributed to the secular ideal in the West were missing in India. There was no doubt a lot of talk about secularism during the freedom movement. But its two greatest proponents, Gandhi and Nehru used the term in different contexts. For Nehru keeping religion out of politics became an article of faith after the politicization of religion had led to India's partition. For Gandhi religion was integral to it.

Though the word secularism does not find a place in the original Constitution adopted in 1950, its entire scheme envisages a secular polity. Nowhere has the state anything to do with religious or educational institutions, nor are religious qualifications prescribed for holding public office or enjoyment of civil rights. Individual freedoms and fundamental rights are not subjected to any religious tests.

But can constitutional provisions or even Herculean endeavours of a great national leader erase traditions nurtured over thousands of years of social history? Once it is conceded that India is a deeply religious country, there are certain consequences that flow from it. In a religious society, religion is not 'what an individual does with his privacy'. It gives identity to its followers. It performs vital social functions. It shapes one's world view — both spiritual and temporal. In such a situation how can religion be kept out of politics? Both occupy a lot of common space.

The Muslim stand on this issue is clear. Islam pervades not only the spiritual realm of its followers, it is an entire way of life, and permeates every facet of human activity. It is also a fact that the Koran, along with Hadith and Sunna, contain specific injunctions on concerns of daily life and conduct of human affairs. Any deviation from these injunctions is apostasy. The state, thus, becomes only an agent for faithfully enforcing the Koranic mandate. Here, since politics is subsumed by religion, how do you keep them apart?

Sikhism was born in response to a grave political crisis. Two of its Gurus, Arjun Das and Tegh Bahadur, sacrificed their lives while defending the basic political rights of the Hindus. Guru

Gobind Singh waged a lifelong battle against the religio-political tyranny of the state. Even subsequently, the Sikhs had to continuously fight the Muslim rulers for their survival. No wonder, then, that the historical experience of the Sikhs is suffused with political turmoil. The politics of the Sikhs has been dominated by the Akali Dal, which is the custodian of both their religious affairs and political interests.

In contrast to Islam and Sikhism, Hinduism evolved over thousands of years in an environment of relative peace, tranquillity and contemplation. Lacking a central orthodoxy and a mandate to spread its message, it remained free from bigotry and proselytizing fervor. Its plurality and openness helped keep its secular concerns free from religious bias.

But is that really so? The Hindu caste system is one of the most enduring social institutions created by man. It derives its sanction from the scriptures, but it serves secular ends. In fact, the social universe of the Hindus is deeply mediated by religion. But the secular and the religious strands have been so finely interwoven that it is impossible to tell them apart. Its most telling illustration is the use that Tilak, Gandhi, and several other Hindu Congress leaders made of the imagery and idiom of Hinduism in their political strategies. This came to them instinctively, and it helped in establishing an immediate rapport with the bulk of the Indian masses for whom Hindu symbols and metaphors were woven into the fabric of their socio-religious consciousness. Gandhi's Ram Rajya, though secular in content, was religious in inspiration.

In the Indian communal matrix, Hinduism, Islam and Sikhism are the three significant religions, and in all of them religion and politics are closely intermeshed.

Nehru pointed out that "Minorities in India...are not racial or national minorities as in Europe; they are religious minorities."[18] In other words it is religion which defines their identity and not ethnic, linguistic or regional factors. In opposition to this phenomenon he repeatedly pointed out: "In what way are the interests of the Muslim peasant different from those of the Hindu peasant? Or those of a Muslim labourer or artisan or merchant or landlord or manufacturer different from those of his Hindu prototype?"

Good logic, and very progressive indeed. But this is not how the workers and landlords of the two communities perceived their situation. Class identity in India has proved a weak cementing force. It is true that mostly the poor from both the communities get killed in communal riots. But the Hindu poor burn the shops of Muslim merchants only and the Muslim labourers kill only Hindu mill-managers. Ascribe it to false consciousness or what have you, but it is much stronger than the true class consciousness.

Nehru placed excessive reliance on the efficacy of the economic factor. "... in his treatment of the communal question, Nehru suffered from a certain economistic, deterministic and reductionist bias. This led him to underplay, if not ignore, the role of communalism as an ideology and the need for an ideological political struggle against it."[19]

Nehru felt that science, industrialization, economic growth and democracy would secularise society. But, as pointed out by Andre Gunder Frank, "The recent past, present and foreseeable future are witness to the widespread growth and increasing strength of new nationalist and religious movements... The fact that the students in Malaysia and elsewhere are becoming Islamic revivalists shows that modernisation theory does not work."[20] The developments in India during the post-Nehru era bear this out. The spread of education and industrialization has been accompanied by a steady growth of the communal and sectarian forces. Though there is no causal relationship between the two, one does not necessarily counter the other either.

Nehru stated, "Personally... I am opposed to the idea of political or economic rights being given to an individual or a group on the basis of religion."[21] This was the accepted policy of the Congress also. But Nehru's commitment to democratic and secular norms was informed by a deep concern for the safety and security of the Muslims. "They were to be not only citizens with equal rights but also a self-governing religious community in charge of its own personal law."[22] In pursuit of this objective, constitutional safeguards were provided under Articles 28 and 30. This implied that whereas no religious instruction could be imparted in educational institutions funded by the state, the minority institutions were exempted from this bar. Further, minorities were given the right to establish and administer their own educational institutions, and were entitled to receive government aid without any discrimination.

This "simultaneous commitment to communities and equal citizenship" led to a "potential contradiction" between Nehru's loyalty to "anti-communal secularism and to Muslim community autonomy."[23] Equality of all citizens before the law is the bedrock of democracy. But special constitutional safeguards for minorities introduced a dangerous conflict between the rights of the individual and the group.

These special provisions are greatly valued by the minorities. They may not amount to much in material terms, yet the minorities consider them basic for the preservation of their culture and identity. But if viewed objectively, they have done more harm to them than any other act of omission or commission of the government. It is these safeguards which have been exploited by the Hindu communalists to convince their co-religionists that they were being discriminated against in their own country; that they were being treated as second-class citizens by the government. As communal issues are highly emotive and nobody pauses to verify the charge of discrimination against the Hindus, it is further argued that the Muslims are a pampered minority. This line of argument has done more to foment majority communalism that anything else.

In this matter, Nehru was placed in a no-win situation. The minorities felt insecure in view of Hinduism's great assimilative power. They had to be assured that their religious and cultural identities would be fully protected. This is what Nehru set out to do. After all, solicitude for the disadvantaged and insecure communities is the hallmark of a civilized society. But these humane measures were misrepresented as acts of discrimination against the majority. Of course, Nehru did not foresee this development. But even if he had, what was the way out for him?

The greatest failure of the Independence struggle lay in its inability to effectively contain the communal forces. Despite all efforts to the contrary, the country got partitioned on communal lines. Each year of the Nehru era was marked by communal riots of varying intensities, and the graph rose continuously. After Nehru the communal situation worsened steadily, reaching its climax with the demolition of the Babri Masjid.

What went wrong with Nehru's secular agenda? Was it conceptually flawed? Quite simply, Nehru neither formulated a comprehensive policy to combat communalism, nor mounted a sustained campaign against it. He came nearest to defining its essence when he wrote in 1937: "... communalism meant that in politics and social and economic matters, Muslims and Hindus must function separately as a group and deal with other (religious) groups as one nation deals with another. So also in trade unions, peasant unions, business, chambers of commerce and like organisations and activities."[24]

This concept has been refined and elaborated by Bipan Chandra in his writings on communalism.[25] He postulates that "communalism is basically an ideology" which consists of three stages, "one following the other." First, the people who follow the same religion have common secular interests, that is, "common political, economic, social and cultural interests." The second element is the "notion that in a multi-religious society like India, the secular interests... of the followers of one religion are dissimilar and divergent from the interests of the followers of another religion." And, the third stage is reached when "the (secular) interests of the followers of different religions... are seen to be mutually incompatible, antagonistic and hostile."

This "unreal communal division" says Prof. Chandra, "obscured the real division of the Indian people into linguistic, cultural, religious and social classes..." With the spread of communal ideology, religious consciousness was transformed into 'communal consciousness'. Economic stagnation and limited job opportunities were exploited to sharpen the awareness of the communal divide.

According to this view, communalism is antithetical to

nationalism, and tends to subvert it. Communal ideology can be dislodged only by a counter-ideology. And that is the ideology of nationalism: "... nationalist ideology must confront and over-power communal ideology." This view of nationalism versus communalism is based on the most exuberant phase of the Independence struggle. Nationalism then was the ruling credo and the talisman for Independence. During this period nationalism united people and communalism divided them. So, the conclusion drawn was that they were inherently opposed.

"Nationalism as an ideology in the service of the established social order is nothing new or surprising."[26] It has been used the world over not only to bolster democracy and socialism, but also fascism, and other types of tyrannies. In the Indian experience itself Jinnah used nationalism in the service of communalism, and the RSS peddles it to shore up its communal ideology.

Communalism may be rooted in communal ideology. But it is simplistic to dub it as 'false consciousness'. This ideology has historical and objective basis. When a religious community becomes the object of widespread and systematic discrimination, it inevitably comes to perceive 'common secular interests', 'common political, economic, social and cultural interests' which cut across class boundaries. The so-called 'false consciousness' then acquires an objective basis and attains its own autonomous existence.

As secularism is entirely a product of Western history and thought, discourse on this subject is mostly conducted in terms of Western idioms and concepts. The precondition of a secular society is separation of church from the state, or religion from politics. But Gandhi, who was as secular as could be, said, "I do not believe that religion has nothing to do with politics. The latter, divorced from religion, is like a corpse, only fit to be buried."[27] And elsewhere, "... for me, politics bereft of religion are absolute dirt, ever to be shunned."

Of course the religion that Nehru abhorred and Gandhi adored were two very different entities. Yet the fact remains that Gandhi, the greatest physician of the Indian psyche, felt that the secular prescription does not work for India. For most of the Western educated elite it is very difficult to abandon this anchor. But this paradigm did not hold good during the freedom struggle, nor later. Gandhi may have been indulging in hyperbole when he said that "politics bereft of religion are absolute dirt". But that is what Indian politics is in danger of becoming. This, of course has numerous causes. Yet there is also little doubt that the unprecedented spread of communalism has become the greatest threat to India's stability.

The secular dilemma of India is born of a contradiction that lies at the centre of her polity. On the one hand we have a society for which religion is still the bedrock of its social consciousness. On the other, India is constitutionally committed to keep religion and politics apart. The effort to resolve this contradiction has led to all manner of fanciful reasoning. For instance, our belief is that the *mantra* of *sarva dharma sambhava*, or equal respect for all religions, will solve communal conflicts. But it offers no solution; it has actually led to further complications. "In the name of toleration of all communities, and their eventual harmonisation, what we finally achieve is reconciliation of multiple communalisms, promotion of multiple obscurantism, universal superstition and mixing of all mythologies."[28] Although Hindus have convinced themselves that their ethos is basically secular, this is certainly not the whole truth. The Hindu cultural tradition is firmly rooted in religion. The confusion arises when 'secular' and 'plural' are treated as synonymous. Hindu religion is definitely very pluralistic and diverse. This has been an important reason for the plurality of the Indian society. But there is danger of overplaying this factor.

Another crucial element which has prevented Hindu society from getting homogenized is the highly divisive power of caste. It is as much the divisiveness of the caste system as the plurality of Hinduism which has prevented it from becoming a communal monolith. Thus, paradoxically, the highly reactionary institution of caste has played a very progressive role: it has served as a bulwark against the majority communalism and saved India the fate of its two neighbours.

The main obstacle in the way of creating a secular Indian society is that the secular agenda was not framed within the parameters of the Indian cultural tradition. "In the West intellectual revolutions have usually taken place in opposition to religion. But in India every aspect of the modern enlightenment, and every movement through which it has been expressed, has been based on the idea of revitalising society through religious reconstruction. Nehru may be described as the first intellectual thinker who has not found it necessary to lean on religion."[29] The Bhakti movement is the most prominent example of this process. The teachings of Shankaracharya, Nanak, Kabir, Swami Vivekananda, and the Muslim Sufi saints are other growing points of this phenomenon. "The ignorance of the secularisation process within religion on the part of the modern elite has created a vast hiatus between the secular forces deriving their inspiration from modern Western thought and those rooted in the Indian Religions Reformation."[30] Further, "Some of the basic failures of contemporary Indian secularism arise from the lack of rootedness in the Indian *cultural tradition* which, to a large extent, still means the Indian *religious tradition*."[31]

This brings us to a typical Indian paradox. India needs a model for the secularization of her society which is constructed within the confines of the Indian religious tradition. Whilst Nehru would consider such a proposition a contradiction in terms, to Gandhi it would appear axiomatic. But the need for such an exercise cannot be over-emphasized in view of the collapse of the politics-without-religion paradigm.

Whichever the model of secularism that ultimately prevails, it will do so only if social policy is integral to it. Unemployed and deprived people fall easy prey to the communal ideology, and fierce competition for scarce resources readily takes the form of communal conflict.

14

Governance and Institutions

$\mathcal{I}$ndira Gandhi regretted that her father was a saint strayed into politics; that he lacked the necessary ruthlessness. But nobody can jump out of his skin, and his daughter's lament notwithstanding, Nehru could not be ruthless. In his view the strongman concept itself was 'something undemocratic and repugnant to the spirit of our country as well as the times.' He was deeply imbued with the Congress culture of compromise and consensus. These traits, coupled with his moral stature, enabled him to hold this country together during very critical times. It was no mean achievement.

On assumption of office Nehru had a host of major problems facing him, and two of these required urgent attention. One was the resettlement of the refugees, and that has been dealt with in chapter one. The second was the coming to terms with hundreds of princely states. With Independence the British Paramountcy over the princely states lapsed, and some princes started dreaming of acquiring independent status. But it was a wild dream. Constituting one-third of the country's area and dotted all over, their independence would have led to the Balkanization of India.

There were three factors which impelled the princes to see reason and to not indulge in adventurism. First was the ferment among the people of these states, as India's freedom struggle had a deep impact on their subjects. Secondly, this was the one issue on which the Government of India took a firm and clear-cut stand. Luckily for the country, the job was entrusted to Sardar Vallabhbhai Patel, Deputy Prime Minister in charge of Home Affairs, who executed it with clockwork precision and thorough professionalism. Thirdly, the princes were promised handsome privy purses and other privileges in perpetuity.

The Ministry of State was created by the Interim Government in July, 1947. Once the broad approach had been decided, Patel worked out the modalities of his strategy with the assistance of V.P. Menon, his gifted secretary. The operation was performed in three stages. After the Sardar had convinced the princes of the futility of any adventurist moves with his tough but persuasive talk, he made them sign the Instrument of Accession. This served as a bridge for the change-over from the British Paramountcy to the Indian Dominion. Almost simultaneously, it was followed by integration of the acceded states with the Indian Union (then Dominion). As it would have been very cumbersome and wholly unviable to have nearly 552 princely states becoming 552 additional provinces of independent India, Patel aggregated them into a dozen provinces. The third stage was the introduction of democratic institutions in the newly created units. Officers from All India Services were deputed to these states to create rule-based, stable administrative structures. All these units participated fully in the first general election in 1952, thus joining the mainstream of Indian democracy.

With the completion of the integration process, the resultant 26 states were grouped under three categories. The old provinces comprising British India were called Part A States; the groupings of princely domains as Part B; and some small, centrally administered areas as Part C.

There were only three states which marred this otherwise flawless operation. They were: Junagadh, Hyderabad and Jammu and Kashmir. Junagadh, a small principality ruled by a Muslim prince, acceded to Pakistan. This was a crazy move as the state, located in Kathiawad, was far removed from the Pakistan border and more than 80 percent of its population was Hindu. After some acrimonious exchanges between the two countries, the Indian army entered Junagadh and conducted a plebiscite. People voted overwhelmingly for India, and this ended the Nawab's misadventure.

Hyderabad was the largest and the richest Indian state with a standing army of 50,000. Its ruler, the Nizam, was a Muslim and 89 percent of the state's population was non-Muslim. Unlike the other princely states, the Nizam did not accede to India on 15 August 1947. He was seeing visions of ruling an independent state, and in this he was encouraged by foreign elements hostile to India.

As tension between the Nizam and the government of India escalated, a standstill agreement for one year was signed between the two parties under pressure from Lord Mountbatten. Instead, hoping to benefit from the India-Pakistan clash over Kashmir, he intensified his hostile activities, and encouraged the Razakars, a fanatical Muslim outfit, to organise themselves into a fighting force.

Whereas Patel advocated decisive military action, Nehru was holding back his hand in view of the international ramifications of this issue and its likely repercussion on the Kashmir conflict. But the Nizam's intransigence increased by the day and even Nehru despaired of a peaceful settlement. The last hurdle in the way was removed when Lord Mountbatten left India in June, 1948. The Indian forces marched into Hyderabad on 13 September 1948 and within four days the Nizam surrendered.

This leaves us with the state of Jammu and Kashmir. In view of its importance, a separate chapter will be devoted to it. But the integration of Goa and Pondicherry may also be noted here. India started negotiations with both Portugal and France for their peaceful pull-out. France ultimately vacated Pondicherry in 1954. But Portugal had no intention of following suit. For fourteen long years Nehru explored every available avenue to solve this problem without resort to arms. Goa was assured of backing by her Western friends in her indefensible stand. In fact Britain conveyed her compulsion under a treaty to support Portugal in the event of a conflict with India.[1] Nehru was still dilly-dallying when, ultimately, the Indian troops moved into Goa on 17 December, 1961 and the Portuguese forces surrendered the next day. It was Krishna Menon, the Defence Minister, who had finally forced Nehru's hand.[2] The Western world reacted strongly, and the US

Ambassador to the UN stated before the Security Council that the Indian use of force was the beginning of the end of the United Nations.[3]

The next important item on Nehru's agenda was the formation of linguistic states. The Congress had all along recognized the validity of this demand. The Constituent Assembly wanted steps to be initiated to create linguistic states even before the adoption of the Constitution. But Nehru maintained, "First things must come first and the first thing is the security and stability of India." However, in view of the mounting pressure, a Linguistic Provinces Commission was set up under S.K. Dar. In its report submitted in 1948, it opposed the formation of linguistic states. Owing to strong public opposition to this report, the Congress party appointed a Committee under Nehru to re-examine this issue. It broadly endorsed the Dar Report. But, with typical Nehruvian ambivalence, it entered the caveat that in the event of persistent demands, this question could be reviewed further.

The Telegu-speaking population of the erstwhile Madras state was the most articulate group demanding the creation of a separate Andhra state. In view of the agreement between the Tamilians and the Andhras on this issue, the Congress accepted the demand. But the two sides could not agree on the location of the new Andhra capital. Meantime the agitation intensified and a respected Andhra leader, Potti Sriramulu, went on fast unto death to press this demand. Typically, it was only after his death that the government awoke to the gravity of the situation, and Nehru himself inaugurated the first linguistic state in October 1952.

There were violent agitations all over for extending this principle to the entire country and the situation seemed to be getting out of hand. The government was forced to appoint the States Reorganization Commission at the end of 1953, and it submitted its report within two years. It accepted language as one of the criteria for the creation of new states. But it did not follow a logical and consistent approach. Whereas on the one hand it recommended the creation of states like Kerala and Karnataka on linguistic basis, it also wanted Bombay to be constituted as a bilingual state. As no solution could have satisfied everybody, there were widespread demonstrations and riots in various parts of the country. The government's approach to this issue was hesitant and inconsistent. The manner in which it handled the situation in Bombay best illustrates this point. The Centre took five years to finally resolve this issue, and changed its stand six times as summarized below:

1. In view of extensive protests, riots and firings, it was agreed to modify the commission's recommendations and convert Bombay city into a separate state.
2. As large sections rejected this proposal, Nehru reverted to the idea of a composite, bilingual state, with Vidarbha as a part of it.
3. But agitations continued and it was announced that Bombay city will be centrally administered for a fixed period and the position reviewed thereafter.
4. This too did not help cool tempers. It was, therefore, agreed to split the province on linguistic lines, with Bombay city automatically reverting to Maharashtra after a fixed period.
5. This again did not help control the situation. So the proposal for a composite, bilingual state was again approved by the Cabinet.
6. This provoked the Gujaratis and there was large-scale rioting in Ahmedabad. Consequently, the state of Bombay was again bifurcated on linguistic lines in 1960. Bombay city was to be the capital of Maharashtra and a separate state of Gujarat was formed.

This tiresome and confusing account throws up in sharp relief the contrast between the management styles of Nehru and Patel. Patel's handling of the princely states and their merger with the Dominion was a neatly executed and efficient operation. By comparison, the reorganization of states was a fumbling, messy and long-drawn exercise.

The main reason for Nehru's uncertain and vacillating approach to the linguistic states was that he did not consider linguistic states to be a major issue, and treated the adjustment of state boundaries as an administrative matter. But he did not realize that language issues could whip up emotions to a pitch which even the freedom movement had not.

Nehru conceived and created on a global scale. Whether it was in the realm of development, or reform, or administration, he initiated grand projects and set up big institutions. But however impressive these plans appeared on paper, their realization on the ground was a matter of strenuous attention to detail and uninspiring drudgery.

In the earlier years, and especially during the lifetime of Patel, Nehru could not have his full say. But in 1956 when a foreign journalist asked him about the slow pace of reforms, he replied, "Considering the influence of this large organization of the Congress, and considering the influence I have, I would say that there is very little that we cannot get through here through the democratic process."[4]

Yet this influence was not fully harnessed to solve the problems facing him. He vacillated and dithered when faced with difficult options. Yet this was only partly true. Look at the way he asked Patel to resign over the communal issue, or forced Tandon to quit, or put Sheikh Abdullah behind bars, or implemented the Kamaraj plan. He certainly could wield the big stick once he was convinced that he should, or he perceived a threat to his position.

Nehru's main constraint as a ruler was that he did not have the makings of a good manager; his judgement of men was unsound; he lacked the art of delegating authority and make others slog for him; he was a poor implementor of his own schemes, and he worked too hard for his own good and the good of the system.

The way M.O. Mathai materialized from nowhere and rapidly acquired great influence as Nehru's private secretary shows how naïve he could be in accepting people at their face value. He over-trusted Sheikh Abdullah and then felt terribly let down. His first cabinet and the Planning Commission included persons who had little sympathy with his goals, and caused considerable embarrassment later.

The larger the enterprise, the greater the delegation of power down the line. In Nehru's case, "A probing interest in every aspect of the Central administration was combined with full acceptance of his obligations in parliament and general surveillance of developments in the country as a whole. Nothing that was happening in India was of indifference to him... He gave orders for a sun-shade to be provided for a policeman on traffic duty; chided the chief minister of Bombay for the arrest of a man and wife found kissing in public, and was concerned that parts of the film *Hamlet* had been censored...He received about 2,000 letters every day, not all concerning official matters. Nehru spent four to five hours every night dictating replies."[5] This sort of exhausting regime was unfair to himself, as also to his job. And then he complained of feeling stale and was left with little time for general reading or fresh thinking. The four hours he spent in replying letters could have been more gainfully devoted to higher affairs of the state. The greatest irony of this situation was that Nehru could not inspire his colleagues to emulate his passion for hard work.

Nehru's major projects, though sound in conception, got derailed in the process of execution. His food policy, his efforts to introduce state trading in foodgrains, and the setting up of an effective public distribution network never got off the ground. His schemes for economic and social reform were not neatly formulated, and no attention was paid to the creation of a suitable delivery system. He did not evolve an efficient feedback mechanism which could continuously evaluate and review the progress of various schemes and alert him in time about any serious malfunctioning. His extreme austerity in respect of his personal staff was some-what misplaced. Looking to the size and complexity of the job, he needed much greater staff support.

In this context one should also not underestimate the resistance offered by the vested interests that surrounded Nehru and be-came increasingly stronger with the passage of time. Also, owing to his distaste for confrontation, he came to equate the democratic system with compromise, accommodation and facile bargaining in which others profited and he lost. And the authority vested in him by the Constitution and his mass support remained consid-erably under-utilized.

This account cannot, of course, detract from some of the great feats of management and system-building performed during Nehru's time. These include resettlement of millions of refugees;

integration of princely states; conducting of three general elections; creation of a host of new institutions, projects and national laboratories, and the entire apparatus for planning and state regulation of economy. The point sought to be made here is that adequate benefit from a number of these great initiatives could not be derived owing to weak and faulty implementation.

Whereas Nehru laid great emphasis on changing the traditional, backward society, he did not show the same awareness about the management of that change. Economic growth, industrialization, social mobility or urbanization are all unsettling processes. Democracy itself introduces a level of individual freedom and permissiveness which may prove subversive of the established system. In such a situation law and order becomes the first casualty. And this inevitably leads to the expansion of the coercive apparatus of the state.

During the heady days of the freedom movement the national leaders were very allergic to the use of the police force. At the Lucknow Congress, 1936, Nehru had declared, "A government that has to rely on the Criminal Law Amendment Act and similar laws ... is a government that has ceased to have even a shadow of justification for its existence."

In a letter to chief ministers of Bihar and Madras, he wrote on 10 August, 1948 "We are getting very unpopular in other countries and our reputation now is that of a police state suppressing individual freedom."

And in May 1949 he told Pandit Pant, chief minister of UP, "More and more we have to rely upon our administrative and coercive apparatus of government ... In this process we become more and more the prisoners of that very administrative apparatus."

Nehru saw the downhill slide with great perspicacity, but he could not stop it. Ten years after becoming the Prime Minister he said, "I do not think anyone in India can dislike this firing business as, I do. I have a horror of it; I think it is a bad thing and I hope that it will be possible to put an end to it."[6]

But how did matters shape after Independence? Whereas the

police dealt with crime and tried to keep in check the disruptive forces on a day-to-day basis, the remedy for these ills lay in the domain of social engineering. All the measures for economic development and social equity introduced by Nehru had their impact on the country's law and order situation also. To the extent they succeeded, they promoted peace and social harmony. And to the extent they failed, they worsened the climate of public order. The tensions and conflicts that lie embedded in the body politic like sticks of dynamite, have been implanted not by professional criminals; their origin lies in the misdeeds of the moneyed classes, the avaricious politicians and corrupt officials. Honest implementation of agrarian reforms could have brought peace and a sense of justice to the countryside. But the landowner-moneylender combine inverted their intent and left rural India smouldering with discontent. It was the millions of deprived tenants and marginal farmers who later supplied ready recruits to Bhoomi Senas, Lal Brigades, the Naxalites and such other outfits.

Basically, this situation arose out of a conflict between the dynamics of social change and the forces of status quo. The only way out of this dilemma for Nehru was his willigness to pay the political price, including the loss of prime ministership, for social transformation. Self-interest as well as excessive emphasis on consensus prevented him from playing the role of such a decisive leader.

Nehru "is as pure as a crystal," said Gandhi. It is difficult to imagine a public man more clean and honest in his personal life than Jawaharlal. But he had a typical aristocrat's disdain for money and those who made money. A person of frugal habits, he did not have much use for it in any case. "It is not that I am against material comfort, but I am not sure that it is too good to have too much of it."[7]

With such indifference to money matters and a high degree of probity in his own conduct Nehru, perhaps, did not realize the extent to which acquisitiveness can become such a consuming passion with other people that it obliterates the distinction between right and wrong.

However one explains it, the fact remains that Nehru showed great tolerance of corruption in public life, especially in people whom he liked.

Soon after he took over as Prime Minister, allegations of corruption and nepotism poured in thick and fast. Many of the persons involved were close to him. As to Nehru's approach to corruption in public, it may be viewed from three angles. First, he never used a single tainted penny to his own advantage. Second, he tried to underplay this phenomenon so as to save the party and the government from getting discredited before the public. In a letter to Jagjivan Ram he wrote, "the people in high office tended to attract wild allegations."[8]

So far so good. As Nehru said, "We are a gossipy people," and a climate of suspicion and charge-sheeting does tend to undermine morale. But there is no defence for the third aspect of Nehru's attitude to corruption. Some of his closest associates were involved in corrupt deals; there was irrefutable evidence against them, and yet he went out of the way to shield them.

The first major scandal of the Nehru era was the purchase of jeeps and other military hardware from the UK. The deal was handled by V.K. Krishna Menon, the Indian High Commissioner and, perhaps, the only close Indian friend of Nehru. He awarded contracts to bogus firms who never met their obligations and the government incurred heavy losses. All norms of financial propriety were violated, requisite sanctions were not obtained and heavy advance payments made without obtaining adequate security.

There was widespread hue and cry against these transactions and the Public Accounts Committee recommended an enquiry by a committee of high court judges. No action was taken on this recommendation and sometime later Krishna Menon was appointed as Cabinet Minister without portfolio. Subsequently he was made the Defence Minister of India.

Another well-known scandal concerns the favour extended by T.T. Krishnamachari, the Finance Minister, to one Haridas Mundhra. It is an intricate and a murky affair. Its highlight was the sale of Mundhra shares worth 1.27 crore to the Life Insurance Corporation of India with the ostensible purpose of buttressing the Calcutta share market. The deal was struck with the help of H.M. Patel, the then Finance Secretary, who had instructed the Chairman, LIC to do the needful. In view of public criticism, press exposures and parliamentary pressures, M.C. Chagla, Chief Justice of Bombay, was asked to enquire into the case. He held that the minister-in-charge must bear the main responsibility for this muddle. Krishnamachari resigned as a result of this finding. But Nehru was gracious enough to reappoint him to his cabinet after some time! This was nothing short of a slap in the face of public opinion.

In these two cases Nehru acted in flagrant disregard of the basic norms of public morality because of his personal fondness for the concerned worthies. In two other well-publicized cases, that of Partap Singh Kairon and Bakshi Ghulam Mohammed, the motivation was political expediency.

Partap Singh Kairon became the Chief Minister of Punjab in 1956 and continued in office till after Nehru's death. Nehru regarded him highly as he was able to contain both the Sikh and Hindu communal forces in this sensitive border state. But his sons and wife made heaps of money, acquired a lot of immovable property and behaved in a very arrogant manner. Repeated complaints made to Kairon produced no results. It was only when the Supreme Court passed strictures against Kairon that Nehru was forced to appoint a Commission of Enquiry in 1963. By the time the Report was submitted, Nehru had left the scene.

Bakshi Ghulam Mohammed became the Prime Minister[9] of Jammu and Kashmir after the arrest of Sheikh Mohammed Abdullah in 1953, and ruled the state as his personal fief for the next ten years. He was wholly authoritarian, corrupt to the core, and his family plundered the luckless state in every way. His only qualification was that he faithfully toed the Indian line on Kashmir. All allegations, representations and enquiry reports were ignored. Ultimately it was in 1963 that he was axed under the Kamaraj Plan.

The above instances do not exhaust the roster of corrupt

ministers who flourished under Nehru's patronage. These are only the most prominent instances and they attracted a lot of adverse public notice and press comment. The saddest aspect of these examples is that the protection given to any of these four persons did not benefit Nehru in any manner. On the contrary, he would have set very healthy precedents and his public image would have improved further if he had taken stern action against them. By condoning high-visibility cases of corruption and extending personal protection to the guilty, Nehru legitimized graft in high places, and this undermined the moral basis of the polity. There were few failings of Nehru for which the country has paid so heavy a price as his acceptance of corruption among his own colleagues and partymen.

Nehru's tolerance of corruption, and the extent to which he tolerated it, highlight another lacuna in his approach to governance. In publicly condoning the misdeeds and improprieties of chief ministers and ministers he was inadvertently undermining the rule of law and eroding the institutional basis of the polity.

It is not that Nehru did not appreciate the value of institutions. He himself created so many of them, and nursed them with great care. Democracy was the greatest institution that he fostered. He was a stout defender of the freedom of the press. Though he was frequently irked at the conservative attitude of the judiciary, especially when it came in the way of progressive land reforms, he never tried to short-circuit the judicial processes. The introduction of Panchayati Raj was again an effort to give an institutional basis to participatory democracy at the cutting edge of administration. The creation of the National Development Council was meant to provide a forum for the state governments to interact with the Centre, and resolve by consensus issues concerning development plans and such other matters of common interest.

Thus, Nehru was certainly not unaware of the relevance of institutions to democracy or the need to foster them. Yet, he did not evolve any consistent approach to institution building, or prescribe inviolable norms of institutional sanctity. At times he behaved not as a constitutional authority but a medieval potentate who, in a fit of generosity, would forgive the greatest misdeeds of his favourites. Here, he failed to appreciate that exception destroys the rule of law; that his deviations would become norms for his minions.

Dismissal of the first non-Congress ministry of India is an ugly blot on Nehru's image as a great democrat. In the 1957 election, the Communist Party of India (CPI) led by E.M.S. Namboodripad, came to power in Kerala. In fact the Namboodripad ministry took a number of progressive measures and did things which Congressmen had been only promising to do. But the measure which really raised a storm was the Education Bill. It was meant to regularize the appointment of teachers, but the Catholic bishops and the Nair Service Society took it as a direct assault on their domain and launched a relentless campaign against the CPI government. This ideally suited the Congress party and it exploited the agitation to its full advantage.

Despite pressures from his partymen, Nehru was disinclined to act against the state government. It was during this period, that Indira Gandhi became Congress President, and she seems to have preferred the anti-CPI line. It is also a fact that owing to prolonged agitations and acts of violence, law and order was breaking down in the state. Ultimately, the anti-Communist lobby won the day and the CPI ministry was dismissed on 30 July 1959 under Article 356 of the Constitution. And thus was set a most unfortunate precedent of pressing a highly potent Constitutional provision in the service of political expediency. Little did Nehru realize that the one-time exception he thought he had made would be repeated a hundred times over during the next forty years.

Nehru not only led the freedom struggle, he was actively involved in the Trade Union movement also. His basic interest in trade unions flowed from his deep humanism and allegiance to socialism. But after Independence the nature of his responsibilities changed, and so did his approach to the dictates of labour welfare. As prime minister, Nehru seems to have viewed the labour problem from three angles: first, ideological; second, growth; and third, political.

As the public sector employed two-third of the industrial workers in the country, Nehru desired it to become a 'model employer'. Public undertakings paid good wages and spent large sums on labour welfare. Various labour laws like the Factories Act, Employees State Insurance Act, Plantation Labour Act and Mines Act were also passed to protect the interests of the workers.

The imperatives of growth require that law and order is maintained and the production apparatus runs without any hitch. Consequently, in this matter Nehru was acting primarily as an employer.

When AITUC called for a one-day strike against the adjudication machinery and decontrol, Nehru remarked, "It seems quite astoundingly irresponsible for any organization... to indulge in strikes at this moment and in this way, even though they may be token one-day strikes."[10]

Politically, Nehru approached labour issues as a Congressman. The All India Trade Union Congress (AITUC) was the mother of trade unionism in India. But owing to its domination by the communists, its activities could be anti-establishment. The Congress, therefore, founded the Indian National Trade Union Congress (INTUC) in 1947, and gave it all possible official patronage to build it into the premier labour organization of India. In 1950 AITUC and HMS (Hind Mazdoor Sangh) organised a strike of Bombay textile workers to press their demand for higher bonus. The strike lasted for 63 days. The INTUC went all out to ensure its failure. And it failed.

The most potent weapons in the government's armoury to influence and mould the course of trade union movement were the Industrial Relations Act (Bombay) and the Industrial Disputes Act. The main objective of these enactments was to identify and resolve industrial conflicts. But by empowering the government machinery to intervene and adjudicate on the merits of the dispute, they gave extensive powers to the 'appropriate government' (mostly Congress) to influence the outcome. And the governments invariably used this clout to ensure that INTUC became the beneficiary of its discretionary powers. The workers also knew that INTUC, being the *Sarkari* (official) union, could get them the maximum benefits. No wonder, then, that it became the largest labour union in country.

This partisan attitude of the government has not only eroded the moral base of INTUC, but also harmed the trade union movement. Of course, a lot of benefits have been extended to the industrial workers, but this has come about more from the intervention of the party in power than the inherent strength of labour unions. In view of the above factors, a strong labour movement has failed to grow in India.

'In the later years of his life, Nehru could not have looked back with much satisfaction on his long tenure. Whatever bounce was left in him, was sapped by the Chinese war. Yet he was not the person to throw in the sponge till the end. He made two major attempts in the last year of his life to turn things around: the Kamaraj Plan and the Bhubaneshwar Congress Resolution. Kamaraj Nadar, the highly regarded chief minister of Tamil Nadu, formulated a scheme for revitalizing the Congress party by inviting senior leaders to give up ministerial office and devote themselves to party work. Even if Nehru was not the inspiration behind this proposal, he welcomed it instantly. So happy was he with Kamaraj at his initiative that he got him elected as the Congress President.

The plan itself was a peculiar hotchpotch: in effect, if not in intent, it was a Machiavellian ploy wrapped up in Gandhian rhetoric. After the Congress Working Committee had approved the proposal in August, 1963, six Central cabinet ministers and six chief ministers were relieved of their charge and asked to work for the party.

The composition of this pack did not carry much credibility with the people. Moreover, the exercise was not followed up by any spurt of activity for refurbishing the party organization. On the other hand, persons like Morarji and Patil criticized it severely as a motivated manoeuvre.

Nehru also tried to strengthen his support base by inducting T.T. Krishnamachari and Ashok Mehta into his cabinet. But it was a case of too little too late. Also, Krishnamachari, who had to resign from the cabinet on corruption charges, could not have lent much lustre to the operation clean-up.

The Bhubaneshwar Resolution on Democracy and Socialism tried to recapture some of the spirit of Karachi and Avadi sessions, and reiterated Congress commitment to democratic socialism. As Nehru suffered a stroke at this session and died after a couple of months, the matter did not proceed further.

As the executive head of state, Nehru was constantly called upon to take hard decisions. This required clarity of goals, firmness, and occasional ruthlessness. Nehru's democratic liberalism and eclectic nature went against these traits. He was a person of sharp perceptions, his political instincts were sound and his moral values beyond reproach. But he had a peculiar faculty to get detached from the events, comment upon them objectively, realize fully the shortcomings of his approach, and yet do little to take corrective action.

As early as 1949 he wrote to a chief minister, "... our standards have fallen greatly. Indeed, we have hardly any standards left except not to be found out... We drift along calmly accepting things as they come."[11]

Two years later he wrote to Rajagopalachari, "We seem to have lost all capacity to consider anything from the point of view of a new approach. We go round in circles and cannot get out of our grooves."[12]

Much before he became the Prime Minister, he was aware of the urgent need to overhaul the administration. Later, in letter after letter to the chief ministers, he emphasized the need to change the old system. Yet he himself hardly took any steps to change the systems and procedures in the Central Secretariat. When he wrote, "The fact is... that the decisions taken are not given effect to, are hung up inordinately. It is difficult to catch the culprit for some suitable excuse is always forthcoming," one feels like asking, 'But who are you complaining to? And against whom?'

One of Nehru's biographers remarked, "India was and still is to some extent unique. The range of radical social and economic policies continually endorsed by the dominant party and ignored in principle is unequalled elsewhere."[13] In fact this trait is an attribute of the Brahmanical mind-set: in the beginning there was the 'word'; the 'word' is primary and eternal; the rest is all illusion. So, speeches, meetings, official circulars — all pay obeisance to the 'word', and serve as subtitute for action and performance.

Nehru's inadequacies in the arena of governance may be attributed to three basic factors. One, the constraints imposed by his temperament and character. He just did not have it in him to use the hatchet. He was an excellent physician; but the country badly needed a surgeon also. Secondly, his philosophy of management placed excessive emphasis on consensus and accommodation. In such a diverse and divided society you cannot always take everybody along with you. At critical moments parting company with old colleagues or enforcing unpopular decisions becomes obligatory. This he could not do. And thirdly, when Nehru complained about the deficiencies of administration and implementation, the fault actually lay with the structures. It is not the fault of a bullock cart if it cannot perform like a steam engine.

15

Science and Culture

In Nehru's order of priorities science, socialism and planning occupied a pre-eminent place. But, in a sense, science ranked the highest, as his love of the other two derived from it. "I am a socialist because I feel that socialism is a scientific approach to the world's problems."[1] And "Planning was science in action."[2]

In his early years Nehru did not show any special aptitude for science. When he was sent to Harrow for schooling in 1905, it was his father's decision that he should study this subject. And the pursuit of science was preferred as it would facilitate his entry into the Indian Civil Service (ICS). "As you know, I want you specially to develop a taste for Science and Mathematics... nothing will please me more than to have in you the first Senior Wrangler of your year. The ICS will then be child's play for you."[3] When Nehru entered Cambridge in 1907, he opted for the Science Tripos: chemistry, geology and physics. But as he found the going tough in physics, he swapped it with botany.[4] Motilal felt let down at this change-over. He wrote, "What I expect from you is a first class."[5] But, to the dismay of his father, Nehru turned in a second. Realizing that his son was "not cut out for the ICS nor for a scientific career," Motilal wrote to his brother Bansi Dhar, "Jae (Jawaharlal) is made of different stuff... (and) he is bound to rise in his father's profession."[6] One obviously cannot be too careful in asking for boons! Who would have heard of Motilal Nehru if his wish for his son to join the ICS had been granted!

It was not only intellectual curiosity which inclined Nehru to the study of scientific literature on his own; he was keenly aware that science held the key to modernity. His inability to study physics at Cambridge also seems to have hurt his self-esteem. To make up for this deficiency, he occasionally fantasised about his love of science in his student days. Addressing the National

Academy of Sciences at Allahabad, he said, "For I too have worshipped at the shrine of science and counted myself as one of its votaries."[7] And on another occasion he recalled, "The days when, as a student, I haunted the laboratories of that home of science, Cambridge."[8] One would imagine that he spent much of his spare time hanging around the Cavendish! And at a press conference in 1945, "I have a scientist's outlook. Long ago I took a degree in science and studied physics..." Incidentally, that is the one thing he did not do!

There were several reasons for science to have such a strong appeal for Nehru. For one, it was the epitome of logic, rationality, enlightenment. It liberated the human mind from old, traditional patterns of thought, thus clearing the way for modernization and progress. In view of the impact of science on human thought, he said, "No person can call himself educated today unless he or she knows something of science and technology."[9]

More importantly, "It is science alone that can solve the problems of hunger and poverty, of malnutrition and illiteracy, of superstition and deadening customs and traditions, the vast resources running to waste, of a rich country inhabited by starving people."[10]

Before one considers Nehru's contribution to the promotion of science and the scientific culture, it will help to look at the state of Indian science on the eve of Independence. "The modern awakening in Indian science," said M.G.K. Menon, "was part of the ferment in Indian society that characterised the freedom struggle."[11] The Indian scientific scene started buzzing with creative activity with the emergency of the Calcutta group of scientists. The Indian Institute for the Cultivation of Science was established in 1876, and it was nursed by such stalwarts as C.V. Raman, Meghnad Saha, S.N. Bose, K.S. Krishnan, among others. This was the heroic age of Indian science, and daring pioneers ventured on their own to create oases of physical research. Jagdish Chandra Bose established the Bose Institute of Calcutta for biophysical research in 1917. P.C. Mahalanobis created the Indian Statistical Institute in Calcutta in 1931, and M.N. Saha founded the Academy of Sciences at Allahabad in 1930. With a grant from Dorabji Tata Trust, H.J. Bhabha started the Tata Institute of Fundamental Research, Bombay in 1945. Leading umbrella institutions like the Imperial (Indian) Council of Agricultural Research (ICAR) and the Council for Scientific and Industrial Research (CSIR) were established in 1929 and 1942. It is really remarkable how a band of gifted and motivated scientists, with meagre resources and facing heavy odds, placed India on the world map of science.

During the freedom struggle Nehru had kept in touch with the Indian and foreign scientists. He associated Saha and Mahalanobis with the work of the National Planning Committee, and addressed various science conferences from time to time. After Independence he could not wait to start promoting the scientific establishment. "... within ten days of assuming office as Prime Minister, in the midst of communal orgy, Nehru found time to attend a meeting of the Council of Scientific and Industrial Research."[12]

There was no dearth of ideas to develop and consolidate India's scientific base; what mattered was the people to give shape to these ideas. Here Nehru was fortunate to have the services of people like S.S. Bhatnagar, Homi Bhabha and P.C. Mahalanobis available to him. They were not only eminent scientists and men of vision; they were also excellent organizers and administrators. It was with their help that the edifice of scientific research, both pure and applied, was built by Nehru.

In concrete terms, Nehru's greatest contribution to Indian science was the creation of seventeen national laboratories under the umbrella of the CSIR. They covered major areas of physical, chemical, biological and engineering sciences and technology. In this field, Bhatnagar's contribution as Director, CSIR, was invaluable.

Nehru paid special attention to the vital area of atomic power. "The government of India attach great importance to the development of atomic energy," said he, "because atomic energy will make a very important contribution to the world's resources of power for industrial use and social use in the future."[13] Bhabha, who had set up the Tata Institute of Fundamental Research in 1945, was the person who headed this programme.

Another thrust area was that of Space Research. A committee to pioneer this research was set up in 1962, and a separate agency entrusted with the construction of rocket launching facility at Thumba.

Then we have a string of Indian Institutes of Technology (IIT), conceived on the model of the Massachussets Institute of Technology. They were a part of Nehru's programme to create a vast reservoir of technical personnel to meet the country's fast growing requirements. "What comes in the way of rapid development of India," he said, "is not so much lack of money as lack of trained personnel."

Though committed to peace and disarmament, Nehru paid adequate attention to the country's requirement for defence production. He advised Baldev Singh, his Defence Minister, to appoint a competent Scientific Adviser. D.S. Kothari, an eminent scientist, was the first person to hold this post. An exclusive outfit, the Defence Research and Development Organization was established under him in 1959. Incidentally, the Subterranean Nuclear Experiment Project (SNEP) was conceived during Nehru's time. It is this project which organized the detonation of an atomic device at Pokhran in May 1974.

In 1958 the government passed the Scientific Policy Resolution which became the sheet anchor for the promotion of scientific research. The opening para of the Resolution stated:

> The key to national prosperity, apart from the spirit of the people, lies, in the modern age, in the effective combination of three factors, technology, raw materials and capital, of which the first is perhaps the most important, since the creation and adoption of new scientific techniques can, in fact make up for a deficiency in natural resources, and reduce the demands on capital. But technology can only grow out of the study of science and its applications.

Nehru's fondness for science led him to romanticize it. His thinking on science was shaped by British scientists of the Fabian era. He loved to talk of the cultural, universal and philosophical dimensions of science. He considered science as a great benefactor of mankind, and ardently believed that it would liberate humanity from the clutches of want and hunger.

This view of science was all right for parlour talk. But it was likely to create fuzziness in dealing with the down-to-earth problems of a poor and developing country. Nehru talked of science incessantly, but seldom about technology. He used metaphors like 'temple' and 'votary' while referring to scientific establishments, but never referred to them as 'workshops.' He created a string of national laboratories, and invested them with a lot of prestige. Housed in air-conditioned and expensive buildings, enjoying far greater autonomy than conventional government offices, and manned by scholars and researchers, they acquired an aura of awe and mystery which raised them far above the common run of old-fashioned, poorly financed research outfits of yore.

It will be churlish to grudge the special work environment created for the country's leading scientists. But in the Indian context it produced three unintended effects. First, it downgraded the status of the universities as the premier centres of learning and research. In the post-independence era the level of university education has steadily declined. This has proved to be a very costly neglect. "In the modern world" says D.S. Kothari, "the universities make by far the largest contribution to fundamental science...In fact the level of science and technology in the universities provides a good barometer to the standard of health of science and technology in the country... Also, there must be close cooperation between universities, and national laboratories and other research organisations so that in the establishment of centres (of excellence), fullest use is made of all available resources."[14]

Secondly, the high priests of science working in the exclusive 'temples' of research acquired elitist traits and moved away from the mundane concerns of the common man. Pure science was at a premium; technology, especially related to the needs of small-scale and cottage industries, was too lowly and pedestrian for the attention of esteemed researchers. This elitist bias of the scientific establishment, including Nehru, also explains the far greater attention paid to atomic energy and space than to agriculture, public health or consumer industry.

Thirdly, by extending generous state patronage to the leading scientists of the country, the government turned them into its faithful employees and, thus, weakened their creative impulse.

It would be silly to suggest that promising scientists should be forced to live in penury to get the best out of them, or that the state should leave them to fend for themselves. Moreover, modern scientific research has become so expensive that the days of Edison or Madam Curie are gone for ever. Yet, the fact remains that excessive solicitude by the government does curb one's spirit of independence and tends to turn the scientist into a courtier. Occasionally, genius is bound to be wayward, erratic and arrogant. It would have done Indian science a world of good if some crazy genius, like the Greek philosopher who rebuked Alexander for obstructing the sunshine, had addressed Nehru in like manner. Instead, we were treated to a spectacle of half a dozen leading scientists fiercely competing for Nehru's favours.

Nehru was not only right in funding scientific research on a large scale; this was the only way to promote it. But, instead of creating huge white elephants of national laboratories, research could have been more usefully financed through universities, autonomous corporations and endowments. The distinguished track record of the Tata Institute of Fundamental Research, Bombay, is a case in point.

The elitist bias of the scientific establishment deflected the focus from the centrality of technology for a developing country. Actually, to reach a stage of self-sustaining technological growth, a close interaction between the national laboratories, the universities and the industry was imperative. But the laboratories became ivory towers, universities were reduced to the status of poor relations, and industry was more interested in foreign tie-ups and import of technology than the local brew.

The laboratories, of course, did undertake research in applied science and technology, but it was not appreciated that if you spend one rupee on developing a product or an appliance, you have to spend ten rupees on its engineering and application. Owing partly to the absence of a research-industry nexus, no system was evolved to test and market the products and processes in pilot projects.

The flip side of the coin is that in the earlier stages the industrial infrastructure was itself feeble and bilateral linkages with industry could not be easily forged. Further, with a weak entrepreneurial tradition and the glamour of foreign technology, the Indian industrialist was unwilling to place his bets on indigenous research.

Nehru passionately believed in the universality of science. This meant that science was neutral and apolitical. In other words, if the direction given to science by one country proves beneficial to it, the same could be replicated by other countries with equal advantage. This approach resulted in all sorts of distortions. A country with surplus labour and scarce capital hooked itself to the technology of capital surplus and labour-scarce economies of the West. This led to the culture of 'gigantism' — large plants, mechanized production and meagre employment generation. What India needed was concentration on refining and developing small-scale, diversified, sturdy and easy-to-maintain machinery with high employment potential. But this was a pursuit which had little appeal for scientists whose vision was dominated by the huge, mass-production, automated plants of the West.

Not only were Nehru's advisers insufficiently alive to the dangers of indiscriminate import of Western technology, the researchers engaged in developing indigenous resources were seldom encouraged. Even after Independence India opted wholesale for the Western system of medicine, ignoring the rich heritage of traditional, local systems. It is only lately that foreign pharmaceutical firms have started rummaging the great storehouse of Ayurveda and tribal remedies, and raking in huge profits by marketing them under their brand names. "People have now stressed the use of biogas, which was laughed at when Gandhi advocated (it). Pillai's work on the utilisation of sewage and its purification was ignored.

So was the work of Mitra on *neem* oil and *neem* products, which is now patented by industry in the USA and for which we may have to pay, or the work of Siddiqui on Raulfia, Bhilawan and other natural products."[15]

Perhaps the greatest lapse of India's institutionalized research was to ignore the vast productive reservoir of craftsmen and artisans. These self-employed, enterprising and innovative people had been meeting for centuries the country's needs for all sorts of artefacts, appliances and objects of daily use. They possessed hereditary skills of a high order and had served the needs of the high and the low with equal competence. But their implements and production methods had remained unchanged for centuries. With a little effort and some dedication, their equipment could have been upgraded, use of new raw materials introduced and production technique improved. It would have not only saved this traditional sector from being swamped by modern machinery, but also generated considerable employment, and transferred a portion of the industrial income to the countryside.

An interesting instance of this neglect is the loss of the traditional export market for rose essence. India had been exporting this item to the European perfumeries for decades. But after the Second World War it lost this market to Bulgaria. Reason: this essence had been traditionally distilled in Hassia, UP, for centuries by hereditary workers employing techniques developed during the reign of Emperor Jehangir. (It finds a mention in Tuzak-e-Jehangiri.) The process remained unchanged over the last four hundred years. No wonder, it was knocked off at the first exposure to modern technology.[16] Had a researcher from National Chemical Laboratory designed a more efficient distillation apparatus for the job, India would have retained her hold in the world market and many jobs would have been saved. But unfortunately neither had the essence-makers in Hassia heard of the great laboratory, nor had the elite researcher heard of Hassia.

All technological research and development is a waste unless you devise efficient channels for its diffusion. There was a lot of airy-fairy talk about scientific temper and industrialization of the

country. But no institutional mechanism was designed to raise
scientific awareness of the masses, or to take the fruits of technology to the people.

Despite all the shortcomings of Nehru's science and technology
policy, it must be recognized that he created a massive institutional base for the growth of scientific culture, and the national
laboratories were able to assemble that critical mass of scientists
which alone could lead to self-sustaining research activity.

Culture

Once Nehru received a letter from Gandhi, enclosed in a
shabby envelope. He wrote back:

> I must protest against the apology of an envelope in which your
> letter came... Forgive me my superficiality. I like my diamonds
> smooth and polished. You have shown us the art and style of
> living life in a grand manner. That is the real thing, but why
> should we ignore style and art in the little things of life? Most of
> us cannot reach the snowy heights. Would you deprive us of the
> flowers in the valley?[17]

Writes Kamaladevi Chattopadhyaya, "Jawaharlal's sensitivity
to culture formed perhaps the tenderest core of his make-up. It
expressed itself in his love of beautiful objects. He derided people
who were fast losing a sense of appreciation for things of beauty".

Anamolous though it may seem, liberation of India dealt a serious
blow to the arts. Princely states, despite being backwaters of
reaction, provided valuable patronage to art and culture. Most of
the eminent Gharanas (schools) of classical dance and music rose
and flourished in these states.

Fortunately, the new state stepped into the shoes of the princes
and gave the much-needed support to the arts in various fields
and across the board. In fact, in the colonial era, patronage was
extended on a selective basis and according to the whims of the
rulers. But after Independence Nehru took several measures to
institutionalize this promotional activity, and even hitherto

neglected traditional art forms were assisted. There is little doubt that but for the dogged persistence of B.V. Keskar, Minister for Information and Broadcasting, classical music would have suffered a serious setback. By making available the forum of All India Radio to the singers, he not only provided them with much-needed succour, he also helped to sustain and encourage public interest in serious music.

At the institutional level, the most publicized initiative was the creation of three national academies: Sangeet Natak Akademy, Sahitya Akademi and Lalit Kala Academy.

With a view to preserving the cultural heritage, as it existed in the form of statuary, monuments, manuscripts, etc., the National Archival Policy was framed. National Museum and Anthropological Survey of India were established and existing museums, libraries and archives were reorganized and strengthened.

This is as far as the purely formal framework of promotion of art and culture is concerned. But the authentic and vibrant culture of the people does not dwell within the confines of museums, Akademies and archives. It is the folk culture, the tribal culture and the popular performing arts which enrich the emotional and spiritual life of the masses. Here again Nehru gave special encouragement to diverse sub-cultures, and regional and local art forms. One of the most innovative practices introduced by him was to invite tribal and folk artists to Delhi from all states of India to participate in the Republic Day celebrations. This provided a unique opportunity to the participants to experience at firsthand the rich cultural diversity of their country, and gave them a sense of participation in a great national festival. In due course the Republic Day parade came to be telecast all over the country, thus exposing the bulk of the population to a remarkable spectacle of their incomparable heritage. This was also a very imaginative experiment in national integration through visual display of the country's vast cultural landscape.

Nehru also used the occasion of various fairs, festivals and routine visits to the rural and tribal areas to join the performers, don their dress, and get into the spirit of festivity. These symbolic gestures were morale boosters for the local people. As these events were shown on films and television throughout India, they helped disseminate folk and tribal culture to very large audiences.

"Nehru often visited exhibitions, be they of individuals or set up by art organisations, and acquired works of art either for himself or for the Indian missions abroad."[18] To relieve government buildings of their drabness, "He directed the unimaginative Works and Housing ministry to encourage the painting of modern murals on the walls of official buildings which would break the decorative tradition with new motifs and forceful themes."[19]

This awareness of the need to relate old to the new, traditional to the modern, scientific to the artistic was always there with Nehru. Therefore the canvas on which he worked had not only a vast spread, but also a lot of depth.

16

Foreign Affairs

$\mathcal{M}$ost of the top leaders of the freedom movement were educated abroad, and their struggle was against a foreign power. Thus, the national movement had a cosmopolitan dimension right from the start. But it was Nehru who lifted foreign relations to a much higher plane and related the national movement to the global crusade against colonialism. In fact he was basically an internationalist. "My outlook was wider," he said, "and nationalism by itself seemed to me definitely a narrow and insufficient creed."[1] He, therefore, viewed even the freedom struggle as a localized version of the worldwide campaign against colonial oppression. "The freedom that we envisage," he said "is not to be confined to this nation or that... but must spread out over the whole human race."[2]

Commonwealth

After Independence, one of the first foreign policy issues facing India was whether to continue her membership of the Commonwealth, or to snap the 30-year-old link. With memories of colonial oppression still fresh, the popular sentiment was opposed to having any such connection. But the mature national leadership viewed the matter differently. Nehru was in favour of retaining the link, but the status of the British empire vis-a-vis a sovereign republic presented difficulties. When Nehru attended the Commonwealth Prime Ministers' Conference in 1949, the problem was overcome by an ingenious formulation. Whereas India's status as a free and sovereign republic was recognized, India accepted 'the King as the symbol of the free association of its independent member nations and as such the head of the Commonwealth.'

Emotional attachment to Britain and British institutions had little to do with Nehru's decision to join the Commonwealth. National interest was the primary consideration. In a world becoming increasingly polarized into antagonistic blocs, here was a free association of nations demanding no commitment to any ideology or group. "If we dissociate ourselves completely from the Commonwealth, then for the moment we are completely isolated."[3] In fact the logic of circumstances favoured India continuing this membership. Even after Independence the country had opted for the British model of democracy, and retained wholesale the institutions left behind by her. Indian armed forces were organized on the British pattern and used British weaponry. India's main trading partners were in the Commonwealth, and her substantial wartime assets were held in pound sterling. India was bound to require a lot of financial and technological assistance, and Britain could serve as a valuable conduit for that.

Also, the Commonwealth of 1949 was not the same entity as it was during the heyday of British imperialism. "When people think of the Commonwealth influencing us in our policies," observed Nehru, "may I suggest to them the possibility that we may also influence the others in the right direction."[4] In fact Nehru did much more than that. The original Commonwealth was a five-member white man's club. It was India's entry that changed it into a multinational body by devising a mechanism under which ex-colonial sovereign states were admitted as full members.

Non-Alignment

Independent India opened her eyes in a post-war world where the old imperialist order was disintegrating and new forms of hegemony were emerging. In the ensuing era of superpower confrontation a large number of countries stood polarized between the capitalist and the communist blocs. Nehru did not think that aligning with either bloc would serve India's best interest. In all modesty Nehru clarified, "It is completely incorrect to call our policy (of non-alignment) 'Nehru' policy... It is a policy inherent in the circumstances of India, inherent in the past thinking of India, ... inherent in the circumstances of the world today."[5]

The insularity provided by the Himalayas had been breached. To the north was hostile Pakistan, aligned with the West. To the north-east was emerging a new China, liberated, monolithic and expansionist. India needed peace if her development plans were to bear fruit. There was also the imperative of securing economic aid, from whichever quarter it was available on respectable terms. India could not afford heavy outlay on buying armament. In such a situation, Nehru repeatedly emphasized that it was essential to "substitute political diplomacy for military defence."[6] Moreover, it was the only policy commensurate with the country's size and status. As Nehru said:

> I can understand some of the smaller countries ... being forced by circumstances to bow down before some of the great powers and becoming practically satellites of those powers...But I do not think that consideration applies to India...India is too big a country herself to be bound down to any country, however big it may be.[7]

Not only was there no question of India becoming a satellite, Nehru perceived her as a stage for the unfolding of global events. Addressing the Constituent Assembly he stated:

> ... remember that India, not because of any ambition of hers, but because of history and because of so many other things inevitably has to play a very important part in Asia ... India becomes a kind of meeting ground for various trends and forces and a meeting ground between what may be roughly called the East and the West.

Korean War

The three-year Korean War (1950-53) turned out to be a test by fire for India's policy of non-alignment. On the day the war broke out, the Security Council took up an American-inspired resolution accusing North Korea of having committed aggression against South Korea. On the basis of available information the Indian representative at the UN supported this resolution. The UN (American) forces not only pushed the North Koreans back, they crossed the international boundary dividing the two Koreas and headed towards Yalu river, which separates Korea from China. The Chinese were not prepared to take it lying down and Chou

En-lai, their Prime Minister, woke up the Indian ambassador in Peking to convey a warning to the Western powers against such a reckless move. India, which was then the only bridge between these adversaries, did convey this message to the Americans, but they laughed at the Chinese temerity to take on the mightiest power on earth. So, the Chinese troops went into action, and in the fierce encounters that followed, over 50,000 American soldiers were killed. The American public was furious and there was talk of using the atom bomb.

Nehru tried hard to defuse the situation and proposed a general conference for the purpose. The USA rejected the proposal and brought forward a resolution in the United Nations declaring China as the aggressor. This time India voted against the resolution, as aggression had been committed by Gen. MacArthur, the American Commander. In first voting for the UN Resolution accusing North Korea of aggression and then opposing the resolution to declare China as the invader, India was not establishing any symmetry of its position between the two blocs: she was only demonstrating her resolve not to get aligned to any alliance, and to judge international issues on merit.

A few months after the Korean war broke out, the Chinese moved their troops into Tibet and annexed it surrepticiously, without informing India. Nehru was very upset at this move. But he did not permit this unfriendly gesture to prejudice his mind and he persevered with his efforts to peacefully resolve the Sino-American conflict over Korea.

The main hurdle to a settlement was the thorny question of repatriation of prisoners of war. Krishna Menon devised a formula which led to a prisoners of war agreement being signed and a Neutral Nations' Repatriation Commission set up with an Indian, General K.S. Thimayya, as its Chairman. This brought the Korean war to an end. Yet such are the norms of power politics that India was not asked to participate in the Geneva Conference on Korea held in 1954.

India's role in the Korean crisis won her neither acclaim, nor many friends. But Nehru's efforts to prevent the Korean conflict from escalating into a larger conflagration, his non-partisan role and transparent sincerity did convince the international community of the usefulness of his approach to international affairs. Whether it was China or the USSR or Britain or America, they all approached India for passing messages across the ideological divide.

It was as a result of his role in the Korean war that Nehru arrived on the international scene as a world leader, and non-alignment became a credible policy.

South-East Asia

Nehru was basically an internationalist, yet Asia was closest to his heart. The Asian Relations Conference, held in Delhi in March 1947 was Nehru's first attempt to define and assert this Asian personality and, incidentally, his centrality to it. More than twenty nations attended it. In his inaugural address Nehru said:

> For too long we of Asia have been petitioners in the Western courts and chancellories. That story must now belong to the past. We propose to stand on our own feet and to cooperate with all others who are prepared to cooperate with us.

The deliberations of the Conference were wrapped up in euphoria and bloated rhetoric. There was no follow-up, no concrete results. Yet it enabled a lot of Asian leaders to come together and be animated by a vague sort of Asian kinship.

Two years later Nehru convened in Delhi a Conference of States bordering the Indian Ocean when the Dutch attacked Indonesia to re-establish their colonial rule. India was able to persuade Ceylon, Burma, Pakistan, Saudi Arabia and Iraq to join her in denying all facilities to the Dutch aircraft and shipping.

The resolutions passed by the Conference were sent to the United Nations, and within a week the Security Council resolved that ceasefire be declared, political prisoners released and Republican government re-established. This was, indeed, a very satisfying moment for Nehru.

Indo-China was a time bomb ticking in the heart of Asia. The confrontation between France and the Vietminh threatened to embroil big powers. America was leaning towards the former and China towards the latter. Laos and Cambodia were also being sucked into the conflict. Nehru tried to secure an immediate cease-fire and participated in the Geneva Conference on Indo-China in 1954. After hectic lobbying it was agreed that all foreign troops from Laos and Cambodia would be withdrawn.

In view of India's contribution, the Geneva conference appointed her as Chairman of the International Control Commission set up to supervise the import of armament into Vietnam, Laos and Cambodia.

In cooperation with the other four Colombo powers, Nehru convened an Afro-Asian Conference at Bandung in 1955. All independent Afro-Asian countries except South Africa and Egypt were invited. Obviously, no concrete results or specific formulations could be expected from such a heterogeneous gathering.

Chou En-lai took full advantage of this opportunity of the first international exposure that he got. He made a great impact on the Afro-Asian leaders and established several valuable contacts. And, undoubtedly, Chou's gain was Nehru's loss. Not only did Nehru not emerge as the central figure of the gathering, he was seen to be over-playing his role as the patriarch of Asia.

West Asia

Indian association with South-East Asia was based on old cultural ties and some trading activities. But her links with West Asia were more substantial. India not only had close cultural and trading bonds with this region, it also served as the corridor to the Occident. After Independence India's trade with West Asia had increased substantially. As three-fourths of her trade passed through Suez Canal, she had a heavy stake in preserving peace in this area.

Politically this area has a special importance for India. First, Pakistan has always tried to use the Islamic card and rally the West Asian states behind her and against India. Secondly, in consequence of the cold war and the lure of oil, the West has sought to re-establish her hegemony over this zone through military alliances. The first move was to create a Middle East Defence Organization, which was rejected by Egypt. Then, with the help of Pakistan, Britain managed to rope in Turkey, Iraq and Iran to sign a five-nation Baghdad Pact, with the USA helping it from the wings.

Nationalization of the Suez Canal Company in 1956 by Egypt in retaliation against the Anglo-American decision to stop financial support to the building of Aswan Dam faced India with a tricky situation. She was the main user of the Canal, and the adversaries were her friends.

The UK convened the London Conference to decide on a course of action. While various options were still under consideration, Israel suddenly invaded Egypt. Britain and France followed suit. Nehru condemned it as "a reversal of history which none of us can tolerate."[8] He called for immediate UN intervention and actively participated in the United Nations parleys. Ultimately, a cease-fire was agreed upon and an international force, including troops from India, asked to oversee it. The three aggressors withdrew their forces and Egyptian sovereignty over Suez Canal was recognized.

Neighbours

Two of India's five immediate neighbours, that is, Pakistan and China, will be dealt with separately in the next two chapters. Of the remaining three, Nepal is almost a continuum of northern India upto the Himalayan foothills. As a landlocked country, its only access to the sea and the world outside is through India. Thus, geography has made India vital to Nepal's existence. On the other hand, sandwiched between China and India, it is crucial to the latter's security interests.

Indo-Nepalese relations, mostly smooth, had their ups and downs. There are two important factors which give occasional jolts: one, the ambitions of her neighbour China to extend her influence over Nepal. Second, the democratic processes in India, which produce an unsettling effect on the Himalayan Kingdom. Then, there is the highly unequal relationship between a small country and its very big neighbour which generates its own strains.

India has normally been sensitive to Nepalese susceptibilities and needs. In 1950 Nehru signed a Treaty of Peace and Friendship with Nepal which recognized her "complete sovereignty, territorial integrity and independence," and stated that "neither government shall tolerate any threat to the security of the other by a foreign power." It also gave Nepal the right to import arms and ammunition after prior consultation with India. In pursuance of this treaty India set up 17 check-posts at the passes between Tibet, Nepal and Bhutan. A Military Mission was also established in Kathmandu. Simultaneously, a Treaty on Trade and Commerce was also concluded, accepting Nepal's "full and unrestricted right of commercial transit of all goods and manufactures through the territory and ports of India." Such trade was exempt from all duties. India has also extended substantial aid to Nepal and undertaken the construction of several roads, power plants, dams and other utilities.

It is the political developments in Nepal that have caused problems in the bilateral relations. King Tribhuvan, who was a virtual prisoner of the Ranas, was beholden to India for helping him to regain his power. But his son Mahendra had no such obligation. He suspected India of encouraging Nepali Congress leaders to demand democratic rule. After the India-China war his bargaining position vis-a-vis India improved, and he was not averse to playing one against the other. Thus, the end of the Nehru era saw the emergence of a less docile Nepal.

Till 1937 Burma was administered by the British as a part of India. One consequence of this arrangement was the inflow of a large number of Indians, who had not only settled in Burma but controlled the bulk of her retail trade. After the country became a republic in January 1948, most of these settlers were forced to go back. It speaks volumes for the mature leadership of the two countries that this unpleasant operation was not allowed to sour the cordial relations between them.

The two countries had a long and ill-defined border, and its demarcation was completed in 1967 without any hitch. Naga rebels used the Burmese jungles as a sanctuary, but Burma co-operated with India in their interception.

With Ceylon (renamed Sri Lanka in 1972) the problem of the ubiquitous Indian settlers, mostly Tamilians, could not be re-solved as amicably. Whereas Sinhalas, the local population, were apprehensive of their large Tamilian neighbour, the immigrant Tamilians felt insecure owing to the rising Sinhala chauvinism. But during Nehru's regime the relations between the two coun-tries remained friendly.

The United States

Nehru had to perform a difficult balancing act in establishing a stable equation with the two superpowers. His socialism inclined him towards the Soviet Union, but emotionally and culturally he had a pronounced preference for the West. After deciding to remain in the Commonwealth, he looked to Britain and America for aid. When Radhakrishnan, the Indian ambassador in Moscow, suggested in 1950 a friendship treaty with the USSR, Nehru mi-nuted on the file, "If there is a world war, there is no possibility of India lining up with the Soviet Union whatever else she may do."

Nehru visited the USA thrice: in 1949, 1956 and 1961. His second visit, when he talked to President Eisenhower for over twelve hours, was slightly more successful than his first visit, which was a disaster. Dean Acheson, the American Secretary of State, described Nehru as "one of the most difficult men with whom I have ever had to deal." One can imagine how his patrician sensibilities were offended when the industrialists invited to a luncheon meeting were introduced to him as "twenty billion dollars collected around this table." His own assessment of the visit was, "They had gone all out to welcome me and I am very grateful to them for it and expressed myself so. But they expected something more than gratitude and goodwill and that more I could not supply them."[9]

And as to his third visit to the States, President Kennedy described his meeting with Nehru as "the worst head-of-state visit I have had."

Of course, the Indo-American differences did not stem from temperamental incompatibility of their leaders. America was not only the most powerful nation in the world, she had a pathological antipathy towards the communist bloc. She cloaked her self-interest in moral rhetoric and posed as a champion of the free world. She was ⁓ncircling the Soviet Union with military alliances and g ʰᵉʳ camp-followers. In pursuit of her objectiv ictum that 'those who are not with ad no such black and white percep He was convinced that military pa tensions, and that non-alignment cated the arms race and campaigneu ear arsenals.

Nehru's refusal to aₙₒ A, his espousal of China's admission to the UN and his knᵥ. ɔocialistic outlook sufficed to convince America that he was anti-American and a crypto-communist. She insisted on arming Pakistan despite Indian protests, consistently adopted an anti-Indian attitude on the Kashmir dispute in the UN, and went so far as to support the Portuguese claim on Goa. America may have been serving her own objective of encircling the USSR by befriending Pakistan, but its net outcome was to heighten Indo-Pak hostility.

On the economic front, trade between the two countries kept growing and, in due course, America became India's biggest trading partner. India also received considerable US aid and shiploads of American foodgrains. Yet the political differences always prevented the growth of cordial relations between the two countries.

The Soviet Union

India's relations with the USSR were far from friendly to begin with. Despite Lenin's view to the contrary, the Soviet communists considered India's freedom struggle as a reactionary movement.

After Independence, the Soviet Union was not averse to encouraging the Indian communists to rise against the national government. Stalin did not receive even once Vijayalakshmi Pandit, the first Indian Ambassador to his country and sister of the Indian Prime Minister. When India decided to remain in the Commonwealth, the Soviet Ambassador in Delhi remarked, "Today is a sad day for India and the world."

The Soviet attitude started softening after Stalin's death. But it was Nehru's role in the Korean war which convinced the USSR of India's bonafides and the usefulness of her policy of non-alignment. Nehru's visit to the Soviet Union in 1955 aroused a lot of public enthusiasm, and the Indians gave an unprecedented welcome to Bulganin and Krushchev, the Soviet leaders, during their visit to India a few months later. Before his departure Krushchev told Nehru, "We want to be friendly with you but not to separate you from your friends. We want to be friendly with your friends."[10]

Starting with the offer to build the Bhilai Steel Plant, the USSR helped India liberally to create her massive public sector enterprises. In defence matters also the assistance has been equally important. In the arena of international diplomacy the two countries have generally seen eye to eye. Whenever the Western powers tried to embarrass India on the Kashmir issue in the Security Council, either the use of the Soviet veto or apprehension of its use saved the day for India.

Indo-Soviet relations have been uniformly smooth and cordial. The Soviet assault on Hungary in 1956 to crush the uprising of democratic forces was the one occasion when Nehru was placed in a quandary. Consideration of friendship, reinforced by self-interest, prevented India from openly condemning the Soviet intervention when America raised the issue in the United Nations. This earned India worldwide censure and her non-aligned credentials were also questioned. Nehru tried to retrieve the situation when he joined the Prime Ministers of Ceylon, Burma and Indonesia in issuing a statement in November 1956, asking for the withdrawal of Soviet troops from Hungary and giving her the freedom to decide her political future.

It will be simplistic to believe that the Soviet Union befriended India out of goodness of heart, or because the Indians happen to be such lovable people. Surrounded by hostile powers, the USSR was perceptive enough to realize that a non-aligned country of India's size and location was very useful in maintaining the balance of forces in Asia. Even the rise of China as a communist giant could pose a threat to the Soviet leadership of the socialist camp. A non-aligned, friendly India was thus the best bet to keep in check the American expansionism and Chinese ambitions.

A wrap-up

The soundness of Nehru's foreign policy is affirmed by its endurance over half a century. And several of its features were innovative in the sense that they marked a distinct departure from the long established patterns of international diplomacy, and pulled the centre of gravity of the world towards the Indian ocean. More than anybody else, it was he who spotlighted the emergence of Asia and Africa as new forces in the post-Second World War arena. There was nothing very original about the concept of non-alignment, yet it was Nehru who gave body to this idea and turned it into a vital force for peace and stability during the hottest phase of the Cold War. The non-partisan and positive role that he played in the Korean, Indo-China and Suez conflicts not only gave credibility to the doctrine of non-alignment, it also established Nehru's status as a world leader. He was the only statesman who was equally at home in the East and the West, and thus served as a bridge between the two.

Nehru himself was prone to exaggerate the role played by India in reordering the world. In a rare moment of modesty he admitted, "We are not, frankly speaking, influential enough to affect international events very much... it is not in consonance with our dignity just to interfere without producing any effect. We should be either strong enough to produce some effect or not interfere at all."[11] He was much more his usual self when he described the Conference on Indonesia as "a turning point in history," or told the chief ministers that "the future of Asia will be powerfully determined by the future of India."[12] His speeches are liberally interspersed with references like, "the emergence of India in world affairs is something of major consequence in world history," "India is growing into a great giant again," "India can play a big part... in helping to avoid war," "India has gone up in the scale of nations in its influence and its prestige."

Two pet projects of Nehru were: shaping the Asian personality and non-alignment. But unlike Europe, Asia was too diverse a region, a battleground of different ideologies, alliances and intrigues, to acquire a cohesive personality. As to non-alignment, lessening of international tensions deprived it of some of its shine. Perhaps the bitterest lesson that Nehru learnt in the practice of international diplomacy was that nations happen to be singularly ungrateful. He convened a conference on Indonesia to condemn the Dutch attack on that country, and Sukarno became one of his harshest critics in later years. He explored all possible avenues to help Laos and Vietnam in the Indo-China war. Later, Laos joined the Western Bloc and Vietnam condemned India as the aggressor in the India-China war. He did all he could to placate the West Asian countries, and they mostly sided with Pakistan. And it must have hurt the apostle of peace terribly to see that India had to go to war with two of her largest neighbours.

"Nehru criticized the foreign policy of big powers on the ground that it aimed at the expansion of their power and influence. He himself was, however, very keen to see that India occupied both status and influential position in international politics."[13] In fact his ambition to play a role larger than warranted by his power-base proved counter-productive.

All these failings notwithstanding, Nehru's contribution in shaping India's foreign policy is one of his most lasting achievements. After Independence, it was for the first time in her history that India was required to interact with the world at large on a continuous basis. And it was Nehru's grasp of the global situation and his vision of India's place under the sun that enabled him to craft a policy-frame which none of his heirs in office has dared alter in any significant manner. Of course, this also points to the conceptual limitations of his successors, as a foreign policy which remains static in a fast changing world tends to develop arthritic stiffness.

17

Pakistan and Kashmir

artition was a one-time operation. After the initial shock, the two severed parts of the subcontinent would have limped back to normality in due course. But the Kashmir dispute has turned the gash into a festering sore, endlessly draining the vitality of both India and Pakistan.

According to the British, the transfer of power implied simultaneous lapse of paramountcy over the princely states. Taking advantage of this construction, the Maharaja of Kashmir neither merged with India, nor Pakistan, and proposed a 'standstill agreement' to both. Pakistan accepted it with alacrity; India did not respond.

Being a predominantly Muslim State, Pakistan ogled Kashmir as her legitimate prize. But there was a fly in the ointment: Sheikh Mohammed Abdullah, a fiercely secular-minded person and a personal friend of Nehru. He had nursed his non-communal National Conference since 1937, and was the most popular leader in the state. As the Conference represented democratic forces, and the coming events foreshadowed trouble, the Kashmir government arrested him in March 1946 when he was proceeding to Delhi to meet Nehru.

So, this is how things stood when India became independent. Apprehending that the Hindu Maharaja may opt for India, Pak emissaries and agents were busy preparing the ground for Kashmir's accession to Pakistan. She was seeking favours from the USA in exchange for special military facilities. India was still fumbling for a proper response to the situation.

Then Pakistan suddenly jumped the gun. She armed a motley crowd of nearly 5000 tribals from the North-West frontier and sent them across to the Kashmir valley on 22 October. The Prime Minister of Kashmir dashed to Delhi to seek help, but Nehru refused to oblige. It was only at the insistence of Patel that Nehru changed his mind, and on 27 October, Indian troops were flown to Srinagar just as the tribal invaders were closing in. Mountbatten was opposed to this move, and when he failed to dissuade Nehru, he made him agree to link military assistance to immediate accession and the offer of a plebiscite after law and order had been restored.[1] Thus, as Kashmir acceded to India, Nehru announced on All India Radio on 28 October that a plebiscite will be held in Kashmir, and a complaint against Pakistan for waging an undeclared war against a neighbour was made to the United Nations Organization.

The manner in which both India and Pakistan bungled the handling of the Kashmir conflict is truly astounding. It is also incredible as to what little thought was given by either side in crafting its approach and strategies. And in India's case there was no clarity about her ultimate objective in slipping into this quagmire.

The fuse was lighted by the Pakistani incursion into the Valley. What did Pakistan hope to achieve by this move? It would have been naïve and unrealistic to imagine that India would not retaliate. And still more foolish to imagine that she would have the better of the Indian Army in an encounter. On the other hand, this misadventure gave India a perfectly legitimate excuse to send her armed forces into Kashmir and establish a strong presence there.

India did one better by rushing to the United Nations and, thereby, walking straight into the labyrinth of the cold war intrigues. And two months before approaching the UN, in an excess of moral ardour, and without any provocation, Nehru broadcast to the world that India would hold a plebiscite in Kashmir.

As if not to be left behind by her adversary, Pakistan bungled again when she refused to comply with the Security Council's resolution of 21 April 1948 to withdraw her forces from the occupied territory of Kashmir. As the progressive withdrawal of the Indian troops was contingent on Pakistani exit, this gave India an pied territory of Kashmir. As the progressive withdrawal of the Indian troops was contingent on Pakistani exit, this gave India an excellent excuse to keep her army stationed in Kashmir. Not only that, it also set an example of casually ignoring Security Council's dictates, which India later used to good effect. If Pakistan had removed her forces from the occupied territory, it would have created an embarrassing precedent for India and obliged her to follow suit.

India's reference to the UN instantly globalized the conflict. The troubled waters of the Dal Lake lured many an international angler to the Valley. And the Security Council became an arena of big power manipulation, arm-twisting and blackmail. In the very first year of the dispute, the Council passed four resolutions, and completely changed the focus of the Indian reference. Whereas India had confined her complaint to the 'Kashmir question' only, the Council enlarged it to the 'India Pakistan Question' in its very first resolution of 17 January 1948. Pakistan accused India of genocide against the Muslims and securing accession of Kashmir by fraud and violence. The British delegate took an openly pro-Pakistani stand. This resolution established a pattern of Anglo-American approach to the Kashmir conflict which has seldom varied despite changes of governments. This approach equates Pakistan with India, takes no note of Pakistan's aggression, and shows a marked concern for the aggressor's interests.

The second Security Council Resolution, passed three days later, set up a three-member Commission. The third resolution passed on 21 April 1948, was the most important. It asked for the declaration of cease-fire, withdrawal of Pakistani forces from occupied Kashmir, followed by a phased withdrawal of Indian troops. This was to be a prelude to the holding of a plebiscite. As Pakistan did not agree to pull out her forces, the rest of the resolution naturally became inoperative. The Council passed eight more resolutions during Nehru's lifetime, but these mostly dealt with procedural matters.

Owing to the uncompromising postures adopted by both India and Pakistan, a deadlock was reached in the Council after five years of wrangling. Thereafter started bilateral exchanges between the two countries. The thaw began with Nehru's visit to Karachi in June 1953. He received a warm welcome, with cheering crowds lining his six-mile route from the airport. This was followed by the Pakistani PM's visit to Delhi in August the same year. Though Sheikh Abdullah was arrested in Srinagar only a week earlier, the two prime ministers discussed matters of mutual interest in a calm atmosphere, without permitting the Abdullah issue to cast its shadow.

These contacts continued for nearly three years but no real breakthrough could be achieved, as neither side was prepared to compromise on any substantive issue.

During the intervening period, things had happened which changed the context considerably. Pakistan had joined the Baghdad Pact and SEATO, and received large quantities of arms from America. The socialist bloc had acquired much greater clout with the explosion of an atom bomb by the USSR and by China going Communist. The Kashmir Constituent Assembly had ratified accession to India, thus strengthening the Indian stand on Kashmir. These developments were obviously not conducive to fostering a policy of compromise and accommodation.

The India-China war provided an ideal opportunity to Britain and America to exploit India's difficulties and pressurize her to reopen talks with Pakistan. Negotiating teams from both sides had six sessions. India proposed partition of the state, but there could be no agreement on the line of division. As the talks failed, Pakistan went back to the Security Council. Owing to the irreconcilable stand of the two countries and the fate of its earlier efforts, the Council this time refrained from passing a resolution and, in May 1964, made a summation of the dispute.

Right from the beginning Pakistan was clear as to what she wanted in Kashmir. Jinnah had repeatedly stated that Kashmir should accede to Pakistan, and he made an attractive offer to the Maharaja in this regard. Pakistani agents were ceaselessly working in the Valley to incite pro-Pak agitations. In August 1947 Jinnah desired that he would like to spend a fortnight's holiday in the Valley, and the state had a difficult time dissuading him.[2] In the Security Council debates Pakistan always asserted her intention to annex Kashmir. Further, "in an effort to coerce the state into accession to Pakistan, the Pakistan authorities cut off supplies to Kashmir of food, petrol and other essential commodities."[3]

On the other hand, India dithered and fumbled for years before making up her mind on this issue. Initially there was no indication that India wanted to hold on to Kashmir. This is amply borne out by the impression that Sardar Patel conveyed to some senior Pakistani leaders. In a recorded interview, K.H. Khursheed, Jinnah's trusted aid, stated that Patel had told Sardar Abdul Rab Nishtar, minister in the first Pakistani cabinet and governor of West Punjab, "Bhai, give up this talk of Hyderabad and Junagadh, and talk of Kashmir: take Kashmir and settle the issue."[4] In another interview, Sirdar Shaukat Hayat Khan, member of Pakistan Constituent Assembly and a minister in Punjab, stated that in October 1947 when Mountbatten visited Pakistan, he conveyed Sardar Patel's message to Liaquat Ali, the prime minister, that if Pakistan kept out of Hyderabad, India would leave Kashmir alone. When Sirdar Shaukat Hayat, who was present at the meeting, commended the proposal to Liaquat Ali, he replied in Urdu, "Sirdar Sahib, have you gone out of your mind? Why should we leave a province larger than Punjab and settle for some mountain rocks?"[5] And here is the authoritative version of V.P. Menon, Sardar Patel's Secretary of States, who personally handled this matter. During the four-day discussions with the Maharaja of Kashmir in June 1947 Lord Mountbatten "... went so far as to tell the Maharaja that if he acceded to Pakistan, India would not take it amiss and he had firm assurance on this from Sardar Patel himself."[6]

Nehru's repeated assurances, especially in the earlier stages of the dispute, that Kashmir will be free to decide its own future, further the landing of Indian troops in the Valley, he told the Constituent Assembly, 'We are, of course, vitally interested in the decision the state would take.'[7]

But it took a long time for India to clearly state her stand on Kashmir. After Nehru had stressed Kashmir's 'intimate connection' with India, his Home Minister, G.B. Pant, stated in July 1955, "The Constituent Assembly of Kashmir which was elected on the basis of adult franchise has taken a definite decision. ... While I am not oblivious of the initial declaration made by the government of India I cannot ignore the important series of facts which I have briefly referred to above. In these circumstances, I personally feel that the tide cannot be turned now." This 'tide' surged forward as Nehru told the Lok Sabha on 29 March 1956:

> ... while we are desirous of settling this Kashmir problem with Pakistan, there was no settlement ...(if) the manner of settling ...would lead to a conflict with Pakistan.

In 1957, in his address to the Security Council Krishna Menon explained the implications of 'self-determination' for Kashmir. Self-determination, he stated, "was a principle which could be applied to dependent territories governed by a colonial power; it could not be used in regard to a constituent unit like Minnesota which forms part of a federal union."[8]

Menon made India's stand still more explicit in 1962 in the Security Council. He explained in detail that India had offered a plebiscite at one stage and Pakistan had then failed to honour its commitments; conditions had now changed so greatly that the earlier resolutions had become obsolete. "On no condition shall we sell our heritage. On no condition shall we open the door for the disruption and disintegration of India..."[9]

It took India 15 years to spell out her position so categorically. Here one cannot fail to notice the sophistication and sophistry of her handling of a sensitive diplomatic issue, and her imperceptibly gradual advance toward her goal.

Sheikh Mohammed Abdullah was the kingpin of Nehru's Kashmir policy. Nehru told the Maharaja of Kashmir, "The only person who can deliver the goods in Kashmir is Abdullah. ... No satisfactory way out can be found in Kashmir except through him."[10]

Nehru had good reasons for this high opinion of the Sheikh. Since 1937 he had fostered the All Jammu and Kashmir National Conference as a disciplined and truly secular party in a predominantly Muslim state. It was this party which helped to maintain peace and harmony when the rest of the subcontinent was rocked by communal riots. But its accession to India was a different issue. It was a measure of last resort. Participating in the Security Council debate in 1948, Abdullah had stated, "We realized that Pakistan would not allow us any time, that we had either to suffer the fate of our kith and kin ... or to seek help from some outside country. Under these circumstances both the Maharaja and the people of Kashmir requested the government of India to accept accession." In other words, if the conditions were normal, he would have acted differently. In fact from the day the Maharaja released him from jail on 29 September, he never unreservedly advocated accession to India. Four days after he was set free, he said at a public meeting in Srinagar that the question facing Kashmir was whether to join Pakistan or India. And despite all his association with Nehru and Gandhi, he said, "My personal convictions will not stand in the way of taking an independent decision in favour of one or the other Dominion." Here the Sheikh was clearly equating India with Pakistan as the two viable options open to the people of Kashmir. A fortnight later, on 17 October, he said in an interview in Delhi, "Kashmir cannot immediately decide the question of accession to either Dominion. ... It is much more necessary at present for Kashmir to secure the establishment of full responsible government."

Even after Kashmir's formal accession to India and his installation as the prime minister, his quest for an independent Kashmir continued. "After meeting the United States ambassador in Srinagar in the spring of 1949, Sheikh Abdullah seems to have got the impression... that the United States and Britain would favour an independent Kashmir. ... He was even reported to have suggested this to Sir Owen Dixon (the UN representative) in the summer of 1950 as one of the possible solutions to the Kashmir issue and to

1950 as one of the possible solutions to the Kashmir issue and to be contemplating bilateral negotiations with the leaders of Azad Kashmir."[11]

Nehru was obviously worried at the increasingly confrontationist posture of Abdullah. He invited him on three different occasions to Delhi to sort matters out, but the Sheikh avoided meeting him on one pretext or the other.

Abdullah's secessionist tendencies resulted in fuelling the Hindu communal elements in India. There were also complaints from the Jammu Hindus against discriminatory treatment. Praja Parishad, a party of Jammu Dogras, prepared a charge-sheet against Abdullah and started a Satyagraha. Hindu and Sikh communal parties joined the agitation and Shyama Prasad Mukherji, the Hindu Mahasabha leader, proceeded to Srinagar to guide the movement. He was arrested while entering Kashmir and died of a severe heart attack on 23 June 1953 while in detention. This aggravated communal tensions and relations with Kashmir worsened further. Ironically, this strengthened Abdullah's support base in the Valley. "For the first time public cries are raised in Kashmir that the Indian Army should get out."[12] As the events moved towards the point of no return, the Sheikh stated in a speech in Srinagar on 10 July that as even Nehru had failed to contain communalism, Kashmir should become an independent state.

The die was now cast and Abdullah could have declared secession of Kashmir any minute. By the time the flash-point was reached, a serious split had developed within the National Conference as several of Abdullah's colleagues did not approve of his policies. Three of the five members of the Cabinet turned against their leader and levelled serious charges against him. Apprehending political instability in the state, Dr. Karan Singh, Sardar-i-Riyasat, dismissed Abdullah from prime ministership on 8 August 1953, and Bakshi Ghulam Mohammed was sworn in as his successor. Next day the new government arrested the Sheikh on charges of "corruption, malpractices, disruptionism and dangerous foreign contacts." Strange though it may seem, "Nehru's consent was neither sought nor given for the arrest of Sheikh Abdullah..."[13]

With the arrest of Abdullah, Nehru's Kashmir policy lay in a shambles. India's strongest argument before the Security Council was that she held a mandate from the people of the state. And now the leader of the people and architect of Kashmir's political identity had to be dismissed and jailed for plotting against India.

In India Abdullah is perceived as a deceiver who stabbed his benefactor in the back. Nothing could be more unfair to the Sheikh. Though highly emotional and somewhat inconsistent, he was a man of integrity, courage and grit. He was wholly secular and a nationalist. But the problem here is that Abdullah was a Kashmiri nationalist and not an Indian nationalist. His basic loyalty was to Kashmir and he wanted an arrangement which best served the interests of the Kashmiris. According to his perception, their interests could be so served if Kashmir became an independent state. And he tried to move towards this goal with dogged persistence. But the problem with Nehru's outlook was that India's national interests subsumed those of Kashmir's. There was a definite element of political expediency in this approach. Whereas earlier, Nehru voluntarily stressed the imperative of ascertaining the wishes of people before deciding the future of the state, gradually he resiled from this principled stand in view of political considerations. It should be noted that the stridency of Abdullah's demand for independence increased as it became progressively clear that India was no longer committed to a plebiscite.

Whenever or wherever India and Pakistan spoke about Kashmir, the statements were full of solicitude for the helpless people of the Valley. But neither of them considered it expedient to ask the poor Kashmiris as to what they wanted. It took Nehru a couple of years to retreat from his offer of plebiscite. Pakistan never wanted it.

For India Kashmir has been a self-inflicted wound which has
bled her white over the years. And it has distorted India's foreign
policy perspective. Kashmir has been a crucial factor in condition-
ing her attitude towards other countries. Further, the weakness
of India's stand on Kashmir has eroded her moral authority. After
Sheikh Abdullah's arrest, India's claim that the people of Kashmir
supported her accession to India sounded hollow. Thereafter, the
ratification of accession by the Kashmir Constituent Assembly on
26 January 1956 was used to legitimise India's dominion over
Kashmir. But this event took place 3½ years after Abdullah's
detention. His successor, Bakshi Ghulam Mohammed, had little
popular following and was wholly beholden to India. Thus, ratification of accession under his leadership had hardly any moral
force. If Abdullah had still been the prime minister of Kashmir,
it is unlikely that the accession would have been endorsed.

India actually became the prisoner of a fallacy of her own
creation. It was argued that Abdullah was completely secular in
his outlook. This was true. It was also believed that the Kashmiris
were by and large a secular people. This was also right. It was
further claimed that the Indians are also secular. We may let that
pass.

Now, from the above premise it was abruptly inferred by a
strange quirk of logic that owing to this common bond of secularism, secular Kashmir, led by secular Abdullah was eager to
merge with secular India. But neither had Abdullah shown any
such inclination nor had the Kashmiris expressed any such desire.
Actually, when accession was announced, the Muslim soldiers of
the Maharaja's army were up in arms, post-offices in Srinagar
went on strike, the Muslim Conference organized widespread
anti-accession demonstrations, and there was a local uprising in
Poonch.

India was justified in arguing that if accession of Kashmir to
Pakistan was accepted owing to her being a predominantly
Muslim state, it would amount to an endorsement of the two-
nation theory. But this principled stand did not justify denial of
the right of self-determination to a state which was never a part
of India even during British rule.

A person of Nehru's perception could not have felt comfortable at the manner India stretched logic to cover the inconsistencies of her stand on Kashmir. He was highly sensitive to international opinion and he realized that his Kashmir policy was not winning friends or influencing people. As early as October 1948, "His visit to London and Paris brought home to him how much India was being judged by her conduct in Kashmir and Hyderabad. He was forced to recognize that his policies did not appear as impeccable to others as they did to him."[14]

It was to justify his Kashmir policy in his own eyes and the eyes of the world that he tried continuously to find some viable solution to this tangle. Towards the end of his days he made a last ditch attempt to get out of this impasse: he released Sheikh Abdullah on 8 April 1964. When President Ayub Khan of Pakistan invited the Sheikh for a visit, Nehru readily approved of it. Abdullah was still in Pakistan, exploring various options, when he got the news of Nehru's death.

The ultimate arbiter may not have solved the Kashmir problem, but he did release Nehru from his predicament.

18

India-China Showdown

*N*ehru felt a historical and civilizational affinity with China that he did with no other country. When China was fighting the Japanese aggression, India was waging her own struggle for Independence. Yet, despite all his preoccupations, Nehru mobilized public support and raised funds to help the Chinese volunteers. Mao Zedong expressed his gratitude to "... you great Indian people and the Indian National Congress for the medical and material aid that you have given."[1] In 1938 the Congress gave a call to boycott all Japanese goods to express its solidarity with China. After China won freedom in 1949, Nehru campaigned tirelessly for her admission to the UN, strove to promote harmonious Sino-American relations, provided China with excellent international exposure at Bandung, and played a valuable mediatory role in the Korean war.

Thus, from Nehru's point of view, the India-China conflict was the most unlikely thing to have happened. Shattered and disillusioned after this combat, the stricken Nehru wailed in pain, "How I worked for friendship between India and China, fought for China's legitimate interests in the world and aggression was my reward."[2] This was not the first time for him to discover that gratitude was not a currency which nations exchanged in their commerce.

Most wars are avoidable: the India-China war was particularly so. A malicious destiny relentlessly drove the two countries towards a head-on collision, despite umpteen sidings available en route. After China's annexation of Tibet in 1950, the two countries had a 3,500 kilometre long border. Broadly speaking it could be divided into three segments. One, the eastern sector, dividing

Tibet from the sprawling north-eastern tribal belt of India, the North Eastern Frontier Agency (NEFA), later named Arunachal Pradesh. At the other end is the western sector, where Ladakh and Aksai Chin are located. Between these two is the middle sector, situated just above the northern boundary of Nepal, Bhutan, and Himachal Pradesh. As the border dispute was mostly confined to the eastern and western sectors, we may ignore the middle sector. Even between the remaining two zones, the real bone of contention was the western sector, though the main brunt of the Chinese attack was borne by its eastern counterpart.

China's proximity to India acquired a new dimension when her troops marched into Tibet in 1950 and declared it a part of China. This annexation was much resented by the Indians. However, the storm blew over, and Nehru's role in the Korean war and his constant espousal of China's admission to the UN helped create a more congenial climate. But the real improvement came with India signing an agreement with China in 1954, recognizing her complete sovereignty over Tibet. [It was in this agreement that five principles of co-existence (Panchsheel) were enunciated for the first time.]

All the gains in goodwill from this agreement were nullified by the Khampa uprising in Tibet, which reached its peak in 1959. As a result of the brutal suppression of this revolt, thousands of Tibetan refugees, including the Dalai Lama, trekked to India. There was widespread sympathy for the Tibetans, openly expressed in public meetings. China viewed this as an unfriendly act, particularly the Indian government's offer of asylum to the Dalai Lama after the Buddhist countries of Burma and Ceylon (Sri Lanka) had declined to do so. This incident marks a turning point in India-China relations.

It was the presence of the British imperial power that had ensured peace along India's frontier with Tibet and China. But the fact of nearly 3,500 kilometre-long undemarcated boundary between the two neighbours was fraught with mischief. And the moment the

British left and China got over her internal problems, trouble surfaced.

Right from the beginning Nehru's stand was that India's frontiers were inviolable and non-negotiable. But he was also fully aware that the borders were fuzzy. For instance, he told Lok Sabha that though the McMahon Line indicated a firm boundary, "in some parts, in the Subansari area or somewhere that it was not considered a good line and it was varied afterwards by us ..."[3]/A little later, in a letter to Chou En-lai, Nehru explained an apparent discrepancy, saying that strict adherence to the McMahon Line would result in transferring to India areas which were under Chinese occupation.[4] In fact McMahon had himself observed:

> The map showing the boundaries of Tibet as a whole, which it is proposed to be attached to Tibet convention, is on far too small a scale to show such boundaries in detail.[5]

As to the western sector, Nehru was more explicit. After the discovery of the road built furtively by China in Aksai Chin Nehru stated, "But the actual boundary of Ladakh with Tibet was not very carefully defined... I rather doubt if they did any careful survey... It is not clear... I cannot say what part of it may not belong to us, and what parts may."[6]

But after the 1959 Khampa rebellion and some border incidents, relations between the two neighbours soured and Nehru's stand on the border issue hardened. When the two prime ministers met in Delhi in April 1960, he was "... willing to discuss any specific dispute, (but) India had no intention of yielding on her general stand that the frontier was a fixed one which had been peaceful for many years."[7]

It is, of course, a fact that on the basis of documentary evidence India's case was stronger. But the absence of documents on the Chinese side, or the availability of maps in India with boundaries drawn during the British rule, could not alter the ground reality. And what was the ground reality? "From March 1956 to October 1957, more than 3000 Chinese workers and soldiers were engaged in building a motorable road, 'cutting across high mountains, throwing bridges and building culverts.' ... All the while India was 'utterly unaware' of the Chinese activities. 'This is eloquent

proof that this area had indeed always been under Chinese jurisdiction.' "[8] (Portions within quotes are from Chou En-lai's letter
to Nehru, dt. 7 November 1959). And how did India learn about
the existence of this road? From a Chinese magazine report noticed by the Indian ambassador in Peking!

What was the Chinese perception of the boundary issue? Speaking at the Bandung Conference in 1954, Chou En-lai said:

> With some of these (neighbouring) countries we have not yet
> finally fixed our border-line and we are ready to do so... But before
> doing so we are ready to maintain the present situation by
> acknowledging that those parts of our border are parts which are
> undetermined. ... As to the determination of common borders...
> we shall use only peaceful means...[9]

Even five years later, while addressing the National Peoples'
Congress, Chou reiterated, "The boundaries between China and
certain neighbouring south-eastern countries remain undeter-
mined and they could reasonably be solved through peaceful
negotiations."[10]

Subsequently, though China became less explicit on this point
owing to worsening relations, she never resiled from this position.
In his letter of 23 January 1959 to Nehru, Chou En-lai wrote:

> In view of the various complex factors mentioned above, the
> Chinese government on one hand finds it necessary to take a more
> or less realistic attitude towards the McMahon Line, and on the
> other hand, cannot but act with prudence and needs time to deal
> with the matter.[11]

The basic point to be noted here is not that India was in the
wrong and China in the right. But one is left with the uncomfortable feeling that Nehru was being unduly rigid and club-footed
in dealing with the border problem, and he had not formulated
an overall policy frame to guide his strategy. On the other hand,
the Chinese stand was consistent, accommodating and well rea-
soned. At least this is the impression the Chinese managed to
convey to the outside world.

Whereas on the one hand Nehru did not always consult his cabinet or its subcommittees on vital national issues, on the other he adopted the dangerous practice of taking live, hot issues to the Parliament. And once public opinion was aroused, popular pressures abridged the government's policy options, and bilateral settlements based on an approach of give and take became difficult. The manner in which the Indian Parliament got gradually involved in the India-China territorial dispute is a case in point. In November 1950 a member of the Parliament asked whether the north-eastern boundary was recognized by Tibet. There was also a query about the borders shown in the Chinese maps. Nehru concluded his reply with the remark: "Our maps show that the McMahon Line is our boundary and this is our boundary — map or no map. That fact remains and we stand by that boundary, and we will not allow anybody to come across that boundary." This uncompromising and belligerent stand in respect of an undemarcated boundary which, in 1950, was not questioned by China in any case, was neither diplomatic nor reasonable.

After the Khampa revolt in 1959, the boundary question figured in a number of letters exchanged between the prime ministers of the two countries. Nehru placed the entire correspondence before the parliament. The MPs were furious and the national press reacted violently.

As a last-minute bid at reconciliation Nehru invited Chou En-lai to Delhi for talks in February 1960. However, he told the Parliament, "... the present positions are such that there is no room for negotiations ... and, therefore, there is nothing to negotiate at present." But when news about the invitation to Chou leaked, there was an uproar in the House. Minoo Masani described it as 'national humiliation', and Kriplani said that the country had been 'betrayed by the present government.' With this sort of public mood one can well imagine as to how much elbow room was left to Nehru for a meaningful exchange with his Chinese counterpart.

Nehru, no doubt, had a very soft corner for China. Yet he never felt very comfortable in the neighbourhood of this mighty giant. He told an Indian cultural delegation before it left for China in

1952, "Never forget that the basic challenge in South-East Asia is between India and China."[12] During an informal chat with journalists who accompanied him to China in 1954, Nehru said, "... some day or other these two Asian giants were bound to tread on each other's corns and come into a conflict, and that will be a calamity for Asia."[13] And in June 1954 he noted on a file that Chinese expansionism had been evident during various periods for about a thousand years, and a new period of expansionism was perhaps imminent. "Let us consider that and fashion our policy to prevent it coming in the way of our interests..."[14]

But despite all his perspicacity Nehru did not fashion his policy to meet the approaching threat. Regardless of the deteriorating situation and massing of troops on either side of the border, Nehru insisted on believing that China would not attack India, and that the border problem was well under control. In 1953 he minuted that "No major challenge to these frontiers is likely in the near future." On concluding the treaty on Tibet, he wrote, "We have gained instead something that is very important, i.e., a friendly frontier and an implicit acceptance of that frontier."[15] When he visited China in 1954, he pointed out to Chou that Chinese maps were showing some Indian territory as a part of China. He was told that these were maps drawn by the old regime and China had not had the time to revise them. In 1956, this issue was discussed again and Nehru got the impression that though China considered the boundary drawn by the British as illegal, one should accept it on practical grounds. This verbal assurance was not only considered "quite clear and precise acceptance of the McMahon Line, (but also sufficient) to conclude that the major border issue had been settled for all practical purposes."[16]

Going by circumstantial evidence, it will be seen that in September 1962 Nehru left India to attend a routine Commonwealth prime ministers' conference, and Krishna Menon, the Defence Minister, also proceeded to attend the UN Session of little consequence. Nehru returned on 2 October. Shooting incidents across the border had started in September. Yet Nehru again left for Colombo on 12 October, to inaugurate an Ayurvedic research centre and returned on the 16th. Lt. General B.M. Kaul, Chief of

General Staff, had proceeded on leave, and the Director of Military Intelligence was sent for a cruise on the Vikrant. And the full-scale Chinese attack commenced on 20 October, 1962! If Nehru had any inkling of the Chinese intentions, the configuration of these stars would have been somewhat different!

The greatest proof of Nehru's 'no war' belief lies in the fact that India did not prepare for the coming event. No regular Command was created, no stocks and stores built up, no feeder roads constructed, no weapons procured, or adequate troops positioned in advance. The Indian army was so unprepared that the soldiers did not have winter clothing and shoes, and even the rations were insufficient.

Tension had been building up on the frontier for quite some time. In October 1959 the Chinese opened fire on an Indian patrol near the Kongka pass, killing five Indian policemen and capturing a dozen others. After these incidents the Chinese premier wrote a letter to Nehru on 7 November, 1959, proposing that the troops of the two countries should withdraw 20 kilometres from the McMahon Line in the east and from the line of actual control in the west. Also, that the status quo should be maintained. This fair-sounding proposal was a clever ploy, as it required India to withdraw from her established border in the north-east. On the other hand, withdrawal of 20 kilometers in the western sector did not harm China's interests, as that would have still left the crucial Aksai Chin segment with the road in her possession. Nehru found these proposals unacceptable and in his reply of 16 November suggested that the Chinese troops should withdraw to the east of the international border and the Indian personnel to the west.

The border incidents were ominous signs of the emerging trends. Both sides were establishing border posts to substantiate their claims to the frontier as perceived by them. In view of a minute of Nehru, the Indian government decided in November 1960:

> So far as Ladakh is concerned, we are to patrol as far forward as possible from our present positions towards the international border. This will be done with a view to establishing our posts

which should prevent the Chinese from advancing any further...
This must be done without getting involved in a clash with the
Chinese, unless this becomes necessary in self-defence.[17]

It is this approach which later came to be known as the 'forward
policy'. When orders in pursuance of the above decision were
issued by the Army HQ, somehow the portion prohibiting the
patrols from getting involved in a clash with the Chinese was
omitted. In pursuance of this policy India raised the number of
posts to 24 along the McMahon Line, and set up 43 posts in the
western sector. At some points, owing to anomalies in the boundary marked on the maps, some Indian posts were established
beyond the boundary, and this led to ugly incidents.

This situation was obviously leading the two countries towards
a major clash. An unusual feature of this development was the
attitude of the Indian army. Normally, the armed forces are raring
to go, and the civilian authorities have to keep them in check. In
this case, the army was all along telling their civilian masters to
avoid confrontation. "Army HQ warned the civilian arm of the
serious military risks entailed in the forward patrolling for which
the government was pressing... the Army pointed out that forward patrolling as called for by the government would invite
sharp Chinese reaction..."[18] And "The Chiefs of Staff warned in
January 1961 that if the policy to resist to the full and evict any
further Chinese aggression led to more than a limited war, it
would be beyond the capacity of the Indian army to hold out for
more than a short period."[19] Further, "Worried by its weakness
in men, materials and logistics, the Western Command warned
Delhi in August that political direction was not being based on
military means."[20] In early 1961, when Nehru told the parliament
that the military situation in the western sector had changed in
India's favour, Corps Commander Lt. General S.D. Verma, 'immediately wrote a strongly worded letter to his immediate superior, General Thapar (saying)... that the Prime Minister's remarks
were optimistic, misleading, and bore little relation to the facts
on the ground."[21] General Daulat Singh of Western Command

wrote to Army HQ in mid-August 1962, "Militarily we are in no position to defend what we possess, leave alone force a showdown."[22]

There was a strange air of unrealism and casualness about the manner in which India stumbled into this war. Somehow Krishna Menon had lulled Nehru into the belief that China would not attack India. But occasionally, the PM was also making off-the-cuff, jingoistic statements which unnecessarily sent the wrong signals to the Chinese. After the occupation of Tibet, Nehru clarified in a speech before the parliament in December 1950 that China should be in no doubt that India would defend the Himalayan borders. "Whether India had the necessary military resources or not," he said, "I would fight aggression whether it came from the mountain or the sea."[23] And a week before the Chinese attack, he told the press at Delhi airport before leaving for Colombo, "Our instructions are to free our country... I cannot fix the date, that is entirely for the army."[24] If accepted at its face value, this was nothing short of an open ultimatum to China.

September 8th 1962 is a landmark in the development of India-China conflict. The Chinese forces attacked Thagla Ridge and dislodged the Indian troops. This was a clear indication that now they meant business. Yet, as noted earlier, unmindful of the threat, Nehru pushed off to London to attend a routine conference. On his return, as the plot was thickening, he again left for Colombo on 12 October for another meeting. And before his departure made that statement about army having been told 'to free the country'! And a week later the Chinese army launched a massive attack, overrunning the Indian posts in the eastern sector. It was a well-calculated, well-planned and a wholly professional manoeuvre. The outcome was a complete rout of the Indian forces all along the line. In the western sector, the situation was no better. On 20 October the Chinese captured 13 forward Indian posts in the Galwan valley, and by the beginning of November they were training their guns at the Chushul airstrip.

Then, as suddenly as the Chinese had descended on India, they declared unilateral cease-fire on 19 November, and started their withdrawal two days later. According to their declaration, the Chinese forces were to withdraw 20 kilometres behind the line of actual control as it existed on 7 November 1959. In the eastern sector they offered to withdraw from the positions held south of the McMahon Line to 20 kilometres to its north. (This was a reiteration of the offer made by Chou En-lai on that date.)

The Chinese assault on NEFA is variously described in India as an act of 'perfidy', 'betrayal', 'a stab in the back'. What a juvenile reaction to the most serious crisis ever faced by free India! This description amounts to blaming your known enemy for not having behaved like a friend! At least from 1959 onwards it had become clear that the border problem would have to be solved bilaterally one way or the other. The Chinese consistently maintained that the common borders were never delimited by a mutual agreement, nor demarcated on the ground. Nehru held that the borders were fully settled, except for minor adjustments here and there and, therefore, there was nothing to negotiate. The Chinese also repeatedly showed their willingness to accept the McMahon Line, provided India left Aksai Chin to them. This was a fair quid pro quo, especially as India's claims in the western sector were weak, and the region had hardly any geo-strategic importance for her.

As border issues are not always decided on merit, India could have taken a conscious decision that 'map or no map', she was going to stick to her stand, come what may. But in that case she should have prepared herself for the consequences. Instead of that, Nehru convinced himself that the Chinese would not wage a real war against India and, therefore, paid no serious attention to gearing up the Indian war machine for a real-life battle. Even when the countdown had started, he was routinely attending international conferences. The basic homework was so completely neglected that the Cabinet Committee on Foreign Affairs, Defence Committee of the Cabinet, Chiefs of Staff Committee and Joint Intelligence Committee, which should have been fully involved in evolving a comprehensive war strategy, were never activated. Repeated pleas and protests by the army commanders about lack of preparedness were ignored. Forward posts were set up by the dozen, without constructing feeder roads linking them to supply depots. Krishna Menon's penchant for working through coteries had destroyed the unity of command at the top. Favourites and upstarts were bandying about 'orders from the top', violating the line of command and demoralizing the senior commanders. Upright generals like S.D. Verma, Daulat Singh and Umrao Singh, who dared question the wisdom of the government's decisions, were humiliated, removed and victimized. And one could be sure that all this chaos and lack of readiness was fully known to the Chinese.

With this sort of higher direction of war, is it any wonder that the Indian forces suffered a humiliating defeat? The fault lay neither 'in our stars' nor the in Chinese perfidy. As Nehru himself told a meeting of state information ministers soon after the Chinese attack, "For some years past we have been living in an artificial world of our own making." And in a letter to Krishna Menon, "I do not know how I shall explain to parliament why we have been found lacking in equipment. It is not much good shifting about blame. The fact remains that we have been found lacking and there is an impression that we have approached these things in a somewhat amateurish way."[25]

As opposed to the 'amateurish' Indian attitude, the Chinese approach was thoroughly professional. Having once defined their target of annexing Aksai Chin, they went for it like an arrow. And in the process they displayed much greater tact, finesse and flexibility. They never resiled from their original offer of settling the border through mutual negotiations, and came up with one proposal after the other. But all along, Nehru stuck to a rigid stand, showed no ingenuity in coming up with quick responses, and did not make any 'give or take' manoeuvres.

Several experts have held that the Chinese had started preparing for this war the moment they occupied Tibet. The existence of an elaborate network of roads, setting up of supply depots, positioning of artillery at strategic points and massive deployment of troops trained in mountain warfare are cited in support of this view. But there exists a much simpler explanation to this phenomenon. After the annexation of Tibet in 1950, the Chinese troops were stationed there on a regular basis to subdue the hostile local population. Later these troops were greatly augmented to suppress the Khampa rebellion. It was also necessary to improve road communication for effective administration of this province. This was naturally accompanied by the establishment of well-stocked supply depots. Thus the Chinese always had a fully acclimatized and well-equipped army deployed in Tibet to meet local contingencies. And it did not require much extra effort to use this well-oiled war machine for marching into NEFA at short notice. It may be that the Chinese had evil designs from the beginning, but the state of their preparedness does not by itself establish their malafides.

There is nothing that the Chinese did which Nehru had not anticipated. But there was a lot that Nehru anticipated that the Chinese did not do. One of Nehru's main failings as a policy maker was that he could not integrate his sharp perceptions and insights into a coherent policy frame. It is said that war is too serious a matter to be left to the generals. But here it is the political masters who bungled and blundered endlessly despite very sober professional advice by the field commanders. Both politically and militarily, this is the one war which should teach India how not to wage a war.

What was the aftermath of the India-China war? Obviously, it brought to an end the Nehru era. Nehru's policies were openly attacked and the Third Plan suffered a serious setback. The Congress lost three parliamentary by-elections in a row, and for the first time a no-confidence motion was moved against him in Lok Sabha in August 1963. Even the Congress MPs sabotaged the government's bid for a constitutional amendment to strengthen legislation on land ceilings. The defeat also gave a handle to the rightist lobby in India, as it could now claim that the entire Nehruvian plank had collapsed. A couple of years after Nehru's death it had gained enough strength to openly challenge Indira Gandhi.

On the international front, the Chinese victory firmly established her status as the premier Asian power. It has been argued that the primary aim of China was to attain this position by beating India in an open conflict. This is a bit far-fetched. Her basic objective all along was to grab Aksai Chin as it was vital to her national interests. The other gains were incidental. Otherwise China would not have tried so consistently for years to settle the border issue through negotiations.

It was in the field of foreign relations that Nehru ruled supreme: his authority, knowledge and judgement in international matters were never questioned. His credentials as a peace-maker were impeccable. Yet it is an irony of fate that this is the one area where his greatest failures lie. Under his stewardship India got into a situation on Kashmir which saddled her with a back-breaking burden of permanently maintaining a large force in the Valley without the prospect of any solution in sight. With China he had to fight a disastrous war. Both these confrontations left behind a legacy of ongoing conflict for his successors. And the issues which led to these conflicts were amenable to peaceful solutions.

Despite having inspired a whole generation of third-world leaders in their struggle against colonialism and espoused so many worthy causes, Nehru found himself friendless when he needed friends the most. Not a single non-aligned country came to his support when China attacked India.

19

Nehru - The Man

*I*t is more than thirty years that Nehru has been dead. Yet today we hardly know anything about his personal life that we did not during his lifetime. In fact his total dedication to the job in hand hardly left him any time for a personal life.

In any profile of Nehru, his courage must get pride of place. Reflecting on the ups and downs of life he wrote, "There is only one thing that remains to us that cannot be taken away: to act with courage and dignity and to stick to the ideals that have given meaning to life..."[1]

And, "...only they can sense life who stand often on the verge of it, only they whose lives are not governed by the fear of death. In spite of all the mistakes that we might have made we have saved ourselves from triviality and an inner shame and cowardice."[2]

In a quarter century of political activeness from 1920-1945, Nehru spent more than one third of this period in prison. These were years of his youth and middle age, the most productive years of a person's life. Yet they left behind no mark of bitterness or rancour, nor dimmed his zest for life or faith in India's destiny.

Even while in prison, he rarely grumbled, felt peevish or lost his poise. And he never indulged in self-pity. "It seems to me" he wrote from the prison cell, "I am getting far too much sympathy from others and I do not deserve it. It is those who work and labour outside who deserve sympathy, not we who laze and eat and sleep."[3] His innate sense of decency revolted at the special treatment given to him in prison, and he repeatedly protested to the authorities against this unjust practice.

It is difficult to find instances when Nehru was petty, vindictive or malicious. After Independence there were no reprisals, no witch-hunting, no settling of scores. The ICS officers, who had imprisoned the national leaders or ordered firings on the Congress demonstrators, were given all respect and trust due to their office, and bygones were treated as bygones. A smaller man would have harboured animus against the British. But Nehru attended his first Conference of Commonwealth Prime Ministers in 1948 as if the colonial era had never happened. Even Churchill, his old adversary, had to concede, "I have always admired your ardent wish for peace and the absence of bitterness in your consideration of the antagonism that had in the past divided us."[4]

Once Ram Manohar Lohia made a very offensive reference to Nehru's ancestry in the parliament. Said he, "The PM pretends to be an aristocrat. I can prove that his grandfather was nothing but a Chaprasi (peon) at the Mughal Court." Unruffled, Nehru replied, "I am most grateful to the Hon'ble Member. I have been trying for years to get him to accept that I am a man of the people. Now he has admitted it himself."[5]

In case he came across an instance of ugly behaviour, he would try to apply a corrective without reprimanding the offender. At the 1961 Republic Day Parade where the Queen of England was the chief guest, some politicians got ruffled as they did not get seats owing to their late arrival. When volunteers requested them to sit on the ground like others, they went protesting to Nehru. "Nehru quietly got his daughter and the Speaker to leave the Queen's entourage and to lead the MPs away and to sit on the ground with them." At a reception at Constitution House some MPs threw banana peels on the ground. "Nehru, seeing this, pointedly got up, came along with a plate and, without saying a word, shamed them by picking up the mess himself."[6]

For a person who was born in luxury and seen so much comfort, he was spartan in his habits, austere in his living and almost miserly where the spending of public money was concerned. In May 1954, Nehru spent three days in Madras on official business. In reply to a parliament question it was revealed that his stay cost the state exchequer Rs. 90,000. He was upset and wrote to the chief ministers to observe economy on his visits, and added, "I shall hesitate to go anywhere if I am so costly."[7]

Describing Nehru's first visit to the United States, B.K. Nehru writes, "... his entourage consisted of Sir Girja Shankar Bajpai, who was Secretary General of Foreign Office, and M.O. Mathai, his private secretary, and that was all. The travel was by commercial airlines... The journey across the Atlantic... involved more than (a) full night of travelling. The plane had sleeping berths available on extra payment. The Indian 'delegation' had bought itself one sleeping berth in order to save money, and the Prime Minister insisted that Sir Girja and not he, should occupy that berth as he was senior in age."[8]

Nehru overlooked laxity in his colleagues, but he was unsparing in his own conduct. As a measure of economy the Finance Minister, C.D. Deshmukh, wanted the ministers to downgrade the post of their private secretary. Dharam Vira was then the trusted Principal Private Secretary of Nehru. Finance Minister wanted the PM to give the lead. Nehru relieved Dharam Vira without demur and downgraded the post.

Much folklore surrounds the great wealth of Motilal and the luxurious life that the Nehrus lived. In fact Motilal was more large-hearted than rich, and once he gave up his legal practice after joining the national movement, the situation gradually became pretty tight at Anand Bhawan. In 1927 he had to think twice before leaving for Switzerland to join his son. Earlier, to finance his trip to Europe, Nehru "had to return to the distasteful practice of law, and for preparing a brief Motilal secured for him the large fee of Rs. 10,000..."[9]

After his release from Naini jail in 1933, Nehru was required to pay closer attention to his household affairs. "I had ignored them completely so far, and I had not even examined my father's papers since his death. We had cut down our expenditure greatly, but still it was far more than we could afford. We were not keeping a car because that was beyond our means..."[10]

However, the insistent demands of life do not wait. So, Nehru took recourse to the last resort which Indian families in distress do: "To improve the immediate financial situation we decided to sell off my wife's jewellery, the silver and other familiar articles that we possessed, as well as many cart-loads of odds and ends."[11]

Nehru's hectic political activity and long terms in jail left little time for family life. And whatever time he could steal to spend at home was clouded by domestic worries. "Eighteen years of married life!" he writes in *An Autobiography*, "but how many long years out of them had I spent in prison-cell, and Kamala in hospitals and sanatoria?"[12] When Nehru got married in 1916, Kamala was seventeen, "a slip of a girl, utterly unsophisticated," without much formal education. In the Anglicized Nehru household, she was a misfit. Referring to great "differences in our mental outlook," Jawaharlal writes, "I hardly realized that this delicate, sensitive girl's mind was slowly unfolding like a flower and required gentle and careful tending."[13]

To be fair to Nehru, life did not give him enough time to work out a smooth equation with his wife. Occasionally, he refers to Kamala with a lot of feeling, and his memories of their togetherness are full of tenderness and remorse. "I thought of the early years of our marriage when ... I almost forgot her and denied her, in so many ways, that comradeship which was her due." And more pointedly, "I had taken from her what she gave me. What had I given to her in exchange during these early years? I had failed evidently and, possibly she carried a deep impress of those days upon her."[14]

They came much closer when Kamala started taking an active interest in the freedom movement. "Our women came to the front and took charge of the struggle... In this upheaval Kamala had played a brave and notable part and on her inexperienced shoulders fell the task of organizing our work in the city of Allahabad."[15]

This shared involvement in a great venture gave the Nehrus a new sense of companionship. "When I was arrested in February, 1934... Kamala went up to our rooms to collect some clothes for me. I followed her to say goodbye to her. Suddenly she clung to me and fainting, collapsed."[16] With his stoic reserve and dread of showing personal emotion, this is the closest Nehru came to giving a glimpse of his conjugal intimacy.

Kamala's death was followed by his mother's two years later. His father had died earlier in 1931. His daughter Indira was pursuing her studies abroad. This left Nehru lonely and forlorn. "I would return to my home from my wanderings almost unwillingly," he writes, "and sit in that deserted house by myself." This was at least partly the reason for his turning into such a workaholic.

Nehru was forty-seven when he became a widower. He was not an ascetic. In fact his views on sex were rather unorthodox for those times. Writing about his student days abroad, he says, "Most of us were strongly attracted by sex and I doubt if any of us attached any idea of sin to it. Certainly I did not; there was no religious inhibition. We talked of its being amoral, neither moral or immoral."[17]

Yet during Kamala's lifetime he remained loyal to her. After her death he did get involved with some controlled affairs. The one with Edwina Mounbatten is widely known. So ardent was his passion for her that even at a formal dinner given by Vijayalakshmi Pandit, the Indian High Commissioner in London, he disappeared with Edwina, leaving the guests high and dry.[18] And the following we have on Pupul Jayakar's authority: "I asked Vijayalakshmi Pandit of Jawaharlal Nehru's relationship with Padmaja (Naidu). 'Didn't you know Pupul?' she replied, 'they lived together for years, for years.' Questioned further as to why he had not married Padmaja, Vijayalakshmi replied, 'He felt that Indu had been hurt enough. He did not want to hurt her further'."[19]

M.O. Mathai, Nehru's private secretary, who was privy to many a household secret, gives instances of Padmaja's extreme jealousy of Lady Mounbatten, and quotes Miss Naidu as telling him, 'Jawahar is not one woman's man.' Mathai also writes about Nehru's affair with one Sharada Mata, from whom he sired a son.[20]

Physically, Nehru enjoyed excellent health and seldom suffered from any illness. His popular image is that of a robust, energetic and youthful person, always walking fast and with a springy gait.

He was sixty-eigh͟   ͟ng Pass, "mostly
on horse-back, wa͟   ͟ne or two miles
and came down on͟   ͟ work schedule,
H.V.R. Iyenger wri͟   ͟.͟y with him during
a period of exceptiͻ   ͟.͟ͻͻ and anguish, I have come to the
conclusion that no purely physical or physiological explanation
is adequate."[22]

Nehru spoke and wrote millions of words. His lively mind bub-
bled with ideas, and he had great faith in their potency. Men of
action normally fulfill themselves through their deeds. For him,
fulfilment came through articulation, philosophizing, conceptualizing. Even the launching of great schemes and projects were
occasions for lighting sparklers of words and firing rockets of
ideas.

This tendency becomes much more pronounced in his
speeches. Most of them are too long and tedious. He is not only
reflective in his speeches, but also discursive and rambling. His
habit of soliloquizing or thinking aloud in public, though attractive at times, could prove harmful in a head of government.

"It would be a good thing for the world," said Nehru, "if all
the Foreign Ministers remained silent for some time. More trouble
is being caused in foreign affairs by the speeches that the Foreign
Ministers ... deliver in their respective Assemblies or in the United
Nations." And he himself provided the best example of this danger when he made so many hasty and ill-advised pronouncements
about India's problems with China. As one observer remarked,
"India's foreign policy was not in the files of the Ministry of
External Affairs, nor even in the head of the Prime Minister but
on his tongue."[23]

Very often Nehru played with words as a child plays with
marbles, and he enjoyed expansive talk just for the love of it. The
German Chancellor, Adenauer, is reported to have felt exasperated when after a masterly expose of international problems,
Nehru would not come down to earth but evaded specific questions of vital importance to the two countries.[24] P.M.S. Blackett,
the famous British scientist whom Nehru used to consult on

India's defence production programme, said, "... he had too much intellectualism to solve any problem. He just chatted. He liked chatting about the world in general... When I was consultant to Defence Ministry, when I stayed with him, he just chatted. It was curious. I was surprised. He chatted."[25]

This love of hearing his own voice and the unchallenged power he wielded for long gave Nehru an exaggerated notion of his own importance and made him somewhat insensitive to the response of others. Malcolm Muggeridge thought he was "rather a conceited second-rate person." Hugh Gaitskell said, "He is a very arrogant man; I think that is one reason he makes such long speeches. He really thinks everyone wants to listen to him."[26]

At the Bandung Conference when Sir John Kotlewala described east European countries as colonies under communist domination, Nehru went up to him and asked with some heat, "Why did you do it Sir John? Why did you not show me your speech before you made it?" Sir John shot back, "Why should I? Do you show me yours before you make them?"

These stray instances of Nehru's arrogance are based on the perceptions of foreigners who never came close to him. But what does one say to this observation by Maulana Azad, his lifelong colleague and friend: "Jawaharlal is, however, very vain and cannot stand that anybody else should receive greater support and admiration than he."[27] Raj Kumari Amrit Kaur, describing him as 'A Friend Without Friends,' said, "he is not averse to flattery and there is conceit in him which makes him at once intolerant of criticism and may even warp his better judgement."[28]

Both during the freedom struggle and his tenure as prime minister, Nehru was occasionally faced with 'make or break' situations. Though at times he did come to the brink, he invariably retreated. "My outlook has always been against conflict," he told a journalist.[29] In 1928 Nehru offered his resignation as General Secretary of the Congress owing to differences over the Simon Commission controversy. The Congress Working Committee did not accept it. "And again I agreed," wrote Nehru. "It was surprising how easy it was to win me over to a withdrawal of my resignation. This happened on many occasions ...."[30]

This penchant for resigning acquired much higher visibility during Nehru's years in power. In 1951 he threatened to resign over the Tandon controversy. In 1954 he desired to quit office as he ̄ ̄ ̄ling stale. In 1957 he wanted to leave when he was ou' ̄ ̄ his attempt to replace Rajendra Prasad by Rʑ ̄ ̄nt of India. And in 1958 he created a fı ̄ ̄e to resign to a gathering of Con-ſ ̄ ̄f the Parliament. "I feel that I must ̄ ̄ ̄e myself from the daily burden and ̄ ̄ ̄ual citizen of India and not as Prime ̄ ̄ ̄d of actually submitting his resigna-tion, ̄ ̄ ̄ ̄ ̄ ̄ the MPs! Predictably, the MPs told him as to how ̄ ̄ ̄able he was for the country, and he faithfully bowed to the pressure from his party. So despite all his resolves and threats, he never actually submitted his resignation to the President.

When a journalist asked Nehru as to why he gave in to public pressure if he really wanted to resign, "His answer was that India needed him, that his constituency was the people of India."[31] And just five days before his death when he was asked at a press conference if it would not be in the country's interest to solve the succession problem in his lifetime, he replied, "My life is not ending so soon."[32]

Nehru was much bigger than the post he held. But power is an opiate, and it was pathetic to see its addictive hold over this colossus. His life's work was over by 1958, and he would have departed in a cloud of glory had he resigned then. And it would have set the healthy precedent that the only exit route for a politician is not through defeat or death.

In the days of individual Satyagraha in 1940 when Nehru's arrest was imminent, he came to see Gandhi at Sevagram. As he was leaving Gandhi's wife gave her blessings and said, "God will look after you." Nehru replied, "Where is God, Ba. If he exists, he must be very fast asleep."[33]

Nehru was not religious — not in the conventional sense. The strife, bigotry and intolerance that he saw practised in the name of orthodox faith gave him a 'horror of religion.' Moreover, his scientific, rationalist outlook could not come to terms with religious faith. Yet he recognized that religion, "... offered... a safe anchorage from doubt and mental conflict, an assurance of future life which will make up for the deficiencies of their life."[34] He goes even further and says, "Whether we believe in God or not, it is impossible not to believe in something..."[35]

Nehru's personal preference was for "the open sea, with all its storms and tempests."[36] Traditional religion's straitjacket was distasteful to his eclectic mind: I was, somewhere at the back of my mind, a pagan, with a pagan's liking for the exuberance of life and nature, and not very much averse to the conflicts that life provides."[37] Thus, "The traditional Chinese outlook, fundamentally ethical and yet irreligious or tinged with religious scepticism has an appeal for me..."[38]

In the strict, formal sense, Nehru was obviously not religious. But so far as the ethical and human dimensions of religion are concerned, he was as religious as any self-proclaimed man of God can be. After he asked Ba 'Where is God,' Gandhi laughed and said, "While Jawaharlal always says he does not believe in God he is nearer God than many who profess to be his worshippers."

Nehru turned his face away from a life of luxury to serve his downtrodden countrymen. He suffered all sorts of privations and insults at the hands of the colonial rulers, and spent the best nine years of his life in jail. He was a man of deep compassion, a thorough gentleman, would not consciously hurt anybody, and was truthful in his dealings. He waged a lifelong struggle against injustice and oppression, and his sympathies embraced the whole of mankind. If such a person was not truly religious, who else could be ?

But there is a terrain of human psyche which lies beyond the reach of logic and rationality where emotion, instinct and intuition hold sway. This is the terrain not accessible to the agnostic; this is the primordial soil in which religion is rooted. But Nehru was candid enough to observe, "It is all very well for the likes of Sapru and me... to talk pompously and in a superior way of our tolerance in matters of religion when neither of us has any religion worth talking about."[39]

Nehru's more radical views about religion are contained in his *Autobiography*, published in 1936. His *Discovery of India*, published a decade later, shows a deeper understanding of it. He writes,

> ... religion had supplied some deeply felt inner need of human nature, and that the vast majority of people all over the world could not do without some form of religious belief... In the wider sense of the word, religion dealt with the unchartered regions of human experience... It was obvious that there was a vast unknown region all around us.[40]

This unknown region did not interest Nehru very much. "I find the problems of this world sufficiently absorbing to fill my mind."[41] And, "Essentially, I am interested in this world, in this life, not in some other world or a future life."[42]

Thus, being a here-and-now person, his focus of attention is Man and the human condition. "God we may deny, but what hope is there for us if we deny man..."[43] Consequently, the enlightened modern mind "is governed by a practical idealism for social betterment ... Humanity is its God and social service its religion."[44]

Science had a decisive influence on Nehru's belief system: "It is the scientific approach, the adventurous and yet critical temper of science, the search for truth and new knowledge, the refusal to accept anything without testing and trial... all this is necessary, not merely for the application of science — but for life itself and the solution of its many problems."[45] But a decade later he stated, "Scientists should note that they do not have a monopoly of the truth...Truth is too vast to be contained in the minds of human beings or in books, however sacred."[46] And while addressing the annual session of the Indian Science Congress in 1963, he observed, "Without science there is no future for any society; but even with science, unless it is controlled by some spiritual impulses, there is also no future."

It is interesting to note that the above three quotations pertain to 1946, 1957 and 1963. And they show how Nehru was gradually moving from a totally science-based, materialistic outlook to a science-tinged-with-spirituality position. In an interview to a journalist he said, "Yes I have changed. The emphasis on ethical and spiritual solutions is not unconscious. It is deliberate, quite deliberate."[47]

In fact the science on which Nehru had built his worldview, had itself undergone a sea change. From Newtonian certitude, it had entered the probablistic realm of 'uncertainities' of quantum mechanics; and the three Euclidian dimensions had been pierced by the fourth one of space-time continuum. As a result of his vast reading Nehru was aware of these developments and this led him to discover correspondences between the modern science and Vedantic metaphysics. He wrote, ... "it is interesting to compare some of the latest conclusions of science with the fundamental ideas underlying the Advaita Vedantic theory. These ideas were that the universe is made of one substance whose form is per-petually changing, and further that the sum total of energies remains the same. Also that the explanations of things are to be found within their own nature, and that no external beings or existences are required to explain what is going on in the universe, with corollary of a self-evolving universe."[48] Further, "All this upheaval of thought," said Nehru, "has led scientists into a new region, verging on the metaphysical."[49] Of course, the process of Nehru's conversion to the Advaita philosophy was slow, and the changeover was never complete.

For Nehru, the ultimate test of a creed, a philosophy or a code of conduct was its social relevance. "The real problems for me," wrote he, "remain problems of individuals and social life ... of the adjustment of relations between individual and between groups, of a something becoming better and higher, of social develop-ment, of the ceaseless adventure of man... A living philosophy must answer the problems of today."[50]

Going back to the roots of the Indian ethos, he says:

> The central idea of old Indian civilization... was that of *dharma*, which was something much more than religion or creed; it was a conception of obligations, of the discharge of one's duties to oneself and to others. This *dharma* itself was part of *rita*, the

fundamental .moral law governing the functioning of the universe.[51]

Thus Nehru expects two things from any coherent system of belief and theory of statecraft: first, that it must answer the problems of today. That explains his aversion to metaphysics and transcendentalism. And second, it must have a sound ethical basis. Any approach which does not satisfy these two criteria cannot be the basis of a stable and just social order.

Nehru's contribution to the building of modern India is unique and enduring. He was handed a very messy slate, and he wrote on it an agenda of gigantic proportions. This made his task exceedingly difficult; but nothing short of it could have met the requirements of this newly liberated subcontinent. There could not be a greater tribute to the global vision of this man than the fact that none of his successors have been able to expand or modify his policy-frame in any significant manner. Perhaps no ruler in history conceived and launched so many and such massive projects for the welfare of his people, and that too in the face of such daunting odds.

In fact our quarrel with Nehru is not that he is not great, but that he was not greater. Especially when he had the capacity to be so. Thus, to borrow Dylan Thomas's phrase, ours has been a 'lover's quarrel' with Nehru.

It is also to be remembered that if several of his initiatives petered out after his death, the blame cannot be placed at Nehru's door. Programmes of social, economic and political reform, especially in the earlier stages, are not self-sustaining forces. The moment you neglect them or put them to wrong use, they lose their momentum and degenerate into empty rituals.

Perhaps none will deny that but for Nehru, India's modernist agenda could have been overwhelmed by forces of revivalism and communalism. When he assumed power, India was a rickety enterprise. It could have disintegrated into warring states, turned into a theocracy, or got saddled by a ruthless dictator. Nothing of the sort happened. To date Nehru has been succeeded by ten prime ministers in a row, and each succession has been completely peaceful and constitutional. This is the ultimate tribute to Nehru's leadership.

Nehru once wrote to G.B. Shaw, "There are too many questions which fill the mind and for which there appear to be no adequate answers, or if the answers are there, somehow they cannot be implemented because of the human beings that should implement them."[52]

The situation in which Nehru found himself was bristling with myriads of such questions. And he was too civilized and eclectic a person to stamp them out with an autocratic flourish. A smaller person and a narrower mind claiming to know all the answers would have handled them with greater assurance and firmness.

When Nehru died on 27 May 1964, his old companion and occasional adversary, C.R. Rajagopalachari said, "Eleven years younger than me, eleven times more important, eleven hundred times more beloved by the nation... I have been fighting Sri Nehru all these ten years over what I consider faults in public policies. But I knew all along that he alone could get them corrected. ... He is gone leaving me weaker than before in my fight."[53]

And Arnold Toynbee wrote: "One must be thankful when a noble soul takes on itself the burden of political leadership, for politics are always in need of redeeming."[54]

When Nehru left the scene, idealism and greatness walked out of Indian politics. Some of his successors were astute practitioners of realpolitik, but their concerns were much narrower. And ever since Indian politics has been in urgent need of 'redeeming'.

20

Interregnum - I

W atched by a galaxy of world leaders and mourned by millions of his countrymen, Jawaharlal Nehru was cremated on 28th May amidst the chanting of Vedic hymns by priests specially flown from Kashi and sprinkling of water brought from the holy Ganga. The funeral pyre was lit by Sanjay, his youngest male heir. As Hindu custom forbids women to perform last rites, Indira Gandhi was ineligible for the ceremony.

The manner of Nehru's cremation was at variance with his wishes. He had clearly stated in his Will, "I do not want any religious ceremonies performed for me after my death. I do not believe in any such ceremonies and to submit to them ... would be hypocrisy ..." Of course he wanted that "A small handful of these ashes should be thrown into the Ganga ..." But here the reason was purely cultural, not religious. "The Ganga ... is the river of India, beloved of her people, round which are intertwined her racial memories, her hopes and fears, her songs of triumphs, her victories and her defeats. She has been a symbol of India's age-long culture and civilization ..."

'The king is dead, long live the King.' Even as Nehru's body was lying in state, an emergency committee of the defunct Cabinet decided to recommend to the President the appointment of G.L. Nanda, the seniormost cabinet minister, as the pro tem Prime Minister. Radhakrishnan agreed to the proposal provided the Congress Parliamentary Party (CPP) duly elected its new leader within a short time.

There was considerable low-key lobbying for the prize post, and some intrigue. Morarji Desai threw his hat in the ring with indecent haste. Nanda kept a low profile. Jagjivan Ram entered the fray late. Shastri did not stake his claim at all.

The Congress President and his close associates wanted a consensus candidate, as an open contest would have created bad blood. This was not acceptable to Desai, as he considered it a violation of the democratic principle. On 31 May Kamaraj convened a meeting of the Congress Working Committee at which most of the Chief Ministers and other prominent leaders were also present. It was decided to authorize the Congress president to ascertain the preference of the partymen and then advise the CPP about a generally acceptable person as its leader. Kamaraj found that the candidate of his choice, Lal Bahadur Shastri, enjoyed overwhelming support. He gently conveyed his findings to Shastri, Morarji, Nanda, Jagjivan Ram and Mrs. Gandhi. Morarji quietly withdrew. Thus was solved the conundrum of 'after Nehru who?' without producing a ripple.

The Congress leaders showed remarkable maturity and restraint in tackling the question of succession. They were fully aware that the world was watching India and the country's image was at stake. So they made a determined effort to achieve unanimity in selecting the new leader.

After his election, Shastri also took good care not to ruffle any feathers. He retained Nehru's cabinet intact, and made his daughter, Indira Gandhi, minister of Information and Broadcasting to enlarge his base. Another new entrant to the cabinet was Sanjiva Reddy. S.K. Patil, removed under the Kamaraj plan, was also reinducted.

Shastri's smooth accession not only testified to the health of the Indian Republic, it led to its further democratization. Nehru was a colossus; he did not need anybody's support to become prime minister. Shastri, a meek, modest and amiable person, did not enjoy a position of predominance in the party. This not only promoted more equal discussion within the cabinet, but also greater autonomy to the state governments.

The closing years of Nehru saw the rise of a caucus which played a decisive role in shaping the course of events. Known as the 'Syndicate', its more prominent members were Kamaraj, party bosses Atulya Ghosh and S.K. Patil, Sanjiva Reddy, Chief Minister of Andhra Pradesh, and Nijalingappa, CM Karnataka (then Mysore). It was this caucus which met in Tirupati in October 1963 and decided that Shastri should be sponsored for Congress presidentship and, if he declined, then Kamaraj should fill the slot. Moreover, it was also resolved that Desai should be kept out at any cost. Although this caucus came to acquire a rather unsavoury reputation, it must be said to its credit that its members never gave precedence to personal ambition over the country's interests. In fact when persons with no stronger claims were manoeuvring to succeed Nehru, none of them aspired for the job. And it was largely owing to the efforts of the Syndicate that the proceedings for electing Nehru's successor were conducted with due propriety and dignity.

Despite all the rich experience and maturity that he brought to his office, Shastri's tenure was doubly jinxed. First, the last years of Nehru saw an overall deterioration in the economy. Agricultural production had become stagnant, industrial growth slowed down, and the balance of payments problem worsened. Pressures for devaluation were also mounting. Secondly, fate did not give him enough time to come to grips with these problems, as death terminated his regime after just nineteen months.

Endemic food shortages, leading to the spectre of famine in states like Kerala, haunted Shastri all along. It was not an overnight phenomenon; it had plagued Nehru as well in his later years. Investment in agriculture had remained inadequate, and populist socialistic postures inhibited the government from openly favouring the market forces.

But the situation became precarious owing to severe drought, and food production declined by 17 percent during 1964-66. This resulted in widespread unrest, and the Communist Party of India launched a nationwide agitation. The government was subjected to severe criticism in parliament and there were loud rumblings within the Congress Party. Nearly 19 million tonnes of foodgrains had to be imported during this period and prices shot up by 32 percent. In November 1964, the government issued the Essential

Commodities (Amendment) Ordinance for summary action against hoarders and profiteers. But as the states did not want to alienate the traders, the main source of party funds, hardly any action was taken under the Ordinance.

On the advice of the Planning Commission, Shastri agreed to create the Food Corporation of India with a mandate to start open-market procurement from January 1965. But there were hardly any arrivals owing to drought, and even the buffer stock built up by the import of four million tonnes of foodgrains under PL-480 got depleted. Further, America suspended all aid as a reaction to the Indo-Pak war. Thus, driven to the wall, the Central government was compelled to introduce statutory rationing in the larger urban centres.

One incidental fallout of the food crisis was that the country was forced to explore all avenues to increase agricultural output. This led to the rapid and extensive introduction of high-yielding varieties of seeds and the adoption of a package of new agricultural practices. C. Subramaniam pursued this approach with great vigour, and it was this path which ultimately led to food self-sufficiency.

Perennial language controversy was another crisis that hit the Shastri government. Unthinkingly, the Home Ministry issued a circular on 25 October 1964 asking various states to report progress made in promoting the use of Hindi, and directed the Central Secretariat Offices to correspond in Hindi with Hindi-speaking states from 26 January 1965. This was seen as another attempt by the Hindi chauvinists to impose their language on the South, and it led to extensive agitation in Tamil Nadu. There were language riots and firings, claiming many lives. Two of Shastri's cabinet ministers, Subramaniam and Alagesan, resigned in protest.

Despite the explosive nature of the situation, Shastri moved slowly and hesitantly. Ultimately, a compromise solution, based broadly on S.K. Patil's formula, was devised. It gave each state the freedom to use English in communicating with other states or the Centre; English was to be used for official purposes by the

Government of India, and the Union Public Service Commission examinations were to be conducted in English and all the national languages listed in the Constitution. A three-language formula was to be introduced in all the states, and a programme for phased development of Hindi drawn up. But owing to the intervention of Indo-Pak war the proposed amendment could not be taken up during Shastri's lifetime.

Shastri had known poverty in his childhood and his sympathies were with the underdog. But in his outlook he was a conservative. When he came to office, there were acute food shortages, foreign exchange was scarce, unemployment was on the rise and the economy in a bad shape. Consequently, India's experiment in planning did not hold much appeal for him.

Shastri began by cutting the Planning Commission to size. Earlier, its members enjoyed indefinite tenure. Now they were given a fixed term. Then, the practice of the Cabinet Secretary acting as ex-officio secretary to the Planning Commission was discontinued. More importantly, Shastri started dealing directly with various ministries, and associated the Vice-Chairman of the Commission only when necessary. He gave a much greater say to the chief ministers and the National Development Council in the process of plan formulation. He constituted a National Planning Council of Experts where only the Deputy Chairman of the Commission was represented.

Two other developments led to a further decline of the role of the Commission. Firstly, the creation of Prime Minister's own Secretariat headed by the eminent civil servant L.K. Jha. He was an expert in economic matters in his own right and favoured market economy. Secondly, Ashok Mehta, the Vice Chairman, Planning Commission, who did not have the rank of a minister, carried little weight.

The Draft Fourth Plan (1966-71) was submitted to the 22nd meeting of the National Development Council in September 1965. There were serious differences of approach to the raising of agricultural production between the Ministry of Food and the Planning Commission. But the government was saved the dilemma of making hard choices by the intrusion of the Indo-Pak war, and Shastri told the Commission to recast the Plan in view of the greatly enhanced defence requirements.

The Indo-Pak conflict of 1965 was a barren, purposeless and ruinous exercise, and it developed slowly over a period of eight months. It started as a border skirmish in the Rann of Kutch, an undemarcated, marshy tract in Gujarat State. The Rann's main attraction for the two countries was the belief that there existed oil reserves under its swamps.

In 1960 the Indian forces had repelled some Pakistani troops from this area. Later, in 1965 it was discovered that Pakistan had built a heavy-vehicle road in this region which passed over a small tract of Indian land. (This was not the first time that the Indian intelligence made such a discovery after the event!) Occasional incursions from across the border had also resulted in the occupation of Indian territory around Kanjarkot. When India asked for the withdrawal of Pakistani forces from the area, there was a direct armed confrontation in which the Indian troops suffered some reverses. As Shastri was unwilling to escalate this border skirmish into a war, he accepted the UN offer to refer the dispute to a three-member tribunal, thus conceding that the territory in question was a disputed area. The tribunal awarded a sizeable chunk of the Rann to Pakistan.

But this was only a prelude to full-scale action on three fronts. To begin with, Pakistan repeated the old trick of sending armed infiltrators into Kashmir through passes in the Uri sector. It was the loyalty of two Kashmiri Muslims whose timely information led to the detection of this incursion and consequent retaliation by the Indian army. The threat from this front was neutralized when Tithwal and Haji Pir, two crucial passes on the border, were occupied by India and the intruders pushed beyond the boundary line.

The second front opened with a massive Pakistani assault in the Chhamb sector of Jammu on 1 September. Here the Indian forces were clearly outnumbered and outmanoeuvred, and there arose an imminent threat to the Poonch-Rajouri Road, which linked Kashmir to the rest of India. It was at this stage that Shastri decided on an all-out war and the Indian army opened the third front with a three-pronged attack on Pakistan. Initially the army advanced all along the line, and in one area it reached the outskirts of Lahore. Then there were some ding-dong battles, stalemate and reverses.

With UN intervention, a cease-fire was declared on 23 September and both sides were required to withdraw to positions held before 5 August. But Pakistan declared that she will withdraw her troops only if the Kashmir problem was also simultaneously settled.

The stalemate continued till Alexi Kosygin, the Soviet Prime Minister, offered his good offices to help work out a mutually acceptable via media. Ayub Khan, the President of Pakistan, and Shastri met at Tashkent in the first week of January 1966 and signed the Tashkent Declaration after a lot of hard bargaining. Both sides agreed to withdraw their forces as per the UN resolution and pledged to observe the 'principle of non-interference in the internal affairs of each other.' Any hope of its promoting good neighbourly relation was snuffed out with Shastri's death from a heart attack within a few hours of its ratification.

This war did not result in an iota of gain for either party. Even the military honours were evenly divided. But the leaders and the media of both India and Pakistan projected it as a glorious victory for their respective countries. And it turned overnight the shy and timorous Shastri into a national hero. It is quite likely that in pursuance of the Tashkent Agreement, the handing back of Tithwal and Haji Pir to Pakistan would have raised a storm back home. But this eventuality was submerged under a wave of national mourning for a man whose basic goodness and sincerity of purpose were never in doubt.

The manner of Shastri's accession to power led to decentralization of the polity. The states and the party regained some of their lost power and prestige. The Central cabinet and the ministries functioned more democratically. But the change came about all too suddenly, and this created problems of adjustment. The chief ministers started pursuing narrow, parochial policies which were detrimental to the country as a whole. Whereas some states were faced with famine, the surplus states refused to mop up excess foodgrains from large producers through compulsory levy. Traders, hoarders, and profiteers had a field day. It was with much difficulty that statutory rationing could be introduced in urban areas, and modest foodgrain stocks built through levy.

This situation highlighted the tricky nature of decentralization in the Indian context. Concentration of power at the Centre robs the states of their initiative. But devolution encourages parochial and fissiparous tendencies which pose a threat to the country's stability. The solution obviously lies in fine-tuning a balance through trial and error, which had not been attempted so far.

Shastri's economic policies and approach to agricultural production marked a break with the past. He favoured a much greater role for the private sector, encouraged foreign collaborations and adopted a more accommodating attitude towards the USA. As to increased food production, he favoured his Food Minister's policy of introducing high yielding varieties of seeds, backed up by imported fertilizers and pesticides, and dependable irrigation facilities. As only well-to-do farmers could afford this package, he was obviously 'betting on the strong.'

What was Shastri's lasting impact of the polity? His brief, 19-month tenure provides a plausible alibi for his inability to solve any of the serious problems that he had inherited from Nehru. His moves towards decentralization of polity and liberalization of economy were reversed by his successor. But on one vital issue the initiative taken during his time produced lasting results. That was the new agricultural policy which ushered in the Green Revolution and made India self-sufficient in foodgrain production. But Shastri did not live to get the credit for this long-gestation scheme, and Indira Gandhi became its main beneficiary.

Indira Gandhi

21

Born to Rule

$\mathcal{O}$n the eve of her election as the Prime Minister, Indira Gandhi wrote to her son Rajiv in London,

'How hard it is from being a king,
When it is in you and the situation?'

This impromptu recall of Robert Frost's verse when various aspirants were still fighting out their grim battle for succession shows how she perceived her position: it was in her to be the 'king'!

When Shastri included her in his cabinet, she was a complete novice holding a junior charge. Yet Indira never recognized his authority as her boss.

Shastri sent T.T. Krishnamachari and Indira Gandhi to attend the Commonwealth Prime Ministers Conference in July 1964. When she was still in London, Shastri shed Foreign Minister's charge and gave it to Swaran Singh. Mrs. Gandhi told a pressman, "Should he not have consulted me and Krishnamachari? I do not want the job. But surely I should have been consulted."[1] Later, when she was attending a UNESCO conference in Paris in October 1964, the Soviet Premier Krushchev was replaced by Kosygin. She wanted to hop across to Moscow, but the ministry of External Affairs opposed the move. Yet she went there all the same, and was the first Asian leader to felicitate the new Premier.

Indira behaved as a national level trouble-shooter and air-dashed all over India to handle complex issues on her own. In early 1965, when language riots broke out in Tamil Nadu, she reached Madras promptly, leaving Shastri and Kamaraj twiddling their thumbs in Delhi. Shastri told friends that 'Indira was exceeding her brief and indeed jumping over the Prime Minister's head.' When a journalist asked for her reaction to this remark, she flared up and said that she did not look upon herself as a 'mere' minister but as one of the leaders of the country. "Do you think the government can survive if I resign today? I am telling you it won't. Yes, I have jumped over the Prime Minister's head and I would do it again whenever the need arises."[2]

Later, in August, when she landed in Srinagar for a holiday, there were reports of Pakistani infiltrators invading the Valley. She was advised to go back. Instead, she stayed put, asked the chief minister of Punjab to send police reinforcement, visited the troops, organized citizen's committees, and went to Srinagar twice again to help the war effort.

Mrs. Gandhi openly censured Shastri on several occasions for not following the Nehruvian line. While addressing the Congress Socialist Convention in October 1964, she warned against "the danger of the Congress sliding away from the socialist path," and stressed the need to "rescue the party from those who do not believe in its policies." And she told a journalist in November 1965 that after Nehru's death "India had swerved from the right path," and "socialism and non-alignment are being forgotten."[3]

Mrs. Gandhi was a very cautious person and seldom criticized anybody openly. But here she was lambasting her own Prime Minister, committing gross breach of cabinet discipline, openly, repeatedly, aggressively. She could not have done it on an impulse; she was certainly conveying a message through these improprieties.

With the sudden death of Shastri at Tashkent, Indira Gandhi heard opportunity knocking at her door. She had all along feigned indifference to ministerial office. Now the time for dissimulation was over. But having closely watched the manoeuvres that preceded Shastri's accession and the way Morarji Desai had ruined his prospects by indecent haste, she held back her horses. In any case, the initiative had to come from other quarters; her job was to guide the flow of events in her direction. And this she did with a degree of finesse, restraint and poise which foreshadowed the shape of things to come.

The Syndicate, as in Shastri's case, tried to be the king-maker again. But unlike the earlier occasion, there was no panic about inducting the new incumbent. If Nehru's succession caused no serious problem, Shastri's would not.

As the Prime Minister's office could not remain vacant, G.L. Nanda, the seniormost cabinet minister, was sworn in as the successor. The final choice, of course, was to be made by the Congress Parliamentary Party (CPP). S.K. Patil wanted Nanda to continue at least till the next general election to be held in 1967. Atulya Ghosh campaigned for the election of Kamaraj. Biju Patnaik and Jagjivan Ram favoured Morarji Desai.

In all this confusion, only one man knew his mind, and moved towards his goal like a soft-footed cat. That was Kamaraj. When he left for Delhi to attend Shastri's funeral, R. Venkataraman, Industry Minister in Tamil Nadu, was travelling with him. He told the latter, "We will have Indira as the Prime Minister." And after a pause, "She knows all the world leaders, has travelled widely with her father, has grown up amongst the great men of the freedom movement, has a rational and modern mind, is totally free of any parochialism — state, caste or religion."[4]

This was as fair and objective an assessment as could be. But he was not in total control of the situation. He had to gently coax and guide various groups and lobbies to accept his view. And he could not make it very explicit, lest there was a backlash.

Nanda was sworn as PM on 11 January, and the CPP met on the 19th to elect its leader. For the first four or five days of this period there was low-key but hectic canvassing by different candidates. Nanda was the first to throw his hat in the ring. But he told Kamaraj that 'if he accepted second place in any cabinet, that would be one headed by Mrs. Gandhi.'[5]

Desai watched the developments for a couple of days. But when he spoke, he left nobody in doubt. 'It was obvious that I would be a candidate' he said. Morarji's high moral pretensions and rigid views were not the best recipe for winning friends. He also realized that if the decision was left to the party bosses, he had no chance. So he wanted the issue to be decided by the CPP through secret ballot.

Indira Gandhi never lobbied openly. But she was not sitting

idle either. Her moves were neatly calculated, well-timed and well
targeted. She met Kamaraj the day he reached Delhi, and also
apprised him about Nanda having approached her. The astute
Chanakya advised, "Just leave things as they are. I will consult
with many people."[6] Sometime later she told D.P. Mishra, the
Chief Minister of Madhya Pradesh and her staunchest supporter,
that "if there is near unanimity and Kamaraj asks me, I would
stand."[7]

As the situation developed, it became increasingly clear that
Mrs. Gandhi would be the winner. But she was a little concerned
owing to lack of support from Atulya Ghosh and S.K. Patil. She
sent P.C. Sethi, Deputy Minister for Steel, as her emissary to the
former, and Dinesh Singh, Deputy Minister for External Affairs,
to the latter. This was just to assure them that she cared for their
goodwill. And her debt to Kamaraj she publicly acknowledged
when she said, 'He has asked me to stay at home until he calls
me.'

Whatever other differences the Syndicate members may have
had, on one point they were agreed: Desai had to be kept out. He
would have been not only inconvenient but also irksome. So it
was crucial to select a candidate who could defeat Desai. Another
important factor was the person's ability to pull votes in the
coming elections.

Nanda was generally acceptable to all, but he could neither
worst Desai in an open contest, nor could he be much of a vote
catcher. Kamaraj himself was firmly opposed to enter the fray.
He repeatedly said that as he neither knew Hindi nor English, he
was unsuited for the job.

Thus, through a process of elimination, Indira Gandhi was the
only candidate to fit the bill. She was the one person who could
defeat Desai. And with her Nehru charisma, she was a truly
national-level leader and the best vote getter.

An important new element that influenced the course of events
was the clout exercised by the state chief ministers. On the earlier
occasion they were sidelined by the Syndicate. This time,
D.P. Mishra told his colleagues: why leave the responsibility
entirely to Kamaraj; we must share the burden. He was thus able

to mobilize the support of eight chief ministers for Mrs. Gandhi, and Kamaraj announced this to the press. This was a critical breakthrough for Indira, and a big psychological boost.

Mrs. Gandhi's chances steadily improved with time. Nanda threw in the towel and assured her of his support. Atulya Ghosh went to her to pledge his fealty. Jagjivan Ram was the last major leader to turn around. Sensing the direction of the wind, he ditched Morarji and told Kamaraj that he would support Mrs. Gandhi. The CPP met in the Central Hall of the Parliament on 19 January under Kamaraj's chairmanship. It took $4\frac{1}{2}$ hours to complete the exercise. As Satyanarain Sinha emerged from the Hall to announce the result to the eagerly awaiting pressmen, someone shouted. 'Is it a boy or a girl?' 'A girl', replied Sinha. Indira had polled 355 votes against 169 by Desai.

While taking the oath of office on 24 January Indira Gandhi did not 'swear in the name of God'; she 'solemnly affirmed'. This was to underscore her progressive, modernist image. She was keenly aware that her succession heralded a generational change.

But the past cannot be switched off with the flick of one's little finger. In the very first exercise after assuming office she realized how firm was the hold of the old manipulators. She could not constitute a cabinet of her choosing. Kamaraj ensured that most of Shastri's ministers were retained. She wanted to shift at least Nanda from Home Ministry; but even this she could not do. She was reluctant to give a cabinet berth to Jagjivan Ram, but yielded on this point also. She dropped Humayun Kabir and A.K. Sen, whose performance had been poor and who had no godfather to back them. Only three new cabinet ministers of her choice, i.e., Ashok Mehta, G.S. Pathak and Fakhruddin Ali Ahmed were inducted. Dinesh Singh was promoted and made Minister of State for External Affairs. Morarji Desai, who could not bear the thought of serving under Mrs. Gandhi, later agreed to be Chairman, Administrative Reforms Commission, with the rank of cabinet minister.

If she did not derive much satisfaction from cabinet formation, the conduct of government business could not have been more gratifying. As a minister under Shastri, she had given a poor account of herself. Things could not improve suddenly on her becoming the Prime Minister. Slips of paper had to be continuously passed on to her to answer questions and supplementaries. Still she repeatedly faltered and bungled. The opposition was none too indulgent to her, and Ram Manohar Lohia was not far wrong in calling her *goongi gudia* (dumb doll). Typical of this period was her performance at the AICC Session, Jaipur, held soon after she became PM. There was bitter controversy about the working of food zones. Even C. Subramaniam, the Food Minister, was roughly treated. Indira was literally pushed to the mike to defend her government's policy. But she dithered, forgot her brief and retreated. Ultimately Kamaraj stepped in and saved the day by assuring the members that the PM had already promised to reconsider the matter.

After Mrs. Gandhi had returned to Delhi, her close friend Pupul Jayakar called on her. In Pupul's words, "She was angry with herself. The shock to her self-image had devastated her. With hurt and bitterness, she began to speak of her aunt Vijayalakshmi Pandit. 'From my childhood' said Indira, 'she said everything to destroy my confidence; she called me ugly, stupid. This shattered something within me. Faced with hostility, however well prepared I am, I get tongue-tied and withdraw'."

After she had calmed down Pupul asked her as to what the three weeks of prime ministership had meant to her. Mrs Gandhi replied, "It is only three weeks? You know I am scared of the coming parliament session. I have no friends in the Cabinet."[8]

When Indira Gandhi became Prime Minister, she was one of the juniormost MPs, with little experience of handling parliamentary business. Being a shy and reserved person, she was unnerved when facing seasoned parliamentarians, quite a few of whom were hostile to her. The above instances of her diffidence and the position of total dominance she reached later are an index of her tremendous growth potential. Within three years she had become the undisputed leader both in and outside parliament. And it could not be otherwise in the case of a person who knew that it was in her and the situation to be the 'king'!

22

Shaky Start

*I*ndira Gandhi could not have chosen a worse time to become the Prime Minister. Immediately on accession, Nehru too had to contend with the aftermath of Partition. But there was the euphoria of Independence to sustain hope. Shastri's main challenge was to not to look puny in comparison to Nehru. But Indira had problems, problems, all the way, without a single redeeming feature in sight. Whereas Shastri could gloat over the make-believe victory of the Indo-Pak war, Indira was left with the management of its ruinous consequences. In 1965-67 severe drought ravaged the country. The food situation became so precarious that India had to live from 'ship to mouth'. There were rice riots in Kerala and the situation in food deficit states was volatile. In the North-East, Mizos and Nagas were up in arms. Akali agitation for the creation of a Punjabi-speaking state had reached a flash point with Sant Fateh Singh threatening to immolate himself. Hindu fanatics, demanding a ban on cow slaughter, were adopting ever more aggressive postures.

For a new incumbent these challenges were indeed unnerving. But the most urgent public issue was the sharp rise in prices. The consumer price index shot up by 14 percent in 1965-66 and showed no sign of abating. Industrial output and exports declined. Budgetary deficits increased, and the Fourth Plan faced drastic pruning.

This desperate situation called for drastic remedies. Mrs. Gandhi had no clue as to what to do. And her panic response to the crises was to jump out of the frying pan into the fire. Much before Indira appeared on the scene, there had been discussions on devaluation of the rupee. Sachin Chaudhary, the new Finance Minister, had little grasp of the matter. Ashok Mehta, C. Subramaniam, L.K. Jha, B.K. Nehru, all favoured this course.

They had sound professional credentials and their word carried weight. The argument that finally converted Mrs. Gandhi to their view was that without devaluation the international agencies would not give aid. And aid Indira could not do without.

The decision to sharply devalue the rupee by a whopping 36.5 percent was announced on 6 June, just $4\frac{1}{2}$ months after Mrs. Gandhi became PM. The public reaction was very adverse. It was roundly condemned by the press, the opposition, the intellectuals and her own party. The main thrust of the criticism was that this decision had compromised national honour as it was taken under external pressure. It was no secret that the USA had been arm-twisting India to devalue the rupee. Indira Gandhi, who had boasted of getting foreign aid without strings was accused of getting strings without aid.

As it turned out, the devaluation was a fiasco. None of the anticipated gains accrued. Exports grew at a measly rate of 2 percent per year between 1966-70. Whatever little prospect there was of revival, got aborted by another failure of monsoon. The 'most unkindest cut' was the American response. Only the first instalment of Rs. 150 crores out of the promised aid package of Rs. 675 crores was received.

Mrs. Gandhi was fully aware of having badly tripped and wrote in *My Truth* 14 years later, "... it (devaluation) was a wrong thing to do and it harmed us greatly."[1] She also gradually eased out Ashok Mehta, L.K. Jha, and other architects of this disaster. Unfortunately it further deepened her distrust of people, with baneful implications for her and the polity.

The state chief ministers and the Syndicate had backed Indira Gandhi as she seemed to have the widest appeal for the electorate. The fast-approaching general election in February 1967 was going to be her test by fire. In the formation of her cabinet, she had seen that it was the party bosses who called the shots. In the selection of party candidates also, she had little say in the matter. She could not get party nomination even for Krishna Menon. Several of her known supporters were denied tickets and some of them left the party. This taught Mrs. Gandhi the lesson that it is not enough to be a prime minister; one had to control the party apparatus as well to wield effective power.

Indira Gandhi mounted a spirited election campaign, covering most of the states and hundreds of constituencies. As there were no other national-level leaders, and the regional satraps did not have much of a mass appeal, she carried the main burden of electioneering all by herself. One incidental benefit of her exposure to large crowds was that she overcame her dread of public speaking and developed her own idiom for talking to the simple village folk. At an election meeting at Rae Bareilly she struck a professional note when she said, 'My family is not confined to a few individuals. It consists of crores of people. Your burdens are comparatively light, because your families are limited and viable. But my burden is manifold, because crores of my family members are poverty stricken and I have to look after them.'

It was at Bhubaneshwar that she was hit on the nose by a stone while addressing an angry gathering. Though she started bleeding, yet she stood firm and finished her speech, while pressing her injury with a handkerchief. Her courage and tenacity won her countrywide acclaim and this incident, in a way, baptized her as a tough fighter.

The meeting at Bhubneshwar was not the only hostile crowd she had to face, nor was she the only leader to confront it. Owing to high inflation and scarcity of foodgrains, the masses were generally disgruntled and agitated. Besides Indira, several other Congress leaders had to brave angry demonstrations. This was an ugly portent and a warning to Mrs. Gandhi to mend matters urgently.

If the election results came as a shock to Indira, they were traumatic for the Syndicate. In the parliamentary election the strength of Congress MPs dropped from 358 to 279 in a House of 520. Congress performance in the states was worse. Out of a total of 3453 assembly seats contested all over the country, the party won only 1661, i.e., less than 50 percent. For the Syndicate it was a wash-out. Kamaraj the king-maker lost in both constituencies from which he contested. Atulya Ghosh and S.K. Patil were defeated in their own states. Sanjiva Reddy and Nijalingappa were the only prominent Syndicate winners.

On the face of it, Indira's position in the parliament was much weakened owing to the loss of 79 seats. Moreover, several of the new Congress MPs owed allegiance to the Syndicate and could any time turn against her. On the other hand her moral standing had improved. When an interviewer asked her about the electoral reverses, she replied, "If you will notice there have been very selective defeats."[2] She was obviously referring to the Syndicate losses in different states. For her it was indeed a 'sweet defeat'.

Now that Indira was her own master, she formed a cabinet of her liking and showed the final list of ministers to Kamaraj at the last minute. Even Sanjiva Reddy was sidelined and made Speaker of Lok Sabha, the lower house of parliament. On Kamaraj's insistance she agreed to include Morarji in the Cabinet, but on her terms. He was made Deputy Prime Minister in-charge Finance Ministry with no special status.

Indira inherited a situation where single party dominance of the Congress both at the Centre and the states was complete. But the 1967 assembly elections changed the scene substantially. The Congress lost more than half the assembly seats in the country. Either through alliances or defections, the opposition parties were able to form ministries in eight states by the middle of the year. Thus half the country slipped out of the Congress fold. This was not a bad thing in itself. Single-party dominance since Independence had weakened the democratic forces. But the way it came about was calamitous. Opportunistic coalitions, called Samyukta Vidhayak Dals (united legislators' parties), were formed to gain power, and legislators were bought and sold like horses. In the first year after the elections 438 state legislators defected from one party to the other, and by March 1970 this figure had reached 1827. This was openly done either for lure of office or money. So quick was the shuffling of legislators in Haryana that it came to be known as the state of *aya Rams, gaya Rams*.

Constitutional provisions were flagrantly abused to subvert and destroy constitutional norms and procedures. The Speaker of the Punjab assembly, when faced with a no-confidence motion for his partisan role, repeatedly adjourned the assembly. In U.P. and Rajasthan there were serious charges of governors acting unconstitutionally at the behest of the Centre.

In the 1967 elections the rightist parties were the greatest gainers. Swatantra emerged as the largest opposition party in the parliament, with Jan Sangh as number two. Compared to 1962, the tally of the former increased from 18 to 42 seats, and that of the latter from 14 to 35. The leftist parties also registered impressive gains. The two communist parties were able to win 42 seats compared to 29 (pre-split) in 1962.

The results also showed that the state and the Central politics were moving on two separate planes. A notable feature of this phenomenon was the emergence of some strong regional parties, or national parties with a strong regional base. Dravida Munnetra Kazhagam (DMK) of Madras destroyed the political base of Kamaraj by reducing the Congress strength from 139 in 1962 to just 50 in 1967. It gained absolute majority in the assembly, renamed the state as Tamil Nadu, and since then the Congress has never come to power in that state. CPI(M) emerged as a major political force in both West Bengal and Kerala, and formed United Front ministries in both the states. But in West Bengal, the revolutionary zeal of the party cadres led to the undermining of civil administration through 'gheraos' (encirclement of factory managers), strikes and lawlessness. This resulted in the dismissal of the first Communist-led government in West Bengal and imposition of President's rule. The same bitter medicine had to be given to Bihar, Uttar Pradesh, Haryana and Punjab. Thus, within two years of her becoming the prime minister, Indira was faced with economic crisis, party dissensions, and political instability of unprecedented dimensions.

The odds that Indira Gandhi faced were formidable. Her capacity to handle them was still untested. Her limitations, as they came to the public notice, resulted from the strain of adjustment of a very private, shy and sensitive person to the challenges of public life. But her inexperience was mainly confined to the formal and procedural aspects of her job. So far as its substance was concerned, she had served a long apprenticeship under her father. Basically she had an amazing capacity to absorb experience. Once she had mastered the nitty-gritty of governance, she grew very fast and within five years acquired a greater hold over the polity of India than her father ever did.

In her *My Truth*, written 15 years after the event, Mrs. Gandhi said, "I think Mr. Kamaraj and others supported me just because they felt that I had the majority in the party, between Mr. Morarji Desai and myself." Gratitude has never been a failing of the Nehru clan. But in her election as Prime Minister, Mrs. Gandhi had good reasons not to burden herself overly with any sense of obligation towards the Syndicate or even Kamaraj. In fact she was to exhibit pretty soon a very different emotion towards these 'benefactors'.

23

The Master Strategist

*C*ommenting on the widening gulf between her and Kamaraj, Indira Gandhi told Pupul Jayakar, "... the fact is he wants to be Prime Minister. He has always wanted to be the Prime Minister."[1] A few months later, after her return from the Bhubaneshwar election meeting, she again told her friend, "Kamaraj is manoeuvring to see that the struggle between Morarji Desai and me becomes so acute that Kamaraj could step in as the concensus candidate."[2]

Human motives are seldom unmixed and several events of the Indira era can be interpreted variously. But nobody could accuse Kamaraj of having any ambition to be the prime minister. He was realistic and patriotic enough to realize that owing to basic limitations in his education, he was not suited for the job.

Secondly, it is equally certain that from the word go, Kamaraj wanted Mrs. Gandhi to be the Prime Minister, and he used all his astuteness to achieve this goal. Yet, pretty early in the day Indira Gandhi started suspecting him of having designs to succeed Shastri. For one thing, this was due to her inherent sense of insecurity and pathologically suspicious nature. For another, it was 'in the situation' that Indira and Kamaraj would fall out. The Syndicate had supported Indira in the hope that an inexperienced and diffident person like her would be a pliable ruler. But Indira had a very different view of her role: she was not prepared to share power.

Problems of adjustment surfaced soon after Mrs. Gandhi became PM. She did not have a free hand in forming her cabinet and could not even shift Nanda from the Home ministry. She was obviously piqued. And she showed her annoyance in several ways. She got an opportunity to put Nanda in his place when a huge procession of Hindu fanatics marched on Parliament House in November 1966, demanding a ban on cow slaughter. It broke into an unruly mob on confronting the security cordon. There was defensive firing, government and private property was damaged, and chaos prevailed. Nanda being the Home Minister in charge of law and order, and known for having a soft corner for *sadhus*, was sacked by the Prime Minister for incompetence.

The decision to devalue the rupee was a major policy issue and Indira did not take Kamaraj into confidence at the discussion stage. When she informed him about it at the last moment, he naturally felt ignored and slighted. In fact this was the decisive act which distanced Kamaraj from Indira. Their relations became so strained that when questioned about the forthcoming elections, she told a journalist on 25 December 1966, "Here is a question of whom the party wants and whom the people want. My position among the people is uncontested."3

Mrs. Gandhi was particularly annoyed at the Central Election Committee for having denied tickets to most of her supporters. And as the Congress fared poorly at the 1967 general election, there were charges and counter-charges from both sides. The election had hit the Syndicate particularly hard on two counts. First, most of the party bosses themselves lost at the polls. Secondly, Indira got elected as the prime minister on her own, without having to rely on the Syndicate for support. No wonder, then, that she did not consult Kamaraj while constituting her Cabinet. As if this was not enough of a rebuff, she successfully opposed his re-election as the party president after his second term expired in December 1968, though he was himself keen on another stint.

In this atmosphere of distrust and hostility, the traditional Congress approach to the resolving of differences through low key, back-room negotiations in a spirit of give and take was replaced by hostile postures and accusatory, populist rhetoric. Thus, every major issue became a pawn in the power game and led to friction. One of the first such problems was the election of the next President of the Republic when Dr. S. Radhakrishnan's tenure came to an end in 1967. The Syndicate favoured re-election of the

present incumbent. Indira opposed his renomination and preferred Dr. Zakir Hussain, the serving Vice-President and a highly
respected scholar. After some wrangling the Syndicate accepted
Mrs. Gandhi's proposal and Dr. Hussain got elected as the
President.

Poor performance in the 1967 elections had caused a lot of unease
among the senior leaders and Nanda submitted a paper on "Lessons of the General Election". He attributed the voter reaction to
the wide gap between the party's promises and performance. He
blamed the leadership for not having a common social outlook or
programme. This theme was taken up by the Congress radicals
and the old leadership was severely criticized. As a result of this
controversy the High Command adopted a resolution which came
to be known as the 10-Point Programme. The main features of
this agenda were: social control of banking, nationalization of
general insurance, public distribution of foodgrains through official agencies, curb on monopolies and concentration of economic
power, and removal of privileges of former rulers.

Indira Gandhi was in no tearing hurry to implement this mildly
leftist programme. In fact for the next two years, except for the
dust raised by the radicals called the Young Turks, almost nothing
was done about it. At the AICC session in June 1967, this group
got the clause for the removal of privileges enlarged to include
abolition of privy purses. The Syndicate members condemned this
change. Morarji called it a breach of faith. Mrs. Gandhi disapproved of the tactics used by the radicals, as most of the delegates
had left when the amendment was moved.

At the Jabalpur Congress session held in October 1967, the
socialists urged the leaders to accept nationalization of banks
instead of their social control. But in view of Desai's firm opposition, it was not approved. When the Young Turks became
vociferous about earnest implementation of the 10-Point
Programme, Indira came to the support of Morarji and advised
that nothing should be done to harm the Congress unity.

Election of the new Congress President at the end of 1967
reflected the latent antagonisms. Indira and Kamaraj had been

asked at the Jabalpur session to come up with a mutually acceptable choice. S. Nijalingappa, the chief minister of Karnataka,
emerged as the compromise candidate, though he was not keen
on the post.

Nijalingappa turned out to be less docile than Indira Gandhi
had expected. While preparing the list of the Congress Working
Committee members he did not consult her, and even ignored
her recommendation to include Dinesh Singh in the Committee.

The first sign of an open rift between the two groups appeared
in April 1969 at the Faridabad Congress session when the
members of the Congress Forum For Socialist Action demanded
immediate nationalization of banks. Desai aborted the move with
his strong opposition. But it was the broadside fired by the new
Congress President at the public sector which signalled the start
of open conflict. This censure created a commotion. Mrs. Gandhi
rebutted Nijalingappa's criticism in detail and emphasized the
need for higher investment in the public sector to achieve self-
reliance. The acrimonious exchanges may have continued further
but for the fire which consumed the huge tent under which the
delegates were assembled.

The basic conflict between Mrs. Gandhi and the Syndicate was
about the sharing of power. But as the controversy raged, it acquired the contours of an ideological divide. Political expediency
makes strange bedfellows. Morarji Desai, whom the Syndicate
had wanted to keep out at any cost, now became its darling.
Mrs. Gandhi's instinctive preference was for left of centre politics,
but she was no intrepid socialist. Things could have drifted for
years in the usual, muddled Congress fashion, except that the
hand of fate intervened. Dr. Zakir Hussain suddenly died of a
heart attack a few days after the Faridabad session. Both sides
immediately realized the significance of the event. In view of the
irreconcilable differences between the Syndicate and the Prime
Minister, the new President could play a crucial role. It was,
therefore, imperative to have one's own candidate in that office.

The Syndicate was keen to sponsor Sanjiva Reddy for the post
and started campaigning for him. Indira Gandhi kept her own

counsel. According to convention V.V. Giri, Vice-President, should have been elevated to this office. But neither the party bosses nor Mrs. Gandhi were keen on him. The reports reaching Indira indicated that efforts would be made to dislodge her after Reddy's election. In the absence of a consensus, the issue was left to the Congress Parliamentary Board (CPB) for decision in the Bangalore session, scheduled for 10-13 July 1969.

Aware of the need to present a progressive image, the draft of the official resolution incorporated the main recommendations of the Bhubaneshwar declaration and a promise to implement the 10-Point Programme. Mrs. Gandhi prepared her own note on Economic Policy which her emissary, Fakhruddin Ali Ahmed, placed before the Working Committee on 10 July, the first day of the session. Indira herself did not attend the meeting that day owing to 'indisposition'. She described her note as 'just some stray thoughts rather hurriedly dictated.' It reiterated some of the less radical proposals of the Forum and, contrary to the earlier under-standing, showed readiness to reopen the issue of bank nation-alization. There was nothing revolutionary in this note, and its populist slant was obvious. The Syndicate saw through the game, endorsed it in toto, and threw the ball back to Indira Gandhi, desiring the government to implement it expeditiously.

But the real battle was joined at the CPB meeting held on 12 July. Out of its eight members, Kamaraj, Patil, Desai and Nijalingappa were on one side, and Indira Gandhi, Jagjivan Ram and Fakhruddin Ali Ahmed on the other. Chavan was the flip-flop man about whose loyalty both the parties had doubts. It was he who had suggested Jagjivan Ram's name to Indira as her candi-date, and Mrs. Gandhi took it for granted that Chavan was with her. But he had actually struck a deal with the Syndicate that he would be made Deputy Prime Minister under Desai on Indira's ouster. When Mrs. Gandhi first learnt about Chavan's pact, she sent her emissary to him and was assured of his total loyalty. On the basis of repeated reports, Chavan was sounded thrice by Indira about his intentions and thrice she was assured that he was with her.[4]

In view of the lurking uncertainty Indira suggested that the issue may be decided at Delhi after fuller discussion. The Syndicate insisted on settling the matter in that very meeting. It proposed the name of Sanjiva Reddy. Mrs. Gandhi pleaded that it would fulfill Mahatma Gandhi's dream if an untouchable was made the President of India, and suggested the name of Jagjivan Ram. When the matter was put to vote, Chavan went with the Syndicate and Reddy won nomination as the official Congress candidate.

The outcome of this tussle was a big setback for Indira. She was boiling with rage and remarked after the meeting that the party bosses would have to face the consequences. Three days later, Nijalingappa recorded in his diary, "She has been taught a lesson now. Being wilful I feel she will do something hasty in a huff."[5]

The very next day Nijalingappa could have complimented himself on his perspicacity. Whether Mrs. Gandhi acted in a huff or not, she did act in a decisive manner. On 16 July she wrote to Desai, "I know that in respect to some of the basic issues that arise you entertain strong reservations and have your own views about the direction as well as the pace of change... in all fairness I shall not burden you with this responsibility in your capacity as Finance Minister, but should take it directly upon myself. I am advising the President accordingly." Simultaneously, the news was given to the press. Desai was indignant at the discourtesy shown to him and sent in his resignation.

In her Note on Economic Policy Indira Gandhi had only hinted at reconsideration of the earlier decision on social control of banking and taken no action on the radical demands of the Young Turks. Now she was suddenly seized with a revolutionary zeal and nationalized 14 of the largest banks on 21 July by a Presidential Ordinance. By doing this after Desai's exit, she also ensured that the entire credit for this popular measure went to her.

Earlier Mrs. Gandhi had prided herself on her pragmatism. Now it was ideology and principles all the way. The news of nationalization had an electrifying effect on the masses. Hordes of poor people from all walks of life came to her house to compliment her on this bold step. There were pro-Indira slogans and posters all over.

For Mrs Gandhi an important benefit of bank nationalization was that it established her socialist credentials. This prompted the Indian Left to pledge support to her. "We have allies in the Congress led by Mrs. Gandhi," said S.A. Dange, the veteran communist leader. Whereas the communists backed Indira to gain respectability by aligning with the ruling party, for Mrs. Gandhi this support proved decisive in the coming contest.

Regarding the Presidential election, the moment Giri learnt that his claim had been ignored, he sprang a surprise by resigning from the office of acting President and declaring his intention to contest as an independent candidate. If the Syndicate had not opted for him, Indira too did not fancy him. However in the current situation Giri's move provided a promising opening to Indira, though she did not yet know how to exploit it.

As the Parliamentary Board had approved the nomination of Sanjiva Reddy, he had become the official Congress candidate. Under pressure from the Syndicate Mrs. Gandhi agreed to file his nomination papers. This was the one tactical mistake she made in this entire game.

Technically, having herself sponsored Reddy's nomination as the official candidate, Mrs. Gandhi had tied her own hands. Now her problem was to somehow get out of this bind. And here the club-footed Nijalingappa committed a fatal blunder and played into her hands. In his over-eagerness to canvass support for Reddy, he started talking to various opposition parties and, in the process, approached the Jan Sangh and Swatantra also.

Indira Gandhi's main charge against the Syndicate had been that this caucus of old party bosses was a conservative and reactionary group, and it was they who stood in the way of her introducing progressive and pro-poor reforms. After Nijalingappa's ill-conceived move she accused him of forging an unholy alliance with communal and reactionary elements. When the Syndicate insisted upon her issuing a whip to the Congress legislators to vote for Reddy, she wrote to Nijalingappa:

It is a matter of deep anguish ... that attempts are now being made at the highest level in the party to compromise with political parties totally opposed to our principles and accepted programmes. Elections are a medium to fight for our values and voting is a process of association with these values. I cannot think of winning election by clouding principles. I do not think therefore that in these circumstances it would be right for me to have a whip issued.

Seldom has self-interest and expediency been clothed in such noble sentiments. Indira would rather that the party candidate lost than that the party values were sacrificed. But at the operational level Mrs. Gandhi still felt awkward in directly opposing Sanjiva Reddy whose nomination papers she had filed. So, she devised a circuitous approach. Jagjivan Ram and Fakhruddin Ali Ahmed, both members of CWC, wrote to the Congress President that his talks with Jan Sangh and Swatantra had tarnished the party's image and this may have grave repercussions on the presidential election. The letter was delivered at midnight and simultaneously released to the press so that it may be published in the morning papers without the recipient having had time to issue a rejoinder. When Nijalingappa protested, a still more belligerent letter was sent to him on the same lines.

As the exchange of these midnight missives escalated, a group of Congress MPs started a signature campaign to permit them free voting in the presidential election as the Congress mandate had been compromised. Matters reached a climax when two days before the election, on 14 August, the CPB appealed to the Congress legislators to vote for Reddy, and the next day Indira openly told them to vote according to their conscience. She wrote to Nijalingappa:

> Instead of enlightening us about your talks with the leaders of the other parties and any understanding you might have reached with them to get their support, you have sought to assure me that you are not going to topple my government ... I must record a strong protest at this attempt to inject power politics into a discussion involving fundamental issues. I need no personal assurance, nor do I seek to retain office at all cost.

So, it was a battle for principles and issue-based politics; it had nothing to do with power or office!

The presidential poll was held on 16 August in an atmosphere of hostility and bitter controversy. The results, declared on the 20th showed that V.V. Giri had polled 4,20,077 votes against 4,05,427 secured by Reddy. The scales in favour of Giri were tilted by the bloc vote of the Communists, Socialists, DMK, a section of the Akalis and Independents. A windfall for Giri was the promise of support by Charan Singh, the President of Bharatiya Kranti Dal in the UP assembly.

The victory of Indira Gandhi's candidate did not bring the faction feud to an end. Actually, now the antagonists were poised for a fight to the finish. The Congress High Command could not sit back and quietly swallow the humiliation of such a blatant flouting of its dictates. And Indira considered it imperative to establish her control over the party, as without it she could not have a free hand.

Now that the two sides were aiming at each other's jugular, there was no room for niceties. So events moved fast towards the tragic denouement. As Indira emerged victorious, Congress MPs from the Syndicate camp started defecting to her side. A solid block of 42 communist MPs was already backing her, and a number of Independents pledged their loyalty to her. Chavan also abandoned the Syndicate, though his group in Maharashtra had voted for Reddy.

The Party bosses realized that they would lose further ground if they did not seize the initiative. Sixty MPs demanded action against Indira Gandhi and others for opposing the party candidate. Nijalingappa sent a show cause notice to her, Jagjivan Ram and Fakhrudin Ali Ahmed to explain their misconduct. A meeting of the Working Committee was fixed for 25 August to consider the issue.

As a head-on collision seemed unavoidable, Chavan initiated last minute unity moves and associated C. Subramaniam with his efforts. At the CWC meeting Nijalingappa agreed to withdraw the show cause notices against Mrs. Gandhi and others, and the Indira faction withdrew the allegations against Nijalingappa. This time again Indira had the better of the Syndicate: whereas the withdrawal of charges against Nijalingappa had no meaning after the event, the dropping of show cause proceedings against her and others was a real gain.

The truce was fragile as it tackled none of the basic points of the conflict. To put an end to this war of attrition the Indira camp started a signature campaign to requisition an emergency meeting of the AICC to elect a new Congress president and Working Committee. With the requisite number of signatures collected by the requisitionists, Nijalingappa was obliged to convene the Working Committee meeting for 1 November to consider their request. As the vilification campaign against the Syndicate escalated, Nijalingappa sent a strong protest to Mrs. Gandhi on 28 October, alleging:

> You have made personal loyalty to you the test of loyalty to the Congress and the country. All those who glorify you are progressives... the bait and threats that the government can use are being used freely and openly to secure regimentation and personal loyalty.

Chavan having already moved over to Indira Gandhi, the Congress President was doubtful of commanding a majority in the CWC meeting. In a clumsy and indefensible move, he removed C. Subramaniam and Fakhruddin Ali Ahmed from the Committee on technical grounds just one day before the scheduled meeting.

As Mrs. Gandhi's faction was now reduced to a minority, she boycotted the CWC meeting and decided to convene a parallel Working Committee meeting of her loyalists. Thus, on 1 November there was the ludicrous spectacle of two CWC meetings being held simultaneously: the Syndicate bloc assembling at the official Congress party office at Jantar Mantar Road, and the Indira camp gathering at her residence. Interestingly, of the 21 members of the CWC, 20 were split equally between the two groups, and K.C. Abraham, the 21st member, shuttled between the antagonists to bring about a last minute patch-up. But his valiant efforts failed owing to the distrust and the rigid postures of the two sides.

As the Syndicate members started arriving at the Congress office, the Indira loyalists raised slogans against them and created unruly scenes by roughing them up. This was a prelude to the sort of mob politics that the country was to witness in ample measure in the days to come.

The upshot of these developments was a vertical split in the Congress. The Syndicate expelled Indira Gandhi from primary membership of the party on 13 November and asked the CPP to elect a new leader in her place. It was not Desai but Ram Subhag Singh who was elected to the post. On her side, Indira held a meeting of the party MPs the very next day. Majority of them turned up to assure her of their support. As the dust settled, it was seen that Mrs. Gandhi had a substantial edge over the Syndicate. Only 68 out of 284 Congress members of Lok Sabha and 46 of 150 Congress MPs of Rajya Sabha voted for the election of Morarji Desai as chairman of the party.

Having thus worsted the Syndicate, Mrs. Gandhi convened a meeting of the AICC on 22 November. About 440 out of a total of 705 elected members attended and passed a vote of no-confidence against Nijalingappa. Subramaniam was appointed as the interim president. As both sides claimed to be the real Congress, the press finally settled the issue by suffixing the letter 'R' (Requisitionist) to the Indira faction and letter 'O' (Organization) to the Syndicate Congress.

Organizationally, this split was the most momentous event in the 84-year history of the Congress — the largest mass-based party outside the Communist bloc. It marked the demise of the Congress culture of consensus and compromise. Now, one person's will to power steamrolled all opposition and established a style of politics which changed the face of the Indian polity. The mass upsurge, whipped up after the bank nationalization also introduced the dangerous practice of exposing volatile policy issues to the politics of the streets.

In one sense the Congress split was overdue. Nehru, despite his socialist professions, had failed to give a radical orientation to the government. To pull the country out of this morass it was necessary to have a clear polarization of forces, and a split in the dominant political party should have hastened this process. But despite all the rhetoric about norms and principles, the actual line-up of leaders of the two sides showed no ideological divide. For instance, Kamaraj was the odd man out in the Syndicate as his leanings were distinctly leftist. Ashok Mehta, Tarakeshwari Sinha and Sucheta Kriplani were not rightists. On the other hand, Jagjivan Ram and Fakhruddin Ali Ahmed were conservatives. So was C. Subramaniam. Of course, Indira Gandhi herself had socialist bias, and so had the members of the Congress Forum for Socialist Action. But Mrs. Gandhi's leftism seldom became a guide to her action. The split, being essentially a struggle for power, led to radicalization of politics only to the extent it helped Indira to consolidate her position.

But it did highlight Indira Gandhi's talents as a master strategist. Once her brilliant Principal Secretary, P.N. Haksar, had convinced her to shift the focus of conflict from personal to ideological issues, she fully exploited the advantage of this approach. The Bangalore session was the turning-point. She sent her Economic Policy Note to the CWC, but did not attend the first day's meeting. This gave her time to assess the reaction without getting involved in any argument. Moreover, as to the most controversial point in the note, she kept the escape door ajar by only showing her willingness to reopen the issue of bank nationalization. Once she was overruled in the Working Committee meeting and Reddy's nomination approved, Mrs. Gandhi moved fast. She sacked her Finance Minister, Desai, who had a pro-capitalist image, and then nationalized the banks. This was a master-stroke, though at that time she did not realize its full potential. It convinced the masses of her desire to use the wealth of the rich for the benefit of the poor. This was also the measure which persuaded the two communist parties to lend her whole-hearted support, which proved critical in Giri's election.

Yet a close look at the events does not provide any evidence of Mrs. Gandhi having worked out a neat, well-planned and long-term strategy in advance and then, to have executed it relentlessly, step by step. Most of the time her responses were crafted on the spur of the moment as contingencies arose. And till the end she tried to avoid risking a rupture. Her Note on Economic

Policy was only a sober reiteration of the accepted Congress agenda. When the Young Turks criticized Desai in the AICC for stalling bank nationalization, she rose to his defence. She tried to get postponed the fateful CWC meeting at Bangalore. She supported the unity resolution of Chavan and it was Nijalingappa who violated the compact. She had never planned to field Giri as her candidate, and till pretty late in the day did not know as to how to openly oppose the official nominee. Further, these instances also show that she was not the firm decision-taker which she is made out to be.

The reason why Indira outsmarted the Syndicate was her ability to better read the public mood and then devise stratagems to heighten and exploit it. Tactically, she was far more resourceful and nimble-footed. In fact it may be more correct to describe her as a master improviser than a master strategist. But, perhaps, all great strategists are first and foremost great improvisers and tacticians.

24

On the Crest

With the syndicate outmanoeuvred and her candidate installed as the President, Indira Gandhi's supremacy was complete. But she knew that the ground under her feet was rather slippery. A Prime Minister rules not with the blessings of the President but on her strength in the parliament. There she was quite vulnerable. It was with the support of 42 communist and 25 DMK MPs that she could muster a majority. And dependence on others was the one thing she found most galling to her pride.

Even otherwise, over 60 percent of the Congress legislators had voted for Sanjiva Reddy, despite all her populist postures. In the states the Congress MLAs were continuously defecting to the opposition parties, leading to the fall of the Congress ministries. Some of her advisers favoured immediate mid-term poll to rectify the imbalance. But, having closely watched the mechanics of three general elections under her father and conducted one herself, she knew better. Eighty percent of the electorate lived in the villages where vote banks were formed on the basis of caste and local influence. Mrs. Gandhi needed time to reach these formations through definite policy initiatives.

In the prevailing confusion and fluid situation, party loyalties had weakened and money power was being freely used to win over wavering MPs. Indira Gandhi now had the resources to play this game better than others. Also, her open invitation to all the ex-Congressmen and dissidents was attracting to her party all types of mercenaries. She therefore wanted to hurry slowly.

Indira devised a multi-pronged strategy to prepare the ground for an early election. Having nationalized the banks, she started several schemes for advancing loans to small entrepreneurs, farmers, etc. As she failed to push through the parliament a bill to abolish privy purses of the ex-rulers, she did this through a Presidential ordinance. She set up Monopolies and Restrictive Trade Practices Commission to check concentration of wealth in private hands. All these measures were widely publicized to reinforce her image as a progressive reformer.

To establish a direct rapport with the masses and convey the message of reforms to them, she toured the country extensively. When the Supreme Court struck down the Act on bank nationalization in February 1970, she turned it into a major election issue. It was cited as an instance of the obstacles placed in her way to transform society. Also, she hastily re-nationalized the banks through an ordinance so as not to lose the popular fallout from this measure.

Having done her spade work Mrs. Gandhi was now looking for a suitable opportunity to play her trump card. This was soon provided by another order of the Supreme Court, setting aside the Presidential ordinance abolishing privy purses of the princes. It was a good, populist issue and re-confirmed the designs of conservative elements to thwart people-oriented programmes. So, after a hurried cabinet meeting, she obtained the President's approval on 27 December 1970 to dissolve the Parliament and go in for a fresh poll.

From January to March, for seven weeks, Indira mounted one of those back-breaking 18-hour-a-day election campaigns for which she earned universal admiration. She empathized with the people's problems, told them all she wanted to do for them, and how entrenched interests had repeatedly foiled her attempts. Realizing the futility of opposing Indira Gandhi individually, the four opposition parties, that is, the Congress (O), Jan Sangh, Swatantra and Samyukta Socialist Party formed the high-sounding Grand Alliance to fight the elections collectively. Though this ill-assorted group could not agree on a common programme, it reached seat adjustments in respect of all but 76 parliamentary seats. The Alliance, obsessed by its own prejudices and petty concerns, made Indira the target of their attack and hurled personal abuse at her. Even more suicidal was their condemnation of her radical measures like bank nationalization and abolition of privy purses. She was accused of aligning with the communist forces and destroying democratic institutions. Their punch-line was 'Indira Hatao' (remove Indira) for all these sins.

None of the above points had any special appeal for the masses. Mrs. Gandhi never indulged in personal invective, and carried herself with dignity, which won her wide acclaim. As to 'Indira Hatao', she replied that the real issue before the country was 'Garibi Hatao' (remove poverty). Thus the Syndicate unwittingly gave her a most potent election slogan which she used to great effect.

Typical of Mrs. Gandhi's style was her two-track election campaign. The Congress (R) manifesto aimed at "the advance of socialism through democratic process," as also giving "scope to the private sector to play its proper role in the economy." After attacking "the vested interests and the business groups" who were opposing the government's economic policies, she stated that "further nationalisation of industry was not on the agenda." She wooed the rich on the promise of giving them "political stability and conditions of economic growth," and held out the hope of a better life to the poor.

The Grand Alliance's tactical blunder in making Indira their main target turned the election into a referendum on an individual who, at that time, was enjoying wide popularity. Mrs. Gandhi herself exuded confidence and when a journalist asked her as to what was the main election issue, she justifiably claimed, 'I am the issue.'

Though Indira was riding the crest of a popularity wave, the odds against her were formidable. Even the pre-split Congress had never secured 50 percent of the votes cast. This time the traditional wing of the party, the seasoned bosses and vote bank manipulators were all opposed to her. For the first time the main opposition parties had formed an alliance against the ruling party. Yet, when the election results came, they surprised her no less than her opponents. Her party got 352 seats in a House of 518. Equally gratifying for Indira was the crushing defeat of her rivals. Congress (O) won just 16 seats. The score of the two rightist parties, Jan Sangh and Swatantra, slumped from 80 in the previous parliament to 30 in the new one.

With her opponents routed and more than a two-third majority in the Lok Sabha, Indira was in complete control of the situation. Now she could enact any laws she fancied, amend the Constitution any way she liked. The presidents of state congress committees, the chief ministers and other party leaders had contributed little to her victory. It was now the party and the chief ministers who needed her charisma to gain power and legitimacy.

  The 1971 election also marked the exit of the old generation of Congressmen with their tiresome tales of jail terms undergone during the freedom movement. The younger generation had a more professional approach to politics and looked upon it as a vocation. It believed in enjoying the rewards of success without feeling squeamish about its lavish lifestyle. Also, as the winner takes all in politics, it became imperative to succeed, no matter what the means or the costs.

As various political parties were fighting their grim battle in the electoral arena, there was a catastrophe brewing across India's borders where East and West Pakistan were moving towards a head-on clash.

  Though East Pakistan constituted about 60 percent of Pakistan's population, the country's defence and civil services were completely dominated by her western counterpart. There was a lot of resentment in East Pakistan against this imbalance and Mujibur Rehman, leader of Awami League, mobilized mass anger into a popular movement. He prepared a Six-Point Charter, demanding complete autonomy for the eastern wing. This was rejected outright by the Pakistani rulers. But as Mujib's movement gathered momentum and the situation seemed to be getting out of hand, Field Marshal Yahya Khan, the President of Pakistan, took a chance and ordered election for the National Assembly. He hoped that no party would get a majority and then he would be able to play one leader against the other. But Mujib won 160 out of 313 seats and, thus, became eligible to form the government. This was not acceptable to Pakistan's ruling class.

In the end, Mujibur Rehman was arrested by Yahya Khan and martial law clamped on East Pakistan. The ruthless General Tikka Khan was appointed the Administrator, and he let loose a reign of terror the like of which had not been seen even during the medieval times.

India awoke to the gravity of the situation only when the victims of Tikka Khan's holocaust started flooding into West Bengal and the North-Eastern states. Indira was not only deeply concerned with the human aspect of the tragedy, the continuous pouring of millions of refugees put a heavy strain on the country's financial and administrative resources. As most of the refugees were Hindus, it also posed the danger of a communal backlash.

General Tikka Khan's barbarous offensive also gave rise to a determined resistance movement within the state. Mukti Bahini, a highly motivated guerilla force composed of young recruits drawn from all over gave the Pakistani army a harrowing time. It blew up bridges and railway lines, interrupted supply vessels and launched surprise attacks. The Indian paramilitary forces maintained a close liaison with Mukti Bahini. Special training camps were organized for its volunteers on the Indian side of the border, and much of its arms and equipment was also supplied by India.

India could not afford to remain a mere spectator of this upheaval on her borders. By November 1971 nearly 10 million refugees had poured into the country. Indira Gandhi realized the international repercussion of any hasty intervention. It would be interpreted as interference in a neighbour's domestic affairs. Pakistan had become friendly with both China and the USA, and at this precise moment was engaged in facilitating a rapprochement between the two enemies. There was a distinct possibility that in any armed conflict between India and Pakistan, these two countries would support the latter.

But Indira Gandhi also saw that the way things were developing, an armed conflict with Pakistan was becoming unavoidable. At the back of her mind must have been the unholy but delectable thought of doing to Pakistan what Jinnah had done to India. But she planned her moves with the utmost caution. She told the Lok Sabha as early as 27 March 1971, "In a serious moment like this the less we as a government say, I think the better it is." The same day she stated in the Upper House, "A wrong step, a wrong word, can have an effect entirely different from the one which we all intend."

Indira had to prepare the ground on both the home and the international fronts. She gave full freedom to her Defence Chiefs to express their views on the subject. She also gave the defence forces adequate time to gear up and get ready for action. But she stipulated that it would have to be a blitzkrieg, as a prolonged combat would create international complications and bring outside players into the field.

In view of the apprehension that foreign powers may come to Pakistan's help, Indira signed a twenty-year Treaty of Peace, Friendship and Cooperation with the USSR in August. The Treaty was widely hailed in India. It was not only a morale booster for the country, but also had a sobering effect on China, especially in view of the border dispute she was having with the USSR.

During these months Mrs. Gandhi kept writing to the world leaders about the situation developing on India's borders. In September she visited Moscow for a frank discussion on the issues involved. On 4 October she went on a 21-day foreign tour and visited Germany, France, Britain, the UK, Belgium and the USA. The approach everywhere was to arouse the world conscience to the merciless butchering of the civilian population in East Bengal and the problems created by the influx of millions of refugees into India. She also emphasized that her country would not start a war, though she was not scared of it either.

Owing to Tikka Khan's savagery, the flow of refugees kept rising. Pakistan also took offence to direct Indian assistance to Mukti Bahini. Despite all the provocations, Mrs. Gandhi behaved with patience and restraint. She permitted the establishment of a government in exile by the Awami League near Calcutta, but did not accord any formal status to it. Later, as the opposition's demand for action became more strident, she told a public meeting in August, "There are some in this country who are attempting to make political capital out of the Bangladesh issue... This is no occasion for irresponsible action ... the government will take any such step (recognition of Bangladesh) only after careful consideration of all aspects of the question."

Meantime, sniping from across the border intensified and General Niazi, the Pakistan military commander, threatened in October that "the war would be fought on Indian territory." On 25 November Yahya Khan boasted that "in ten days I may not be here in Rawalpindi — but off fighting a war." It was only at this stage that Indira Gandhi formally asked the Indian troops to chase the Pakistani intruders across the border, and that too in self-defence.

Ultimately Pakistan's impatience and bluster got the better of her discretion. On 3 December 1971, she launched a pre-emptive strike in the western sector by attacking eight airfields from Srinagar to Barmer. These were hastily planned raids and inflicted hardly any damage on the Indian Air Force. But by attacking India Pakistan relieved Mrs. Gandhi of the odium of starting the war. Mrs. Gandhi, who was in Calcutta at that time, dashed back to Delhi and in a midnight broadcast appealed to the nation to fight valiantly in the 'war forced on us.' The President declared a state of Emergency and India recognized the independent state of Bangladesh on 6 December.

After the initial Pakistani air-strikes, the Indian counter-attacks gave a severe blow to the Pak Air Force. But in the western sector the Pakistani forces, armed with the latest American weaponry and in high spirits, inflicted heavy damages on the Indian troops in the Chhamb sector. The Indian army soon recovered lost ground, and fighting erupted in several parts along the western border.

In this war the Indian Navy's performance was spectacular. It attacked and sank the Pak submarine Ghazi off the Vishakhapatnam harbour, and launched a surprise attack on Karachi, the premier port of Pakistan. Several ships were sunk, oil dumps in the city set ablaze and the city itself thrown in disarray. In the eastern sector, Indian aircraft carrier Vikrant attacked the two major ports of Khulna and Chalna and blocked Pakistan army's escape route to the sea.

The real scene of action, of course, was the eastern sector. Here India was on the go right from the start. Pakistan had to fight the Indian army from outside and the east Bengali insurgents from within. Ably assisted by the air force, the Indian army rapidly advanced towards Dacca, avoiding direct contact with Pak troops by skirting around the cities where they were concentrated.

As the campaign was proceeding according to plan, the USA tried to throw a spanner in the works. She had already stopped all aid to India, and four days after the war started Nixon ordered the US Seventh Fleet to proceed towards Bay of Bengal. But Indira did not panic and chose to ignore the threat. America had hoped that the presence of her fleet in the Indian ocean would encourage the Chinese to venture forth. But China was obviously not prepared to go that far in support of her friend.

The USSR gave all possible moral and material support to India and ordered her fleet to sail from Vladivostok to meet the challenge of the US armada. She also vetoed two anti-Indian resolutions moved by the US in the Security Council, though America was able to get through the UN Assembly a resolution calling for immediate cease-fire and withdrawal of troops.

Meantime, India had got the upper hand in both the western and eastern sectors. With the Pakistani defences collapsing fast and the Indian army racing towards Dacca, an ultimatum was served on the Pak commander Niazi on 13 December to surrender by the 16th. The instrument of surrender was signed that day in Dacca.

While the country was exulting in this victory, Indira Gandhi played another ace. The very next day after the surrender she declared a unilateral cease-fire. Several of Mrs. Gandhi's advisers wanted her to drive home the advantage by pulverizing the Pakistani defence forces. But her ambitions were not territorial.

She had gained her objective and now wanted to show the world that she was neither vengeful nor expansionist. Also, further pursuit of war would have invited UN sanctions and American reprisals. Even the Soviet Union did not want her to proceed further.

It was Mrs. Gandhi's superb leadership qualities, her uncanny sense of timing and the meticulous preparations made for the campaign that enabled India to completely knock out the Pak war machine. She gave maximum weight to the advice of her military commanders and did nothing in panic. The execution of this campaign stands in marked contrast to the confused, ill-planned and amateurish manner in which the India-China war was fought in 1962.

This magnificent victory made Indira Gandhi the unrivalled leader of her people. Even the opposition parties lauded her and Atal Behari Vajpayee of Jan Sangh hailed her as Durga, the Hindu goddess of power. It was also a commendable achievement to have promptly sent back the ten million refugees to Bangladesh. Thirdly, though unexpressed, it was a matter of great satisfaction for Mrs. Gandhi and the Indians that Pakistan, their implacable foe, was broken and maimed. This was the clearest refutation of Jinnah's two-nation theory. Lastly, this victory altered the power balance in South Asia, with none left in the region to challenge India's supremacy.

Magnificently victorious, decorated with Bharat Ratna, riding the crest of the wave, Indira Gandhi reached the pinnacle of glory and public adulation which few mortals had ever known.

25

The Downhill Slide

*1*971 was unquestionably the year of Indira Gandhi. From a stunning electoral victory to the magnificent triumph in the Bangladesh war, she zoomed to the peak of glory. But a peak is an unsteady perch. And she soon rolled back on a steep gradient into the morass of intractable problems. These were partly inherent in the objective conditions then prevailing, and partly they were of her own creation.

The economy was certainly in a bad shape. The burden of feeding 10 million refugees for months had been a severe financial strain. It had also depleted the overflowing granaries. The war had been no less a financial drain. In 1972 the monsoon failed, resulting in a shortfall of 15 million tonnes of foodgrains compared to the previous year. Next year again there was drought and, actually, the lean period extended upto 1975. This naturally led to a drop in power generation and a slowing down of industrial growth. Then there was the oil-shock of 1973 when the OPEC suddenly raised the price of crude fourfold.

With half the population living below the poverty line and unemployment steadily on the rise, the Indian polity had inbuilt elements of instability. Added to this was the burden of a war and drought, making the situation even more precarious. But this was not the first time that the Indian economy was faced with a crisis. What made matters grave was the political management of the country.

Mrs. Gandhi had learnt three lessons from her experience of the 1967 elections and encounter with the Syndicate. First, she must control the party organization if she was to gain full sway over the government. Second, the state chief ministers should not be allowed to become independent centres of power. And third, she must acquire personal control over party funds so as not to look to others for financing elections and other political activities. With this three-pronged strategy she could not only become a supreme ruler in her own right, but make everybody else dependent upon her for survival and support.

After the creation of Bangladesh and the prompt return of all the refugees, the first major task facing her was the holding of the state assembly elections. The Congress again swept the polls, securing 70 percent of the seats contested. Every other party got a drubbing except the CPI which had gone in for seat adjustments with the Congress. The Swatantra and the Congress (O) were wiped out. In its stronghold of West Bengal, CPI(M) got only 14 seats as against 111 won in the previous election.

After the split the party organization lay prostrate at Indira's feet : the Congress president and the Working Committee members were all her nominees. As to the taming of the state Congress committees, she superseded them in the problem states and appointed ad hoc committees in their place. This was done with the ostensible purpose of revitalizing the party apparatus. The Congress election manifesto had stressed the need for "organizational support to the Government in carrying out reforms at the grassroots level." To give substance to this promise, Mrs. Gandhi started the long-drawn process of organizational elections in December 1972. She was flooded with complaints of malpractices, corruption, enrolment of bogus members, etc. Consequently the elections were cancelled midway and ad hoc committees appointed instead. Never again did she undertake this exercise during her long years in power.

Mrs. Gandhi replaced four senior chief ministers with an independent base by much younger persons. They were Mohan Lal Sukhadia of Rajasthan, Brahmanand Reddy of Andhra Pradesh. S.C. Shukla of Madhya Pradesh and M.M. Choudhary of Assam. They were replaced by Barkatullah Khan, Vengal Rao, P.C. Sethi and S.C. Sinha, respectively. These incumbents were not only junior politicians without much following, they owed their office entirely to Mrs. Gandhi's munificence. This was only the beginning of a trend that established a set pattern for the selection of chief ministers.

In the Central cabinet also changes were made to promote loyalists and downgrade influential ministers. Babu Jagjivan Ram had a solid, independent base among the Scheduled Castes, and wielded considerable influence in Bihar politics. Indira started building up L.N. Mishra, her fund raiser and a junior leader from Bihar, as a counter weight to him. Later he was raised to full cabinet rank as Railway Minister. She also inducted Bhola Paswan, another Scheduled Caste leader from Bihar, as a cabinet minister. Uma Shankar Dixit, an old family loyalist, was given charge of Home Ministry, politically the most important portfolio. D.K. Barooah, another faithful, was also given a cabinet berth.

Along with establishing total command over the party organization and political executive in both the states and the Centre, she also ensured that never again would her style be cramped for shortage of funds. Even during Nehru's time money was collected for party work and elections. But he himself never got involved in the exercise. Sardar Patel, Rafi Ahmed Kidwai and S.K. Patil were his prominent fund raisers. But Indira centralized donations to the party and herself supervised the operation. Dinesh Singh, Minister of State for Commerce, was her first important fund collector. Then came in the much smarter L.N. Mishra. Later several other wheeler-dealers got into the act, and filling the party coffers became a highly visible and much talked-about activity.

Indira Gandhi was perceptive enough to realize that her three-pronged strategy to secure her flanks may neutralize challenges from within the party and the government, yet her real battle was to be fought in the public arena. On the eve of 1971 elections Indira Gandhi had promised to introduce radical reforms to remove poverty and reduce excessive income disparities. Indira's own political instinct also indicated that the masses would be with her if she adopted a socialistic stance. Consequently she embarked on a radical programme — the only such undertaking in her political career.

It was not just her perceptions which led her on to this course;

the availability of a set of brilliant leftist advisers was a major factor. P.N. Haksar replaced L.K. Jha as her Principal Secretary in May 1967, and was largely responsible for crafting Indira's strategy in her clash with the Syndicate. After the parliamentary poll, D.P. Dhar was inducted as the Planning Minister and Mohan Kumaramangalam as Minister for Steel. They were joined by Siddharth Shankar Ray, Minister for Education, in the new cabinet.

At the organizational level, the agency available for spearheading radical reforms was the Congress Forum for Socialist Action (CFSA). The basic approach of the Forum was shaped by Kumaramangalam's thesis which he formulated before leaving the CPI in 1966. He had argued that as the communist party could not usher in socialism by itself, it should align with the progressive, leftist elements in the Congress to achieve this goal.

The Forum aimed at a comprehensive amendment to the Constitution so that the relationship between Fundamental Rights and the Directive Principles of State Policy was reversed, and the larger social good placed above the good of the individual. There was no reason why the individual rights should be considered more fundamental than the society's rights.

The main hurdle in the way of radical reforms was the Supreme Court's judgement delivered in the celebrated *Golak Nath* case in 1967. The court had held that the Parliament had no authority to amend fundamental rights, and that this could be done only by convening another constituent assembly. It was on the basis of this ruling that bank nationalization and abolition of privy purses were set aside in two separate judgements in 1970. Mrs. Gandhi's think-tank came up with two constitutional amendments to remove this hurdle. The twenty-fourth amendment excluded from judicial review any modification of fundamental rights made under article 368 of the Constitution. And the twenty-fifth amendment replaced the word "compensation" with "amount" for compulsory acquisition of property. So far, the courts had related "compensation" to market value. Henceforth the "amount" and mode of payment for such acquisitions were to be fixed by law. And while the going was good, privy purses and other privileges of the former Rulers were also abolished under the twenty-sixth amendment.

This onset of revolutionary amendments was severely jolted when a 13-judge special Constitution Bench of the Supreme Court gave its judgement in the *Keshavananda Bharati* case in April, 1973. The order struck a compromise between the extreme conservatism of the *Golak Nath* case and the radicalism of the new amendments. In short, it was held that whereas the parliament had the right to amend any part of the Constitution, yet in so doing, it could not alter or destroy its "essential features" or "basic structure". Thus legislation pertaining to this area was still subject to "judicial review".

To meet this challenge, her advisers like Kumaramangalam and Law Minister, H.R. Gokhale, evolved the concept of "committed judiciary". It was argued that radical legislation could produce results only if it was interpreted by judges with a progressive outlook. As luck would have it, Justice S.M. Sikri, the Chief Justice, was due to retire two days after this judgement was delivered. Mrs. Gandhi used the opportunity by promoting Justice A.N. Ray as the Chief Justice, ignoring the claims of three other judges senior to him. It was for the first time that the seniority principle was violated. The three superseded judges resigned, and the government's action was roundly condemned by legal experts, the press and the parliament.

During the interval between the *Keshavananda Bharati* case and the landmark amendments, General Insurance was nationalized in August 1972, and the coal mining industry followed suit after five months. The guarantee to protect the service conditions of Indian Civil Service officers under article 314 was withdrawn, and an ill-conceived proposal to extend control over the press by diffusing the ownership pattern of newspapers was also prepared.

The rise of radicalism in the Congress was viewed with apprehension by other elements in the party. Both the Congress socialists and the traditionalists accused the Forum of conspiring for a communist take-over of the party. However, several factors led to the Forum's decline. Indira Gandhi herself was none too happy at the emergence of an influential, cohesive and radical group which seemed to be setting the pace for her.

Kumaramangalam's sudden death in an air crash in 1973 hurt the Forum badly. He was not only a person of great conviction and dynamism, he was also very close to Indira. This robbed the Forum of its prime mover.

The increasing involvement of Sanjay Gandhi, the PM's younger son, in politics also meant trouble for the Forum. He was young and dynamic, and committed to free enterprise. To counter the influence of the CFSA, he associated himself with the launching of the Nehru Study Forum. Its declared objective was to propagate Nehru's policies.

The two forums created the impression that two antagonistic coteries had emerged within the Congress, and this was not considered good for the party. After the 1972 elections Mrs. Gandhi herself suggested that as the split of 1969 had purged the Congress of anti-socialist elements, there was little point in having activist groups propagating policies which were already a part of the Congress manifesto. The message went home. There was some behind the scenes activity, and both the forums agreed to wind themselves up. This also marked an end to Indira Gandhi's affair with radicalism.

At the ground level the abnormal rise in prices, shortage of essential commodities and other problems facing the economy had driven the common man to desperation. Scarcity of foodgrains resulted in the looting of godowns and riots in several states. The Central government did not have sufficient stocks to meet the demand, as the granaries had emptied in feeding the refugees form East Bengal. Panicked at the emerging situation, the government decided to adopt the policy of state trading in foodgrains from 1973. Wholesale traders were delicenced and the state took over the direct purchase of foodgrains.

It was an ill-timed move as the country was passing through a long spell of drought. The moment the scheme was notified, market arrivals declined and the prices shot up. Farmers were not prepared to sell their produce at the procurement price, and they made windfall gains through illegal trading. So did the hoarders. Ultimately the scheme had to be scrapped within one year.

It was a combination of all these factors which resulted in prolonged and violent agitations, and breakdown of civil administration in some parts of the country. Serious trouble first started in Uttar Pradesh. Owing to student unrest Lucknow University was closed from 21 May 1973. This provoked the students and they went on a rampage, setting several buildings on fire. The state government posted a battalion of Provincial Armed Cons-stabulary (PAC) in the University campus. But the constables were themselves a disgruntled lot and joined the students. This was open revolt by the law-keepers and it created an unprecedented crisis. Army and Central police forces were deployed to control the situation. There were armed clashes between the two sides resulting in 37 deaths. The state administration was badly shaken. Three battalions of PAC were disbanded and Chief Minister Kamlapati Tripathi resigned. It was just good luck that no political party used this explosion to ignite pent up public discontent.

The student agitation in Gujarat, which followed a few months later, and gradually developed into a powerful mass movement, spotlighted the pitfalls of Indira's style of political management. After the 1972 assembly elections, the conservative but stable and experienced Chief Minister, Hitendra Desai, was replaced by Ghanshyam Oza, a minister of state at the Centre. He was a clean and well-meaning person, but had no mass base or following among the party MLAs. His main rival was his Industry Minister, Chimanbhai Patel. He was a highly unscrupulous manipulator and succeeded in weaning away more than half the Congress MLAs from Oza by heavy bribes, kidnapping and other means. Despite being Indira's nominee, Oza had to be replaced by Chimanbhai owing to his majority in the legislative party. Mrs. Gandhi was much displeased, but felt helpless. Soon an occasion arose to make use of Chimanbhai's talents, as funds were required for the approaching elections in UP and Orissa. He collected the desired amount from the cooking oil producers in lieu of giving them a free hand in 'fixing' oil prices.

As the state continued to be rocked by agitations and disorder, the police had to be used to tackle the situation. The student community came up with a charter of demands, asking the government to proceed against the black marketeers and the corrupt, and make essential commodities available at controlled prices. As invariably happens in such situations, the general public, politicians and the anti-social elements also joined the student agitation. A call for a *bandh* (closure of all establishments) in Ahmedabad was given for 10 January.

Now that the fuse was lighted, trouble spread to all parts of the state. The students formed a Nav Nirman Samiti (Committee for Reconstruction) and the movement spread to the whole state. On top of its agenda was the dismissal of the corrupt chief minister and dissolution of the state assembly. MLAs were subjected to harassment and threats, and they started resigning under duress. Ultimately, the chief minister was asked to step down, the state assembly was suspended and President's rule imposed. But this did not solve the problem as the assembly was not dissolved. As the agitation again picked up, Morarji Desai decided on 11 March to go on a 'fast unto death' to press the demand for the assembly's dissolution. Four days later the Centre conceded this point and thus ended a landmark mass movement against the government.

The start of the student agitation in Bihar coincided with the dissolution of the Gujarat Assembly. The students in Patna had been agitating for academic reforms. In view of the government apathy, and encouraged by the events in Gujarat, the Students Action Committee decided to demonstrate before the state legislature on the opening day of its budget session. Alerted by the events in Gujarat, the police used excessive force to break up the demonstration and arrested a large number of students. This sparked off violence, arson and looting in Patna, and the state of lawlessness continued for nearly three weeks. The Army and Central police forces had to be summoned to prevent the situation getting out of hand.

Jayaprakash Narayan (JP) agreed to lead this agitation when the students approached him in early April 1974. He came out of his 20-year retirement form active politics and led a silent march on 8 April. Owing to his charisma and moral stature, this raised a mere local agitation to the level of a statewide movement aimed at cleansing the political life of Bihar. Jayaprakash gave a call for *Sampurna Kranti* (total revolution) and the introduction of 'party-less democracy' by creating 'permanent institutions of people's power.'

A notable feature of this movement was that it enjoyed the support of all non-Congress parties except the CPI, ranging from the RSS on the right to the CPI(M) on the left. The organizational support for this campaign was provided by the Jana Sangh. Its students wing, the Bharatiya Vidyarthi Parishad, formed the backbone of the Chhatra Sangharsh Sangh, the students' action committee.

JP wanted the movement to steer clear of party politics and remain non-violent. But the political parties had joined him to use his personal prestige to their advantage. And his call to *gherao* government offices, paralyse the government and pay no taxes, injected an element of bellicosity in the agitation which inevitably led to violence.

The students soon got tired of the commotion and, instead of heeding JP's call to leave their studies for one year, went back to their classes. The movement was mostly sustained by the unemployed youth, opposition parties and the lumpen elements. Demand for the dismissal of the state ministry and dissolution of the legislative assembly was something which Indira Gandhi was determined not to concede this time. She repeatedly denounced the extra-parliamentary approach of Jayaprakash Narayan and challenged him to seek his mandate from the people in the next general election.

As the movement in Bihar began losing steam, JP thought of raising his crusade to the national level. The country was disillusioned with Mrs. Gandhi, the press was hostile to her and the campaign in Bihar had evoked countrywide response. Even some regional parties like the Akali Dal, DMK and Bharatiya Lok Dal pledged their support to him. So a multi-party National Coordination Committee was formed. Having accepted Mrs. Gandhi's challenge for a trial of strength at the next election, Jayaprakash started visiting various states, addressing huge rallies. The burden of his theme was that as Indira Gandhi was destroying democracy and promoting corruption, she must be thrown out to save the country. The opposition parties, dejected and demoralized after Mrs. Gandhi's landslide victories in the 1971 and 1972 elections, saw JP as a messiah who could lead them to the promised land.

The JP movement was too much of a hotchpotch, and he himself had no clear idea as to the direction it would take. It was the widespread discontent and economic harships of the masses which gave it a fillip. And it was some unforeseen developments which lent it the dimensions of a revolutionary force.

26

Emergency: Phase-I

As troubles do not come singly, in 1974-75 Indira Gandhi's cup of woe was overflowing. The All India Railwaymen's Federation, led by the firebrand socialist, George Fernandes, served a strike notice in April 1974 demanding hike in pay and dearness allowance, grant of bonus, etc. The strike, coming as it did on the heels of Gujarat and Bihar agitations, would have disrupted the movement of foodgrains and other essential commodities and created chaos in the country. Mrs. Gandhi acted with speed and fury and declared the strike illegal under the Defence of India Rules. Never before had workers been dealt with so harshly. Thousands of them were arrested, severely beaten, thrown out of their quarters, and hundreds of them dismissed. As a result of these repressive measures the strike was withdrawn after three weeks. Not a single demand of the strikers was conceded.

The after-effects of this strike had not yet worn off when L.N. Mishra, the Railway Minister, was assassinated at a function in Samastipur, Bihar. The opposition parties claimed that the murder was engineered by Mrs. Gandhi herself, as she wanted Mishra's secrets to be buried with him. This was a far-fetched allegation and Indira retorted, "When I am murdered, they will say I arranged it for myself."

A controversy that bugged Mrs. Gandhi the most concerned Sanjay's ambition to produce an indigenous car. Whether it was the issue of letter of intent, or acquisition of land for the factory, or raising of funds, everything smacked of nepotism, high-handedness and corruption. Indira was repeatedly censured in the parliament for all these malpractices and the press exposed one scandal after the other. A beleaguered Mrs. Gandhi asked

Subramaniam, Haksar and Chandrajit Yadav to examine this issue. They recommended that the manufacture of this car be given to a public sector company. Indira Gandhi said that if Sanjay is not allowed to make the car, he will commit suicide. Haksar felt that Sanjay was welcome to become the Ford of India but then he should not operate from the Prime Minister's house. Indira Gandhi was a national asset and it was necessary to safeguard her position. Of course, the advice was not accepted. When Sanjay learnt about this matter, he ensured that Haksar was marginalized, and henceforth important papers came to be routed through P.N. Dhar, PM's Economic Adviser.[1]

It was during this period of 1972-75 that Sanjay's influence gradually rose and a new style of governance emerged. People who gave independent and unbiased advice were sidelined and the Sanjay coterie came to control access to Mrs. Gandhi. Delhi, being the hub of Sanjay's operations, received his special attention. As the Lt. Governor is the Chief Executive of the Union territory, the current incumbent Baleshwar Rai was the first target. He was an upright person who could not adjust to Sanjay's style. To get rid of him, all sorts of canards were circulated against him and he was projected as a BJP supporter. Mrs. Gandhi told N.K. Mukarji, the Home Secretary, that he should be replaced, and asked him to suggest a suitable substitute. But before he could respond, she proposed the name of Kishan Chand, a retired ICS officer. Mukarji said that he was not at all suitable for the position. So she did not persist. But after six months it was Kishan Chand who replaced the inconvenient Baleshwar Rai. It was common knowledge that his name had been proposed to Sanjay by his school-mate Naveen Chawla, a junior civil servant. It was also known that Kishan Chand had been interviewed by Sanjay. And Naveen Chawla, who had got the Lt. Governor his job was posted as his personal assistant.[2]

As the Home Ministry held the key to power it was necessary to have one's own man there. Brahmananda Reddy, the Home Minister was a mild person, but too senior for Sanjay to feel comfortable with. So, Mrs Gandhi ordered that all files of the Ministry should be routed through Om Mehta, Reddy's Minister

of State. Thereafter Mehta directly received instructions from the
'PM's House' and became de facto Home Minister.

These isolated incidents show the direction in which things
were moving. Indira Gandhi's style of working was becoming
increasingly arbitrary, personalized and autocratic, and Sanjay
had come to acquire a lot of clout.

The exte[nsive mobi]lization campaign had succeeded [and it had beco]me to Mrs. Gandhi by the
five-mile [long procession in] March to present a charter
of deman[ds to the Loksab]ha. Mrs. Gandhi was worried not so [much by the popu]larity of Jayaprakash as by
his bellige[rent posture. He t]reatened, 'If Mrs. Indira
Gandhi do[es not take ste]ps to change radically the system and
persists in standing in the way of revolutionary struggle, she
cannot complain if, in its onward march, the movement pushes
her aside with so much else.' He repeatedly asked the people to
paralyse the government by all sorts of agitational means, and
exhorted the civil services, police and armed forces not to obey
orders of the government in case they considered these as unlaw-
ful or unconstitutional. This was a clear incitement to rebellion
and anarchy, and things could not have continued like this for
long.

Here, destiny took a hand in settling the issue. On 12 June, three
unconnected events occurred which made it a fateful day for
Mrs. Gandhi. As she was having her morning tea, she learnt that
her trusted adviser, D.P. Dhar, had died of a heart attack. Later,
before lunch, she was informed that her election as member of
parliament from Rae Bareilly had been set aside as a result of Raj
Narain's election petition. And after the evening tea she was told
that her party had badly lost the assembly election in Gujarat.

Obviously, the event that shook her the most was the
Allahabad High Court judgment. She was no longer an MP
and was debarred from holding any elective office for six years.
It stunned the country as never before. The operation of the

judgment was suspended for 20 days to enable Indira to file an appeal.

When Sanjay returned from his Maruti factory and learnt about these developments, "He took his mother to her room and told her angrily that he would not let her resign."[3] From then onward Sanjay was in control of the disaster management operation and Indira Gandhi placed her full trust in him. The first task before Sanjay was the creation of a popular wave in favour of his mother remaining in office. All available road transport was deployed to bring crowds from the adjoining states to stage demonstrations for Mrs. Gandhi's continuance.

Subhadra Joshi, an old friend of Mrs. Gandhi and a local MP, learnt that microphones had repeatedly failed when Indira was addressing groups of her 'supporters'. So Mrs. Joshi went to 1 Akbar Road, the PM's residential office, to set things right. There she saw workers from the Maruti factory squatting all over. Outside the bungalow there was a row of new, unregistered cars supplied by a Delhi businessman. Jeeps loaded with posters were parked nearby. And she saw two persons carrying buckets of adhesive paste. On enquiry, she learnt that the workers were to carry pro-Indira posters in the cars to different parts of Delhi and plaster the city walls with them. Mrs. Joshi thought that it was a crude and ill-conceived exercise. If any pressman learnt about it or took photographs of the vehicles, people would laugh at the Prime Minister mounting a campaign from her own house to project her mass popularity. She told Sanjay about it, but he went ahead with his plan all the same.[4]

Another chest-beating loyalist arranged the strike of Delhi Water Supply workers so as to bring them over for a big demonstration. When Mrs. Joshi learnt about it, she went running to Indira and complained that such tactics would boomerang. Dislocation of Delhi's water supply for a day would create bedlam. Mrs. Gandhi listened to this complaint impassively, but did not react. Mercifully, the plan to mobilize water supply workers was dropped.[5]

The future course of JP's crusade depended on the outcome of Indira's application to the Supreme Court for absolute stay of the High Court judgment. On 24 June the court passed an order granting only a conditional stay: whereas Mrs. Gandhi could continue as the PM, she could not vote in Parliament. This gave a big jolt to her moral authority. What sort of leader of the House was she if she could not even vote like an ordinary MP?

Jayaprakash and his followers were ecstatic and started planning the final phase of their struggle to dislodge Indira Gandhi. The five-party Janata Front went into a huddle and set up Lok Sangharsh Samiti (committee for the people's struggle) under Morarji Desai's chairmanship. It was decided to launch all-India anti-Indira movements from 29 June. Another mammoth rally was organized at the Ram Lila Ground where JP again called upon the people to make it impossible for the corrupt Government of India to function, and repeated his call to the police and army to disobey illegal orders of the government.

With all this turbulence around her, Mrs. Gandhi was not sitting idle either. Closeted with her confidantes she drafted her own response in total secrecy. Accompanied by S.S. Ray, Chief Minister, West Bengal and a legal expert, she went to the President of India on the night of 25 June and obtained his approval for the proclamation of an Internal Emergency under Article 352 of the Constitution. In a midnight swoop most of the important opposition leaders including Jayaprakash Narayan and Morarji Desai, were arrested. As power supply to most newspapers had been disconnected, people had no clue as to what was happening. The Cabinet ministers received the summons early morning on 26 June for a meeting at 6 a.m. They heard the PM's announcement in silence and endorsed her unilateral decision without a squeak. Only Swaran Singh made some innocent query and lost his job subsequently. Two hours later Mrs. Gandhi went on the radio and informed the people, "The President has proclaimed Emergency. There is nothing to panic about." She referred to the "deep-rooted and widespread conspiracy which has been brewing since I began to introduce certain progressive measures of benefit to common men and women."

In its secrecy, speed, and spread it was a remarkable operation. Even the seniormost officials including the Cabinet Secretary knew nothing about it. Yet it is also a fact that a large number of persons were involved in this exercise. After all, the preparation of lists of hundreds of leaders to be arrested, detailing of police parties separately for each one of them, cutting of power supply to newspapers, flying out messengers to various states with secret instructions, could not have been done by only a handful of people. This shows how a core of 'trusted' officials had been created in advance. The fact that the Home Minister, the Cabinet Secretary and many other top officials had no inkling about it also shows how this 'core' operated outside the normal chain of command and accountability.

It is generally believed that Mrs. Gandhi decided to clamp the Emergency after Justice Iyer granted her only a conditional stay of the High Court judgment, and in view of the extremely threatening speeches made at JP's rally on 25 June. But circumstantial evidence shows that, in one form or other, the matter had been under consideration for months. It was in January 1975 that K.D. Malviya told I.K. Gujral, a fellow leftist, that the country had had enough of this bourgeois system and "why not finish it off."[6] In May 1975, D.P. Dhar, India's Ambassador to the USSR and Indira's close confidante, happened to be in India. He told Nikhil Chakravarty, a highly respected journalist, that there was a 50 percent chance of the election petition judgement going against Mrs. Gandhi. Discussing the options open to her, Nikhil said that she should file an appeal against an adverse judgement. Dhar thought that the litigation was a lengthy and dicey affair, and it may be preferable if the President of India suspended the Constitution and assumed the executive powers himself. After the situation had normalized he should revive the Constitution. Necessary constitutional amendment could be made to ensure Mrs. Gandhi's continuance.[7]

Though this was not a very neat arrangement, it shows the thinking in the inner corridors of power. As a specific anticipatory step, "the security arrangement around No. 1 Safdarjang Road (were) taken in hand from the night of June 11 and a conference of police top brass at the PM's house (was held) on the morning of 12 June, much before the Allahabad flash landed in New Delhi."[8]

Sanjay was not a person to sit idly and mope. It was from 15 June that Sanjay started working on "some plan to set things right," as he later told a friend. His idea was to "restructure the government at the political and official levels."[9] The surest indication of advance planning is given by the fact that Home Secretary, N.K. Mukarji, was told on 21 June to immediately hand over charge to S.L. Khurana, Chief Secretary, Rajasthan. He did so on the 23rd as 22nd was a Sunday.[10] Obviously, the search for a suitable successor must have started a few days earlier. According to the Lt. Governor of Delhi "even as early as 23rd (June) a decision had been taken to take the opposition leaders into custody soon after the opposition rally... all arrangements in connection with the impending arrests were discussed at a meeting in the afternoon of June 25 in the room of Shri R.K. Dhawan, in the presence of Shri Om Mehta ...Shri Bansi Lal and Shri Bajwa, SP (CID), Delhi Administration."[11]

On 18 June there was a meeting of chief ministers in Delhi when they were alerted to get ready for taking some strong action. A password was given to them, and they had to get cracking on hearing it.

In view of the above facts it may be inferred that looking to the growing instability in the country, Indira Gandhi had been contemplating some drastic move much before the proclamation of Emergency. This definitely involved detention of opposition leaders and far-reaching constitutional changes. Most of the arrangements for emergency had been completed before the JP rally of 25 June. With his inflammatory speeches, he walked into a trap of his own laying and provided Mrs. Gandhi with an excellent pretext for doing what she had been wanting to do.

The Prime Minister's residence on the night of 25 June 1975 was the scene of some weird and bizarre happenings which pointed to the shape of things to come. After the President had approved the declaration of Emergency a little before midnight, Indira Gandhi sat with S.S. Ray and Barooah to draft her speech to the nation. In the adjoining room Sanjay was discussing follow-up measures with Om Mehta and senior officials, including the Lt. Governor. Indira completed writing her speech around 3 a.m. and retired. In the corridor, S.S. Ray met an agitated Om Mehta, who said that electricity to the newspaper offices was being cut off and the doors of the High Court were being locked. Ray was very upset and insisted on seeing Mrs. Gandhi. Meantime Sanjay also came out and told Ray, "You people do not know how to run the country." By the time Indira Gandhi came out, he was gone. Ray apprised the PM of Sanjay's decision. She was shocked, went inside and emerged after 20 minutes. Ray 'noticed' that her eyes were red, as if she had been weeping. She said, "Siddhartha, the electricity to the newspapers will not be cut and the High Court will remain open."[12] Next morning, the courts remained open, but the electricity was cut.

This incident, reported by Pupul Jayakar, Mrs. Gandhi's close friend, is very significant. It shows the emergence of two command centres within the PM's house — one, under Sanjay, the other under his mother. Sanjay's commands were abrupt, impulsive, authoritarian. Indira's approach was naturally more mature, restrained and practical. But wherever the two came into conflict, it was invariably the Sanjay line which prevailed. More importantly, this dichotomy did not persist for long. Gradually the two centres coalesced, at least outwardly.

All the pre-Emergency preparations focussed on the modalities of striking the first blow. Very little thought was given to the implications of this step on the governance of the country. Though de facto censorship had been imposed, no ordinance to this effect was issued. The lacuna was later rectified in the meeting of Political Affairs Committee of the Cabinet held at PM's residence on 26 June. As I.K. Gujral, came out of the meeting Sanjay turned to him and desired to see all the news bulletins of All India Radio before they were broadcast. Gujral explained that this could not be done as the bulletins were confidential.[13]

The same day in the evening Dhawan rang up Gujral to come over to the PM's house. When he reached there, Indira Gandhi was not at home. Sanjay came out and said in Hindustani, "Dekhiye, aisa nahin chalega" (Look, this won't do). Gujral replied that 'he was doing the right thing. He added, "you are younger than my son and you will not be rude to me."[14] Next morning Gujral was replaced by V.C. Shukla.

Having imposed Emergency, Indira's first concern was to make herself legally invulnerable. Soon after the event, she suspended constitutional rights regarding equality before law (Art. 14), right of life and liberty (Art.21), and protection against arbitrary arrest and detention (Art. 22) through a Presidential ordinance. A couple of days later, Maintenance of Internal Security Act (MISA) was amended to provide for the detention of a person upto two years without disclosing the grounds for doing so. Further, parliamentary proceedings were censored and rules of procedure suspended. Question Hour and motions by private members were discontinued. When the Parliament met on 21 July for the monsoon session, the more vocal of the opposition MPs were already in jail and two days later most others also walked out. Thus the PM was left with an emasculated, rump Parliament which approved all the new legislative measures without demur.

The first act of the Parliament was to make the imposition of Emergency non-justiciable. It also amended the Representation of the People Act with retrospective effect to remove the provisions which resulted in Indira's conviction. Further, all election disputes involving the President, Vice-President, Speaker of Lok Sabha and Prime Minister were taken out of the jurisdiction of the courts.

But the landmark legislation was the marathon 59-clause 42nd amendment which swept away the constraints imposed by the *Keshavananda Bharati* case, removing all checks on the Parliament's powers to amend the Constitution, including its basic structure. It also subordinated the Fundamental Rights to Directive Principles of State Policy. The words 'secular' and 'socialist' were affixed to 'Democratic Republic' in the Preamble. The term of the Lok Sabha and state assemblies was increased from five to six years. All these changes made Mrs. Gandhi the supreme ruler of the country without any check on her power.

Addressing the Rajya Sabha on 22 July 1975 Indira Gandhi said, "We have not been able to give the people the food they need or shelter or education... but we have given them a new self-confidence and I think that is a very big thing." But Mrs. Gandhi knew as well as anybody else that 'self-confidence' without food cannot sustain a people for long. According to her, the whole rationale of Emergency was to remove obstacles in the way of people-oriented reforms and policies. She realized that the intelligentsia could be ignored provided there was a perceptible improvement in the lot of the people and the general law and order situation improved.

Indira needed to do something dramatic to make Emergency palatable — and do it fast. All the ministries were asked to immediately prepare popular, high visibility schemes to be included in an attractive package. Within five days of Emergency a comprehensive 20-Point Programme was launched with great fanfare. It was an expanded version of the 10-Point Programme framed in 1967, and covered pro-poor and social reform schemes contained in the Five Year Plans. Highest priority was given to bringing down prices of essential commodities. Other items included land reforms, removal of rural indebtedness, abolition of bonded labour, provision of house sites to the landless, development of the handloom sector, action against tax-evaders and smugglers, and tax relief to the middles class. Detailed instructions were issued to chief ministers and state Congress committees to create agencies for execution and monitoring of these programmes. Members of AICC were sent to various states to report on the progress of implementation. For the first time extensive powers were delegated to non-official local committees to decide a variety of cases on the spot.

It was a tremendous effort, and the entire administration of the country was geared to implement the programme. It produced some quick results. Owing to large-scale dehoarding operations, detention of smugglers and raids on tax evaders, prices started coming down, essential commodities became freely available, and tax collection went up. Further, three million house sites were allotted to the landless and one million acres of surplus land distributed to them. Thousands of bonded labourers were freed, moratorium placed on small farmers' debts, and payment of minimum wages enforced.

The 20-Point Programme had the effect of aspirin. It suddenly reduced the social temperature and gave immediate relief. But it failed to cure the chronic ailments of the body politic. The poverty alleviation items like allotment of surplus land under the ceiling laws, payment of minimum wages, release of bonded labour, remission of debt, depended on the active cooperation of the bigger landowners for their success. But this was the class whose interest was directly hit by these measures, and they had the least stake in them. Further, official agencies supplied exaggerated accounts of the benefits accruing under the Programme so as to fulfil the prescribed targets. Several schemes were single-shot affairs and their potential was soon exhausted. Dehoarding of foodgrains or black money could not go on for ever. Identification of house sites and distribution of surplus land were self-limiting operations.

At the end of the day what people remembered about the Emergency was not the benefits that materialized under the 20-Point Programme, or better maintenance of law and order, but the mindless brutality to which it degenerated. Indira Gandhi never anticipated such an outcome. It shows how little this astute player of the power game understood the dynamics of absolute power.

27

Emergency: Phase-II

*E*mergency removed the constraints of rules and procedures, and streamlined administration to that extent. The suspension of various legal safeguards, which could also be used to abort justice, made it easier to apprehend known criminals. The tone of civil administration improved, cities became more peaceful, the crime rate went down, trains ran on time, commuters queued at the bus stands, the number of *gheraos* and strikes went down, industrial production increased and exports picked up. Once the initial shock of Emergency and arrest of leaders like JP and Desai wore off, people came to look upon it as a boon. After all, how did the people benefit from democracy?

But soon things started changing. Emergency had placed unlimited power in the hands of the executive, and removed all checks on its exercise. When Sanjay had brusquely told S.S. Ray, "You people do not know how to run this country," the obvious implication was that he did. At the age of 29 one is not assailed by many doubts, and his lack of experience and natural arrogance gave him tremendous confidence to set things right.

Sanjay knew what should be done and how to do it. The democratic processes were too cumbersome. Short-circuit them. Swarms of beggars in Delhi scared away the foreign tourists. Banish them. The capital was dotted with slums all over. Remove them. Certain parts of Delhi were too congested and dirty. Bulldoze them. The poor bred like rabbits. Sterilize them. Some people jabber too much. Shove them in jail. The press was too critical and scurrilous? Censor it.

And Sanjay had all the power for his short-cuts and instant solutions. Now it was he and not Mrs. Gandhi who called the shots. She had joyously admitted at the Chandigarh session of the Congress in December 1975, "You have stolen my thunder."

Politicians and bureaucrats were quick to perceive the change, and adjusted accordingly. Though Sanjay issued only verbal instructions, they were eagerly obeyed by Central ministers, chief ministers, and senior executives. As oral orders replaced written laws and procedures at all levels, administration acquired the character of medieval autocracy. But whereas earlier there was only one autocrat, now every official and local politico became a potentate within his domain.

The Turkman Gate tragedy not only marks the high point of the Emergency rule, it also typifies its worst features. The action was confined to the Ajmeri Gate, Jama Masjid and Turkman Gate areas of Delhi. This was the oldest part of the city and people had lived there for centuries. They were neither squatters, nor were the buildings unauthorized.

Sanjay had a dream — a dream to beautify the face of Delhi by removing the pock-marks of congested colonies and dirty slums. And he refused to see this dream meet the fate of the earlier plans. So, he straightaway swung into action, without taking the affected people into confidence, without developing alternate sites for them, and without having any legal authority to do what he did. Rumours of the proposed action were already circulating and when bulldozers were assembled outside Turkman Gate, people got panicky and gathered in large numbers. As invariably happens in such cases, one thing led to the other, and the police opened fire. All hell broke loose and screaming men, women and children ran in all directions. The police chased them into their houses, beating whomsoever they could seize, molesting women, looting property. The bulldozers moved in and centuries of living history was reduced to a heap of rubble.

According to the Shah Commission's estimates nearly 1,50,000 houses and shops were demolished and 7,00,000 people rendered homeless. They were all carted 15-20 kilometres away to new settlement colonies. The 'beautification' operation was undertaken in the middle of April 1976, and by the time people were able to improvise some sort of roof over their head, monsoon arrived and inundated several of these habitations.

Sanjay's actions were keenly watched and avidly emulated by the state chief ministers. Several large cities were 'beautified' by demolishing thousands of houses. But the case of Benaras merits special mention, as it may have overshadowed the Turkman Gate tragedy but for the last minute intervention by a friend of Indira.

As Pupul Jayakar was going to Benaras, Mrs. Gandhi asked her to look into some disturbing reports coming in from the city. The Divisional Commissioner and Chairman Municipal Corporation took her to Vishwanath Gali which leads to the holiest of holy Hindu temples. "The Governor desired to drive by car to Vishwanathji," the Commissioner explained. Pupul was aghast. To drive by car through a narrow, meandering lane with centuries old buildings jutting on either side? "We shall break the walls of some of the houses and pave the road so that a car could go through," said the Commissioner. Bulldoze these ancient structures and the numerous mini shrines lining it? "Sanjayji wants the city made beautiful," the Commissioner clarified.[1] A revenue Commissioner working under the state government, complying with illegal oral orders of Sanjayji conveyed through some underling!

Mrs. Jayakar was then taken to see the 'beautification' work done on Kamacha road. It "looked as if a bomb had fallen on it." She reported the situation to Indira and showed her the photographs of the demolition work done in Benaras. "She hit the ceiling" and asked Narain Dutt Tiwari, the chief minster of UP to come over immediately. "What is happening in this country? No one seems to tell me," she moaned. Even the chief minister did not know what was happening in his state.[2] Sanjay did not believe in going through the circuitous 'proper channel'. Orders were conveyed directly to officers on the spot. And the state officials also did not check back with their bosses, who were in any case eagerly anticipating Sanjayji's wishes.

The campaign that caused the deepest and most widespread offence was that of sterilization. In a traditional society where potency is the essence of manhood, vasectomy was supposed to lead to impotence. Forcible sterilization was an attack on a person's human dignity and self-esteem. Thus, hardly anybody came forward voluntarily to be sterilized. In view of the colossal effort required for the job, the police, teachers and revenue officials were mobilized to produce candidates. In case they failed to meet the targets, salaries were withheld, increment stopped, and all sorts of other pressures applied. Widows, unmarried girls and boys and old persons, were all made sacrificial goats to fulfil the targets. As the public anger rose against this brutality, there were riots in several places. Forty people were killed in police firing in Muzzafarpur and a dozen in Sultanpur districts in UP. Hundreds died owing to faulty operations.

Demolitions were selective and localized. Sterilization programmes covered the whole of north India, and the villagers were the main target. But it was more than a coincidence that both the campaigns were mainly targeted at the poor and the defenceless.

The declared objective of Emergency was to set things right. But with so much power invested in so many hands, it was used as a pretext to set the people right and settle old scores. Thousands of individuals were arrested, humiliated, tortured, maimed and killed without any specific charges levelled against them. Take for instance, the case of Inder Mohan, a highly respected and dedicated social worker. He met Sanjay and narrated to him the travails of the shopkeepers of the Jama Masjid complex. Two days later, the police picked him up from his flat, gave him a severe beating, put him in the police lock-up, and then transferred him to Tihar Jail. That was in September 1975. His release came only in January 1977 along with other political detenus.

The Secretary, Delhi Students Union, was arrested while organizing a peaceful meeting. In his words, "the police tied my hands between my knees and dangled me from a stick, which they kept swinging to make me sick. They poured water with chilli powder in it down my nose and I became sick. Many student prisoners were treated in the same manner."[3]

The reverse of Sanjay's demolition campaign was the victimization of S.C. Chhabra, Chairman, New Delhi Municipal Corporation. Sanjay's cronies were creating their own constituencies by settling squatters on government land, with the promise to get these unauthorized clusters regularized. Chhabra resisted this and approached the Lt. Governor and ministers to prevent this outrage. Sanjay wanted him to be dismissed. Several cases of graft were fabricated against him and the poor man was totally shattered. Romesh Thapar sought C.D. Deshmukh's advice to save Chhabra. Deshmukh said, "You must approach Indira Gandhi like a supplicant. And you must address her as if she were an empress." Thapar drafted an appeal accordingly, and all cases against Chhabra were dropped.[4]

Janata Coffee House, New Delhi, was the favourite haunt of journalists, intellectuals, authors and the like. Word reached Sanjay that people who assembled there indulged in loose talk about Emergency. The structure was bulldozed one morning.

When the Emergency excesses were brought to light during the Janata rule, Mrs. Gandhi came up with three responses. One, that the horror stories were concocted by the opposition to defame her and Sanjay. But this was a wholly untenable stand, as the official records refuted her claim. For example, she repeatedly denied having met a single person who was forcibly sterilized. But big targets were fixed for the states and compliance reports sent back to the Central Government. Yet if none of the victims complained to her, there must have been good reasons for that.

Secondly, Mrs. Gandhi took the plea that these excesses were never brought to her notice, that even official agencies colluded to keep her in the dark. This is a very specious argument, as any number of cases show that whenever an adverse report was brought to her notice, she not only refused to believe it, but the messenger got discredited in most cases. When Subhadra Joshi repeatedly told her about the excesses committed in her constituency comprising Turkman Gate-Jama Masjid area, Indira retorted, "What to do. The MPs do nothing. When somebody does it, then these people get angry."[5]

K. Seshan, Indira's devoted Private Secretary who had worked with Nehru also, told Pupal Jayakar that whenever he brought to her notice any instance of wrongdoing, she would brush him aside or would behave as if she had not heard him.[6]

Once Chandrajit Yadav complained to her about forced sterilizations and cited specific cases from his own district. Mrs. Gandhi flared up on hearing this, thumped the table and said that these canards were being spread by people jealous of Sanjay's fast-growing popularity.[7]

In view of complaints coming from the Turkman Gate area, Mrs. Gandhi asked Mohammad Yunus to visit the site personally and report his findings to her. Some officials were also in attendance. As the word spread, people came forward to tell their stories. Two victims offered to accompany Yunus and show him around. At the end of the visit Yunus saw that one of those persons was picked up by the police from under his nose, and the other managed to slip away. When Yunus narrated this incident of police high-handedness to Mrs. Gandhi, she tried to verify it from the officials. They flatly denied the report of Yunus. Indira expressed her helplessness in view of these contradictory versions.[8]

With these and other such instances it had become clear to persons with access to Mrs. Gandhi that any report of Emergency excesses would be disbelieved and, at times, construed by her as censure of Sanjay's actions. So people preferred to remain silent and keep their peace. On the other hand, the sycophants around her gave glowing reports of the wonderful work being done by Sanjay and his growing popularity among the masses. And then Mrs. Gandhi took the stand that the misdeeds of Emergency were not brought to her notice!

And third, she blamed the bureaucracy for the people's sufferings. On the one hand the officials were given stiff performance targets, which forced them to resort to coercion. And then they were blamed for exceeding their brief.

Another reason why Indira Gandhi came to believe her illusions was the nauseating flattery of even her seniormost colleagues. It was at the Congress Parliamentary Party meeting held one week before the declaration of Emergency that D.K. Barooah uttered his immortal words: "Indira is India and India is Indira." Later, when Sanjay was launched as the youth leader at the Guwahati Session, Barooah wanted youth to take over the party and compared Sanjay to Shankaracharya, Vivekananda and Akbar. During a visit to Bombay, Y.B. Chavan, India's Prime Minister in waiting, hailed Sanjay, a mere lad compared to him, as a "Leader of the people." In March 1976, Brahmanand Reddy declared, "She (Indira) is the Adi Shakti prepared to crush anybody, however great he might be, who meddles with the solidarity, integrity and welfare of the people." During Sanjay's visits to the states, the entire cabinet used to receive him at the airport and the chief ministers awaited his commands. Huge public meetings were arranged for him and glowing reports of his mass appeal sent to his mother.

The basic problem of Indira Gandhi during the Emergency was that she wanted reality to conform to her perceptions. But the parallax between the two was so wide that a congruence could be achieved only by torturing the truth out of shape.

More than the self-created barriers to free communication it was the rigorous press censorship which cut off Indira from reality. In fact, she had seldom felt comfortable with the press. Nor did she appreciate its role in an open society. Indira told Rajya Sabha on 22 July 1975, "Once there was no press, there were no agitations. The agitation was in the pages of the newspapers. If you ask why there is censorship today, this is the reason." So, press was the villain of the piece. She therefore put pressure on newspaper proprietors to sack obstinate editors, tried to change ownership of unfriendly papers like *The Indian Express* and *The Statesman*, imposed strict censorship, ordered the closure of several papers, and cancelled the accreditation of scores of journalists. To control the news at source, it was decided to merge the four news agencies. As the Press Trust of India resisted the move, its power supply was stopped and AIR served a notice to discontinue its news services. Thus browbeaten, the PTI Board passed a resolution in favour of a merger. The remaining three smaller agencies offered no resistance. And thus was born 'Samachar,'the omnibus news agency. After the event, the Minister for Information and Broadcasting said that this will eliminate duplication of reporting and serve the people.

Indira's media policy was wholly counter-productive. The one area where only cajoling and persuasion could have worked, she wielded the big stick. This antagonized the whole press, both Indian and foreign. It denied her the only channel through which she could receive useful feedback about the public reaction to the Emergency regime. Most importantly, in the absence of authentic news, rumour mongering flourished and people believed the worst about the Government's actions and intentions.

Mrs. Gandhi could shut out the world and run away from reality, but she could not run away from herself. Like her father, she was acutely conscious of her place in history. Freedom, democracy, elections, public opinion were the concepts she had grown up with. Her own political instinct was still sound enough to tell her that the Emergency was wrong, and that things were slipping out of hand. When Pupul took her to meet J. Krishnamurti, Indira confessed, "I do not mind the tiger killing me, but I do not know how to get off its back."

The murder of Mujib and his family on 15 August 1975 had shaken her deeply. She had been talking of a conspiracy against her for quite some time. "They would like to destroy me and my family," she told Pupul Jayakar. At the other end, Bhutto had announced elections in Pakistan. What was the world coming to? Pakistan a democracy and India a dictatorship?

Indira had planned the Emergency to be a short-term affair. But the people around her developed such strong vested interests in it that they wanted it to go on and on. In November 1975 she got the life of the parliament extended by one year. Then, in November 1976 she again postponed election by another year. But she was aware that after the initial impact of the Emergency had worn off, prices had again started rising and the economy got into the old rut. People had started defying the authorities and disturbances were reported from more and more places. She decided to dismount the tiger and, without consulting Sanjay or anybody else, threw in the sponge. On 18 January 1977 she abruptly announced the holding of general election after two months. Opposition leaders and MISA detenus were released and press censorship relaxed. The veil of darkness had suddenly lifted and the country began bubbling with political activity once again.

Sanjay is generally endowed with great powers of evil and intrigue. But there could not be a more uncomplicated youngster than him. During his visit to UP after the declaration of Emergency, somebody asked him about his priorities. "At present there are no elections," he replied, "when the elections come we will see about it." When, at the instance of Mrs. Gandhi, C. Subramaniam, the Finance Minister, tried to help him with his Maruti venture, the outcome was hilarious. To the minister's query about the project report, Sanjay replied, "There cannot be a project report before the project starts." When Subramaniam wanted to explain the position, the youngman retorted that those were all old methods of operating, they were not necessary.[9] If this boy was pushed into the thick of political turmoil and given unlimited authority to run the country's affairs, it was not his fault that he made a hash of things. The blame for this has to be laid at the door of his doting and insecure mother whose shrinking circle of trust gradually narrowed down to the single point of her younger son. Despite all the flak she received in the Parliament over Sanjay's Maruti car project, Indira stoutly defended every action of his. "What shall I do," she said, "if my son does not happen to be a professor type." And, "You see, Sanjay is not a thinker, he is a doer." She, in fact, considered it obligatory to help Sanjay. "When my son has taken a risk," she said, "I could not say no to him. We have got to encourage our young people." It did not matter of course that her son happened to be the only young man being thus encouraged.

To make life easier, Sanjay had evolved an ingenious method of influencing government decisions. In the three important ministries of his interest, that is, Home, Finance and Industry, he got appointed Om Mehta, Pranab Mukherjee and A.P. Sharma as ministers of state under the Cabinet ministers in-charge. They were all beholden to him and did what he wanted. Then, he got Bansi Lal shifted from Haryana and appointed as Defence

Minister. Obviously, he arranged these changes through his mother, and she was fully aware of the purpose behind these moves.

A sizeable and well-meaning section of the Indian intelligentsia believes that the slow-moving, cumbersome processes of democracy are not suited to a poor and developing country, and it is a luxury only the industrialized, affluent nations can afford. Further, if democracy has to be accepted as a necessary evil, then we must have a very strong Centre so as to keep in check the fissiparous tendencies. Emergency rule provides the biggest refutation of this premise.

With the suspension of democracy during the Emergency, it was the poor who really suffered. It was they whose houses were demolished, who were forcibly sterilized, whose right to go on strike or protest against injustices taken away. In the beginning some economic offenders and hoarders were also hauled up. But this phase soon came to an end. In July 1975 the PM had threatened that tax evaders would be severely punished, and "we are thinking of summary trials." Nothing of the sort happened. In fact, by 30 March 1976 an income tax settlement commission had been set up to enable assessees to seek a compromise and secure immunity from prosecution. Further, a 'voluntary disclosures' scheme was introduced under which habitual offenders could get immunity by paying income tax on concealed income at concessionary rates, thus penalizing the honest taxpayer who had paid tax at the normal rates.

In fact the business community was quite happy with the Emergency. Law and order was under control, workers did not go on strike, slums had been removed from the vicinity of posh colonies, and the trains ran on time. The rich will flourish under any regime. It is the poor, the weak and the defenceless who need care and protection. This is best ensured under democracy, and this shield the Emergency had removed.

Emergency was not an act of aggression; it was an admission of defeat. The provocations Mrs. Gandhi faced and the odds against her were grave indeed. Student agitations, industrial unrest, *gheraos*, *bandhs*, strikes, continuous sniping in the parliament, increasing resort to unparliamentary methods of protest — the entire country was being churned up by turbulence and civil strife. And then came the Allahabad High Court judgement, disqualifying her from holding elective office for six years on the basis of two minor technical lapses. Indira Gandhi's anger and frustration were understandable. But the situation required application of skills which her party had honed over decades and her father had used with such finesse. Dialogue, wide consultations and accommodation of dissent were needed to bring down social and political temperatures, and hammer out a consensus. But these are the tools Indira had progressively abandoned since the Congress split in 1969, and switched over to the politics of confrontation. Consequently, people who differed with her were her enemies; opposition parties were anti-national; she was surrounded by conspirators and traitors. This narrowing of horizons brought her to a stage where the only person she could fully trust was her younger son. In such a situation there could be no communication, no dialogue, no give and take. This marked a divorce of politics from governance, and governance from institutions. The system had obviously failed and Indira saw no prospect of reviving it through the democratic processes.

The Emergency has been called an 'aberration' — a spasm which seized the Indian polity. Perhaps it was that. But it also highlighted a deep fault line in the country's political structure. The ease with which the entire democratic framework was dismantled, the people cowed down and the press silenced, showed how shallow the roots of democratic culture in India were. There were victims galore, but hardly any martyrs. To vary L.K. Advani's famous jibe, it was not only the press which crawled when asked to bend, the intelligentsia and the academia behaved no better.

The deepest scar that the Emergency left on the Indian polity was in the area of human rights. Here I am not referring to the innocent detenus whose number according to the Amnesty International's estimates, stood at 1,40,000 at one time, nor demolitions and sterilizations. Real, lasting damage was done by the misuse and perversion of the organs of state power. The police and other government agencies, officially violated the basic laws of the land. The rise of heresy from the *Kaaba* ate into their moral fibre and corrupted them to the core. They lost respect for law, human dignity and the rights of the individual. And this blight did not vanish with the disappearance of the Emergency. It got permanently lodged in the tissues of the system and became a part of the country's administrative culture.

28

Interregnum-II

*O*nce the parliament was dissolved and elections announced, events moved fast. Opposition leaders and most of the MISA detenus were released and press censorship relaxed. The opposition parties were confused. Mrs. Gandhi had given them just two months to get their act together. The leaders had to renew their contacts with the field workers, raise funds, work out a viable strategy and cobble some sort of alliance. They felt that the crafty Prime Minister had again tricked them by this sudden manoeuvre.

Jayaprakash made it clear that he would campaign for the opposition parties only if they merged into a single unit. This they ultimately managed to do and four parties, that is, the Congress (O), Jan Sangh, Sanyukta Socialist Party and Bharatiya Lok Dal came together on 23 January 1977 to form the Janata Party. They convened their first public meeting at Ram Lila Ground a week later with JP as the star attraction. It also happened to be the first public meeting held there after JP's rally of 25 June 1975. It was one of the largest mass gatherings and indicated the direction in which the wind was blowing.

Sanjay had a major say in finalizing the lists of Congress candidates. He wanted most of the old fogeys to be shunted out and his own cronies given precedence. But before this exercise could be completed, Babu Jagjivan Ram dropped a bomb by resigning from the Congress on 2 February. A senior, respected leader with a large following ditching Mrs. Gandhi midstream! The impact was shattering. And a great morale booster for the opposition. Bahuguna and Nandini Satpathi, former chief ministers of UP and Orissa, also joined Babuji. They formed a new party called Congress for Democracy. Vijaylakshmi Pandit, Indira'a aunt, joined the Janata Party. Shaken by these developments, the Congress hastily revised the lists of its candidates and most of the sitting MPs were accommodated at the cost of Sanjay's nominees.

Indira held her first election meeting at the Boat Club, New Delhi. The crowd was large, but the response was feeble. Then she mounted her usual 18-hour-a-day punishing election campaign. She clearly saw that the tide was moving away from her. Even when the meetings were well attended, the electricity of a mutual rapport was missing. At places the people were openly hostile.

As the counting of votes progressed on 20 March, it became clear that the Congress was going to lose badly. By the evening something unbelievable seemed to be happening. The Congress was trailing behind in all the constituencies of North India. As excitement mounted, large crowds assembled outside the newspaper offices in Delhi. The latest position was being displayed on large score boards. It was past midnight when Mrs. Gandhi's defeat was confirmed. The crowds spontaneously roared 'gayee' (gone), and started dancing deliriously.

The election results were truly stunning. The Congress did not get a single seat in UP, Bihar, Punjab, Haryana and Delhi, and one seat each in Madhya Pradesh, Rajasthan and Kashmir. Its overall tally was 153 against 350 in the dissolved house. On the other hand, the Janata Party and its ally, Congress for Democracy, bagged 298 seats — thus giving it absolute majority. Not even the most wildly optimistic Janata leaders had dreamt of such a windfall. In a midnight cabinet meeting on 20 March it was decided to immediately recommend to the President the lifting of Emergency, and Indira herself resigned on 22 March after the last results had come in.

The Congress Working Committee met two days after the defeat to take stock of the situation, but adjourned after affirming faith in Mrs. Gandhi's leadership. It was also decided to discuss party affairs in the next meeting of the committee on 12 April. During the intervening period the leadership polarized into two factions: one led by Indira, and the second by S.S. Ray, Barooah, and others. Apprehending that Sanjay and his associates may be attacked in the meeting, Mrs. Gandhi sent a letter to the Congress president, saying, "As one who led the government, I unreservedly own full responsibility for this defeat."

Indira Gandhi came to the meeting only when Chavan, Barooah and Kamlapati Tripathi went specially to fetch her. Nobody spoke against her. Sanjay, not being a Congress member, was not even mentioned. But in a later session not attended by Mrs. Gandhi, Bansi Lal was expelled for six years and V.C. Shukla reprimanded. Owing to mounting pressure, Barooah resigned as the Congress president, and Swaran Singh was given interim charge.

Two months later Brahmananda Reddy was elected as the new president, defeating S.S. Ray by a wide margin. Y.B. Chavan became leader of the Congress Parliamentary Party. These two persons were fully backed by Indira, and she hoped that they would act as her puppets. But in the changed context both wanted to be their own masters — they had licked her boots long enough. And this clash of ambitions led to the second Congress split.

The first cracks appeared when the Janata Government dissolved nine Congress assemblies and ordered a fresh poll. During his election meetings Chavan denounced Emergency rule and blamed tight press censorship for his inaction. When the CWC meeting was convened to review the election results, Reddy said that even the cabinet ministers had no prior inkling of the Emergency. A month later he announced his decision to revamp the Pradesh Congress Committees. In this process he appointed H.K. Patil, an old adversary of chief minister Devraj Urs, as Pradesh Congress President of Karnataka. This was an affront to Mrs. Gandhi, as Urs was one of her staunch supporters.

So the fat was in the fire. Whereas earlier, both Reddy and Chavan used to regularly consult Indira on important issues, the practice was discontinued with the gain of greater self-confidence. Chavan had gone so far as not to inform Mrs. Gandhi when he endorsed Morarji Desai's proposal to elect Sanjiva Reddy as the next President of India. At one point Brahmananda Reddy remarked that he would not be a 'rubber stamp (Congress) president.'

Indira realized that she must acquire a formal base to wield influence. Not being an MP, she could not be the leader of the Congress Parliamentary Party. The other slot was that of the party president. So her supporters started a campaign for the resignation of Reddy in favour of their leader. This move was justified on the ground that only Indira could save the party in this hour of crisis.

In view of her inability to have things her own way, Indira resigned from the Congress Working Committee on 18 December, but continued to be a primary member of the Congress. Three days later her followers declared their intention to hold a National Convention of Congressmen. This Convention met on 1 and 2 January 1978 with Indira Gandhi as the chairperson, and it claimed that her party was the 'real Congress'. This provoked the CWC to expel Mrs. Gandhi from the party the very next day. She, in turn, expelled Reddy, Chavan and others from her party and designated it as Congress (I), 'I' denoting Indira. The other faction came to be known as Congress (S) after Swaran Singh succeeded Reddy as the president. This was almost a virtual replay of the first Congress split in 1969. It also led to the bifurcation of the Congress Parliamentary Party, with 76 MPs supporting Reddy's faction. Congress (I) was left with 70 MPs.

The mighty Indira was mortally scared after her defeat. Mujib's murder had haunted her during the Emergency. She genuinely believed, and not without reason, that some foreign powers were plotting against her. Late on the night of 20 March, when her defeat seemed imminent, she asked Rajiv and Sonia to take their children with them and spend the night with friends.[1] To soften the hostility of the Janata party, she sent a letter to Morarji assuring him, "I am gradually disengaging myself from politics and those who predict a political come-back for me are perhaps deliberately doing so to alarm both the govenment and the Congress."[2] Later she personally met Morarji and Charan Singh with the same objective.

In the beginning Indira told several friends of her desire to retire to some 'sylvan spot in the Himalayas'. But that she could not, even if she had wanted to. The Janata government had launched numerous cases against Sanjay and several enquiries were started against her. When J. Krishnamurti advised her to quit politics, she said, "I have only two alternatives, to fight or to let them destroy me like a sitting duck."[3] So, the indomitable fighter in her took over.

She knew that her real battle lay in the public arena. She must win back the people who had become alienated from her. Her political instincts revived, and she started visiting places which would fetch her the maximum goodwill and publicity. A welcome opening appeared in the form of an invitaton from Vinoba Bhave. She went to his Ashram in Paunar and spent two days there. She was welcomed by a large crowd at Nagpur airport and this naturally lifted her spirits.

Her visit to Belchi, a village in Bihar, was a landmark event. Eleven Harijans had been murdered and burnt in that village. It was August and she travelled through a heavy downpour by jeep and tractor, crossed a river in spate on elephant back, and reached the remote, Godforsaken place in the evening. She listened to the woes of the villagers, gave them solace, and it was late at night by the time she returned. Everywhere people welcomed her with garlands, sang her praises, craved forgiveness. Next day she called on the ailing JP at Patna and addressed a public meeting. Later she travelled to Rae Bareilly by train and road to meet her constituents. She received a big welcome at the Lucknow railway station and people everywhere seemed to have already forgotten the Emergency excesses.

She went to Hardwar to spend some time with Anandmai Ma, her spiritual preceptor. Later she visited Kashmir and complained against Janata misrule and the partisan attitude of the press. In October, when she went to Agra by train, there was a stampede at the railway station. While addressing the public meeting, she was modest enough to confess, 'People come to Agra to see Taj Mahal and Agra Fort. People go to Delhi to see Qutab Minar and Indira Gandhi.' During a three-day tour of the tribal areas of Gujarat, she spent a lot of time with the tribals, addressing meetings, discussing their problems, sharing their frugal meals. It is some measure of the animus of the press that whereas she was mostly welcomed by large crowds wherever she went, the newspapers generally reported black-flag demonstrations against her.

An American caller, seeing the stream of poor people visitng Indira Gandhi, asked her that something must have been done for them as they were coming to her even now. "No," she replied, "those for whom something was done are nowhere to be seen." Her greatest chagrin must have been to see her former senior ministers depose against her before the Shah Commission.

The manner of the Janata government's birth foreshadowed its future: Desai, Jagjivan Ram and Charan Singh, three old and embittered egoists, each aspiring to be the prime minister. It was only the intervention of Jayaprakash Narayan and J.B. Kriplani which solved the tangle and Desai was sworn in as Prime Minister on 23 March. But this was a decision forced from above. In an open contest Jagjivan Ram would have been the clear winner. Thus, the first major act of these champions of democracy was an undemocractic decision.

The more vocal and aggressive section of the Janata Party was full of Emergency hurts and a spirit of vengeance. Several Commissions were set up, and dozens of cases registered against Sanjay on half-baked charges. The most notable of these was the Shah Commission, appointed in April 1977 to enquire into "allegations of abuse of authority, excesses and malpractices" committed during the Emergency. But Indira Gandhi was not mentioned by name.

The Janata also started a campaign of calumny against Indira. Charan Singh as Home Minister accused her of a plan to shoot all the opposition leaders in jail. It was alleged that Jayaprakash's kidneys were deliberately damaged when he was under treatment in a government hospital at Chandigarh. On the basis of a photocopy published in a newspaper, Sanjay was charged in the Parliament of having issued a cheque on a Swiss bank in favour of his wife Maneka. The Finance Minister later clarified that the bank concerned had described the photocopy as a forgery. Mrs. Gandhi was constructing a farmhouse outside Delhi. Its floor was dug up on the suspicion that she had buried cash chests there. In May 1977, Col. T.S. Anand, Sanjay's father-in-law, was found dead in an open field. A little later, Kishan Chand, Lt. Governor of Delhi during the Emergency, jumped into a well and died. It was sought to be made out that Sanjay had contrived these deaths as he wanted to shut the mouth of people who knew too much. None of the allegations could be proved and some were based on forged evidence.

In the Shah Commission enquiry the Janata pulled out all stops to indict and damn Indira. Large and vociferous crowds used to attend the Commission's hearings, which were broadcast on loud-speakers. The government media regularly publicized the allegations made against her. As the witnesses were not allowed to be cross-examined, they were free to level the wildest accusations against Indira.

But Mrs. Gandhi acted with dignity and defiance. When Justice Shah summoned her, she insisted that she would appear only as a witness. When he wanted her to depose before him, she objected that she was under oath of secrecy of office and would not say anything about the decisions taken by her as Prime Minister. Moreover, she could not be asked to give incriminatng evidence against herself. The Commission submitted its report in April 1978, holding that the declaration of a state of emergency was a fraud, as there was no evidence of a breakdown of law and order.

But the incident which really turned the tide in Indira's favour was the shabby and amateurish manner in which the Janata govenment arrested her on 3 October 1977 on two silly charges. As the police went to her house to apprehend her, she took her time to get ready and, in the meantime, a number of her followers were intimated on phone. A convoy of vehicles started from her house and came to a halt at a railway crossing near Haryana border to make way for two trains. Her lawyers argued with the police that in case it was intended to cross over to Haryana, this could not be done without a proper court warrant. This the police had not anticipated. So the convoy turned back after some wrangling and Mrs. Gandhi was finally brought to the Police Lines rest-house at Kingsway Camp.

Next day when she was produced before the Court at Parliament Street, there was a large slogan-shouting gathering of both pro and anti-Indira demonstrators. The magistrate found that the charges against the accused had no supporting evidence and even the First Information Report was not signed. And the police did not even ask for a remand. So the Magistrate ordered unconditional release of Mrs. Gandhi and she went back triumphant, with the Janata government having suffered a humiliating rebuff.

Though the Janata had come to power at the Centre, most of the states were ruled by the Congress. And real power lay in the states. Moreover, it was the state legislatures which elected members to the Rajya Sabha, where the Janata was in a minority. Thus, it contrived to issue a proclamation one month after coming to power, dissolving Congress governments in nine states. The justification for this indefensible step was that the Congress having miserably lost at the Centre, had ceased to represent the people in the country. This was a bad precedent and a plea of doubtful Constitutional merit. Worse still was the Supreme Court's approval of such an action conveyed in a reference made to it for advisory opinion under Article 143 of the Constitution. As the people were still very angry with Indira, the Janata party was able to sweep the assembly polls held in these nine states.

The first indication that Mrs. Gandhi was gaining ground came from the assembly elections held in five states in February 1978. The Congress (I) won absolute majorities in Karnataka and Andhra Pradesh, and formed a ministry in Maharashtra in coalition with Congress (S). Next month, Indira's candidates won two assembly seats and a by-election to parliament in UP.

Janata leaders were too busy fighting one another to take much note of these developments. But they were really rattled when Indira Gandhi got elected as member of Lok Sabha from Chikmaglur, a rural constituency in Karnataka. Devraj Urs, Chief Minister of Karnataka, worked hard for her, and George

Fernandes campaigned vigorously against her. Indira was sworn in as an MP on 20 November 1978 and hoped that this would give her some respite from the relentless harassment. But that was not to be. The very next day the Lok Sabha was presented with a report of the Privileges Committee of the House, holding her guilty of breach of privilege. This finding referred to a privilege motion moved against her in early 1978, alleging harassment of four officials when they were collecting information in reply to a Lok Sabha question. On this flimsy charge the Janata expelled her from Parliament on 19 December and imprisoned her till the House was prorogued. So Mrs. Gandhi spent one week in Tihar Jail.

But the Janata inflicted much deeper wounds on itself by incessant infighting. Desai, Charan Singh and Jagjivan Ram just could not pull together, as each was trying to pull down the other two. Charan Singh accused Desai of shielding his son Kanti who was indulging in open corruption. Desai levelled a similar charge against Charan Singh's wife. Jagjivan Ram attacked Charan Singh for the riots in his state which had alienated the minorities. At one time Charan Singh had called Bahuguna a KGB agent; later they joined hands to dislodge Desai. Sanjay, and Jagjivan Ram's son Suresh carried on their own negotiations for an alliance. In the states, the functioning of Janata ministries was made impossible, as they were being repeatedly asked to seek votes of confidence by rival constituents.

While the senior Janata leaders were tearing one another apart, Morarji Desai failed to provide effective leadership to the Parliamentary Party, resolve differences and work out compromises. The only time he climbed down from his high moral pedestal was when his son Kanti was attacked. Once he told his critics, 'You are possessed. You need to be exorcized.' But even he was stirred into action when Charan Singh described his cabinet colleagues as a 'bunch of impotent people' for their failure to punish Mrs. Gandhi. Two days later, on 29 June 1978 Desai asked him to resign along with Raj Narain. This led to the exit of two other Bharatiya Kranti Dal cabinet ministers and four ministers of state.

But Charan Singh was too important a partner of the coalition to be kept out. So efforts were immediately started to bring him back and seven months later he rejoined the cabinet.

Jan Sangh was the only constituent of the Janata Party which behaved with dignity. It had long-term goals. It quietly recruited a large number of its camp followers to the police, educational institutions and government media. But its strong ties with the RSS got it into trouble with its partners. These ties violated the Janata Party code which debarred its members from joining any other organization whose objectives were at variance with it.

With so much energy spent in mutual squabbles and Indira-baiting, little time was left for new policy initiatives or even routine administration. Prices started to rise sharply, law and order deteriorated, and people became increasingly disenchanted with the Janata rule.

Weird things were happening in this atmosphere of instability and political adventurism. Indira Gandhi had opened a channel of communication with Bahuguna, and Sanjay had become a friend of Raj Narain. The prospects of Charan Singh replacing Desai were openly discussed. Mrs. Gandhi sent him a bouquet on his birthday from Tihar Jail and he, in turn, invited her to celebrations of the birth of a grandson.

It was in this air of unpredictability that on 11 July 1979 Y.B. Chavan, leader of the opposition moved a routine vote of no-confidence against the Desai government. But owing to the split within the Janata Party, the motion was carried and Morarji resigned. The President invited Charan Singh to form the government. His strength rested on his alliance with the Congress (S) and a promise of support by the Congress (I).

Charan Singh was required to seek a vote of confidence within one month of his assuming office. Indira Gandhi made her support conditional on the scrapping of the Special Courts Act, which was passed mainly at Charan Singh's behest. For her it was a matter of survival to have the Act removed. But Charan Singh, found it impossible to oblige. So, at the last minute Indira withdrew her backing. Unable to muster adequate strength for a vote of confidence, Charan Singh resigned on 20 August. He also recommended the dissolution of Lok Sabha which the President accepted, ignoring Jagjivan Ram's strong claim to form the government. And thus came to a sorry end the term of the first non-Congress government.

The Janata rule marked not only the first break from the single-party dominance, but also the ascendance of the rural lobby in the government's priorities. Several ameliorative schemes were prepared in this connection and large foodgrain stocks left by Indira Gandhi were gainfully used for 'food for work' programmes. Its *Antodaya* scheme aimed at helping the poorest families in each village by creating productive assets for them. During the first two years the production of foodgrains reached a record of 125 million and 130 million tonnes. Further, 2.6 million hectares of additional land was brought under irrigation. There was a substantial rise in the consumption of fertilizers and expansion of agricultural credit.

The Janata government also tried to remove the more obnoxious provisions of the 42nd Amendment to the Constitution by the 44th Amendment Act. (It could not go all the way as it did not have a two-third majority in the Rajya Sabha.) Earlier, internal emergency could be declared under article 352 if the country's security was threatened owing to 'internal disturbance'. This was substituted by 'armed rebellion'. A cabinet decision was made a pre-condition for declaring a state of emergency. Further, the citizen's access to the courts on matters concerning rights to life and liberty could not be suspended. Persons arrested under preventive laws could not be detained for more then two months without review of their cases by the courts. The five-year term of Lok Sabha and assemblies was also restored.

An interesting innovation in planning was introduced by adopting the concept of rolling annual plans. Industrial growth during this period slowed down as more funds were diverted to

agriculture and investment in key industrial sectors was reduced.
Heavy deficit financing resulted in unprecedented spurt in prices.

The Janata was born out of a massive political movement and its
basic failure also lay in the political domain. It had a number of
highly experienced and able ministers, and the masses were with
it. But its leaders showed little appreciation of the historic opportunity that had unexpectedly landed in their lap.

Despite all the worry, uncertainty and hostility that Indira Gandhi
faced, she conducted herself with remarkable courage and dignity
during the Janata rule. She never tripped, fully exploited the
lapses of her tormentors and made very skilful use of the media.
It was a superb performance and proved once again that she
fought best when she fought with her back to the wall.

29

The Come-back

$\mathcal{A}$fter the sort of drubbing that the electorate gave Indira Gandhi in 1977, and the trail of bitterness that the Emergency had left behind, her return to power in January 1980 was truly a spectacular performance. This time it was not only the opposition she had to fight, most of her former cabinet ministers and senior Congress (S) leaders were also pitched against her. Yet she won 350 seats in a House of 529, thus securing almost two-third majority. Sanjay won from Amethi by a wide margin.

Despite the harrowing experiences during the Janata rule, Mrs. Gandhi had forgotten little and learnt even less. Even when she was in the wilderness, she refused to accept an arrangement where she was not in absolute command. Several attempts were made to unite the two factions of the Congress. But the efforts failed as she would accept nothing short of total control of the organization. It was owing to the failure of the unity talks that the Congress (I)-Congress (S) ministry in Maharashtra fell. Again, the Janata was able to get the requisite two-third majority in the Rajya Sabha to pass the Special Courts Bill only because Congress (S) members, piqued at Indira's attitude, voted for it. This exposed her to the risk of a summary trial and conviction. But even for reasons of expediency, she refused to accept party unity except on her terms.

Then, she would not permit anybody to point a finger at Sanjay. At an AICC meeting in April 1979 Devraj Urs raised the issue of Sanjay's continued involvement in politics. As some other members also joined him, Mrs. Gandhi walked out of the meeting. Later, on a visit to Karnataka she wanted Urs to resign from the office of President, Pradesh Congress Committee, as he was also

chief minister of the state. When he raised some questions of
propriety, a show-cause notice was served on him. In a stinging
reply Urs told Mrs. Gandhi, 'You have forgotten that while dealing with us you were not dealing with your domestic servants or
satraps.' Indira's immediate reaction was to expel Urs from the
Congress (I) for six years. It was of no consequence that she had
contested parliamenary elec[   ]nstance
and he had used all his reso[   ]sure her
victory. Nor was she bother[   ]what she
needed was to befriend ene[   ]riends.

Thus, when Indira return[   ]es of any
interaction with her were cle[   ]uthority
or aspire to create an indep[   ]nd never
breathe a word against Sanjay.

She returned the Janata's compliment by dismissing all non-
Congress state ministries. Fresh elections were held in these states
in May, and the Congress won everywhere hands down, except
in Tamil Nadu. Sanjay not only had a major say in the selection
of party candidates, but also the appointment of chief ministers.

Most of the worries nagging Mrs. Gandhi vanished with her
accession to power. Just one day after the event, a judge of the
Special Court suddenly discoverd that he had no jurisdiction to
try cases against Mrs. Gandhi and dissolved the court. His
brother-judge presiding over the second Special Court did not
take long to emulate his learned peer. Both Sanjay and V.C. Shukla
had been sentenced to two years' imprisonment and had appealed
against this judgment to the Supreme Court. The apex court did
not take long to set aside the convictions.

Indira Gandhi shifted to her previous residence at 1 Safdarjung
Road and life seemed to settle into the familiar, old groove. Sycophants were fawning all around, beating their chests louder than
ever before. Sanjay, MP and General Secretary, AICC, was holding court, appointing chief ministers, shuffling officials, issuing
orders. And then came the crash. On the morning of 23 June, while
doing aerobatics in his two-seater plane, Sanjay crashed into a
drain behind 12 Wellingdon Crescent, his residence during the

Janata regime. Indira rushed to the spot and saw her cherished dream lying in a mangled heap. She was shattered. But she soon gathered herself and was her usual, composed self again. At Ram Manohar Lohia Hospital, as doctors were tending to the torn bodies of Sanjay and his co-pilot, she took aside Chandra Shekhar and said, "I have for some time been wanting to speak to you about Assam. The situation is very grim."[1] This was the quintessential Indira: a picture of indomitable courage in the face of crisis, and never oblivious of history watching her over the shoulder.

After the accident Indira asked her friend, "Where do I go from here, Pupul?" But the show must go on. After three days she was at her desk in South Block, disposing off files, issuing instructions, holding meetings. And gradually the smithereens of her dream were put together again when her elder son Rajiv was asked to 'help mummy' and he resigned as pilot in the Indian Airlines. The following year he was elected as MP from Amethi and later appointed General Secretary of the Congress (I).

The concluding five years of Indira Gandhi's tenure as Prime Minister were not only the most disturbed, but also the least rewarding. She had come to power on the slogan: 'elect the government that works.' But few things seemed to work smoothly this time. During the previous five years the country was first battered by the Emergency excesses and then the Janata misrule. A sizeable number of Congress MPs in the new parliament were Sanjay's nominees. They were not only young, inexperienced, and lacking in any ideological anchorage, they took their new status as a licence for plunder and misconduct.

Even otherwise, it was a tired Indira who became the Prime Minister in 1980. The Emergency was a period of great inner turmoil for her. She had helplessly watched things going out of control. The Janata rule was one long nightmare, and she lived in continuous dread of her own and her children's safety. All these harrowing experiences had scarred her soul and broken her spirit. And on top of that came Sanjay's devastating crash. She obviously could not be her old self again.

The way Indira quickly got over the trauma and learnt to live with her sorrow goes to her credit. But the country was becoming ungovernable, and the rot could be stemmed only by a leader at the peak of his powers. At one level India's basic problems of poverty, scarcity and sluggish growth remained unaltered. At another, the spread of democratic consciousness, rise of new demand groups and re-adjustment of rural-urban equation injected ever new discords in a society already rocked by numerous conflicts. Indira's accession to office was preceded by a year of severe drought. The huge foodgrain stocks left by her in 1977 were mostly used up by the Janata government in its 'food for work' programme. Owing to high levels of deficit financing by Charan Singh, the prices were rising steeply and despite her election promises, she just could not bring them down. The situation was not helped by the oil prices reaching new peaks in the international market.

These were familiar problems which the country had faced several times earlier. So were the recurrence of communal riots, atrocities on the weaker sections, tribal unrest and peasant insurgency. But this second set of problems had changed in character. For one thing, they had become more persistent and their spread had increased. For another the class character of some of the adversaries had also altered.

Land reforms of the fifties had benefited the upper layer of the Shudra peasants the most. Millions of them had become influential, middle-level land owners. On the other hand, the landless, mostly comprising Scheduled Castes and other deprived sections, had become more conscious of their rights and resisted oppression by their employers. This confrontationist situation further aggravated caste conflicts, leading to an increase in cruelty to Harijans. Whereas Mrs. Gandhi had tried to get political mileage from the Belchi outrage during the Janata regime, similar barbarities were committed at Parasbigha and Pipra soon after she came to power.

Prolonged exploitation of the tribals by contractors, moneylenders and avaricious farmers had driven them to desperation. It was mainly the combination of the landless and the tribals which led to the re-surfacing of Naxalism in several states. Their activities were largely confined to the tribal areas, and the People's War Group in Andhra Pradesh was the most aggressive of the lot. In 1981 alone more than 300 incidents of Naxalite violence were reported, resulting in nearly one hundred deaths.

It was not only the dispossessed who felt aggrieved and angry. The landowning classes with their rising aspirations, wanted a larger share of the state's resources. They organized countrywide agitations demanding higher procurement prices for their produce and supply of subsidized agricultural inputs.

Perhaps the most worrisome development was the worsening of the communal situation owing to communalization of politics. Two specific factors may be noted here. One, Jana Sangh had fully exploited its position as the senior partner of the Janata Party. It had not only broadened its organizational base, it also inducted a large number of its followers in the government services. Secondly, the conversion of nearly 1300 Harijans to Islam in Meenakshipuram in April 1981 severely hurt the Hindus. No other incident has given such a fillip to Hindu communalism or done so much damage to the cause of communal harmony.

As to the situation on the ground, there were 2185 cases of communal riots during this period, and they resulted in 2394 deaths. These figures are higher than any other 5-year period since Independence. The severity of communal violence in Muradabad, Aligarh, Biharsharief, Baroda, Malegaon, Bhiwandi, Belgaum, and the occurrence of frequent riots even in south India showed how the cancer of communalism was spreading in the body politic.

It was also observed that whereas earlier Mrs. Gandhi used to rush to the site of serious riots and show special solicitude for the minority community, now her responses were milder both in word and deed. Perhaps, owing to the alienation of the Muslims as a result of the Emergency onslaught, she was now trying to cultivate the Hindu constituency. A clear indication of this change was given by C.M. Stephen when in 1983 he declared, "...the wave-length of Hindu culture and Congress culture is the same."[2]

In August 1980 Moradabad was rocked by one of the worst communal riots. Mrs. Gandhi paid a hurried visit to the city two months after the event. She described the riots as a part of a conspiracy to undermine the stability of the government.[3] In May 1984 she assured the majority community that "If there is injustice to them or if they did not get their rights, then it would be dangerous to the integrity of the country."[4]

The economic and social problems facing the country, or the class, caste and communal conflicts, were not of Indira's creation, though she could have exerted harder to contain them. But on the political and administrative fronts the situation deteriorated largely as a result of her misjudgement and mishandling.

Mrs. Gandhi never appreciated that only strong states make for a strong Centre, and strong states can be built only by capable and strong chief ministers. In her anxiety to remove all challenges to her authority she never favoured the emergence of able leaders with a popular base. Karnataka and Andhra Pradesh were the only states with chief ministers of some standing. Devraj Urs of Karnataka, one of her most loyal supporters during the Emergency, was destabilized when he criticized Sanjay. After coming to power she eased out Chenna Reddy of Andhra Pradesh who had stood by her during the Emergency but acted a little cocky. Indira replaced him by T. Anjiah, who was a well meaning nonentity. He was openly reprimanded by Rajiv Gandhi when he held a grand reception for him at the Hyderabad airport. But Rajiv obviously overdid his act and the public humiliation of the chief minister enabled N.T. Ramarao (NTR), a popular film actor, to launch his Telugu Desam Party to safeguard the self-respect of the Andhras. Instead of an apology, Anjiah got the boot. He was removed from office and replaced by B.V. Reddy, who was soon replaced by V.B. Reddy.

Sanjay had a major say in the appointment of chief ministers, and his nominees seldom brought any credit to their office. Jagannath Pahadia of Rajasthan had to be removed owing to serious charges of corruption. But it was A.R. Antulay who brought the maximum odium on his benefactors. He floated various trusts and collected millions by issuing permits of controlled commodities, accepting large donations, granting exemptions, etc. The media and parliament repeatedly demanded a judicial enquiry against him. But Indira was reluctant to offend the Muslims by sacking a chief minister from their community. Ultimately it was the Bombay High Court's strictures against him that led to his exit.

"Rajiv lacks Sanjay's dynamism and his concerns," she told her friend Pupul Jayakar, "yet he could be a great help to me." Rajiv's grooming for a political career proceeded on two tracks. One, the large corps of Sanjay's henchmen was systematiclly disbanded and Maneka Gandhi was downgraded to pre-empt the emergence of a rival focus of power. In this process the treatment meted out to Sanjay's young widow forms one of the least edifying episodes of Indira's life. Maneka was a spirited lass, ambitious and pushing, aspiring to inherit her husband's mantle. This was anathema to Mrs. Gandhi, and their differences led to some very ugly incidents. So incensed was Indira with Maneka that she threw her out of the house and passed some very coarse remarks about her family. It was sad to see such a refined and cultured lady losing control over herself and making public a family quarrel.

The second track she followed was the building up of Rajiv by exposing him to various facets of governance and political management. Besides his election as an MP and appointment as General Secretary of the Congress, Indira Gandhi drafted his cousin Arun Nehru and his close friend Arun Singh to help him in his work. One of the major organizational tasks given to Rajiv was to monitor the preparations for the IX Asian Games. I was the Secretary General of the Organizing Committee and spent hundreds of hours in his company. The Games proved to be a spectacular success and Mrs. Gandhi was very proud of her son's contribution.

Rajiv's next important assignment was the conduct of assembly elections for Andhra Pradesh and Karnataka in January 1983. He was placed in overall charge of the operation, and Arun Nehru was asked to assist him. "They will make mistakes, they will learn," she confided to a friend. "Why are we so afraid of making mistakes?"[5] When the results came, the Congress (I) had lost in both the states. N.T. Ramarao made a clean sweep in Andhra Pradesh and the Janata Party won in Karnataka.

Obviously the Indira charisma was wearing off. This raised the hopes of the oppostion parties, and NTR started dreaming big. He renamed his regional Telegu Desam as Bharat Desam Party. Mrs. Gandhi was quite allergic to him and ticked him off when he raised the question of the Kashmir chief minister's dismissal in the National Development Council. This created a big rumpus and all the non- Congress CMs walked out of the Council meeting in protest.

Few months later Ram Lal, governor of Andhra Pradesh, sacked NTR without any provocation and installed N. Bhaskar Rao, his Finance Minister, in his place. Bhaskar Rao's claim that he had defected to the Congress (I) along with his followers and outnumbered Telegu Desam was accepted without verification. But he could never prove his majority in the House. Later NTR paraded his followers before the President in Delhi, and was sworn in again as the chief minister.

The removal of NTR was severely criticized by all sections of public opinion. Indira Gandhi informed the parliament that she learnt about the Governor's action only from a news report and had nothing to do with this episode. Nobody believed her. But this seems to have been true. Her Principal Secretary, P.C. Alexander has written, "The truth is that she came to know of Governor Ram Lal's action for the first time when I got the news from the Intelligence Bureau and brought it to her notice."[6] It is believed that Arun Nehru, anticipating her wishes, phoned the governor to do the dirty job. This badly exposes the workings of the PM's coterie and shows its political naïvety and absence of scruples.

The three border states of Assam, Jammu and Kashmir and Punjab had problems with the Centre since Independence, and these worsened with time. Whereas the situation in each state had its own peculiar features, yet there were two factors in common. One, the local population's perceived threats to their identity. And two, Mrs. Gandhi's persistence in placing the party interests above the larger national good.

The North Eastern region is a cauldron of ethnicities, ever on the boil. Though Indira Gandhi tried to satisfy local aspirations by creating the states of Meghalaya, Mizoram and Arunachal Pradesh, and conferred full statehood on Manipur and Tripura, yet these were only partial solutions.

But it is the developments in Assam during the Indira era which occupy the centre stage in the North East. Before reorganization, it comprised the whole of this region except the two small pockets of Manipur and Tripura. By 1972 four states, i.e., Nagaland, Meghalaya, Mizoram and Arunachal Pradesh were carved out of it.

In Assam it was not the political parties which led the struggle, but the All Assam Students Union (AASU) had mounted one agitation after the other, and in 1978 it came up with a 16-point agenda, which included the question of continued infiltration by the foreigners. So strong was AASU's hold over the state that when election to the parliament was held in 1980, the poll could be conducted in only 2 out of 14 constituencies.

When Indira Gandhi returned to power in 1980, she made earnest efforts to reach a settlement with the agitators. The crux of the AASU demand was that all aliens who entered Assam after 1951 should be disenfranchised and expelled from the state. After prolonged negotiations the students agreed to 1961 as the cut-off point. The Centre insisted that the date should be pushed to 24 March 1971, when a pact was signed between Mrs. Gandhi and Mujibur Rehman. At times a compromise mid-point of 1966 was also discussed. In the midst of this stalemate the time came for holding assembly election in the middle of February 1983. The state had already been under President's rule for one year, and it could not be extended as a result of the 44th Constitutional Amendment passed by the Janata government. Prudence required that the Constitution should be amended again to overcome this hurdle. As the Congress(I) did not have a two-third majority in the Rajya Sabha, Indira made a half-hearted attempt to seek the support of the opposition parties. But as no agreement could be reached, Mrs. Gandhi announced the holding of election on schedule.

The state was rocked by agitations and there were all-round appeals to defer the poll. In the statewide violence that followed, thousands were massacred and tens of thousands rendered homeless. Whole villages were burnt and wiped out. The worst carnage occurred in Nelli, a remote village in Nowgong district. It was predominantly a Muslim habitation and the tribal marauders butchered all the inhabitants, including women and children. The holocaust attracted international attention and shocked the country.

This was the most violent election in India's history. And the attendant savagery was largely avoidable. Mrs. Gandhi was not new to the process of constitutional amendment. An earnest appeal would have secured the cooperation of all the parties to make the necessary change. In fact several leaders pleaded to this end. Even if the opposition had backed out, she could have held it responsible for what followed. Why did she do it?

The simple explanation lies in political expediency. Most of the infiltrators from Bangladesh were Muslims and they voted en bloc for the Congress in the hope of receiving its patronage. The Congress leaders from Assam were confident of winning the election. Of course, a Congress ministry under Hiteshwar Saikia was installed after the polls but it was a ghost outfit. Despite heavy voting in the Bengali-dominated Cachar district, the Congress came to power with the support of just 17 percent of the registered voters.

Towards the end of his life Nehru had released Sheikh Abdullah from prison and allowed him to go to Pakistan to reopen negotiations. As Nehru died when the Sheikh was still in Pakistan, the initiative never got off the ground. The following year Abdullah was re-arrested by the Shastri government on suspicion of hobnobbing with foreign powers. In her effort to rebuild bridges,

Indira Gandhi again released him on 2 January 1968, and started a dialogue. The Sheikh had also mellowed. Whatever illusions he had of ruling an independent state were put paid to by Pakistan's crushing defeat in the Bangladesh war and the subsequent Simla Pact. The door to an understanding with Abdullah was opened by D.P. Dhar's note to the Prime Minister in which he listed some concrete proposals for the settlement. Mrs. Gandhi deputed G. Parthasarathy, an eminent diplomat and a trusted adviser, to negotiate with the Sheikh. It was in February 1975 that a six-point Kashmir accord was finally announced in the parliament. It enlarged the area of power-sharing between the state and the Centre.

At that time the state had a Congress Ministry headed by Syed Mir Qasim. Realizing that only Sheikh Abdullah could restore normality in the state, he showed unusual magnanimity for a politician in power, and stepped down in the former's favour on 25 February.

Mrs. Gandhi had acted with wisdom and foresight in rehabilitating the Sheikh. But strangely, after the Janata party came to power in 1977, the Governor of Jammu and Kashmir was informed that the Congress was withdrawing support to the chief minister. This came as a shock to Sheikh Abdullah and he recommended the dissolution of the state assembly. In the fresh election held in July 1977 he trounced his opponents. He remained chief minister of Kashmir till his death on 8 September 1982.

In keeping with the hallowed practice of Indian politicians, the Sheikh had made his son Farooq Abdullah the President of his party in August 1981. So, the succession was quite smooth. Indira Gandhi again acted wisely and supported this arrangement. But the prospect of young Farooq consolidating his position was not to her liking. After all, her party could be completely sidelined in the state. As the assembly elections approached, both sides tried to cobble some sort of alliance, but failed. Farooq swept the board and again became the CM in June 1983.

Feeling insecure, Farooq tried to create a larger base for himself. He attended the opposition CMs' conclave arranged by NTR in Vijaywada in May 1983. A couple of months after his electoral victory, he held a similar session in Srinagar. Mrs. Gandhi found Farooq growing too big for his boots. As his brother-in-law G.M. Shah himself had ambitions to be the Chief Minister, Indira's hatchetmen formed a pact with him and it was agreed that he would defect to the Congress along with his group to topple Farooq. But the Governor, B.K. Nehru, refused to go along with this plot. He was therefore transferred to Gujarat and the 'not-to-reason-why' Lt. Governor of Delhi, Jagmohan, posted in his place.

Early morning on 2 July, G.M. Shah met Jagmohan along with his 12 supporters and claimed majority support in the assembly. A Congress leader accompanied him to confirm his party's backing to the defectors. Farooq was not given an opportunity to engage in a trial of strength on the floor of the House, and Shah was sworn in as the Chief Minister the same evening. Arun Nehru confessed, "Indira Phuphi (aunt) asked us to get rid of Farooq at all costs and we did."[7] Later, he was to repeat the same caper against NTR with disastrous results.

Earlier Mrs. Gandhi had shown great sagacity and political acumen in re-establishing cordial relations with Sheikh Abdullah. But the messy, short-sighted and vindictive act againt his son revealed the other side of Indira. By overthrowing a democratically elected government through such political skulduggery she convinced the Kashmiris that the Centre would never allow them a government of their choice. Of all the blunders committed by the Indian Government in handling the Kashmir situation, this was the costliest and the most self-destructive.

Thus whether it was the economy, or political management of the party and the states, or law and order, or communal relations, or the problems of the border states, the last phase of Indira Gandhi's regime saw an overall deterioration in the situation.

30

Operation Blue Star and After

*O*peratic   1956   ic episode in the post-
Independence   ıd its saddest part is
that it was wh   *Reorganized*   t highlights so sharply
the complexit   *linguistic*   e of governance, the
simultaneous ı   ional interest and the
limitations of I

The genesis .. ... ғ unjab problem lies in the history of the
Sikhs, the partition of Punjab, and the perception of the Sikh
leaders about the denial of a fair deal to their community. In 1956
all the states of India except Punjab were reorganized on linguistic
basis. The Akalis felt that this was an act of discrimination and it
would not have happened if the Hindus were in a majority in this
border state. Later, in the 1961 census a large number of Punjabi
Hindus gave their mother tongue as Hindi. It further confirmed
the Akali belief that this was a ploy meant to prevent the formation of a Punjabi-speaking state.

From 1947 to the end of Indira's rule the Akalis never won
absolute majority in the Punjab assembly. Yet they formed a
government five times in alliance with other parties. But not once
did the Congress-ruled Centre let it complete its full term. This
convinced the Akali Dal that the Sikhs will not be allowed to rule
Punjab, though they constituted 61 percent of its population.[1]

As a result of frequent agitations and threats of fasts unto death
by Akali leaders, the demand for a Punjabi Suba was conceded
in March 1966, soon after Mrs. Gandhi became the Prime Minister.
The credit for this fair decision is given to her. This is only technically correct. The fact is, as stated by Indira in *My Truth*, "When
the Punjabi Suba demand was on, I was very worried ... I went
to Mr. Chavan and said I had heard that Sardar Hukam Singh
was going to give a report in favour of Punjabi Suba and that he

should be stopped." This was in 1965 when Mrs. Gandhi was a minister under Shastri. He had appointed a Parliamentary Committee under Hukam Singh, Speaker, Lok Sabha, to examine this issue. Her apprehension was that "once the Prime Minister's appointee had declared himself in favour of Punjabi Suba, how could we get out of it?" But why was Mrs. Gandhi so agitated over this issue? Again, in her own words, "...to concede the Akali demand would mean abandoning a position to which it (Congress) was firmly committed and letting down its Hindu supporters in the projected Punjabi Suba. ... This startling reversal of Congress policy was totally unexpected."[2]

Indira wrote these words not as a junior and inexperienced minister in 1965, but as a seasoned politician in 1980 after she had served as Prime Minister for 11 years. The most significant aspect of her observations is the distress at the "startling reversal of Congress policy" in "letting down its Hindu supporters in the projected Punjabi Suba." This solicitude for Hindu sensitivities coloured many of her decisions and not on Punjab only. The concern, though, was certainly not communal but electoral.

The linguistic state of Punjab was formed by splitting the original Punjab into the three states of Punjab, Haryana and Himachal Pradesh. As Haryana had no capital of its own, it was decided that Chandigarh would be administered Centrally, and serve as a capital of both Punjab and Haryana. This was a messy arrangement, and caused serious complications later.

Soon, Akali leaders started agitating for giving Chandigarh to Punjab, as a state must have a capital of its own. When an eminent Sikh leader threatened self-immolation, Mrs. Gandhi announced her award in January 1970: Chandigarh would go to Punjab, but the Tehsils of Fazilka and Abohar would be transferred from Punjab to Haryana. This was an even messier solution than the previous one. These two Tehsils were not contiguous to Haryana, and could be linked with that state only by a 10-mile corridor.

Sant Jarnail Singh Bhindranwale, an obscure Sikh priest from a remote village of Punjab, became the most dreaded person in the state in the early eighties.

Giani Zail Singh, another qualified Sikh priest, had more or less the same academic and cultural background as Bhindranwale. But he joined politics and rose to be the chief minister of Punjab from 1972-77. In the 1977 assembly election the Congress lost to Akali Dal.

During the Janata regime, when Sanjay Gandhi was working on various schemes to topple the ill-assorted Janata coalitions in the states, the Giani advised him to split the Akali Dal by creating a rival focus of Sikh leadership. That is how the Congress started nursing Sant Bhindranwale, a fiery zealot, then attached to Damdami Taksal, a famous Sikh seminary. He created his own party, Dal Khalsa, in April 1978, and soon thereafter assaulted a congregation of Nirankaris, a sect accused of apostasy by the Sikhs. Twelve of his followers were killed in this clash.

In the 1980 general election Bhindranwale actively campaigned for several Congress candidates. Later, when BBC questioned Mrs. Gandhi on this point, she conceded, "Bhindranwale did go and speak for one of our candidates in the elections."[3]After the Congress returned to power in 1980, his star rose fast. He settled his score with the Nirankaris when his men shot dead their Guru, Baba Gurbachan Singh, in April 1980.

The event which created a sensation in Punjab was the murder of Lala Jagat Narain, editor of the influential Hindi daily, *Punjab Kesari*, and a respected spokesman of the Hindus. Bhindranwale was suspected of the foul act and Darbara Singh, the chief minister of Punjab, ordered the police to arrest him. Giani Zail Singh, for whom Sanjay had got the home ministership at the Centre, interceded on behalf of his protégé. Bhindranwale was hiding in Haryana, and the crafty CM of the state helped him to escape the police dragnet at Giani's instance.[4] Ultimately, when the police managed to corner him, he agreed to surrender, but on his terms. His arrest was followed by large-scale violence in the state. Yet, one month later, Zail Singh informed the parliament that charges against Bhindranwale had no substance, and he was being released.

Bhindranwale let loose a reign of terror in Punjab. His followers indulged in wanton killings of Hindus to create panic. His strategy was to provoke Hindu-Sikh riots in Punjab so that the Hindus fled the state. This, he hoped, would result in a backlash against the Sikhs in the rest of India who, in turn, would seek shelter in Punjab. Through this exchange of populations he hoped to achieve his cherished dream of turning Punjab into Khalistan, a euphemism for a Sikh homeland. The height of Bhindranwale's audacity was reached when his men shot dead A.S. Atwal, the seniormost police officer in Amritsar, inside the precincts of the Golden Temple on 23 April 1983.

The chief minister wanted the police to enter the Temple and round up the terrorists, but he was prevented from doing so by the Centre. This was a rare opportunity missed by the government to go into the Shrine and flush out the terrorists.

The rise of Bhindranwale meant the decline of the Akali Dal. That was the objective with which the Congress had started this game. But when the Akalis saw that Bhindranwale's militancy was attracting a lot of Sikh adherents to him, they also tried to strike aggressive communal postures. For reasons of expediency, they could not openly oppose Bhindranwale, whom many Sikhs had come to regard as a selfless crusader. Thus, when Bhindranwale was arrested, the Akalis demanded his release.

During the entire Bhindranwale phase, Sikh politics was dominated by three persons. Sant Harchand Singh Longowal, President of the Akali Dal; Gurcharan Singh Tohra, president SGPC; and Prakash Singh Badal, the former chief minister of Punjab. They were basically moderates and despite a general impression to the contrary, they never raised the demand for Khalistan. But they were all self-seekers, and none of them had the courage to challenge Bhindranwale openly. And their task was not made easier by the consistently hostile attitude of the Centre.

The conflict between the Akalis and Bhindranwale resulted not only from their rivalry for Sikh leadership, but also the divergence of their objectives. Akalis wanted political power; Bhindranwale aimed at establishing a Sikh state. "For the former (Longowal) Hindu-Sikh unity was important, but for Bhindranwale it only stood in the way of Sikh supremacy."[5] In April 1984, Longowal was able to persuade the five High Priests to issue a Hukamnama (edict) to end the violence inside the temple and to order Bhindranwale to leave the Akal Takht. But the killing of a former High Priest scared the priests and the edict was never issued.[6] Simultaneously, the Akali Dal began raising high-visibility demands to upstage the Sant. They resurrected a resolution passed in October 1973 at Anandpur Sahib, the place where Guru Gobind Singh had baptized the Khalsa and given the Sikhs five external symbols of identification. This Resolution was later revised in October 1978. As few documents have raised so much controversy, or been so widely misunderstood and misinterpreted, it would be useful to examine it in some detail. Here I am going by the revised and authenticated version as reproduced in Government of India's "White Paper on The Punjab Agitation."[7] The main charge against this Resolution is that it seeks a separate homeland for the Sikhs and is secessionist in intent.

The Anandpur Sahib Resolution actually comprises twelve separate resolutions. Only the first two refer to political and territorial demands, the rest are just hot air. As to the charge of secession, the operative part of the Resolution says that the government should "recast the constitutional structure of the country on real and meaningful federal principles to obviate the possibility of any danger to nationl unity and the integrity of the country and further, to enable the states to play a useful role for the progress and prosperity of the Indian people..." The second resolution is mainly concerned with territorial claims on Punjabi-speaking areas, sharing of river waters with other states, etc. Contrary to what critics say, there is absolutely no reference to the creation of a state where 'Raj Karega Khalsa' (the Sikhs will rule), or limiting the Central jurisdiction to three or four subjects only. Several states have repeatedly asked for enlarging the federal content of the Constitution, and any number of them have mutual territorial or river-water disputes. Yet they have never been blamed of any separatist designs. Further, the resolution was only a bargaining counter and there was nothing sacrosanct about it. (There are other versions of this Resolution which contain some extreme demands. But the one referred to above is the authentic version, and the government's White Paper describes it as such.)

The Akalis, when they ruled Punjab during the Janata regime, did not bother about the implementation of this Resolution, though it was updated during that period. It was only when they lost power and faced Bhindranwale's challenge that it was pulled out of the archives. But as the Resolution itself was too nebulous. When Indira Gandhi held a meeting with the Akalis in Chandigarh on 21 September 1981, they gave her a memorandum of 15 points. Interestingly, as Bhindranwale had been arrested only a day earlier, the first demand of the Akalis pertained to his unconditional release. Mrs. Gandhi told the Akalis, "Bhindranwale is not a good man; you have been supporting him unnecessarily." The Akalis replied, "You have supported him for four years, we have supported him for 20 days."[8]

The fast deteriorating law and order situation in the sensitive border state of Punjab, with its distinct communal overtones, had the Centre greatly worried. In keeping with her style, Mrs. Gandhi did not give Darbara Singh, the balanced and secular chief minister of Punjab, any freedom in tackling things on his own. In October 1983 he was sacked when the terrorists hijacked a bus, pulled out the Hindus and shot six of them in cold blood. President's rule was imposed and B.D. Pande, a former Cabinet Secretary and a very able administrator, was appointed as the Governor. He had even less freedom of action than the chief minister.

Mrs. Gandhi realized that a settlement with the Akalis was a pre-condition to the return of normality in Punjab. Endless negotiations were held between the two sides at various levels in search of a solution, and the failure of these efforts are primarily responsible for the tragedy of Punjab. What were the basic demands of the Akalis? One set of demands were religious, the other purely secular. The only substantial religious demand was the amendment of the Gurudwara Act to bring Sikh shrines all over India under SGPC's control. This was not a critical issue, and never figured as a make-or-break hurdle in the negotiations.

As to the major secular demands, there were three. The first demand was territorial, i.e., the transfer of Chandigarh to Punjab. The second pertained to the sharing of river waters between Punjab, Haryana and Rajasthan. And the third concerned the decentralization of powers. Mrs. Gandhi had three rounds of direct talks with the Akali leaders. The first time she met them in October 1981, and the second time a month later. Talks were held in a cordial atmosphere, though no agreement was reached. The third round was held in April 1982. This time Indira was cold and reserved. "The most obvious explanation of the change in Mrs. Gandhi's attitude," writes Mark Tully, "is that politics came before statesmanship. The following month elections to the state assemblies were due in Haryana and Himachal Pradesh. Both the states had sizeable populations of Punjabi-speaking Hindus who would certainly not have favoured concessions to the party of the Sikhs."[9]

But the efforts for a solution continued. The most notable of these was the talks that Swaran Singh, a former cabinet minister of Indira, had with the Akali leaders in October 1982.

It had been all along conceded by Indira that Chandigarh would go to Punjab, provided the Tehsils of Fazilka and Abohar were transferred from Punjab to Haryana in exchange. The Akalis agreed that the question of the two Tehsils be referred to a judicial commission for decision on merits. They also agreed to refer the river water dispute to a Supreme Court Judge for an independent decision. Decentralization was essentially a question of Centre-State relations, and the Akalis consented to the appointment of a Parliamentary committee to look into the matter. A settlement on these lines was acceptable to Mrs. Gandhi. But she said that the matter would have to be placed before a Cabinet sub-committee. The sub-committee also approved it. Then she wanted to have the approval of the parliament. "But the statement placed before the parliament was materially different from what had been shown to the Akalis."[10]

The Akalis were shocked and called it a betrayal. Swaran Singh swore never to offer his good offices again. Several agreements had been reached with other states and they were never ratified by the parliament beforehand. In fact, a drastic decision like the imposition of Emergency was taken without consulting the cabinet. But here Mrs. Gandhi wanted to pilot this agreement through all the democratic channels of discussion and debate before giving her approval. And what was there to discuss in this agreement in any case? All the three controversial issues had been left for decision by commissions, tribunals or committees. Never before had Indira's political acumen deserted her so completely, and seldom had she been swayed by such narrow concerns.

But, with so many well-meaning persons around, the efforts for a solution continued. Encouraged by the success of his earlier agitations, Longowal threatened to disrupt the Asian Games due to commence on 19 November 1982. Rajiv Gandhi was supervising the arrangements and the project was very dear to Indira Gandhi. So talks with the Akalis were again resumed to defuse the situation. Again, agreement was almost reached but for the last-minute pressure by Bhajan Lal for the transfer of the two Tehsils to Haryana. A couple of months later a third effort also got aborted at the last moment. Harkishan Singh Surjeet, MP, told a BBC journalist, "Three times in six months an agreement was reached and three times the Prime Minister backed out. Each time the interests of the Hindus of Haryana weighed more heavily with her than a settlement with the Sikhs."[11]

The failure of the Akali Dal to reach a negotiated settlement with the government was fully exploited by Bhindranwale. He could now convincingly tell the Sikhs that the Hindu government at Delhi would not concede their legitimate demands through peaceful means. The Akalis were also forced to show greater belligerence so as not to lose further ground to the Sant.

Meantime the extremists were stepping up their reign of terror and the Hindus had started moving out of Punjab. Bhajan Lal, the champion of Hindu interests, made his own contribution to the worsening of the communal tensions. In view of the Akali threat to disrupt the Asian Games, a security cordon was thrown around Delhi. As the route from Punjab to Delhi passes through Haryana, Bhajan ensured that every Sikh coming from Punjab was frisked. In the process the Sikhs were made to remove their turbans and humiliated in every manner. This gratuitous and organized insult to the Sikhs was deeply resented by the whole community and gave Bhindranwale the excuse to claim that the Sikhs could live with honour in Khalistan only.

On 8 February 1984 the Akalis called a general strike to press their demands. It was a peaceful demonstration. "The strike in Punjab was followed by the first serious outbreak of anti-Sikh rioting in Haryana — rioting which the Chief Minister provoked ... warning the Akali leaders the Hindu's patience was running out and that retaliation was near. Hindu mobs burnt down the Gurudwara in Panipat... Sikhs (were) pulled out of buses and forcibly shaved ... Eight Sikhs were clubbed to death."[12]

Bhindranwale's terrorists, joined by all sorts of criminals, were holding the state to ransom and killing the hapless people at will. Provocations from Haryana further stoked communal passions. Having failed to make any breakthrough in the negotiations with the government, the Akalis stood discredited in the eyes of their community. As the civil administration broke down, the whole state was declared a 'disturbed area'.

With the Akalis reduced to a nullity and the state government paralysed by indecision, Bhindranwale was pressing the accelerator all the time. His men burnt down 27 railway stations in one day, derailed the Kashmir Express resulting in the death of 19 persons, shot dead V.N. Tiwari, MP, and gunned down Romesh Chandar, the son of Lala Jagat Narain. With an increasing number of Hindus leaving the state in panic, the Sant saw his dream of a Sikh state taking shape.

As rumours began floating that the army may be deployed to arrest him, Bhindranwale started smuggling arms into the Temple and turned it into a regular fortress. In this venture he was assisted by General Shahbeg Singh, an expert in guerilla warfare, who had trained the Mukti Bahini at one stage, but had to leave the army later in disgrace.

It is surprising that whereas the fortification of the Golden Temple was going apace in the open, the government could neither prevent the smuggling of arms nor stop construction of bunkers and pillboxes.

Almost till the end Indira Gandhi told her advisers that entry of the army into the Golden Temple was unthinkable. Rajiv Gandhi was actively associated in this exercise and his team talked to a number of persons on this subject. But a powerful lobby was advocating that in view of the awesome power acquired by Bhindranwale, there was no option to the army storming the Temple. Lt. General K. Sundarji, GOC-in-C Western Command assured the PM that it will be a 'knock-out blow' and the whole operation would be over in two hours.

In a last-minute bid to wrest the initiative from the Sant, Longowal announced the launching of an agitation to stop the movement of foodgrains from Punjab to other states. He also beseeched Indira Gandhi "to make some concession for which he could claim credit so that he could call off the Morcha and isolate Bhindranwale."[13]

But events were hurtling towards their tragic denouement, as if driven by a malevolent fate. On 2 June Indira Gandhi broadcast an appeal to Akali leaders not to stop the movement of foodgrains, offered to refer the dispute about Chandigarh and the two Tehsils to a commission, and advised the Punjabis "don't shed blood, shed hatred." But the die had already been cast and the Akalis had no time to respond. Next day the army laid siege to the Temple and thirty-seven other Gurudwaras in Punjab, and the state was cut off from the rest of the country. Giani Zail Singh, the President and Commander-in-Chief of the armed forces, was not informed about this operation, code named 'Blue Star'. The army made a full-scale entry into the temple on 5 June. The government could not have chosen a worse time: it was the martyrdom day of Guru Arjun Dev, and the place was packed with devotees. This shows the nature of expert advice available to the PM. Every time the troops tried to advance, they met a strong barrage of fire and suffered heavy casualties. An armoured car was knocked off by Bhindranwale's rocket launchers. Ultimately, the army ordered its main battle tank, Vijayanta, to move in. Six tanks trundled down the marble steps and on the Parikarma (the walk way skirting the holy tank), and started firing at Akal Takht. To this assault with heavy 105 mm guns Gen. Shahbeg Singh had no answer. The best part of the building was reduced to rubble, fire raged, and this put an end to Bhindranwale's crazy career.

The dead bodies of Bhindranwale and Shahbeg Singh were discovered on 7 June. They met an amply deserved end. But what about the large number of devotees who died in the crossfire. The temple staff and pilgrims were treated as if they belonged to the enemy side and tortured. "The army locked up 60 pilgrims in that room and shut not only the door but the window also. Electric supply was disconnected. The night between June 5th and 6th was extremely hot ... the door of the room was opened at 8 a.m. on June 6th. By this time fifty out of sixty had died."[14] The Blackhole of Calcutta is history; this incident was hardly noticed.

The entire Sikh community was stunned and outraged. Some sections of the population and the government showed gross insensitivity to this trauma. Some Hindus in Amritsar and several other cities celebrated the event by distributing sweets and a show of jubilation. The government, in its anxiety to justify its action, mounted a publicity campaign which created the impression that all Sikhs were secessionists. Whereas the civilian Sikhs just clamped up after the Operation, some Sikh soldiers, mostly fresh recruits, could not bear this shock and rose in revolt. Particularly tragic was the mutiny at the Sikh Regimental Centre at Ramgarh, Bihar, where Brigadier S.S. Puri, the Commandant, was shot dead by his soldiers.

I was Secretary, Ministry of Infomation and Broadcasting when all this happened. On 11 June I took a plane-load of Indian and foreign journalists to the Golden Temple. I saw old Sikhs with dishevelled hair clutching chunks of the demolished Akal Takht, and wailing 'We have lost all; we have become paupers.'

The government decided to rebuild the structure as its sight was provocative to the Sikhs. So Buta Singh, Minister for Works and Housing, was given the task. As the Sikhs were most averse to cooperating with a government agency, he got hold of a sect leader and started *Kar Sewa* (service of work). Despite the facade of a contrived *Kar Sewa*, the structure was actually rebuilt by contractors. Later it was demolished by the community and reconstruction started with solemn rites by voluntary service of devout Sikhs.

Indira Gandhi was assassinated five months after Operation Blue Star. But she had been having premonitions of the approaching end for quite some time. Her close friend Pupul Jayakar has sensitively captured her sombre moods of this period. When Pupul met her towards the end of 1982 Indira said, "For the last month I have not slept. I feel great uneasiness, a sense of foreboding ... Night after night I dream of a venomous old woman, full of hatred, reaching out to destroy me."[15] She had been under too much stress for too long, and the fairy-tale ogres, closeted in her mind since childhood, were wriggling out of her subconscious and preying on her sleep. "I have been receiving secret reports" she continued, "of tantric rituals and black magic rites being performed to destroy me and my sanity."[16] Pupul took her to meet the sage J. Krishnamurti. The meeting stilled her mind. It is around this time, Pupul feels, that Indira wrote, "I have never felt less like dying ... if I die a violent death as some fear and a few are plotting, I know the violence will be in the thought and the action of the assassin, not in my dying!"[17]

In the last week of October 1984, she went to Srinagar. She roamed among the mountains she loved so dearly, drank of the autumnal beauty of the Valley, went on a pilgrimage to her family shrines. Before she left, Indira told Pupul, "Once again a feeling is rising in me, why am I here? And now I feel I have been here long enough."[18]

On her return she left for Bhubaneshwar, where she delivered her prophetic speech, "I do not care whether I live or not ... as long as there is breath in me, so long will I continue to serve, and when my life goes I can say that every drop of blood that is in me will give life to India and strengthen it." She was still in Orissa on 30 October when news reached her that her grandchildren's escort jeep had met with an accident. She was always worried about their safety and she rushed back to Delhi. She cancelled her appointments for 31st except for a TV interview with Peter Ustinov. And on that fateful morning, as she left her house for the adjoining bungalow office, two of her security guards, Beant Singh and Satwant Singh, pumped twenty lethal bullets into her.

Much has been written about the non-availability of a doctor or an ambulance at hand, as also the absence of the mandatory security ring around her when she came out of the house. Utter confusion prevailed after the shoot-out and there was bungling all around. Mrs. Gandhi was bundled into a car and driven to the All India Institute of Medical Sciences (AIIMS). At that end there was nobody to receive her, as none had thought of using the wireless link between the PM's house and the Institute.

With a kilo of lead inside that frail body, she could not have been saved even if the situation had been handled to the last letter of the official drill. Yet it is important to stress the above lapses, as they point to the failure of not only the prime minister's security regime, but the breakdown of the system itself. So does the needless reference made to Mrs. Gandhi about the removal of her Sikh security guards. She very rightly turned down the proposal on the ground that it would smack of communal bias. But where was the need to refer the matter to her? A VVIP is never involved in arrangements concerning her own security.

31

Economy and Development

It is generally not realized that though Nehru was the author of the 'socialist pattern of society' approach, it is Indira Gandhi who introduced the series of measures which have come to be associated with that concept. Nehru initiated planning, established the public sector, and passed the Industrial Policy Resolution, 1956. But the actual regulation and control of the economy, and the more obtrusive features of state intervention belong to the Indira era. She not only nationalized banking, but also general insurance and the coal industry. Government take-over of the three foreign-owned petroleum companies was done in the teeth of severe resistance from international oil interests. More than a hundred sick private textile mills and various other loss-making companies were also taken over. State trading in foodgrains, their distribution through fair-price shops, and opening of a chain of super-bazaars was also done during her time.

Two major enactments to regulate the economy were passed by Mrs. Gandhi. They were : Monopolies and Trade Restrictive Practices (MRTP) 1970, and Foreign Exchange Regulation Act (FERA) 1973. She also modified the tax policies with the objective of reducing income disparities and mobilizing higher resources to fund the Plans.

Indira sought to serve three objectives by these reforms. One, to increase the hold of the public sector on the economy. Here the difference in approach from Nehru is worth noting. He concentrated on creating new industries; Indira brought under government control those private undertakings which were vital for the growth of the economy. Second, by taking over the purchase and distribution of essential commodities, she wanted to ensure their assured supply to the vulnerable sections of the population at stable and reasonable prices. Third, MRTP empowered the state to regulate the growth and dispersal of industry, channel investment into priority sectors, and prevent the concentration of economic power in private hands. FERA controlled every aspect of the outgo, inflow and possession of foreign exchange, and prescribed limits for foreign equity participation. It is mainly with the operation of these two Acts that the rigours of 'licence-permit' raj are associated.

Two features of this grand design to control and regulate the national economy in the interest of a balanced and equitable growth may be noted. First, most of these measures were conceived and implemented during Mrs. Gandhi's 'radical phase' (see chapter 25). Second, whereas these measures look sound and progressive from the socialist point of view, in actual operation their real intent was not only diluted but sometimes even reversed. Whatever reform government touches, becomes bureaucratised. These well-meant reforms led to the growth of a jungle of rules, regulations and controls, which not only became a check on growth, they also spawned widespread corruption and massive generation of black money.

It is again a part of this process of reversal that whereas on the one hand the Indian industrialists chafed under the 'licence-permit raj', on the other they developed a vested interest in it. Sheltered behind protective policies, controls and high tariffs, the established industrial houses grew enormously by easily getting around restrictive laws and blocked the entry of new aspirants into their preserves.

MRTP and FERA, coupled with a sharp rise in import duties, created a protected market in which the Indian industrialists had neither the compulsion to improve quality, nor upgrade technology, nor lower costs to enter the competitive export market. As a result of this restrictive and negative approach the "policy instrument to control monopolies has focussed on checking investment by large houses at the margin rather than on the alternative instrument which would guarantee the reduction of monopoly power, i.e., threat of the free entry by new firms and a measure of foreign competition."[1]

It was around 1976-77 when the balance of payments position eased and the economy recovered from the energy crisis that there was a turn-around in industrial growth. This was also the time when the rate of domestic savings rose above 20 percent of GDP and public investment in industry was again raised substantially. No less important was a perceptible change in the government's approach. The regulatory system of controls was gradually relaxed and a degree of import liberalization introduced. Much greater emphasis was laid on exports and several incentives given to exporters. The rate of industrial growth picked up during the last phase of Mrs. Gandhi. The forced social discipline of the Emergency was partly responsible for giving the initial push in 1976-77.

Three Five Year Plans and three Annual Plans were prepared during Indira Gandhi's tenure. None of them was framed or executed under normal conditions. Indira's accession to power coincided with the completion of the Third Plan. The Draft Fourth Plan was ordered to be recast by Shastri owing to the intrusion of the 1965 war with Pakistan. As no approved draft of a plan was ready and Mrs. Gandhi had yet to settle down, she switched over to the practice of making Annual Plans from 1966-1969. The Fourth Plan (1969-74) projections were upset by the torrent of refugees from East Bengal and the Bangladesh war. The Fifth Plan (1974-1979) was jolted by the Emergency and Indira's electoral defeat. The Janata government terminated this plan two years ahead of time, and introduced the concept of Rolling Plans. In 1980, on her return as Prime Minister, Indira Gandhi discarded the Sixth Plan prepared by the Janata government and formulated her own plan (1980-85).

These repeated interruptions and chopping of the Plans robbed the planning process of much of its coherence and impact. Even otherwise, planning had lost its gloss. Failure of the country to acquire self-sufficiency in such a basic sector as foodgrains production after the completion of three Plans was its severest indictment.

These constraints were duly reflected in the future Plans. Despite a rapid rise in prices, allocations for the three Annual Plans remained at the level of the final year of the Third Plan. In view of the resource crunch, mounting criticism from the business community and the approaching general election, finalization of the Fourth Plan was postponed, and a new Planning Commission constituted after the 1967 election. Morarji Desai as Finance Minister got D.R. Gadgil appointed as the new Deputy Chairman. This marked a radical change in the approach to Planning. Gadgil, an eminent economist, was a staunch critic of the Planning Commission and held that it should be only an expert advisory body, without any political leanings or clout.

With Indira Gandhi's impressive victory in the 1971 general election, the Fourth Plan underwent a major mid-course change. The Planning Commission resigned after the election, and a new Commission was constituted with C. Subramaniam as the Deputy Chairman and Planning Minister. There was reversion to the socialistic approach and stress was laid on institutional changes. A new scheme was prepared to enforce ceiling on land holdings. It was estimated that this would release 40 million acres of land for distribution to the landless. Nothing of the sort happened.

Only the first half of the Plan could be implemented under normal conditions. From mid-1971, the upheaval preceding the creation of Bangladesh, the Gujarat and Bihar agitations, and the spread of the JP movement created a level of turbulence which was not conducive to smooth plan implementation. Then there was the oil shock of 1973 which unsettled most world economies.

Owing to the overall decline in public investment, economic growth slackened, resulting in a lower demand for capital goods. Thus there was heavy under-utilization of capacity. The high rate of inflation and limited spread of the benefits of development also depressed the market. Consequently, the rate of industrial growth during the Fourth Plan dropped from 8 to 4 percent.

The Fifth Five Year Plan (1974-79), mired in controversy from the start, got fragmented in the course of implementation. Its ambitious provision was unrealistically high and projections of raising resources were so inflated that B.S. Minhas, a distinguished economist and Member, Planning Commission, refused to sign the Plan document and resigned in protest.

The Plan was published in 1975, one year too late, and then scrapped by the Janata government two years before completion. During the Emergency Mrs. Gandhi paid special attention to the Plan and introduced the 20-Point Programme to emphasize the benefits accruing from enforced social discipline. The Plan achieved an annual growth of 3.36 percent. Industry grew at 5.9 and agriculture at 4.5 percent. These figures were much below the proposed targets.

The Sixth Plan (1980-85) gave top priority to the power sector and preference to the completion of ongoing projects. It made deprived sections the direct targets of investment and framed schemes specifically designed to relieve poverty and create employment. It recommended part withdrawal of subsidies on fertilizers and raising the prices of the public sector products.

During the Indira era (1966-84) consumption of fertilizers increased from one million to 8.4 million tonnes, and irrigation potential from 82 million to 170 million acres. The production of foodgrains, which stood at 72 million tonnes in 1966, rose to 145 million tonnes in 1984. As a result of bank nationalization in 1969, bank advances to the agriculturists increased from Rs. 162 crores to Rs. 5,500 crores for this period.

These figures may present an unduly rosy picture of the impact of the Green Revolution. Even if one leaves aside the larger problems of soil degradation, pollution and ecological damage which result from prolonged use of chemical fertilizers and pesticides, it gave rise to a host of problems in the Indian context. First, its impact was mostly confined to the wheat-growing, well-irrigated areas of Punjab, Haryana and Western Uttar Pradesh. Even in these states, it was the larger landholders with money to invest in expensive inputs who mostly benefited from the new package.

By the mid-eighties the northern region contributed 97 percent of wheat and 65 percent of rice procurement. This phenomenon naturally increased the existing regional disparities.

As to the disparities arising from the Green Revolution, Indira Gandhi was quite explicit on this point. She told an interviewer,

"I don't think we could have expected anything else, because the urgent need was for grains, and so we had to help those who could provide it immediately."[2]

Whereas the public sector laid a solid foundation for industrial growth, its inability to generate adequate surpluses has hurt the economy. It started making regular profits only from 1981-82, and in the last year of Mrs. Gandhi's term it earned a return of 2.5 percent on an investment of Rs. 43,000 crores spread over 207 public enterprises.

As a result of the oil shock of 1973, Mrs. Gandhi took special interest in developing the energy sector. Whereas India's self-sufficiency index in oil and oil products stood at 5 percent in 1960-61, it rose to 70 percent in 1984-85. Ashok Mehta, the Petroleum Minister, wanted to hand over Bombay High to a multinational for oil exploration. Indira wisely insisted on giving it to Oil and Natural Gas Commission.

Whereas coal and petroleum are core industries, the public sector has unthinkingly barged into the consumer sector. For instance, what national interest does it serve for the government to produce bicycles, scooters, cars, bread, footwear, television sets, films and textiles? One of the main compulsions was to save jobs, and hundreds of private indutries were taken over with this intent. But this was a very costly approach, as the funds sunk in these bottomless pits could have been much better utilized in creating new assets and job.

The policy of import substitution did help in building up indigenous production capability, but it also resulted in wasteful expenditure on items and processes which could be imported at a much lower cost.

Though the performance of the public sector has steadily improved, a lot more needs to be done. There is a general tendency to blame low investment for low profitability. But much more important is the urgent need to improve the efficiency of the public enterprises. The entire infrastructure, ranging from state electricity boards and road transport corporations, to railways, coal and communications sectors can show much better results if more attention is paid to renovate outmoded organizational structures and streamline management practices. The comparative performance of the Central and state-run power plants is a case in point. Whereas the former earn the largest profits next to the oil sector, the latter are among the heaviest losers.

In framing her approach to science and technology, Indira Gandhi followed in Nehru's footsteps. But, being a more pragmatic person, she tried to make scientific research more result-oriented. She always stressed the need for self-reliance: to develop the capacity to absorb, indigenise and modify imported technology, and use scientific research in the service of rural India. She created several new organizations like the Department of Electronics, Science and Technology, Space, Environment and Ocean Development. Looking to the need for greater freedom of action, numerous autonomous bodies with independent governing boards were also set up.

With her sharp political instinct, Mrs. Gandhi realized the importance of the international politics of science and took several steps to register India's arrival on the scene. India sent expeditions to the Antartica and set up a base camp there. She actively participated in treaties for exploitation of ocean resources, and launched an ambitious space exploration programme. Mrs. Gandhi herself took an active part in international deliberations for the preservation of global environment and earned deserved recognition for her contribution. The hitch-hiking by Capt. Rakesh Sharma in a Soviet spacecraft was significant only in the sense that it symbolized the country's resolve to keep up with the Joneses of the scientific world. The explosion of a nuclear device showed her determination to join the world's most exclusive technology club.

But Indira did not have Nehru's robust rationalist outlook, nor was her faith in the scientific method that strong. With advancing years she came to rely increasingly on astrologers and tantrics, performed 'yagnas' to avert evil and attract good fortune, visited shrines and sought the blessings of all types of godmen. This sent out the wrong signals in a traditional and superstition-ridden society, and violated the spirit of scientific temper.

Also, despite her repeated emphasis to harness science in the service of the common man, she could not coax the researchers to leave their cloistered laboratories to solve the production problems of the butcher, the baker and the candle-stick maker.

In the global context the share of Indian trade and industry has steadily slipped since Independence. In 1950 India ranked as the tenth industrial nation in the world. In 1980 it occupied the 27th position. Her share of world trade was 2 percent in 1950 and only 0.42 percent in 1980.[3] According to an international survey of industrial performance and productivity in developing countries, India was among the worst performers between 1950-82.[4]

There are two main reasons for this phenomenon. One, misconceived state intervention and inability to evolve strategies in line with the changing global trends. Second, the character of the Indian entrepreneurial class itself.

Also, both the Indian government and private entrepreneurs have unnecessarily suffered from 'export pessimism'. The Second Five Year Plan argued that India's export mainly comprised primary products and raw materials, and the world market was weighted against them. But in respect of non-traditional items the planners believed that export could significantly pick up only when the country's industrialization had made substantial progress.[5] This overly pessimistic view continued to prevail even when the situation had become more favourable. "The Indian tragedy ... is not that we adopted an anti-export bias in the 1950s, when everyone did, but that we did not change in the 1960s when world trade grew by leaps and bounds."[6]

Owing to various structural and performance snags, India's Net Domestic Product (NDP) grew at an average of 3.57 percent per annum from 1950-51 to the end of the Indira era. Adjusted against the average annual growth of 2.24 percent in population over this period, it gives an annual rise of merely 1.33 percent in the per capita NDP. And what a mountain of effort had gone into producing this mouse!

Howsoever modest the Plan provision, it was always a back-breaking task to raise funds. Yet the objective was to double or treble the outlay for each successive Plan. It was Rs. 24,882 crores for the Fourth Plan, Rs. 47,561 crores for the Fifth and Rs. 1,58,710 crores for the Sixth Plan. Yet, instead of accelerating economic growth, the capital/output ratio from 1969 to 1985 rose from 2.81 to 6.21. In other words, with the accumulation of experience and creation of ever-growing assets, the economy became less and less efficient.

The other important cause was the government's burgeoning consumption expenditure. Non-development spending of the government had grown from 6.5 percent of the GNP in 1960-61 to 15 percent in 1989-90. Bureaucracy had proliferated unchecked since Independence. Whereas the number of civilian employees was 14 lakhs in 1947, it had risen to 27 lakhs when Indira Gandhi came to power, and reached 40 lakhs when she left the scene. The cost of back-up services has risen proportionately. The outlay on Defence had grown in the same manner.

Another disturbing aspect of the Indian economy has been the rising debt burden, both internal and external. In 1960-61 the internal debt stood at Rs. 6,188 crores and jumped to Rs. 1,10,074 crores in 1984-85. For the corresponding period, the external debt rose from Rs.782 crores to Rs. 16,637 crores. The increase in external debt in the eighties had been especially alarming, as it had escalated from US$ 20.6 billion in 1980 to US$ 34 billion in 1984, a rise of 65 percent in four years. For the same period, the debt service charges as percentage of exports doubled. The situation was bound to worsen in the future, as not only had the borrowings gone up rapidly, the international lending agencies had also reduced the flow of concessional aid to India. Another contributing factor was the steady rise in trade deficits which had gone up from Rs. 1,295 crores in 1966 to Rs, 4,534 crores in 1984.

Inflation has been a constant feature of the Indian economy. It is a chronic problem of developing countries, as development expenditure takes time to fetch returns. In India's case this has happened to be a painfully slow process. Add to this large borrowings, growing budgetary deficits and the feeble effort at raising resources, and you have a sure recipe for a high rate of inflation. The sharpest price rise took place during the Fourth Five Year Plan (1969-74) when the consumer price index zoomed by 58 percent. The government was forced to take stringent anti-inflationary measures and a number of ordinances were promulgated. Compulsory Deposit Scheme for the salaried employees was introduced. Ceiling on dividends was prescribed and money supply restricted by raising lending rates. Grant of licences, clearances for expansion of capacities, etc., were also expedited. Obviously, it has made the living conditions of the salariat and workers in the organized sector increasingly difficult.

In any civilized society the bottom line of all welfare and developmental activity is the poverty line. And despite the implementation of six Five Year Plans by the end of Mrs. Gandhi's tenure, this line had only declined from 60 to 45 percent of the population since Independence.

Based on a certain level of caloric intake, the Planning Commission had estimated that in 1970-71, 59 percent of the rural and 46 percent of the urban population was living below the poverty line. Later, in a heroic bid to prove the efficacy of poverty alleviation programmes, the Commission stated in 1987-88 that the situation had considerably improved with the poverty line coming down to 32.7 percent for the rural and 19.4 percent for the urban people. This projection was challenged by several scholars, and in a celebrated article B.S. Minhas et al furnished a solid basis to prove that in 1987 the poverty line stood at 49 percent for rural and 38 percent for urban India. For the country as a whole this figure had dropped only from 56 percent in 1970-71 to 46 percent in 1987. In other words, the poverty line declined by 10 percentage points over a period of 16 years. But in absolute terms, whereas 308 million Indians lived in poverty in 1970-71, sixteen years later their number had grown to 361 million.[7] In other words the country's misery index had been rising all the time. (Subsequently, the Planning Minister informed Rajya Sabha in December 1991 that

39.34 percent of Indians lived below the poverty line as against the earlier Planning Commission estimate of 29.9 percent.)[8]

Even this drop of 10 percentage points was a distinct improvement on the earlier situation, and it resulted mainly from a number of poverty alleviation programmes that Indira Gandhi had launched. Starting with the Rural Works Programme (1967), more than twenty schemes were initiated by her to create rural employment and generate durable community assets. This also enabled the government to utilize huge foodgrain stocks for paying wages in kind.

At the beginning of the First Five Year Plan, the number of unemployed was estimated to be five million. The figure rose to 13 million at the end of the Indira era. In other words, population had grown faster than employment. The most disturbing aspect of this phenomenon is that the trends of growth do not provide any let-up in this situation. The Indian economy grew at the rate of 3.5 percent per year till 1970 and employment at 2 percent. During the seventies these figures stood at 4 and 2 percent, and in the eighties at 5.5 and 1.8 percent. Thus, the rise in employment not only lagged far behind the growth of economy, this gap had been steadily increasing.[9]

Agriculture still employs two-thirds of the labour force. In this sector the rate of increase of employment had come down from 2.32 percent to 1.20 percent for the above period. Industrial growth was supposed to siphon off surplus labour from agriculture. But in the organized sector growth of employment declined from 2.5 percent in the seventies to 1.3 percent in the following decade. And even this is almost entirely accounted for by the public sector.[10]

Thus, from whichever angle one looks at it, the growth in population is out-pacing rise in employment and, consequently, the number of the unemployed is constantly going up. Earlier it was assumed that employment would be a natural spin-off of development, and the Plans gave the highest priority to growth. Gradually it was realized that poverty alleviation and employment generation had to be directly built into the Plans, and a number of 'minimum needs programmes' were started from the late seventies onwards. They have produced results, but much below the expected levels.

Whether one considers Indira Gandhi's tenure only, or combines it with that of her father, the per capita NDP grew at a rate of 1.33 percent per annum over these four decades. And this is only a statistical average where a billionaire and a pauper are lumped together. In terms of relieving mass hunger, the consumption of cereals during Mrs. Gandhi's time increased from 408 to 454 grams per head per day. But the intake of pulses, the main source of proteins for the poor, actually declined from 48 grams to 38 grams per head per day over this period.

Many people feel that these bloodless statistics do not conform to reality. Taking a commonsense view based on general observation, they point out that go anywhere in the country and you find many more people having shoes, better clothes, bicycles and even tractors. Thus, they conclude, the lot of the people has visibly improved. There may be two reasons for this impression. In absolute terms there has been some improvement in the general condition of the masses. Compounded at 1.33 percent per annum the product doubles in fifty years, though its major gainers are the upper income groups. More importantly, cycles and tractors are high visibility items: even the addition of six cycles and one tractor in a village hits the eye. But the abject poverty of the vast majority is not that readily visible.

There is, of course, another way of looking at the Indian poverty scene. Experts have increasingly come round to the view that the above methods measure inputs like income, and not outputs, like welfare. A more reliable measure of improvement is the Physical Quality of Life Index (PQLI). It is a fact that average life expectancy of an Indian was 32 years when planning started, and in 1985, it was 55 years — an increase of 71 percent in the average longevity of the people. Much of it, no doubt, is attributable to a substantial drop in infant mortality and better health care, and not to radically improved nutrition levels. But that itself is a substantial gain.

32

Foreign Policy

*f*or Nehru India was a part of the world. For Indira Gandhi, the world was an extension of India. Her thinking was not encumbered by any global vision or grand design. International peace and cooperation were integral to Nehru's view of foreign policy. Indira was not much fascinated by these nebulous concepts. She thought in concrete terms. Being an ardent nationalist, the country's honour, security and clout were the goals for which she strove. Also, by the time Mrs. Gandhi became Prime Minister, most of the colonies had won freedom and the old style colonialism and imperialism did not evoke strong emotions. Thus, hardly any great causes remained over which the world community could be mobilized. Non-alignment had its major appeal for the newly liberated countries. But as they got bogged down with their internal problems and were forced to seek aid from one super power or the other, it became something of an encumbrance.

In this ideologically sanitized environment, Indira's pragmatism served her well. Moreover, her foreign policy did not have to carry the burden of her domestic ambitions; her obsession with personal power and her dynastic designs did not cloud her perceptions of the country's interests.

Pakistan

India's most immediate foreign policy concern has always been Pakistan. When Indira Gandhi came to power, the two neighbours had already fought two wars, the second one only four months before Indira's accession. The Tashkent Declaration did restore peace, though it would be more correct to call it a truce. Z.A. Bhutto, the then foreign minister of Pakistan, first rocked the boat by resigning in protest against the Declaration, and the following year launched his own People's Party of Pakistan.

In August 1968, Mrs. Gandhi offered to sign a no-war pact with Pakistan. President Ayub Khan agreed provided 'the countries could resolve the existing problems and those that might arise in the future.' This was a very tall order and put paid to any attempt to work out a durable basis for peaceful relations.

There are several critical factors which render normalization of relations difficult. First, the perennial Kashmir irritant, which has been getting worse with time. Second, India considers non-alignment as the linchpin of her foreign policy. It does not suit Pakistan at all. To her way of thinking she can ensure her security only by erecting a barrier of alliances around her. That explains her membership of the Baghdad and SEATO pacts, and her close alliance with the USA.

Thirdly, despite her much smaller size and resource base, Pakistan seeks parity with India. Thus it looks for allies and arms from wherever they are available. Fourthly, Pakistan occupies a crucial position in the United States' geopolitical calculations. With the Soviet attack on Afghanistan, Pakistan became a front-line state for America and reaped hefty rewards for her fealty. To these factors may be added the break-up of Pakistan as a result of the Bangladesh war. Both militarily and territorially, it was a deep wound suffered by her. She cannot live down this humili-ation, but would love to return the compliment to India.

It was after the break-up of Pakistan in 1971 that Indira reached the peak of her power and crafted a foreign policy that bore her distinctive stamp. In pursuit of enduring peace she signed the Simla Agreement with Bhutto, the then President of Pakistan, on 2 July 1972. For her the most important part of this settle- ment was "that the basic issues and causes of conflict... shall be resolved by peaceful means," and both sides "will refrain from the threat or use of force against the territorial integrity or political inde-pendence of the other." Further, "all differences will be settled through bilateral negotiations" and "in Jammu and Kashmir the actual line of control resulting from the cease-fire line of 17 December 1971 shall be respected by both sides without preju-dice to the recognised position of either side." This was the equivalent of a no-war pact based on the principle of bilateralism, and it rendered the UN observer group redundant.

Bhutto was careful to get the agreement approved by the Pakistan National Assembly. Pakistan's major gain was the withdrawal of troops from territories under each other's adverse possession. Bhutto was in no hurry to ask for the repatriation of 93,000 prisoners of war as their sudden arrival in Pakistan would have raised several awkward questions. A number of other agreements were subsequently signed to tie up the loose ends. Gradually trade links and travel facilities between the two countries were also resumed and ambassadors exchanged in July 1976.

There has always been a suspicion that some sort of secret understanding was also reached at Simla between Indira and Bhutto. This impression has been confirmed in an article by P.N. Dhar, who was present at Simla during the negotiations as Principal Secretary to the PM. According to Dhar, "Bhutto agreed not only to change the cease-fire into a line of control... but also agreed that the line would be gradually endowed with the 'characteristics of an international border' (his words). It was thought that with the gradual use of the LOC as the de facto frontier, public opinion on both sides would be reconciled to its permanence... when Mrs Gandhi finally asked Bhutto, 'Is this the understanding on which we will proceed?' he replied, 'Absolutely, Aap mujh par bharosa keejiye'[1] (Please trust me)."

Looking to the credibility of the source, this report seems to be correct.[2] Yet, as later events showed, to have 'bharosa' (trust) in Bhutto's oral assurance was like relying on a compact written on sand. Even when he took the agreement to the National Assembly, Bhutto stated that it did not prevent him from raising the Kashmir issue in the UN. He also said "... if people of Kashmir start a freedom movement, we will be with them."[3]

Large arms supplies by China had enabled Pakistan to recoup the heavy losses suffered in the war. Whatever little chance there was for the survival of the Simla spirit was blasted by India's explosion of a nuclear device in 1974. The reaction in Pakistan was violent and Bhutto swore to catch up with India 'even if the people of Pakistan have to eat grass.' He also used it as a pretext to convince the USA to lift the embargo on arms supply clamped after the Indo-Pak war of 1965.

The imposition of Emergency by Mrs. Gandhi in 1975 and the subsequent Janata rule marked a relative lull in Indo-Pak relations. In July 1977 General Zia-ul-Haq staged a military coup in Pakistan, arrested Bhutto and hanged him in April 1979. Tension again started building up when the US resumed large supplies of arms to Pakistan consequent on the Soviet attack on Afghanistan at the end of 1979. When Indira returned as PM next month, General Zia was sitting atop a growing mountain of armaments. He pursued a two-track policy. On the one hand he signed an agreement with America in September 1981 for military and economic aid worth US $ 3.2 billion, yet the very next month he offered a no-war pact with India. Indira vacillated and missed a good opportunity to call Zia's bluff. After some diplomatic exchanges, Mrs. Gandhi offered to sign a treaty of peace and friendship with Pakistan. But in view of the wide divergence in the perceptions of the two countries on almost all issues, these efforts were stillborn. Ultimately, when General Zia visited India in March 1983 to attend the seventh Non-aligned Summit, an agreement to set up an Indo-Pak Joint Commission was signed.

The second track that Zia followed was to steadily beef up Pakistan's defence capability and concentrate on developing the atom bomb. By the early eighties it had become clear that Pakistan had acquired the capability of manufacturing atomic weapons. China rendered the greatest help in this matter, and sensitive devices were also secretly procured from Holland, West Germany, and some other countries. The American Democrat senator Alan Cranston alleged that Pakistan had clandestinely expanded its uranium enrichment facility at Kahuta.[4]

A more insidious plot was the incitement and help that the Sikh militants in Punjab received from Pakistan. Training camps for the terrorists were set up across the border, and they were helped liberally with arms and ammunition. Some extremist Sikhs living abroad were welcomed and encouraged by the Pak rulers to escalate terrorist activities against India.

On her side, Indira Gandhi supported the violent agitation that

erupted in the Sindh province of Pakistan in 1983 for the restoration of democracy. Pakistan accused India of fomenting this
trouble and interfering in her domestic affairs. Thus, during the
closing phase of the Indira era Indo-Pak relations were quite tense.

China

Mrs. Gandhi was well aware that India's relations with China,
her second most important neighbour, must improve. She consistently tried to follow this line, did not react to provocations, and
did nothing to give offence to China. She adhered to the traditional Indian approach of endorsing China's stand on Tibet and
Taiwan, and supported her admission to the UN.

Although China also saw no advantage in following a collision
course with India, she did not refrain from making hostile moves
if these served her purpose. Here, her growing closeness to Pakistan and later with the USA proved inimical to the restoration of
cordial relations. In 1969, she helped Pakistan build a road linking
the occupied Kashmir with Sinkiang.This not only posed a security threat to India, but the entire road passed through territory
which India claimed as her own.

China also lent open support to insurgent forces in India. She
trained and armed Naga rebels to create trouble in the North-
Eastern States. She projected the Naxalites as the vanguard of
resurgent peasantry trying to overthrow a reactionary feudal
order and gave official recognition to the Communist Marxist-
Leninist Party which treated the Chinese revolution as its model.

Despite having developed her own nuclear arsenal China toed
the Pak line in condemning India's testing of an atomic device.
And when Sikkim was integrated into India, the Chinese reaction
was fierce. She was strongly opposed to the Indo-Soviet Friendship Treaty and described it as an attempt at encirclement of
China.

Some of this hostility was symbolic, some an expression of
solidarity with an ally, and some a reaction to acts of perceived
unfriendliness. But a large part of it also stemmed from China's
hegemonic outlook and her strategy to prevent India from emerging as a strong rival.

However, China also realized that chronic hostility to India was not in her interest. The first indication of change in the Chinese mood was given by Mao Zedong when, at the May Day parade in 1970, he chatted with the Indian chargé d'affaires (the ambassador was withdrawn after the India-China war) and expressed his hope for the restoration of traditional friendly contacts between the two countries. India was uncertain about her response, and perhaps, let slip a good opportunity for early improvement in relations through over-caution. In 1975 a Chinese pingpong team led by a Vice Minister visited India. He again harped on the theme of traditional friendship between the two countries. Next year India appointed K.R. Narayanan as Ambassador to Beijing and China reciprocated the gesture.

After Mao's death in 1976 Deng Xiaoping emerged as the leader following a longish power struggle. His pragmatic approach marked a turnaround in China's attitude towards India. He held the view that the border problem can be solved through peaceful negotiation if both countries make concessions, 'China in the eastern sector and India in the western sector on the basis of actually controlled border line.' He suggested that the two countries should start improving relations in economic and cultural fields and the prickly boundary issue could be tackled later.

In concrete terms, China agreed to the Indian proposal to adopt a sector by sector approach to the settlement of the border issue. But hardly any progress was made on this front. Several agreements were signed between the two countries on cooperation in the economic and cultural fields, and visits by delegations and experts were exchanged. On balance, the closing phase of the Indira era saw some improvement in India-China relations.

Bangladesh

India had played a decisive role in the creation of Bangladesh, and then taken good care to underplay her contribution. One expected a long spell of good neighbourly relations between the two countries, and the start was quite promising. Mujib signed a Treaty of Friendship with India in 1972, and Indira Gandhi extended generous aid in the form of credit, foodgrains, fertilizers, crude oil, etc., to tide over the drought.

Mujibur Rehman was a great demagogue, but an incompetent administrator. As things got out of hand, he declared emergency in 1974, and introduced the Presidential system by amending the Constitution in January 1975. But the situation steadily worsened. Encouraged by Pakistan and, probably the USA, the army staged a coup on 15 August 1975, killing Mujib and his family, as also most of the prominent leaders of his party, the Awami League. General Zia-ur-Rehman became the new ruler, but was killed in another coup in May 1981, when General Ershad became the Martial Law Administrator.

There was always a strong anti-India lobby in Bangladesh, and it became more vocal after Mujib's assassination. The country was beset with all sorts of problems, and India was blamed for most of them. But the greatest irritant between the two countries was the sharing of the Ganga waters on the completion of the Farakka dam. For India, adequate discharge from Farakka was crucial to save the port of Calcutta from silting. But Bangladesh felt that withdrawal of large quantities of water, would hit her interests. As the controversy sharpened, Bangladesh approached the UN. The issue was temporarily resolved by the two countries signing a Memorandum of Understanding.

With the stabilization of the military regime, relative normality returned to India-Bangladesh relations and in January 1976 the two signed a trade protocol to step up bilateral trade. But the main focus of Bangladesh gradually shifted from India to the US, China, Saudi Arabia and Pakistan. As America became the largest aid giver and trading partner of Bangladesh, it naturally came to exert more and more influence over her policies. Yet, surrounded as it is by the Indian landmass, the two countries have to interact, negotiate and cooperate on several issues. By and large it has been an uneasy relationship.

Nepal

India's relations with two of her important smaller neighbours, Nepal and Sri Lanka, illustrate the constraints that beset cooperation between two unequal parties. Towards the close of the Nehru era, King Mahendra of Nepal was trying to establish closer links with China and Pakistan to acquire greater elbow-room against India. He was also upset at the activities of Nepali Congress rebels who had sought asylum in India. In a bid to assert Nepal's sovereignty, the king asked India to withdraw the Indian Military Liaison Group and the personnel manning the check posts. India conceded these demands without any fuss.

Indira Gandhi maintained a low profile and kept up the usual flow of assistance to Nepal. But to send King Mahendra the right signal, India imposed several trade restrictions and discontinued the supply of petroleum above a certain quota. The Nepali leaders realized that it would be counter-productive to push matters beyond a certain point. India too was wary of tightening the screw too hard. As greater sobriety and realism returned to mutual relations, a new Treaty of Trade and Transit was signed in Kathmandu in August 1971.

Subsequent developments helped harmonize Indo-Nepalese relations to a large extent. In 1972 King Mahendra was succeeded by his son King Birendra. He understood better the value of Indian friendship and Indira Gandhi also enhanced aid to Nepal. Another factor that helped normalization was India's decisive victory in the Bangladesh war and her testing the atomic device. These happenings induced her neighbours to take her more seriously.

India is not only the largest aid donor to Nepal, but also her major trading partner. Her contribution in setting up irrigation dams, power plants, industrial units and construction of roads is quite substantial. More than six million Nepalese live in India. Above all, the lifeline of this land-locked country passes through India. Thus, Nepal's economy is deeply integrated with that of her big neighbour. Though Indira Gandhi had been quite sensitive to Nepali susceptibilities, the unequal relationship created its own strains. Whereas India has always disapproved of Nepal's ambition to be declared a zone of peace, the latter has incorporated this concept in her constitution framed in 1981.

Sri Lanka

With twenty percent of Sri Lanka's population comprising Tamilians demanding autonomy, there is an inbuilt discordance in the Indo-Sri Lankan relations. Not that the two sides have not tried to cultivate good neighbourly contacts. The most notable achievement towards promoting friendly relation was the signing of an agreement in 1974, defining maritime boundary between the two countries and India's recognition of Sri Lankan sovereignty over the tiny island of Kachchativu.

But despite all goodwill on both sides, the problem of Tamil immigrants fouled up mutual relations. Whereas the Tamilians wanted autonomy, the Sinhalese looked upon them as interlopers. Several militant outfits, and especially the Liberation Tigers of Tamil Eelam, LTTE, resorted to increasingly violent means to assert their rights and, at times, the Sri Lankan government adopted severely repressive measures. Owing to the emotional involvement of Indian Tamilians with their Sri Lankan counterparts, the Indian government felt constrained to espouse the cause of the latter. It is also a fact that these militants received arms from India, and training camps were set up for them in Tamil Nadu. This was naturally much resented by the government of Sri Lanka.

Matters came to a head in 1983 when Sri Lankan forces inflicted heavy casualties on the Tamil militants. Thousands of victims fled to Tamil Nadu in panic and loud protests were raised in India against this carnage. Apprehending retaliation by India, Sri Lanka approached several countries for help and charged India with encouraging insurgency before the UN. India conveyed her firm opposition to involving foreign powers in this affair and offered her good offices to normalize the situation. The two countries set up an All Parties Conference for this purpose, but it failed to produce results.

USSR

Indo-Soviet relations, always cordial, were further strengthened by two new developments. One, the increasing estrangement between the USSR and China, which led to border clashes along the Ussuri river in 1969. Secondly, the signing of the Friendship Treaty in 1971 on the eve of the Bangladesh war. India was now the only large and dependable friend that the USSR was left with in the whole of Asia. And India, faced with the hostility of Pakistan, China and America needed Soviet friendship more than ever before.

But the relationship was not free from occasional hitches. In 1968 when the Soviet troops marched into Czechoslovakia, it became difficult for India to avoid openly criticizing her friend in the UN. The Soviet attack on Afghanistan at the end of 1979 faced Mrs. Gandhi with a tough choice when she returned to power a month later. Her considered stand was that the situation in Afghanistan required a political rather than a military solution, and withdrawal of foreign troops should be accompanied by stoppage of arms supplies to that region. Gradually her stand stiffened. When the Soviet Foreign Minister, Andre Gromyko, came to Delhi seeking endorsement of his country's action, Mrs. Gandhi replied, "On this I cannot help you." Later, during her visit to the USSR in 1982, she publicly demanded withdrawal of Soviet troops from Afghanistan.[5]

But these minor differences notwithstanding, relations between the two countries continued to grow. A Joint Declaration at the end of the Soviet Party Chief Brezhnev's visit in November 1973 gave a fresh impetus to economic co-operation. Assistance in the fields of petro-chemicals, metallurgy, power and engineering was enhanced. Under a new five-year trade agreement for 1976-80, areas of co-operation were further expanded and the Soviet Union overtook the USA as India's largest trading partner. In May 1980, the USSR signed the biggest arms supply contract with India. The most attractive part of these trade agreements was the Soviet willingness to accept payment in rupees.

USA

Just ten weeks after she became Prime Minister, Mrs. Gandhi paid a five-day visit to the USA. This was her most serious bid to mend fences with the States. India badly needed foodgrains and foreign exchange. The response of the American President, L. Johnson, was effusive and patronizing. At a party in her honour, he announced his resolve to ensure that "no harm comes to this girl."[6] Later, he told the Indian Ambassador, B.K. Nehru,

"We must get her elected. You tell me what to do...send her food, attack her. I will do whatever you say."[7]

As to the actual American approach "Johnson believed that India had to be pressurised for its own good to make significant changes in her economic policy. He used pressure (to ensure this)."[8] Pressure was applied in good measure to persuade Mrs. Gandhi to devalue the rupee and refrain from "publicly criticizing US policies in South East Asia." She was also persuaded to use part of the accumulated PL-480 funds for setting up the Indo-US Foundation to "promote progress in all forms of learning." Later an agreement was signed to supply 3.5 million tonnes of foodgrains and give a loan of $48 million to finance some projects.

Back home, Indira was severely criticized for compromising India's sovereignity. Whereas she went ahead with devaluing the rupee, the proposal to set up the Indo-US Foundation was dropped. Subsequently, the activities of the US Peace Corps were also curtailed. The USAID mission and, except in Delhi, the US Information Service libraries, were also closed. What hurt the US the most was a reference to "imperialists in Southeast Asia" in a joint communique that Indira Gandhi signed in Moscow in July 1966.

Lyndon Johnson, having failed to get his way, dragged his feet on the release of aid to India. Each shipload of foodgrains was cleared by him personally and India was made to live from 'ship to mouth' during a period of acute drought. This taught Mrs. Gandhi the hard lesson that India had to acquire self-sufficiency, especially in foodgrains, if she was to retain her self-respect.

Indira paid two more visits to the States. In 1971, she went there as part of a wide-ranging public relations exercise to awaken the international community to the problems created by the vast refugee exodus from East Pakistan. President Nixon's response was cold. Her third visit in July 1982 was in response to an invitation from President Ronald Reagan. She tried hard to put across India's concern at the enormous arms supply to Pakistan. As she told the National Press Club, "Against whom would Pakistan use this military hardware? They cannot be used against Afghanistan because the Soviets are there, and they cannot be used against the Soviet Union." The only concrete gain of the visit was an agreement on the supply of enriched uranium to the Tarapur Atomic Plant. As the USA was not prepared to make it available, it was agreed that France would supply it in future.

At the conceptual level there was no reason as to why the largest and the strongest democracies in the world should not pull together. But India not only did not fit in the global strategic plan of the US, she stood out like a sore thumb. She criticized the American action in Vietnam, recognized the Heng Samrin government in Kampuchea and backed the Palestinian Liberation Organization against Israel. America found this stance offensive. In earlier years the US was one of India's major aid givers and the largest trading partner, and she found India's response singularly lacking in any expression of gratitude.

For India, the most provocative of US actions were the frequent delivery of arms to Pakistan which India considered far in excess of her legitimate defence needs. President Johnson had placed an embargo on the supply of arms to both countries after the 1965 war. In October 1970 President Nixon made a one-time exception to this embargo, and more exceptions were made later. In 1975 President Ford lifted the embargo altogether. In reply to India's protest, Henry Kissinger said that she had been importing 'nearly a billion dollars worth of arms every year, and it was necessary to set the balance right for Pakistan.' Later, in 1981 Pakistan and the USA signed an agreement for $ 3.2 billion for the provision of arms and economic aid.

Whereas politically the relations between the two countries have been seldom very smooth, on the economic and trade front it has been business as usual. Though US aid to India declined substantially, America again overtook the USSR as India's largest trading partner in 1983-84.

Southeast Asia

Indo-China was Nehru's main focus in Southeast Asia. His strong diplomatic support of the Vietnamese nationalist struggle was aimed at keeping it free from big-power rivalry. Indira Gandhi pursued the same line and promptly gave recognition to unified Vietnam and Kampuchea, much to the annoyance of the USA.

Other Southeast Asian countries, small and vulnerable, but strategically located, wanted security and aid. This the United States could provide best and, after the Vietnam debacle, was most interested in doing. These countries, therefore, drifted towards the United States. Also, common interest impelled six of them to form the Association of South East Asian Nations (ASEAN) in August 1967. This was primarily an economic union and, coupled with American aid, helped them grow into prosperous nations.

However, Mrs. Gandhi was able to create a more friendly environment in this region, particularly in relation to Indonesia and Malaysia. Bilateral trade was upgraded and an agreement for some joint ventures signed. India completed the demarcation of the continental shelf with Indonesia, and the latter also lifted restrictions on the immigrant Indians imposed by President Sukarno. But the gains were nominal and Southeast Asia has mostly lived and grown apart from India.

West Asia

Compared to Southeast Asia, India has much heavier stakes in West Asia. Her large Muslim population makes India specially responsive to Islamic concerns. Most of her oil supplies come from this region. An increasing number of Indians have sought employment there, and several private and public sector companies have undertaken a number of construction projects in this region. Pakistan has repeatedly used her Islamic card to create ill will towards India, and the task of countering this propaganda throws up tough challenges to the Foreign office.

India has taken a consistently pro-Arab stand. When the Arab-Israeli war broke out in 1967, Indira Gandhi fully supported the Palestinian cause. The close personal friendship between her and the PLO leader, Yasser Arafat, was the outcome of this support.

However, whether as a result of communal riots in India or Pakistani incitement, most West Asian countries have opposed Indian policies at one time or the other.

Two critical developments in West Asia produced shock waves in India. One was the quadrupling of the price of crude by OPEC in 1973-74. In a major effort to restructure her relations with the Gulf countries, Mrs. Gandhi succeeded in ensuring three-fifths of her crude supplies from Iran, Iraq and the United Arab Emirates on medium-term credit at stable prices. Much of this payment was made through the earnings of Indian workers and professionals employed in the Gulf, whose number in 1983 stood at three-quarters of a million. Indian companies also secured a number of contracts in these countries, and the Indian entrepreneurs considerably increased the range of their products exported to West Asia.

The second shock came with the start of the Iran-Iraq war in 1980. These two countries were then supplying more than two-thirds of India's requirements of crude. Also, several Indian projects were being executed in Iraq. India had to buy crude on the spot market and diversify her sources of supply. Indian exports to the Gulf countries were also affected. Large payments to Indian companies working in Iraq were held up and it took the country quite sometime to absorb the shock.

Non-alignment

For six years after Nehru's death not a single Non-aligned Summit was held. This is some indication of the change in the global political environment. Colonialism and the Cold War no longer excited the people very much. Politics was being subsumed by economics all over, and the European Economic Union best signified this change.

Indira Gandhi first met the two stalwarts of non-alignment, Nasser of Egypt and Tito of Yugoslavia, at the Tripartite Conference held in Delhi in November 1966. The three leaders expressed concern at the sufferings of the Vietnamese people, and highlighted the problems of economic growth faced by the newly liberated nations.

The emphasis of the Non-aligned Movement, NAM, also shifted towards economic issues, and it was at the Non-aligned Summit held in Algiers in 1973 that the idea of a New International Economic Order was first mooted. The seventh Non-aligned Summit, orginally scheduled to be held in Baghdad, was shifted to New Delhi at short notice owing to the Iran-Iraq war. The conference was held in March 1983, and Indira Gandhi as the chairperson made a magnificent job of it. Not only had the movement lost its drive, there were highly contentious issues like Afghanistan, Kampuchea and the Iran-Iraq war which could rock the Summit. Mrs. Gandhi conducted the proceedings with great skill and ensured that there were no serious snags or ugly controversies. No sharply focussed statement could be expected from such a heterogeneous assembly, but it did help revive the sagging image of NAM.

Commonwealth

Whereas NAM did occasionally pay lip-service to political issues, the Commonwealth began skirting them altogether and focussed on matters of economic cooperation and development only. Indira Gandhi was much less enthusiastic about this organization than her father. She skipped several Commonwealth Heads of Government meetings (CHOGM). At one time there were rumours about India withdrawing from the Commonwealth when Britain was actively considering arms supply to South Africa. When the CHOGM was held in Delhi in 1983, she criticized the wastage of huge funds on arms race, when the same money could be profitably used to help the developing countries. Earlier she had regretted that the North had 'pushed aside' the Brandt Commission Report which had recommended that the countries of the North should set aside 0.70 percent of their GNP for development aid to the South.

European Economic Community

Indira was quick to percieve that the real focus of economic issues had now shifted to the European Economic Community, EEC, set up in 1958. India established full diplomatic relations with it the same year to settle matters regarding tariffs, trade quotas, etc. When the world trade was expanding rapidly, India was able to bring about a shift in her export to the EEC countries by increasing the proportion of finished products like engineering goods, garments, chemicals, etc.

In 1973 India and the EEC signed a General Trade Agreement to deepen and diversify economic relations, and a Joint Commission was also set up for this purpose. But worldwide recession in later years slowed down the tempo. Many EEC members imposed restrictions to protect their domestic market. China and Taiwan also offered increasing competition to the Indian products. Structural rigidity in India's manufacturing sector made rapid adjustments to fast-changing demands difficult. Yet EEC has become India's largest trading partner and figures prominently in her economic diplomacy.

Whereas Indira Gandhi's international outlook lacked the splendour of Nehru's global concepts and his deep concern for peace, she operated on a more down-to-earth plane. She correctly judged the changing direction for world trends and gave much greater economic content to India's foreign policy.

33

Statecraft and Style

*I*ndira Gandhi was a politician par excellence. No other Indian leader ever played the power game with as much astuteness and finesse as she. From the day she got into active politics, she was in her element. The Syndicate stalwarts found her reassuringly dumb and helpless, and she gave Kamaraj the impression of being a puppet in his hands. But once Indira got into the seat of power, she left nobody in doubt as to who was the master. One by one she removed every obstacle in her way and did not permit any feelings of gratitude or old loyalties to weaken her resolve. She could have been a little softer on Kamaraj; she owed him so much. A concession here and there would have mollified the Syndicate. She should have recoiled from breaking the great Congress organization which her father and grandfather had so lovingly nursed. But no. Emotion is the enemy of realpolitik. Indira was too thorough a professional to be swayed by feeble sentimentality.

When the pursuit of power did not cloud her judgement, Indira's only guide to action was the national good. And the touchstone of that good was pragmatism. Soon after becoming PM she visited the USA, where she was very well received by the American President. Several Indian leaders accused her of moving close to the States and giving up the Nehruvian path. She told a Congress workers' meeting in Poona, "I do not see myself in the role of an imitation to Nehru. If I think it is necessary to depart from his policies in the interest of the country, I shall not hesitate to do so..."

She was keenly aware of the urgency to normalize the situation in the border states. Whatever her personal views on the matter, once the Hukam Singh Committee gave its report in favour of Punjabi Suba, she did not drag her feet and immediately conceded the demand. She released Sheikh Abdullah and then paved the way for him to take over as Chief Minister of Jammu and Kashmir. This was a rare instance of a democratically elected government voluntarily abdicating in favour of the rival party. Even when she was still in the process of settling down as the PM, she resumed peace talks with the rebel Nagas. Contrary to the earlier government stand, no pre-conditions were laid and, in deference to the Naga demand, she herself conducted these talks. Even if a settlement could not be reached, it softened the Naga hostility, and a split occurred within their ranks. Then, in the early seventies she granted full statehood to Manipur, Meghalaya, Mizoram, Tripura and Arunachal Pradesh. Realizing the value of having the non-Congress Chief Minister of Tamil Nadu on her side, she shed the earlier reservations and went out of the way to befriend M.G. Ramachandaran.

On the other hand, Mrs. Gandhi was tough where the national interest so demanded. Her open defiance of the Seventh US Fleet during the Bangladesh war is the most prominent instance of this trait. Her annexation of Sikkim was characteristic of her concept of pragmatism. This small Himalayan kingdom was strategically located between India and China. It was a monarchy and an Indian protectorate. Its ruler, the Chogyal, married an American and, after that, started staking his claim to sovereign status. The local Congress was quietly encouraged by Indira to agitate against him to create instability. Indira Gandhi did not stand on ceremonies and went ahead to merge Sikkim with India in 1975, wasting no time worrying about Panchsheel or the international reaction.

Having shared her father's agony during the India-China War, Indira Gandhi showed much greater concern for national security. She allocated additional funds for the modernization of the armed forces and improvement of service conditions of defence personnel. But her most noteworthy act in this field was the underground explosion of a nuclear device at Pokhran in the desert of Rajasthan in May 1974. It was a powerful signal of India's resolve to acquire self-sufficient defence capability. She knew that by forcing entry into the exclusive nuclear club, she would be inviting censure by the superpowers. But after China's acquisition of the Bomb, she was not prepared to see India lagging behind. Further, in 1980 India developed a satellite-launching vehicle, SLV-3, and placed the Rohini Satellite into orbit. A communication satellite, APPLE, was also launched in cooperation with France. These developments, significant in themselves, were also meant to announce to the world India's entry into the age of high technology.

Three factors contributed to the shaping of Mrs. Gandhi's political style. First, her deeply suspicious nature. Second, her innate sense of insecurity. Third, lack of seniority. When she formed the government in 1966, all her cabinet ministers were senior to her in age and experience. It was more or less the same Cabinet which Nehru had assembled in 1962, and Shastri continued without much change. She naturally did not feel too comfortable bossing over such seasoned grey heads and devised her own system of bypassing them.

Indira introduced the practice of having a group of advisers whom she shuffled continuously. Her first batch comprised D.P. Misra, Dinesh Singh, I.K. Gujral, Uma Shankar Dixit, Romesh Thapar, and others. It was this coterie which S.K. Patil derisively called the 'Kitchen Cabinet'. To begin with she relied on Dinesh Singh the most, and ordered all official papers to be routed through him. This was naturally resented by the senior ministers, as Dinesh was only a minister of state at that time.

Indira was very careful that the Kitchen Cabinet should not weld into a cohesive group and kept sowing seeds of suspicion among its members. For instance, after she had discussed an important issue with some members of the coterie, she would tell one of them 'Aap zara ruk jaeeye' (you please stay back). She had nothing particular to tell that person, but it made the others suspect that the fellow may have sneaked on them.[1] Once she told Gujral, "You know I am angry with you." As Gujral kept quiet, she asked, "You know why ? Because you are Dinesh Singh's friend." When Gujral said "Only you introduced him to me and wanted us to work together," she remarked "There is no social relationship in politics."[2]

Mrs. Gandhi ensured that nobody remained close to her for long. When she found that Dinesh Singh had started putting on airs, she cancelled the order about sending all official papers through him. Then he lost his ministership. After he ceased to be an MP in 1971, she asked Gujral, who was minister of state for Housing at that time, to throw him out of his official residence.[3] She once told Chandrajit Yadav, "I start judging people from the point of doubt."[4] In other words, she considered everybody untrustworthy unless proved otherwise. And none seems to have passed her rigorous test of loyalty. Even such a trusted and devoted aide as P.C. Alexander wrote, "I always had the feeling that she never trusted any person completely or unreservedly."[5]

Indira never allowed anybody around her to strike roots or create a constituency of his own. She frequently reshuffled her cabinet, and even if a minister continued with her for long, she kept changing his portfolio. Once she told I.K. Gujral, "We must learn from the Communist system. There should be circles within circles."[6] Whether it was the Central cabinet, or the Congress party, or the state ministries and Pradesh Congress committees, there were factions within factions. Each had access to Mrs. Gandhi and each got a crumb from her. Whereas she suppressed dissent against herself with an iron hand, in all other forums a thousand flowers of discord and infighting merrily blossomed around her. There was, therefore, no rival to her anywhere in sight within miles. She discontinued the practice of preparing a warrant of precedence of ministers so that nobody emerges as number two to her. Instead of listing them according to seniority, their names came to be arranged in alphabetical order.

Nehru found it very painful to abandon colleagues. Indira could not retain anybody for long. The list of persons who worked with her closely and were then discarded unceremoniously reads like a Who's Who of that period. They were: Kamaraj, D.P. Misra, Chandra Shekhar, Morarji Desai, Swaran Singh, Ashok Mehta, P.N. Haksar, Siddharth Shankar Ray, H.N. Bahuguna, Mohan Dharia, Krishna Kant, Dinesh Singh, I.K. Gujral, Chandrajit Yadav, D.K. Barooah, Nandini Satpathi, Romesh Thapar, Subhadra Joshi, Karan Singh, Yashpal Kapoor, among others.

The decline of the Kitchen Cabinet started with the appointment of P.N. Haksar as Indira Gandhi's Principal Secretary in May 1967. Two things happened during Haksar's four-year stint in that office. First, he gradually inducted leftists like Nandani Satpathi, K.R. Ganesh, Nurul Hasan and Chandrajit Yadav as advisers to the PM. This team was later joined by Mohan Kumaramangalam and Siddharth Shankar Ray. This period marks the most radical phase of the Indira era. Second, with Haksar's prestige and stature, the Prime Minister's Office, PMO, became the pivot of the decision-making process, and the bureaucrats came to acquire considerable influence on policy formulation at the PM's level.

This system was suddenly disrupted with Sanjay's rise as the main power centre. Haksar was sidelined and Sanjay-nominees appointed as number two in important ministries. He short-circuited the established lines of command and communication, and the more obnoxious features of Emergency flowed from this phenomenon. After Mrs. Gandhi's return in 1980, Sanjay resumed calling the shots. Not only in politics, but in administration also he interfered without any restraint. N.K. Mukarji, who served as Cabinet Secretary under Mrs. Gandhi also for some months in 1980, has a revealing incident to tell about Sanjay's style of intervention. Mukarji learnt that P.S. Bhinder, a Sanjay faithful of Emergency days, was being appointed as Inspector General of Police, Delhi, superseding 40-50 IPS officers. He saw the PM and pointed out that this would demoralize the police force. Mrs. Gandhi said that according to her information Bhinder was the next officer in line of promotion. When Mukarji showed her the official list, she was shocked. But Bhinder was promoted all the same. N.K. Seshan, PM's private secretary, later told Mukarji that when Sanjay learnt about his mother's decision to withhold Bhinder's promotion, he came charging into her office and shouted, "How is this? Something is decided in the morning and you can't hold on for a day. You keep changing all the time."

Sanjay's tragic death restored the earlier system, with the difference that Indira had become even more distrustful. Also some godmen made their way into the charmed circle, exercising an evil influence. And Mrs. Gandhi came to rely more and more on bureaucrats. This inevitably robbed her advisory apparatus of political depth.

Indira generally avoided giving instructions directly to her senior ministers, chief ministers, state Congress chiefs, and others at that level. Instead, she used her minions to act as her conduits. Yashpal Kapur and R.K. Dhawan were the two best-known messengers. This saved her the discomfort of directly transmitting unpleasant or awkward decisions, and if things went wrong later, she could always blame the courier for miscarrying her message. Though Mrs. Gandhi felt more at ease with this arrangement, it had two serious snags. First, it denied her the benefit of the other party's reaction. Second, it placed great power in the hands of her henchmen which they could, and did, use to their own advantage.

Indira Gandhi was one of the most successful practitioners of populist politics. The radical rhetoric accompanying the 1969 Congress split, her slogan of Garibi Hatao, 20-Point Programme, vote for the 'government that works,' sweeping Constitutional amendments, repeated warnings of danger to national unity, intervention by 'foreign hand', are some of the better-known instances of this genre of politics. Her one sure-fire mantra was that when in trouble, talk radicalism.

There is nothing wrong with populism per se. It is a hobby-horse of democracy. Politicians ride it to woo voters and go places. And not many leaders are known to fulfil their election promises. Mrs. Gandhi's skill lay in using variations on the same theme of poverty and social justice, year after year, election after election, with remarkable effect. And this, despite the fact that she did not implement most of the promised reforms.

Such consistent separation of word and deed was bound to give her a somewhat split political personality. As the problems thickened and she got into more and more difficult situations, Indira increasingly economized on the truth and, at times, made statements which she knew to be patently wrong. In this process the gulf between fact and fiction was abridged, forcing her at times to take indefensible positions. It was in defence of Emergency and Sanjay's excesses, the two most indefensible episodes of her regime, that Mrs. Gandhi strained credibility the most. When Sanjay was controlling the levers of political power, Mrs. Gandhi said, "My family has been very much maligned and, of course, my son is not in politics at all." Having become the only power centre in the country, she told an Education Conference on 19 September 1975 that "nowhere in the world had the head of government less power than I."

In a long interview to Mary Carras, her American biographer, Indira made a number of starkly incorrect statements. She was always very sensitive to international opinion. But she told Carras, "Nothing bothers me less than international publicity."[7] As to the reasons for the news of Emergency excesses not reaching her, she said, "The other problem was that our party did not function."[8] And this after having herself made the party dysfunctional. Defending her democratic credentials Indira stated, "I don't think there is anybody who is less authoritarian than I am. I don't know a single person who has consulted more people over anything — except perhaps Emergency."[9] Regarding the problems created by Sanjay's Maruti car project, she said, "There was a problem because the Government was dead against it."[10] It was of no consequence that ministers and officials were bending over backwards to help Sanjay by giving false certification reports.

The Indian political tradition, as fostered by the Congress, was a true reflection of the country's social ethos. It was essentially consensual and accommodative. The Constitution itself formalized that approach by wide dispersal of political authority, and provision of checks and balances at every stage.

In 1969, Indira Gandhi broke not only the party of which she was an offspring, but also the culture of consensus. From then onwards, step by step, she increasingly centralized the government and cultivated a highly personalized style of working. This inevitably drained off the vitality of various institutions of the state, and rendered quite a few of them ineffectual. Mrs. Gandhi, in all probability, did not realize the long-term implications of this process. But there is little doubt that de-politicization, de-institutionalization and de-ideologization of the polity were its direct and inescapable results.

Whereas the concentration of power in Mrs. Gandhi's hands weakened the party and state governments, this process itself created a situation where more and more power flowed to her. Nehru at least relied upon the Congress party for electioneering; Indira rid herself of that dependence also. Her election strategies and campaigns were single-person enterprises. It was she who brought the party magnificent victories and enabled the Congress leaders to become ministers and chief ministers. This gave rise to the belief in her indispensability. For the Congress there was no alternative to Indiraji.

Then Mrs. Gandhi skilfully cultivated the myth that national unity was under threat, and popular movements of protest only weakened the nation. Any group opposing the government policies or agitating for greater autonomy was dubbed as anti-national or secessionist. The antidote to all such threats was to strengthen her hands.

This approach seriously damaged the institutional frame of the polity. Whether it was the judiciary or the executive, personal loyalty was preferred to competence and integrity. Under Sanjay's dictates, officials were promoted, demoted, suspended or transferred for reasons other than the interests of good administration. Rules and procedures were bypassed to accommodate favourites and punish uncooperative officials. Pliable and discredited politicians were frequently appointed as governors, who submitted biased reports for the supersession of duly elected non-Congress state governments.

Mrs. Gandhi's refusal to respect the Allahabad High Court judgment and later to amend the Constitution and Representation of the People Act to nullify its effect, not only lowered the judiciary's prestige, it set the precedent that if you are strong enough to get around the law, do it. This was a clear repudiation of the principle of equality before law, which is the cornerstone of democracy. Her unabashed promotion of Sanjay in defiance of all norms of propriety spawned a culture of nepotism, and senior leaders no longer felt inhibited in pushing their progeny into ministerial berths, or securing lucrative contracts for them.

Indira was still serving her apprenticeship as the Congress President when she spoke to G.B. Pant, Home Minister, about the need to eradicate corruption in the government. Pant told her gently, "Beti (daughter) you do not understand, you are too young. It is only when you grow older that you will realize that complex issues are involved."[11] The advice was well-meant, and well taken. How well, of this the old man could have no idea!

In her personal life Mrs. Gandhi was austere and frugal. Her own wants were few and she hated ostentation. She first felt the need to have large funds under her control when the Syndicate tightened the purse strings on the eve of the 1967 elections. After her victory, with the Syndicate still in control of the party, she started building up her own reserves through her minions. L.N. Mishra, independent minister of state for Commerce, became her main fund raiser. In the licence-permit raj he put a price tag on each clearance and collected mountains of money. This was the beginning of institutionalization of corruption. Daily 'sealed envelopes' were sent from his house to a variety of beneficiaries, who included not only politicians, but also journalists and all sorts of hirelings.

As this practice spread, several ministers and Indira aides became fund raisers 'for the party'. Quotas were fixed for various chief ministers before every election. There is little doubt that these worthies did not pass on all the money they collected to the party treasurer.

How big money got tossed about was highlighted by the Nagarwala scandal. In May 1971, the chief cashier of State Bank of India, got a telephone call, supposedly from Indira Gandhi, to withdraw sixty lakh rupees and hand them over to a person waiting at a particular spot. The cashier took the money to the designated place, a person waiting there identified himself, and the cash was given to him. The cashier later learnt that he had been the victim of a hoax. The trickster was soon caught; he was one R.S. Nagarwala, an army captain. The culprit was tried and sentenced in just three days. And he died in jail.

This was a weird case and the mystery was never solved. How can a cashier, even if he receives a genuine call from the PM, take out a trunkful of money all by himself from a bank? What was the origin of that money and to whose account was it debited? Were there earlier transactions of this nature? This incident raised a stink and gave credence to rumours of murky deals involving the Prime Minister.

There are several reasons for the spread of this culture of official corruption. First the elections had become more and more expensive. Mrs. Gandhi's personal style of electioneering required elaborate arrangements and ever increasing crowds at her meetings. Chief ministers vied with one another to organize huge rallies, transporting people from all over. Then, the party apparatus itself became very expensive with the replacement of dedicated workers by mercenaries. The candidates also had to be given ever larger amounts by the party to fight elections. Most importantly, fund raising in itself became a very lucrative pursuit and all sorts of politicians took upon themselves the duty to fill the party coffers.

The next stage in corruption was reached with the decision to stop running after Indian 'donors', and arrange kickbacks in foreign contracts. Here the sums involved were colossal, and it saved the embarrassment of striking dirty bargains with your own countrymen. I was myself a witness to one of the earlier deals during my stint as Joint Secretary, Ministry of Shipping. My minister of state finalized the purchase of a ship from Singapore for the Shipping Corporation of India. Later, Admiral S.M. Nanda, Chairman of the Corporation, obtained a substantial reduction in the agreed price. The minister was furious and threatened to teach Nanda a lesson. The Admiral, a Bangladesh war hero, met Mrs. Gandhi and explained that he had acted wholly in the interest of the country. The PM admired his devotion to duty but advised that if after his best efforts the party is able to get some donation from the suppliers, he need not bother.[12]

India had massive trade with the USSR. It was common knowledge that in several shady rice deals huge profits were made by the Indian side. A substantial part of these profits was 'donated' to the 'Party'. But real killing was made in defence deals. When I.K. Gujral was the Indian ambassador in Moscow, a paper landed on his desk where a Soviet official had asked for his commission on the purchase of AN-12 transport planes. The official obviously was not familiar with the Indian channels of communication.[13] The practice of receiving commission from foreign contracts spread fast and scores of ministers and officials became the privileged holders of secret numbered accounts in Swiss banks.

Indira Gandhi probably never spent a penny of the tainted money on herself. Yet, under the wholly mistaken belief that money wins elections, she started a process which corrupted the moral fibre of the Indian polity. That her belief was mistaken, is shown by the fact that in 1977 the Janata Party won with a large majority, though it was penniless. In 1980 Indira swept the polls, though her war chest was empty and the Janata had all the money. After her, in 1989, the National Front won when the Congress had enormous funds. Yet the myth persists that winning elections requires heaps of money. There are strong vested interests whom this myth benefits enormously.

A most pernicious side-effect of political corruption has been the legitimization of black money. It is this ill-gotten wealth that goes into the party coffers. The donors have found it more productive and benign, and the donees have to pass no receipts for accepting it. The recipients, when returned to office, not only shut their eye to its generation, but zealously help the process in the hope of receiving more of it in the next round.

Mrs. Gandhi was always hesitant to define her political credo. She told an interviewer, "I don't really have a political philosophy. I can't say I believe in any ism."[14] When Mary Carras asked her about the absence of any coherent economic and social philosophy behind the 20-Point Programme, Indira replied, "This is where I always get into trouble. I don't think you can label under separate philosophical categories. All these things are so interlinked."[15] In fact if the things are so 'interlinked', it should be easy to fit them into a political philosophy. It was the absence of interlinkages that the interviewer was referring to.

She told a conference of Congress leaders on 14 May 1972, "Once equality has come in, then opportunities should open out for everybody to be enriched. How this will be done, I don't know." It is not known what the delegates got out of this statement. It is not equality which will lead to the opening up of opportunities, it is the opening up of opportunities that will lead to equality. And then she admits that she does not know how this will be achieved!

Her onetime Information Adviser, George Verghese, once remarked, "She has no consistent vision; everything is tactics." A wag said that Indira was 'left of self-interest'. There is no denying the fact that her 'will to power' was not conducive to the single-minded pursuit of national goals. With the appearance of Sanjay on the scene in the early seventies, dynastic considerations further narrowed her perspective. That is the main reason why, unlike Jawaharlal, no great themes run through her era. And she launched no major developmental or social-reform initiatives. Her rule was mainly episodic. It is marked by such episodes as the Congress split, Bangladesh war, the Emergency, her remarkable return to power in 1980 and Operation Blue Star. Themes are as much inherent in the politics of ideology as episodes are in the politics of pragmatism and expediency. De-ideologization of politics was, therefore, inherent in Mrs. Gandhi's style of working.

The problem with pragmatism is that when worked to excess, it degenerates into opportunism, ad hocism and expediency. It is only ideology which helps you formulate a coherent world-view, a long-term perspective and an exalted reference point. Indira was a forward-looking person, had a modern mind, and she instinctively empathized with the poor. But in the absence of a vision and commitment these fine attributes got sidelined under stress of circumstances or the lure of immediate gain. She had guts and grit enough to defy the grimmest of threats, but she never fought a pitched battle in defence of an ideological position. Even nationalization of banks, her most radical reform, was introduced to gain a tactical advantage in her combat with the Syndicate. The twenty-fourth and twenty-fifth amendments to the Constitution, which gave her sweeping powers to restructure the polity, were hardly put to any progressive use.

She told an interviewer, "How can anybody who is the head of a nation afford not to be a pragmatist. You have to be pragmatic, you have to be practical, every day. But you have to marry your pragmatism with some sort of idealism, or you would never get people excited about what you want to do."[16]

How revealing! Indira wanted to lace her pragmatism with ideology only as it helped to 'get people excited.' Here, instead of being the prime mover, ideology becomes a convenient ploy. There could not be a more pragmatic approach to idealism.

"Mrs Gandhi depleted India's political capital by eroding the autonomy, professional standards, and procedural norms of political institutions and state agencies... Jawaharlal Nehru was the school master of Parliamentary government, Indira Gandhi its truant."[17] This depletion of 'political capital' produced two baneful results. First, the vacuum created by the erosion of long-established institutions and norms was filled by the rise of informal structures. The proliferation of conmen and touts, creation of local armies by landlords and Dalits, spread of personal security outfits, growth of private agencies offering services earlier provided by the State, are symbols of this decay.

Second, even at the personal level, the more power Indira concentrated in herself, the weaker she became. Its best illustration is the Emergency regime. She was never so powerful as during this period; yet she felt so helpless, and had little control over the march of events. And this could not be otherwise. With the party apparatus dismantled and chief ministers emasculated, the channels of communication and command got choked, and mini-tyrants sprang all over. So devastating was the impact of this institutional decay that the last phase of Mrs Gandhi's prime ministership was devoid of any notable achievements.

34

The Person

*I*ndira Gandhi is the most tragic figure of Indian politics. She was Prime Minister of India for sixteen years and enjoyed tremendous power. She had charisma and her countrymen adored her. The world leaders gave her standing ovations at the UN. Yet she knew little happiness. For the first three years of her tenure she was battling with the Syndicate. In 1969 she managed to vanquish her opponents, but remained in office only with the help of the CPI. It was in 1971 that her party gained a solid majority in the general election. The same year she won her magnificent victory in the Bangladesh war. This was the only period when she experienced true happiness and a sense of fulfilment. Thereafter followed droughts, economic distress and civil disturbances. And then the violent agitations, which led to the declaration of a state of Emergency. She was extremely disturbed during this period, assailed by all manner of doubts. In the process of dismounting the tiger she lost power. Persecuted by the Janata, hounded from pillar to post, friendless and insecure, this was the most harrowing time of her life. When she returned to power in 1980 she was broken in spirit, seared all over, full of bitter memories. Hardly had she time to settle down, when her great white hope, Sanjay, crashed to death. She got over the trauma somehow, attended to the chores of office and performed superbly at some international forums. But this was her least productive term as Prime Minister, and the assassin's bullets ended a life whose creative phase was already over.

During her courtship days she had told Feroz that what she wanted from marriage was children and companionship.[1] Children she got, but not companionship. She had no siblings. In the absence of regular schooling, she made no friends. Her father whom she adored was too preoccupied with the national movement. She did get very close to her mother, but she was a consumptive and there was always the dread of losing her. Her marital life also did not give her the companionship she craved. "I have been and am deeply unhappy about my domestic life," she wrote to a friend. And "I am sorry to have missed the most wonderful thing in life, having complete and perfect relationship with another human being..."[2] So strained had become her relations with her husband that she wrote, "Feroz has always resented my very existence, but since I have become (Congress) President, he exudes such hostility that it seems to poison the air."[3]

Indira grew up in a joint family and she found little sympathy and understanding in it. A skinny, sensitive and self-willed child, she was quick to take offence. She could never forgive her overbearing aunt Vijayalakshmi for calling her 'ugly, stupid'. "This shattered something within me," she told Pupul nearly forty years later, when she had become the Prime Minister.[4] As a result of this shattered self-confidence, "I was so sure that I have nothing in me to be admired."[5]

Carrying all these hurts within her, it was no wonder that Indira suffered from an acute sense of loneliness and insecurity. In fact loneliness came first, the insecurity was born out of it. This also taught her to keep her own counsel and create fortifications within.

Nehru once wrote to his sister Vijayalakshmi from his jail barrack, "During the last fourteen months I have written to Indira regularly... It has been a very one-sided correspondence...I have sent books for her birthday and on other occasions. They are not acknowledged... Indira I feel is extraordinarily imaginative and self-centred... quite unconsciously she has grown remarkably selfish."[6]

Growing up in a world which she perceived as unsympathetic, friendless and hostile, her instinct for self-preservation made her selfish. Writing to Padmaja Naidu about the rarity of any close relationship in his life, Nehru said, "The reason for this failure is my incapacity to give." This was much more so in Indira's case, though she would have never confessed to it. The stress of her childhood circumstances had hardened the core of her heart into a crystal of ice. She was invariably courteous, she could be gracious and charming. But never warm.

Mrs. Gandhi often referred to herself as a 'tough politician', with a 'hard core'. She nursed her toughness with such care that it became an integral part of her persona. After a brief meeting, Charles de Gaulle told her Principal Secretary, "... your Prime Minister is a woman of amazing strength. She has something ... she will make it."[7] And Kissinger considered her 'cold blooded and too tough' to become anyone's stooge.

Mrs. Gandhi was courageous in a very basic sense. During partition riots, she worked tirelessly in refugees camps, saved lives at considerable personal risk, and berated irate mobs into silence. During the Chinese attack when the Indian Army was retreating in confusion and the district collector had fled, she dashed off to Tezpur despite strong opposition by her father and the army authorities. She just could not bear that the Assamese had been left in the lurch. She behaved in the same manner when she landed at Srinagar in 1965 and learnt that the Pakistani infiltrators had attacked the Valley. When she was hit by a stone at an election meeting in Bhubneshwar in 1967, she pressed her bleeding nose with a handkerchief and insisted on completing her speech. Indira displayed courage of a different order when in 1971 she defied the US Seventh Fleet in the Bay of Bengal and went ahead with winning the Bangladesh war. Her composure at Sanjay's death showed yet another facet of her courage. Operating in a male-dominated world, cultivation of a tough exterior was also an occupational compulsion. And so well she performed the act that she came to be known as the only man in a cabinet of old women.

Another trait which lent Mrs. Gandhi great strength was her power of silence. She was an excellent listener, and knew how to draw out the other person without revealing her hand. In 1967 when the West Berlin Chancellor visited India, he spoke to her for an hour against giving recognition to East Germany. She listened with great attention and when he had finished, looked out of the window and said, "Oh dear, it has stopped raining."[8]

When Zia-ul-Haq met Indira at Zimbabwe in 1980, he repeated at length the same piece about the impossibility of Pakistan achieving parity with India which had so impressed Morarji Desai. After having said his piece, as Zia looked up expectantly at Mrs. Gandhi, she said, "I am listening, General Sahib, please continue."[9]

In her official life Mrs. Gandhi was a very organized person: systematic, precise and punctual. "I am always direct," she told an interviewer, "I never spend my time on preliminaries...and I have no time for flowery things."[10] She was a meticulous speech writer. The drafts prepared by her staff were thoroughly revised and in parts rewritten by her. When she visited Paris in 1961 to receive an honorary Doctorate from the Sorbonne University, she worked for nearly a month on her acceptance speech. Her address to the Stockholm conference on Environment went through 18 drafts.[11]

After her return to power in 1980, the Cabinet was given a draft of the President's inaugural speech to the parliament. The paper was prepared by N.K. Mukarji, Cabinet Secretary. It was considered unsatisfactory and a Cabinet committee prepared another version. Indira was not happy with that either and, in the presence of her Cabinet colleagues, worked on it intensively for three hours before approving it. In Mukarji's words, "It was a great improvement on our draft. It was then really the PM's draft."[12]

Meticulousness was not only a hallmark of her official work; it was a part of her whole being. She was equally fastidious about her looks. "Her sari, her blouse, her shoes, her bag were selected for every single function." Before her first visit to the US, she had "written to a few of her friends to locate the latest make-up that would lessen the shadows under her eyes and make her long nose less prominent."[13] In fact so conscious was Indira of her long nose that after she was hit by a stone at Bhubaneshwar, she asked the doctors to perform plastic surgery on it. Of course, they wisely shied away from such a sensitive and hazardous undertaking.

Indira Gandhi was a much better judge of character than her father. "I am an expert in dealing with people," she said in an address at the Administrative Staff College in June 1966. "This is something I think, I was either born with or I learnt from my very childhood." There were any number of high-profile crooks, fixers and swindlers she had to deal with and none of them ever got the better of her. And despite all the shady deals struck during her time, she never became hostage to any blackmailer.

A refined, cultured and sensitive person, Mrs. Gandhi had a genuine feeling for the arts. During her foreign trips she would always find time to visit museums and art galleries, watch plays, and meet artists, intellectuals and scientists. She took a special interest in tribal art and culture and started the practice of organizing tribal dances as a part of Republic Day celebrations. In a bid to make the West aware of India's cultural heritage, she organized the Festival of India in the UK.

She was one of the first world leaders to get involved in environmental issues, and showed deep concern for the conservation of ecology. In 1972 she delivered the keynote address to the UN Conference on Human Environment at Stockholm, and presided over the World Conservation Strategy meeting in New Delhi in 1980. It was at her instance that work on the Silent Valley dam in Kerala was stopped and conservation projects started in several places. The Indian National Trust for Art and Cultural Heritage (INTACH) was established with her help and she became its first patron.

One of the several Indira enigmas is how could such a refined and sophisticated person have a clutch of such coarse, corrupt and slimy characters working so close to her? Nikhil Chakravarty repeated to me the story that P.N. Dhar, Principal Secretary to the PM, had narrated to him. Once he informed Mrs. Gandhi that the family of Sadiq Sahib, former chief minister of Kashmir, was in dire straits, and it would help if his son could be given a job in

Mohan Meakins' agency in Srinagar. She called Yashpal and asked him to do the needful. Ten minutes later Yashpal reported that the job was done. Then she told Dhar, "You look down on these people, but they are useful." This was a very innocent instance of such 'usefulness'. These henchmen indulged in the dirtiest of deals and with the full knowledge of their master. How come?

Then, Mrs. Gandhi wallowed in the most blatant kind of flattery poured on her by the bucketful by the swarm of sycophants that surrounded her. How did a sensitive and cultured person like her not feel nauseated at all the slime spewed around her?

"Because of political struggle, my own life was an abnormal one. This is why I was determined to devote full time to my children."[14] No brothers and sisters, no friends, ailing mother, elusive father, disloyal husband — Indira found refuge in her children. Only the intensity of her love for them could melt the ice-crystal at the core of her heart. Her devotion to her children was total and blind. Sanjay was a scapegrace, and some of his youthful pranks could have landed him in jail but for his connections. His Maruti car project was a disaster. His excesses during the Emergency ruined his mother's political career. Yet the judgement of this highly perceptive woman was paralysed where Sanjay was concerned. In his case, Indira not only condoned all his faults, most of them she saw as virtues. All reports against his misdeeds she construed as a mark of envy against his growing popularity.

She was a great nationalist, and the good of the country was very dear to her. But she worked tirelessly to promote her son as her successor in office, never doubting that this may gravely hurt the country's interests. In fact there runs a strong streak of nepotism through the Nehru family. During the civil disobedience movement when several Congress stalwarts had been arrested, Jawaharlal nominated his father Motilal as 'acting president' of the Congress in April 1930.[15] Earlier, in 1927, Motilal suggested to Gandhi the appointment of his son as president of the Madras Congress Session. Welcoming the idea, Gandhi tactfully replied, "... but I wonder whether it would be proper in the present atmosphere to saddle the responsibility on him."[16] Two years later Motilal again wrote to Gandhi "... the need of the hour is the head of Gandhi and the voice of Nehru... There are strong reasons for either you or Jawahar to wear the 'crown'."[17] Knowing that Gandhi would never accept the 'crown' (as Congress presidency was then called), the fond father hoped that his son would be the next choice.

Jawaharlal Nehru never openly canvassed for his daughter. As he told Norman Cousins, "This business of picking an individual successor is something I find quite alien to my way of thinking. I am not trying to start a dynasty." And he told R.K. Karanjia of *Blitz*, "All this talk of Indira in the matter of succession is totally absurd and quite unlike my nature. Even if I desired to make way for Indira...do you think I have the power to force my choice on the people of India."[18] But in another interview to the same journalist, one notices a subtle shift. He says, "I am certainly not grooming her (Indira) for anything of the sort. That does not mean she should not be called to occupy any position of responsibility after me."[19]

In fact Indira Gandhi was very much 'called to occupy a position of responsibility' during Nehru's lifetime. In 1959 she was 'elected' as the Congress President. Durga Das, the doyen of Indian journalists, gives an interesting insight into this development. Originally, S. Nijalingappa was chosen to be the next incumbent, and he was felicitated for the honour by various delegates. But later the outgoing president U.N. Dhebar called a Congress Working Committee meeting at which Shastri quietly suggested that Indira might be asked to become president. G.B. Pant, unaware of the background moves, was surprised by Shastri's proposal and said, "But Indiraji is not keeping good health. She must first..." Before he could complete the sentence, Nehru agitatedly interrupted to say, "There is nothing wrong with Indira's health. She will feel better once she has work to keep herself busy."[20]

Morarji Desai was convinced that the Kamaraj Plan was designed especially to get him out. Nehru wanted his daughter to succeed him.[21] After Nehru's stroke in 1964 when Kamaraj suggested the name of Shastri to assist him, he asked about Indira also. "No, not yet Indira, probably later" replied Nehru.[22] When Shastri was asked whom Nehru wanted to succeed him, he un-hesitatingly replied, "His daughter."[23] Uma Shanker Dixit met Nehru after his last visit to Dehra Dun before his death, and he spoke about Indira among other things. "Indu can take decisions," said Nehru, "Help her, help her."[24] In fact people freely talked about Indira succeeding her father. As Welles Hangen wrote, "No public figure in India disclaims political ambition so insistently. and none is more disbelieved."[25]

Whereas Nehru felt shy of openly promoting his daughter, he had no inhibition in offering a string of prized jobs to his favourite sister, Vijayalakshmi Pandit. She twice became minister in UP in 1937 and 1946. Then she got the three most important foreign postings as Ambassador of the USSR and the USA, and High Commissioner of the UK. And lastly, she was given the high-profile governorship of Bombay to provide her with a spot of rest and recreation after her exhausting assignments.

Indira Gandhi never had any qualms about grooming her son Sanjay as her successor. She did it assiduously, relentlessly and brazenly. And after the shock of his death, she started the same exercise all over again for her elder son, Rajiv.

The point at issue here is not that Motilal Nehru or Jawaharlal were not fit to be Congress presidents, or that Indira Gandhi did not deserve to be prime minister of India. All of them were emi-nent persons in their own right and they brought credit to which-ever post they held. But it was not proper for the son to promote his father, or the father to promote his daughter, or the daughter to promote her son in public life. It sent out the wrong messages and created unhealthy precedents. It was, in fact, obligatory for such eminent persons to set the highest standards of rectitude. Compare this with the attitude of Mahatma Gandhi. He never drafted any of his children to 'assist' him in his political work and not one of them became a minister. In fact, knowing the man as his colleagues did, none dared suggest anything of the sort to him.

One of the most persistent myths about Indira Gandhi is that she was a very decisive and firm ruler. Actually, by and large, she hated to take hard decisions. She acted firmly only when either she was pushed to the wall or there was somebody around to force her hand. Some of her most critical decisions were taken after prolonged wavering. In 1969 she tried her best to skirt the issue and find a via media before the Congress was split. She never sponsored Giri's candidacy for presidentship, and was uncertain till the end as to how to support him. Emergency was imposed when the situation had almost got out of hand and she found that the opposition was going to remove her from office by force. Even then, it was Sanjay who ultimately compelled her to take the plunge. In the case of Punjab, settlement was almost reached on at least three occasions and then aborted as Indira did not hold her ground.

As to radical reforms, she followed the line of least resistance and was normally wary of hurting any vested interests. So long as P.N. Haksar and Mohan Kumaramangalam were with her, she introduced several radical measures and far-reaching constitutional amendments, and promised effective land reforms. But once they left the scene, matters were allowed to drift.

Her distaste for decisive action also explains her reluctance to craft a cohesive political philosophy or long-range action plan. Her pragmatism and adhocism were best suited to her piecemeal approach. She also tended to get out of difficult situations demanding firm action on the plea that the time was not yet ripe for such a move, or the state chief ministers would not go along with a particular decision.

The one critical situation where Indira acted systematically, decisively and according to a set plan was the Bangladesh crisis. And here she produced brilliant results. She failed to do so in the case of Punjab and the outcome was disastrous.

Indira was more inclined towards religion than her father. Kamala, her mother, was a traditional Hindu lady and followed formal religious practices. Whenever the family was together, Gita and Ramayan were regularly recited in the house. She took Indira along during her visits to the Ramakrishna Mission Ashram and the savant Anandamai Ma. Her ill-health in the earlier years and domestic unhappiness also, perhaps, accentuated her religious bent.

Whereas Mrs. Gandhi had a feeling for religion, she was not religious in the conventional sense in her youth. But as generally happens in life, it was adversity and misfortunes which turned her towards formal religion. After the declaration of Emergency she was under great strain and started lending her ear to astrologers and godmen. One famous astrologer, P.M. Dhumal, conveyed to her that if she and Sanjay continued to live under the same roof, one of them would be destroyed. Later, after Sanjay's crash, somebody brought to her notice a Gujarati newspaper that had foretold Sanjay's end.[26] There were also rumours of Yagnas and Tantric rites being performed by her enemies for her destruction. People played on her fears and organized secret counter-Yagnas for her well-being. The entry of Dhirendra Brahmchari, a Yoga expert and a Tantric, in Indira's inner circle was much talked about in this context. He taught Nehru and Indira the finer points of Yoga and thus secured access to the PM's house. He got very close to Mrs. Gandhi, interfered in administrative matters and made a lot of money through shady deals. He had, perhaps, influenced Indira Gandhi by working on her phobias and his Tantric claptrap. But as Pupul Jayakar, who was a witness to Brahmachari's influence over Indira observed, "... the presence and access of Dhirendra Brahmachari to Prime Minister Indira Gandhi's home and table has never been explained."[27] It was only under Rajiv's pressure that this Rasputin was eased out of the PM's household.

There is nothing unusual about Indira getting interested in esoteric religious practices in her later years. In any case, normally it should not have been of much public consequence. But side by side there appeared another trait which caused genuine concern to her well-wishers. Her pronounced religiosity and frequent visits to temples came to be interpreted as her pandering to the Hindu vote bank. It was a fact that unlike earlier times, now she mostly visited Hindu shrines. Her reaction to communal riots was no longer as sharp and prompt as in the earlier days.

As a child Indira was frail and had to be occasionally admitted to the sanatorium, as sometimes X-rays showed a shadow on her lungs. The fear of her mother's consumption visiting her was always there. Even as a young woman she kept indifferent health, and this was one reason for her giving up the Congress presidency before completing the full term. But once she became Prime Minister, her health improved rapidly. In fact, she soon became famous for her gruelling election campaigns and the heavy work-schedule she followed. Power, as Henry Kisinger said, is the greatest aphrodisiac. In Indira's case it was particularly so. It turned a delicate, ailing and tiny woman into a tough, tenacious and formidable fighter. Accumulation of power was for her an emotional compulsion. It was a condition of her growth. She loved it in all its forms, the more the better. She absorbed it continuously from her environment. Thus she sucked the party, the state, the institutions dry of their power, leaving only empty shells behind.

Indira's exercise of power was obviously amoral. Power being the ultimate objective, it could not be otherwise. She depoliticized politics and institutionalized corruption to control the levers of power. She dragged the country through the nightmare of Emer-gency when her power was threatened. It was the impulse to perpetuate her power by encoding it in her genes which drove her to sedulously nurse her dynastic ambitions.

Mrs. Gandhi's philosophy of pragmatism served her well in this regard. Not having set herself distant goals and lacking ideo-logical commitment, she did not have to sacrifice immediate per-sonal gains to long-term objectives.

"I cannot understand how anyone can be an Indian and not be proud," Indira Gandhi said in her will. She was a staunch nation-alist and had an exalted view of India's destiny. And she was very clear that there were two essential preconditions for its fulfilment. First, India must become self-reliant. Shortage of foodgrains made the country particularly vulnerable to external pressures. To her lasting credit she worked tirelessly to achieve self-sufficiency in foodgrain production through the Green Revolution. She also improved India's balance of payment position and, at one point, the country did not draw the second tranche of a large world bank loan.

Secondly, she knew that India would be respected for her inherent strength and not for any fine speeches made at the UN. Mrs. Gandhi, therefore, modernized the defence forces, diversified sources of a weapons' supply and improved facilities for indigenous manufacture of sophisticated armaments. India's resounding victory in the Bangladesh war, her bold defiance of the US Seventh Fleet and testing of an atomic device sent out clear signals of the country's defence capability and self-confidence.

Indira was also much concerned about national unity and this was a major factor in her continuous efforts to concentrate power at the Centre. She may have overplayed the dangers posed by external powers, but there is little doubt that destabilizing forces were at work within the country and outside.

Mrs. Gandhi was no feminist but she did more to raise the status of women and build their self-confidence than any feminist could have. The fact that a woman was ruling a country with a strong hand, was always well-groomed, dignified and charming, did a world of good to the self-image of Indian women.

A talent for empathy with the poor and an abiding concern for their plight gave her ready access to the hearts of the people. And the poor also related to her instantly. At her public meetings, lakhs came just to behold her with their eyes. When she was out of power, the poor came to visit her in their thousands. Millions wept at her death. Even eleven years later bus-loads of common folk daily come to 1 Safdarjung Road, her official residence, which has now been converted into a memorial.

Mrs. Gandhi may not have had a strong sense of history, but she was acutely aware of making history and her place in it. In this pursuit she identified herself closely with her country. "No hate," she wrote in her will, "is dark enough to overshadow the extent of my love for my people and my country." And a day before her death she told a public meeting at Bhubaneshwar, "And as long as there is breath in me so long will I continue to serve and when my life goes I can say that every drop of blood that is in me will give life to India and strengthen it."

The problem with her identification with India was that, as a corollary, she identified India with herself. Whether Barooah believed in 'Indira is India and India is Indira' or not, she certainly did. So, by a quirk of logic she came to equate her good with the country's good and that is where the mischief lay.

Every giant carries a midget within. Sadly, Indira Gandhi allowed the midget to overpower the giant.

Rajiv Gandhi

35

Tragic Accession

*C*ertain post-assassination television images are deeply
stamped on my mind: Indira Gandhi lying in state and her prominent nose looking still more conspicuous on her bloodless,
pinched face; the incongruity of the chandeliered resplendence of
Ashoka Hall where Rajiv Gandhi took the oath of office, and the
funerary solemnity of the occasion; silhouetted against the setting
sun, Rajiv standing stoically by the funeral pyre of his mother.

Rajiv Gandhi was addressing a rally at Contai in West Bengal
when a policeman gave him a wireless message about the attack
on his mother. Pranab Mukherjee and Ghani Khan Chaudhary
were with him at that time. They rushed to Calcutta airport, where
a special plane was waiting to take him to Delhi. It was during
this journey that he learnt the bitter truth from a BBC broadcast.

As Rajiv was heading for Delhi, a number of central cabinet
ministers, chief ministers, and other bigwigs had assembled on
the eighth floor of AIIMS. The question agitating everybody was:
what next? Arun Nehru was in the lead: consulting, canvassing,
counselling. The two cabinet ministers present there, Shiv
Shankar and Shankaranand, felt that there should be no stopgap
arrangement, as it might lead to complications. Others, including
the four chief ministers, held the same view. They all agreed that
Rajiv Gandhi should be straightaway installed as the new Prime
Minister. As Giani Zail Singh, the President, was out of the
country, and his relations with Mrs. Gandhi had soured, Arun
Nehru suggested that R. Venkataraman, the Vice President should
immediately administer the oath of office.

This unseemly haste was occasioned by several factors. As
Indira Gandhi had discontinued the practice of preparing a

warrant of precedence of her ministers, there was no unchallenged number two in view. Then, there was no national leader of stature who could be acceptable to others as the PM. Moreover a general election was in the offing and the Congress needed a vote catcher. Rajiv, with his clean image and Nehruvian mantle was the best bet for the post.

In all these confabulations, P.C. Alexander, Principal Secretary to Indira Gandhi, played the crucial role of a credible mediator. He was opposed to Arun Nehru's suggestion of the Vice President swearing in Rajiv as the Prime Minister. This would have amounted to lack of faith in the President, and may have led to a Constitutional crisis. Giani Zail Singh was already on his way to India and would be reaching Delhi any time.

Rajiv reached Delhi around 3 pm and went straight to the hospital. Alexander suggested that it would be advisable to seek his opinion in the matter. So, he went to the room adjoining the operation theatre and the scene he witnessed is best described in his own words. "Rajiv was clasping Sonia by both hands in a corner of that room and talking to her very animatedly. Sonia was holding him tightly and with tears rolling down her cheeks was ardently pleading with him not to agree to be the Prime Minister. Rajiv was kissing her forehead and trying to convince her that he had to accept the office as it was his duty to do so in that hour of grave crisis."[1] Rajiv readily agreed that the oath should be administered by the President, as that was the right thing to do.

Giani Zail Singh reached Delhi from S'ana, North Yemen, around 5 pm, and drove straight to the All India Institute. It appears that after discussing the Constitutional position with his officials while in flight, the Giani had also decided to make Rajiv the Prime Minister, and informed the journalists accompanying him of his resolve. After condoling Rajiv Gandhi, the Giani took him aside and informed him of his decision to induct him as the PM.

Before he took the oath of office, the Congress Parliamentary Board passed a resolution electing Rajiv as the leader. Actually, this resolution was a bit of a farce. There were four vacancies in the nine-member board, and with Mrs. Gandhi gone and Kamalapati Tripathi and M. Chandrashekhar out of station, the prime minister of the world's largest democracy was formally elected by the remaining two members, Pranab Mukherjee and P.V. Narasimha Rao. Subsequently, the decision was endorsed by the Congress Working Committee on 3 November and by the Congress Parliamentary Party on the 5th. Two weeks later he was elected the party president by the CWC.

In the beginning Rajiv Gandhi desired that all members of his mother's council of ministers should be invited to take the oath of office along with him. Later, he decided that only P.V. Narasimha Rao, Pranab Mukherjee, Shiv Shankar and Buta Singh would be inducted in the first instance. So the rest had to be told to bide their time.

After the swearing in ceremony Rajiv held a brief cabinet meeting where a resolution of condolence was adopted.

Late that might the new Prime Minister made his first broadcast to the nation. "Indira Gandhi, India's Prime Minister, has been assassinated. She was mother not just to me but to all of you, my countrymen," he said. "Nothing would hurt the soul of Indira more than the occurrence of violence in any part of the country."

But the countrymen were not overly concerned about the feelings of the departed soul. Even as Rajiv was addressing the nation, there were sporadic acts of violence against the Sikhs. The clearest indication of the impending trouble was the stoning of the President's car as he approached the Medical Institute. The car of his Press Secretary, Tarlochan Singh was damaged and set on fire.

Whereas on the evening and night of 31 October, there were only isolated incidents of the Sikhs being assaulted and their property burnt, by the next day a regular pogrom against them was launched. It ultimately ended with the massacre of 2733 Sikhs in Delhi alone, and the destruction of their property worth hundreds of crores.

Two aspects of this holocaust are significant. One, the systematic
and organized manner in which the Sikhs were targeted. Second,
the apathy and, at times, active connivance of the administration
in giving the communal goons a free hand. Rahul Kuldip Bedi, a
journalist, who was an eye witness to these happenings, reported,
"On 1 November all exit points from Trilokpuri had been sealed
off by massive concrete pipes...to ensure that no Sikh escapes
...Two lanes of Block 32, an area around 500 square yards inhabited by around 450 Sikh families, is littered with corpses, the drain
choked with dismembered limbs and masses of hair. Cindered
human remains lie scattered in the first 20 yards of the first lane.
The remaining 40-yard stretch of the street is strewn with naked
bodies, brutally hacked beyond recognition." When Bedi went to
the nearest police station, he was told, "Nothing to worry about,
only two people have been killed." In the premises of the police
station was parked a truck loaded with "... several corpses charred
beyond recognition."

When Bedi met H.C. Yadav, Additional Commissioner of
Police, he was told that he (the officer) "has just returned from
a tour of the trans-Jamuna colonies, particularly Trilokpuri.
Nothing is amiss."[2]

Further, "Led by Congress-I Pradhans and Youth Congress-I
leaders, mobs armed with voters lists began their putsch. The local
police collaborated with the rioters, as numerous evacuees in
camps swore afterwards in affidavits."[3]

According to an eminent journalist, late on the evening of 31
October a decision was taken to "teach the Sikhs a lesson."[4] Perhaps this expression was used in anger by a key member of the
Rajiv coterie, and the 'loyalists' took it for an 'official' command.
"... through the dadas and criminals, with whom several politicians have a regular liaison, groups were contacted that
night...targets were identified and the groups mobilized on the
morning of 1 November, they were given a free hand till after the
funeral was over on the evening of 3 November."[5]

Some apologists argue that the Sikhs themselves invited this
backlash by celebrating the assassination of Mrs. Gandhi. It is a
fact that some misguided Sikhs distributed sweets to mark the

occasion. But "If all the sweets in India had been distributed that would not have justified the burning alive of a single Sikh."[6] When the army entered the Golden Temple and demolished the Akal Takht, the event was widely celebrated by the Hindus, and sweets were openly distributed even in Amritsar. Would such provocation have justified the Sikhs butchering the Hindus in their thousands?

The fallout of the Delhi carnage affected nearly 80 towns in the country and in Kanpur alone 140 Sikhs were killed. But it is also a fact that several Hindus gave refuge to their Sikh neighbours and saved hundreds of them from a gory death. Later, when the government refused to set up a commission of enquiry, it was the Hindu voluntary agencies and social activist groups which performed this onerous task.

Rajiv Gandhi was suddenly burdened with a most difficult charge: he was totally inexperienced; his mother was lying dead, and he had to attend to elaborate obsequies. It was the people around him and especially his senior ministers, whose duty it was to themselves assume the responsibility of maintaining order with a firm hand. But they issued no clear instructions and did not visit the affected areas. A wholly ineffective curfew was imposed and the ghouls violated it freely, with the police watching them indulgently. The army was called, but given no clear instructions. Only on 3 November it was asked to shoot at sight, and this immediately brought the situation under control.

The accession of Rajiv Gandhi was attended by three gruesome tragedies: his mother's assassination; the pogrom against the Sikhs, and the Bhopal gas leak. The last, though the most serious industrial mishap ever, where more than 2,000 persons died, was completely overshadowed by the two other calamities and thus did not get the attention it deserved. Not a very auspicious start for the youngest and the most inexperienced Prime Minister of India.

Rajiv's election to rule one of the most ungovernable countries was an astounding act of dynastic allegiance. He had been an MP for just 38 months, held no ministerial charge, and took no interest in politics till Sanjay's death. Indira Gandhi herself never thought of a political career for him. After the crash when Sanjay's friend Dumpy Akbar suggested that Rajiv may be put up from Amethi, she said, "Don't be silly. His politics are not like ours." And she told Pupul Jayakar, "Sanjay was very frugal, but Rajiv and his wife need certain comforts."[7]

Yet the aborted dynastic dream was quietly rising again in the fond mother's heart. Rajiv resigned from Indian Airlines to 'assist mummy'. He dutifully observed, "I felt that there was a void and I couldn't see anybody else filling it; there was in a sense an inevitability about it."[8]

As Indira left Rajiv free to make up his mind, the Amethi parliamentary seat was left vacant for one year, despite the constitutional obligation to fill all such vacancies within six months. Then, in the beginning of 1983 he was made the General Secretary of the Congress, and formally anointed as leader of the Youth Congress at the Bangalore session of the party. Simultaneously, the Sanjay caucus was gradually liquidated and his widow Maneka, who was aspiring to wear the family mantle, was thrown out of the house. Mrs. Gandhi also exposed Rajiv to major organizational ventures like the IX Asian Games, Non-aligned Meet, the Commonwealth Heads of Government Meeting, etc. He was actively associated with important policy matters, and took a keen interest in the affairs of various states. He was put in charge of the Andhra and Karnataka assembly elections, which the Congress lost by a handsome margin.

Rajiv also started assembling his own team during this phase. Arun Nehru, his cousin and a former executive of a paints company, became his political adviser. Arun Singh, Marketing Controller of Reckitt and Coleman, and an old classmate, left his job to assist his pal. Satish Sharma, a pilot friend of Rajiv; Vijay Dhar, a professional and son of Indira's confidante D.P. Dhar, and Romi Chopra, an advertising executive became other members of the Rajiv coterie.

After accession, the first major task before Rajiv was the holding of the general election. Though the event was due in January 1985, he advanced it by a month, and election was held on 24, 26 and 27 December. It was a shrewd move as Mrs. Gandhi's assassination had generated a tidal wave of sympathy, and public emotion tends to quickly dissipate.

The selection of candidates created the usual acrimony and grievances. Kamalapati Tripathi, the working Congress President felt ignored and slighted, and A.R. Antulay floated a new party on being denied the party ticket. Only 80 of the sitting members were dropped; so it was not much of a shake-up. Owing to very disturbed conditions, Punjab and Assam did not go to the polls. The Congress-I contested 485 of the 508 seats to which election was held.

Contrary to the earlier impression of being a friendly and pleasant person, Rajiv Gandhi unnecessarily mounted a very aggressive and hard-hitting campaign. "Rajiv had made much play in his campaign meetings of Sikh demands for a separate state. Indeed in what has been described as the dirtiest election campaign in Indian history, Rajiv came within a whisker of blaming the opposition for his mother's death by accusing them of supporting Sikh separatism."[9] As a leading journalist observed, "This time round the Congress-I had succeeded in doing to the caste Hindus what it had usually done to the Muslims and the Harijans: it had succeeded in making them insecure and in convincing them that it was the only available saviour."

Rajiv's victory was unprecedented, exceeding the best performance of both his mother and grandfather. The Congress-I polled 49.2 percent of the total votes and 52 percent of the votes cast in the 485 seats contested by it. With 401 Congress-I candidates victorious, it captured 79 percent of the seats in the Parliament.

How much the 'sympathy wave' contributed to this magnificent victory was highlighted by the results of the assembly elections in 10 Congress-I ruled states just three months later. With a view to extracting maximum advantage from the prevailing public mood and hoping to repeat Mrs. Gandhi's performance of 1971-72, these states went in for elections a couple of months ahead of time. But a receding wave only pulls you down and the Congress-I fared badly at this poll. Compared to its share of votes in December 1984, its overall loss was 26.8 percent in March 1985. And this erosion of Congress-I's hold on the states continued throughout the Rajiv regime. By the middle of 1987 there were non-Congress-I governments in eleven states. The whole of the south and most of eastern India had slipped out of the Congress fold.

These elections also highlighted an increasing trend towards regionalization of state politics. Starting from the north, Jammu and Kashmir was ruled by the National Conference, Punjab by Akali Dal, Haryana by Lok Dal, Andhra Pradesh by Telegu Desam, Tamil Nadu by AIADMK, Assam by Assam Gana Parishad and Sikkim by Sikkim Sangram Parishad. Another significant aspect of India's political map at that time was that the BJP did not rule a single state. Even in the general election it had secured only two out of 508 parliamentary seats.

Rajiv Gandhi came to his job untested and untrained. Though this was a handicap, it had some obvious advantages in the Indian context. His name was not associated with any controversial issues, he was not aligned with any caucus, and he had not yet created a coterie of his own. A strikingly handsome person with a sensitive face and tendency to blush like a schoolgirl, he started with a big advantage. His dignified demeanour, unfailing courtesy and openness enhanced his public appeal. People loved to watch him on television. They empathized in his loss and they were only too ready to give him a fair chance.

His initial moves convinced the masses that he wanted to give the country a clean and efficient administration. In the selection of party candidates for the general and assembly elections, he insisted that "A commitment to a clean public life and personal probity were a must." He was quite aware of the malaise afflicting the Congress party and earnestly wanted to rejuvenate it. Having seen the confrontationist politics of his mother, he tried to promote a culture of accommodation and conciliation.

When R.K. Hegde, Janata Dal chief minister of Karnataka, offered to resign on moral grounds after the Congress-I had swept the board in the general election, Rajiv asked him to continue till the next assembly poll. In view of the adverse public reaction to the supersession of non-Congress-I state governments, and with memories of the dismissal of NTR still fresh in his mind, he openly stated that his party would never again destabilize an opposition state government. After assumption of office when he found various chief ministers hanging around him, he asked them to go back and attend to their jobs.

Rajiv also made earnest efforts to modernize the party and systematize its office work. He computerized the bio-data and performance appraisal of each candidate aspiring for the party ticket, and prepared elaborate political profiles of each constituency. He used the system of interviews and questionnaires for the selection of candidates for general election. Though this managerial approach was much resented by the rank and file, Rajiv's aim was to introduce an element of objectivity and fairplay in the process of selection.

After watching Rajiv Gandhi in action for a couple of months the general opinion was that here was a fine gentleman, thoroughly well-meaning, earnest and honest. In view of this impression his indulgent countrymen stuck the label 'Mr. Clean' on him. Clean in politics! And that too, Indian politics ! It was a needless provocation to the jealous gods.

36

Breaking Fresh Ground

$\mathcal{R}$ajiv Gandhi was a very very contemporary person. His job as a pilot had spurred his interest in electronics and tele-communications, which happened to be the frontier areas of technology at that time. In his first address to the nation after the 13-day mourning for his mother, he said, "... together we will build an India of the twenty-first century." This futuristic thrust became the leitmotif of his agenda for change. And naturally, the team of advisers he assembled also comprised young persons, imbued with the corporate culture of a modern industrial society.

At the ground level, Rajiv's most ambitious and comprehensive initiative was the creation of six 'technology missions'. These missions were assigned the task of applying technology to six well-defined areas of underdevelopment to achieve specific, time-bound results. The Drinking Water Mission was to make potable water available to all the Indian villages according to a set time-table. The Literacy Mission was asked to speedily improve literacy levels, and use satellite linked communication aids like radio and television for imparting mass education. A nationwide immuni-zation programme for children and pregnant women was launched to cover the entire population. Another mission was designed to usher in the 'white revolution', by increasing the supply of milk and other dairy products through improving the stock of milch cattle and eradicating diseases of livestock. As the country was spending large amounts of foreign exchange on importing edible oils, a separate mission was set up to develop and introduce improved varieties of oil-seeds. And lastly, in view of the increasing importance of communications, a technology mission was set up for indigeneous manufacture of telecom equipment so as to bring the telephone within the reach of all villagers.

A lot of thinking had gone into the creation of these missions and there is no doubt that the areas of underdevelopment identified by the government merited urgent attention. Even after forty years of Independence, 28 percent of the villages had no access to drinking water, half the population was still illiterate, millions of children and expectant mothers perished for want of elementary health care, per capita milk consumption was only 160 grams per day, and the country was not producing enough cooking oil to meet its bare requirements.

These missions have done a lot of useful work, but they suffered from two handicaps. First, the approach to solving the problems of underdevelopment was techno-managerial. No effort was made to build in components of social and cultural change in this vast effort. Secondly, only the existing delivery system was used to implement the programmes, without introducing any structural changes, or seeking the active involvement of the people. Thus, the moment official pressures slackened, the missions also lost much of their impetus.

Rajiv was very ably assisted in this project by Sam Pitroda, a brilliant telecom engineer settled in the USA, who also happened to be a man of great enterprise and commitment. He helped the PM start the Centre for Development of Telematics, and undertook the development of digital switching equipment for telephone exchanges. Rajiv also gave a big boost to computer culture. He was totally fascinated by the power and potential of the microchip, and a lap-top for him was as much a part of his personal gear as a watch is to others.

One of the first things he did on becoming PM was to formulate a new computer policy. The main thrust of this policy was to rapidly increase the use of computers in offices, banks, railways and other such establishments. He therefore encouraged the indigenous manufacture of computers by reducing duties on components. His own example had a powerful impact and it soon became a status symbol to own a personal computer.

Concrete benefits from computerization were already apparent during Rajiv's regime. The 'Electronics City' of Bangalore, the

Indian version of 'Silicon Valley', developed fast and became a growing point for the development of electronics industry. Rajiv had placed high hopes on the growth of software production, and it has already become one of India's leading foreign exchange earners. An integrated computer network for the railways, RAIL-NET, was created for computerized reservations and keeping track of wagon movement. The Indian Banks Association also opted for computerization of its entire accounting system. But NICNET is the most important computer network which provides countrywide linkages right down to the district for the storage, processing, retrieval and exchange of data between various government departments and field agencies.

For years India had been unsuccessfully pressing America to clear the sale of a super-computer for weather forecasting. It must have been a matter of much satisfaction for Rajiv when, during his first visit to the USA in 1985, he was able to persuade President Reagan to waive the US objection to this deal.

The other areas of high-technology which received special attention were that of space and nuclear research. India was able to place in orbit its first indigenously manufactured remote sensing satellite in 1988 with the help of a foreign launch vehicle.

Though India's nuclear power programme has an uneven record, the government signed an agreement with the USSR in 1988 for the construction of two giant enriched-uranium power stations. This deal went against the 'self-sufficiency' approach, yet Rajiv considered it necessary if India was to meet 10 percent of her electricity requirements by the beginning of the 21st century by nuclear power.

Mrs. Gandhi had already started opening up the economy and simplifying procedures, and Rajiv went in for liberalization in a more systematic manner. He relaxed import controls, encouraged foreign participation and allowed imports even in the consumer sector. This had a stimulating effect on the electronic and the white goods industry. Colour TV sets and Maruti cars were the most high-visibility symbols of the resultant growth. Simultaneously, he relaxed controls, simplified import-export procedures and reduced duties to make life easier for the entrepreneurs.

All these measures led to a middle-class consumer boom and

conspicuous consumption for which Rajiv was much criticized. In fact here he was playing a no-win game. Having abjured the path of state regulation, the alternative of market economy appeared the only viable option. The main beneficiaries of this policy were bound to be the moneyed classes. But it must be remembered that his six technology missions were targeted entirely at the deprived sections of society.

In view of his lack of academic credentials, not many people would have thought that Rajiv would be much concerned with mass education. Yet he took a keener interest in the subject than even his much better educated grandfather. Soon after assuming office, his government started working on a new education policy, and within eight months it produced a report, 'Challenge of Education'. It forcefully brought out the deplorable state of school education in the country. Leave aside the luxury of buildings, the report revealed that a large number of village schools had no teachers, no blackboards, and not even drinking water. No less depressing was the fact that despite low enrolment rates, more than three-fourth of the students dropped out by the time they reached the VIII standard.

The government promulgated a three-pronged approach to improve matters. The Literacy Mission was assigned the task of achieving 100 percent literacy by the time India entered the 21st century; secondly, to rapidly expand facilities for vocational training so as to tackle the problem of the unemployed; and lastly to launch 'Operation Blackboard' to provide basic amenities and teaching aids in all the schools. He laid particular stress on extending the concept of 'distant education' through radio and TV, and established the Indira Gandhi National Open University for providing well-designed educational material to those who could not attend colleges.

But two things happened to this highly laudable new education policy. First, adequate funds were never allotted to achieve the desired goals. Secondly, the PM did not show the requisite stamina and perseverance to push through his reforms. Consequently during the 5-year term of Rajiv Gandhi the literacy levels crawled up by a few percentage points only.

It was from his mother that Rajiv imbibed his concern for the environment. One of Mrs. Gandhi's pet conservational projects was the cleansing of the Ganga, India's river of life. The report on the Ganga Action Plan was ready for presentation when she was killed. In his first speech to the nation Rajiv promised to give top priority to the Ganga project. He set up a ten-member high power Central Ganga Authority with himself as its chairman. A budgetary provision of Rs. 250 crores was made for the first phase of the scheme. Even if the project has lost some its earlier drive, it has significantly lowered the pollution level of the Ganga.

Rajiv also set up a Ministry of Environment to prepare and enforce an environment protection regime. It was made mandatory for industrial projects, other polluting undertakings and dams to obtain clearance from this ministry before going ahead with construction. At the ninth summit of the Non-aligned Movement he proposed the institution of a Planet Protection Fund to provide the latest conservation technologies to the developing countries for the protection of global environment.

Looking to the metro-centric and elitist bias of state patronage to the arts, Rajiv Gandhi tried to correct the imbalance by opening seven zonal cultural centres in the country for the promotion of artistic activities specific to the respective regions. He also ordered a thorough review of the cultural policies pursued by the three National Akademies set up during Nehru's time. A 23-acre site was chosen near India Gate to set up the Indira Gandhi National Centre for Arts. It was meant to be a focal point of research and promotional activities relating to all forms of Indian art.

Rajiv continued the initiative taken by his mother in holding spectacular Festivals of India abroad. So completely were the organizers swept off their feet in their enthusiasm to display a poor country's rich artistic heritage in the great white man's lands that the rarest of Indian sculptures were sent to the USA and France. At the end of the exercise it was found that 27 of them had been damaged in varying degrees in the process of handling.

During his tenure Rajiv launched three major projects. One, the creation of six technology missions. Two, giving a big push to the electronic revolution. And three, framing a bill to give a constitutional basis to Panchayati Raj institutions. This last scheme was a part of his move to establish 'Responsive Administration'.

There were several factors which impelled Rajiv to pay serious attention to this subject. Having failed to hold the party elections, this was the only other area where he could create an impact over a vast canvas. He had acquired a pro-rich, pro-urban image, and Panchayati reform was the best antidote to it. There was also the need to start a major populist programme in view of the approaching general election.

But these factors do not detract from Rajiv Gandhi's very sincere desire to institutionalize Panchayati Raj because it was good for the country. He started his crusade by holding free and frank deliberations with district collectors, and between December 1987 and June 1988 he had met nearly 400 of them at five different venues at one-month intervals. He discussed their recommendations with the state chief secretaries in July 1988. Then, at a Panchayati Raj Sammelan held from 27-30 January 1988, the matter was debated by nearly 8,000 delegates. A two-day conference on Panchayati Raj for Women was held at Delhi on 3 and 4 May, 1989. After that the recommendations made by the collectors and chief secretaries were reviewed and endorsed at the AICC session held in May 1989. And lastly, the outcome of this massive exercise was presented at a meeting of chief ministers convened at Delhi soon thereafter. At the end of this marathon exercise, Rajiv rightly claimed, "... never before has a government at the highest level taken so carefully into account the views of so many tens of thousands of people at every level about democracy and development at the grass roots."

The Panchayati legislation sought to give a Constitutional sanction to Panchayati Raj, the third tier of the government. Panchayats were to be created at three levels, i.e., the district, the block (intermediate) and the village. The Constitution (64th

Amendment) Bill proposed to insert a new (ninth) schedule to the Constitution to make elections to all the three levels mandatory at 5-year intervals. The Panchayats were to have assured sources of income and invested with adequate powers to effectively discharge their functions. They were to prepare their own development plans and control the agencies for their implementation. A special feature of the bill was the 30 percent reservation of seats for women, and proportional reservation for Scheduled Castes and Scheduled Tribes. It was for the first time that reservations were introduced at the level of the third tier of government.

The proposed amendment was passed by the Lok Sabha on 10 August 1989, but failed to get Rajya Sabha's approval as the government did not have a two-third majority there. Whereas this deprived the Congress from claiming credit for this popular legistation at the 1989 general election it, gave the party a stick to beat the opposition with for sabotaging such a progressive and people-oriented measure. It was only after Rajiv's assassination that the Amendment Bill was ultimately passed by the next Congress Government under P.V. Narsimha Rao in December 1992.

There was a peculiar contradiction at the core of Rajiv's plan to 'empower the people' through Panchayati Raj. The ostensible objective of the legislation was a massive devolution of power to the grass-root level institutions. But this did not mean that Rajiv was moving towards a more federal polity. In fact in one sense it was a step towards greater centralization. The Panchayati Raj Bill was a brain-child of the Centre. The Prime Minister directly interacted with the collectors and chief secratries to flesh out the concept. The Congress party and the state governments were never actively associated with its formulation. It was only when the scheme had taken a final shape that a meeting of AICC and the chief ministers was convened to obtain their formal approval. It is a measure of the extent to which the districts were sought to be controlled by the Centre that cheques towards funding Jawahar Rozgar Yojana for the states of West Bengal, Karnataka and Andhra Pradesh were despatched to the collectors and Panchayat presidents directly instead of being routed through the state governments.

Rajiv's distrust of state governments in this matter had some basis. From Nehru's days all proposals to introduce Panchayati Raj had been initiated by the Centre. In fact the states had mostly soft-pedalled them, as strong Panchayats encroached upon the power of the local MLAs and MPs. Secondly, the states were also guilty of diverting funds meant for rural development to non-productive schemes. But the remedy to this situation did not lie in wishing away the state governments. Under the Constitution the districts were administered by the states, and the district officials were accountable to their state governments. Thus the elimination of state governments in such a perfunctory manner was neither Constitutional nor politic. In fact, Rajiv's approach was driving a wedge between the district and the state administration.

Also, how could you have decentralization at the grass-roots, without introducing it at the Centre and keeping the states on such a tight leash? Again, in the drive to 'empower the people' the Congress party itself was wholly centralized and least empowered. Rajiv's Panchayti Raj concept, though informed by the best of intentions, was based on confused and compartmentalized thinking. Its greatest weakness was that it was built upon a basic distrust of the people and their representatives. Despite all the *sammelans* and seminars, only the bureaucrats were used as the sounding boards for this scheme, and they alone were associated with its formulation.

Another notable initiative of Rajiv was the introduction of Jawahar Rozgar Yojana during the birth centenary of Nehru. This scheme aimed at providing employment to at least one member of each poor rural family for 50-100 days in a year. It was funded by the Centre to the extent of 80 percent, and an outlay of Rs. 2,100 crores was initially provided to give it a big push.

Recognizing the need to upgrade the status of women, the National Perspective Plan for Women was prepared in 1988. Among other things it recommended that 50 percent of the grass-root functionaries should be women, and 30 percent of elective seats in all Panchayat bodies should go to women. It was as a result of this recommendation that the Panchayat Bill provided for 30 percent reservation for women in Panchayats at all levels.

Three factors shaped the modern outlook of Rajiv. First, though he belonged to a most distinguished political family, he entered politics with a purely professional background. Secondly, he not only never took any interest in matters political, he had a marked disdain for the tribe of politicians. Thirdly, having studied in Doon School and Cambridge, and then opted for a career in the airlines, his contact with India's ground reality was minimal.

The problem with Rajiv's modernity was that Western technology was the product of more than two centuries of unbroken tradition rooted in a particular socio-economic milieu which had very little in common with India. Moreover, technology had an important political dimension and upheld a specific value system. This again was very different from that of India. Consequently this resulted in a dichotomy between Rajiv's affinity for modern technology and his political universe. Whereas he was in his element setting up technology missions or promoting computer culture, he was unable to adjust to the Indian political ethos, much less evolve a distinct political style of his own. For the same reason he was perceived as an outsider by his party, and on his side he could not relate even to the Congress politicians.

If Rajiv did not have deep roots in the cultural soil of India, his understanding of the Western industrial civilization was also superficial. He did not realize that the technology-driven modernity is as much a product of the mind as machines. His technocratic team which had such a high admiration for the Japanese model did not sufficiently appreciate that what India needs to import from Japan is not technology but her industrial culture, work ethics and attitude to the challenges of modernization. A society mired in the feudal ethos, hierarchical social structures and crippling levels of illiteracy cannot become 'modern' just by the introduction of machines. And in this vital sphere of social engineering the government never prepared a comprehensive agenda to bring about the necessary changes.

37

Administration

$\mathcal{R}$ajiv had the advantage of looking at the Indian political scene as an outsider. He conveyed the impression of an open-minded, fair and receptive person who was eager to show results. And results he showed in ample measure in the first phase of his tenure. By the time he had completed one year in office, he had more achievements to his credit than any other Indian Prime Minister in a comparable period. What is more, his credibility as an honest, purposeful and efficient ruler was well established, and he just could do no wrong. The fickleness of public adulation! After 18 months in office, he just could do nothing right.

He formed his new 40-member Council of Ministers on 31 December, 1984. Its composition showed restraint, maturity and foresight. The key portfolios of Home, Defence and Finance were given to tested war horses like S.B. Chavan, P.V. Narasimha Rao and V.P. Singh. Owing to Pranab Mukherjee's close association with some business tycoons, he was not included in the cabinet. The second line of ministers contained a number of young persons who shared his perceptions. He wisely gave junior assignments to his two closest friends and advisers: Arun Nehru he appointed as Minister of State for Power, and Arun Singh as his parliamentary secretary. He also declared that the performance of his ministers would be constantly monitored and appropriate changes made in due course.

In a major reshuffle nine months later, Rajiv dropped six ministers, reinstated old loyalists like N.D. Tiwari and Sitaram Kesri, gave the much more sensitive charge of Internal Security in the Home Ministry to Arun Nehru, and made Arun Singh the Minister of State for Defence. He introduced the practice of specifically defining the charge of ministers of state so that junior ministers were able to grow by carrying independent responsibility.

One of the first things he did as Prime Minister was to relieve R.K. Dhawan of his charge. Generally perceived as Indira's chief manipulator and fixer, the move confirmed Rajiv's desire to usher in an era of clean politics.

After the general election he immediately introduced the Anti-defection Bill. Before that he held extensive consultations with the opposition leaders and accommodated their suggestions. Thus the bill had a smooth passage in both the Houses. This landmark legislation inserted the Tenth Schedule in the Constitution which made floor-crossing by legislators punishable with disqualification. Only a split within a party was allowed, provided at least one-third of its members in the legislature defected from the parent body. This further confirmed Rajiv's desire to cleanse the country's political culture.

Concerned at the high cost of justice for the poor, he introduced the system of Lok Adalats and Free Legal Aid to provide them with speedier and cheaper justice. The Consumer Protection Act was passed and consumer courts set up. The Anti Dowry Act, passed in 1986, prescribed deterrent punishments for dowry seekers.

Though rated as the least educated of the Indian Prime Ministers, the Rajiv Government framed a New Education Policy within a couple of months of assuming office, and an approach document on the subject was placed before the Parliament in October 1985. This was followed by Operation Blackboard and several other reforms. He further stressed the importance of education by restructuring the Ministry of Education into the Ministry of Human Resource Development, and added the charges of Youth Affairs and Women and Sports to it. P.V. Narasimha Rao, one of the seniormost ministers and a man of learning, was placed in its charge to emphasize its enhanced status.

Rajiv Gandhi seemed genuinely interested in open government and gave unprecedented freedom to the government media. He asked me to show on Doordarshan 'Yes Minister', a delightful

BBC TV serial lampooning ministers and bureaucrats. With his support we started the programme 'Janvani', where ministers were grilled by the people about their performance. Another television serial, 'Sach Ki Parchhaiyan' (Shadows of Truth) exposed corruption and malfunctioning of various government departments. M.J. Akbar's 'Newsline' was another popular programme in the same genre. The trend not only raised the credibility of the government media, but also won kudos for the PM's initiative to expose his government to public criticism.

Rajiv and his advisers from the corporate world strongly felt that India's ritualistic adherence to socialism had not done much good even to the have-nots. His team favoured market economy and wanted the Indian industry to be thrown open to competition. So the PM appointed V.P. Singh as his Finance Minister to pep up the economy and purge the business world of its major ills. Whereas on the one hand some steps were taken for liberalization, on the other economic offenders, even at the highest level, were hauled up under V.P. Singh's 'raid-raj'. His initiative to relax controls and permit greater play to the market forces propelled the economy towards better performance.

The power of technology greatly fascinated Rajiv and, more than anybody else, he instilled the imperative of upgrading obsolete production processes and adopting technological innovation if the Indian entrepreneurs were to survive in the face of international competition. He repeatedly reminded the people that the 21st century would be dominated by electronics and telecommunications, and India must keep pace with new developments to hold her own.

The most outstanding achievements of this phase were the signing of the Punjab Accord in July and the Assam Accord in August, 1985. The country went delirious with joy, and Rajiv was hailed as a great statesman and peace-maker. Thus his first year's record was a remarkable sprint of creative activity and reformist zeal.

The excellent impression that Rajiv created during the first phase of his rule rested upon some admirable policy initiatives, progressive legislation and the two accords. These were essentially expressions of good intent, the equivalent of sowing the seeds. The harvest had yet to be gathered. And that is where lay the rub.

Rajiv had hardly settled in office when the government was rocked by a serious spy scandal. For years Coomar Narain, a conman of an Indian firm, had been passing on sensitive state secrets to some clients, including foreign missions. He used to get photocopies of classified documents from the office of Principal Secretary to the PM, and then hand them over to his patrons. There was a big blow-up; P.C. Alexander owned moral responsibility and resigned; the French ambassador was recalled.

Rajiv was in no way concerned with this ugly episode. But it led to an arrangement which jolted the established hierarchies. After Alexander's exit, nobody was posted in his place. Gopi Arora, the next officer in the pecking order, was only an Additional Secretary at that time, whereas the Principal Secretary ranks higher than all the secretaries. Consequently, Arun Singh, the Prime Minister's principal adviser, automatically took over the functions of the Principal Secretary also. But the secretaries could not interact with him as freely as they would with a member of their own tribe. So the feedback to the PM from the bureaucracy got constricted and the chain of command was distorted.

At the operational level, Rajiv took several steps to improve the efficiency of government departments and make the system more result oriented. With the help of his back-room boys he designed training and reorientation courses for all levels of officials, and asked his ministers also to attend some senior-level programmes. A system of periodic performance review of the ministries was introduced at which the concerned minister and secretary were required to make a presentation. Computers were given to all offices and the officials encouraged to use them as a management tool.

These well-intentioned measures suffered from three drawbacks.

They were bodily lifted from the corporate world and paid scant heed to the traditions and work culture of the system on which they were grafted. Secondly, they only amounted to tinkering with the existing order, instead of changing it structurally. For instance, there was no point in giving the secretary a computer when a telex was kept lying in the dealing assistant's tray for a week before he attended to it. Or, when a file passed through nine levels before it landed on a minister's table. Thirdly, all the monitoring and review at the PM's level not only further centralized an already top-heavy organization, it saddled the PM with excessive detail. At any given time there may be 10,000 important issues pending with the government of India. Rajiv tried to review each important case dealt with in each ministry. Inevitably, he got lost in a jungle of detail in this process. As he did not establish priorities among the major issues that he should attend to, he spent too much time on pursuing matters which were best left to the Cabinet Secretary and his own staff.

The result of this approach was that he was always in a tearing hurry. He came to be known as the 'highlight' Prime Minister, as he not only wanted very brief notes, but important portions of those notes to be picked up by highlighter pens. In fact to save time he came to rely increasingly on audio-visual presentation. Now, such a mode is all right in a boardroom where a company's financial performance, sales effort or project implementation are to be shown graphically. But ministries deal with complex policy issues which have to be analysed, the pros and cons debated and views of other ministries accommodated.

Rajiv Gandhi undertook a massive exercise in fleshing out the concept of 'Responsive Administration'. In 1988 he addressed five large workshops of district collectors in five different states, and encouraged the government officials to share their thinking and experience with him. "... a truly responsive administration must have two essential characteristics," he said, "it must be representative, and it must be responsible." The focus of the whole effort was to establish Panchayati Raj institutions and remove the 'dependency syndrome of the people.'

Whereas 'representative administration' was to be the engine of self-sustaining development, references to paternalistic administration were all the time creeping in. For instance the collectors 'must educate the community to improve its quality of life;' 'the farmers must be made more flexible;' 'we must involve the people in some way;' you actually must be 'meaningful to the human beings whose life you are there to improve'. And, as a wrap-up, behind the implementation of programmes, "... there must be a basic realisation of the ideology, the philosophy from which it flows."[1] But the specific elements of a cogent ideology or philosophy were never spelt out, nor a scheme outlined for infusing that philosophy with the life-blood of a viable action plan.

One should not underestimate the difficulties inherent in implementing Rajiv's plan for Responsive Administration. Neither Nehru nor his successors had been able to evolve a viable model. As a Collector and District Magistrate in the fifties, I belonged to the first crop of officials which was exposed to these ideas and tried to implement them. Since then they had been bottled and rebottled with different labels, but with the same results.

Rajiv was not a conceptualiser or builder of systems. He had a better grasp of concrete issues, and performed well where a single-shot approach was required. His signing of the Punjab and Assam accords best illustrate this point. He did very well in wrapping up these accords as a one-time operation. But he could not view them in the longer perspective, nor could he ensure their neat implementation by adhering to the basic issues. His most notable single-shot performance was the handling of the extremely severe drought of 1987. He personally visited all the affected states, created an elaborate machinery for efficient movement of foodgrains and their distribution, and monitored the entire exercise from a central point. Being a wholly apolitical operation, it was amenable to an entirely managerial solution.

Another weakness in his thinking was the lack of political depth. Rajiv did not rely on his cabinet for formulating his views on major policy issues. Instead, he depended upon his nonelected, non-political advisers for this purpose. Here, on the one hand a group of people exercised a lot of power without responsibility, and on the other the institutional organ of the cabinet system was downgraded.

On an average Rajiv reshuffled his cabinet every two months and replaced sixteen chief ministers during his tenure. Thus he showed little regard for continuity, experience and specialization. Such quick changes bred a sense of insecurity among his ministers. It is rather strange that a person who swore by the virtues of corporate management culture, paid such scant attention to its basic norms. A serious fallout of this approach was that the PMO became much stronger at the cost of the cabinet.

Handling of the Thakkar Commission enquiry report on Indira Gandhi's assassination shows how even sensitive matters were treated without much forethought. Appointed soon after the event, the final report was submitted in February 1986. But instead of placing it before the Parliament, the government passed an ordinance which authorized it to withhold enquiry commission reports in the interest of the country's security. Three years later *The Indian Express* published excerpts from the Report which implicated R.K. Dhawan in the conspiracy to murder Mrs. Gandhi. It proved highly embarrassing for Rajiv Gandhi, who had just rehabilitated Dhawan as Officer on Special Duty.

A second Commission of Enquiry, set up under Justice Ranganath Mishra, was asked to probe into the Delhi riots which followed Indira Gandhi's killing. Its Report implicated 19 Congressmen, but no action was initiated against them. This confirmed the Sikhs in their belief the Rajiv was guided more by party loyalty than dictates of justice.

Then, contrary to the recommendation of the Law Commission, Indian Post Office (amendment) Bill, 1986, seeking to enlarge the government powers to intercept private mail, was passed by the parliament. Giani Zail Singh, whose relations with the PM were already strained, made his displeasure obvious by asking the concerned ministry to explain as to why the Law Commission's recommendations had not been implemented.

On assumpion of office Rajiv had struck everybody as a suave, affable and courteous person. But soon he started showing flashes of temper, and some of his actions became impulsive and hasty. Partly, this was due to pressure of work, and frustration at the unresponsiveness of the system. But it was also a temperamental trait. When still a nobody in the government, he had blasted Anjiah, CM Andhra Pradesh, in full view of the public. As PM he gave a dressing down to two government secretaries in a meeting. At an open press conference, he announced the removal of his Foreign Secretary in a very curt manner. He summarily sacked Delhi's Lt. Governor, M.K.K. Wali, without assigning any reason. During his Andaman holiday, he humiliated the Deputy Director of his Special Protection Group while he was only doing his duty. At times he used to drive his powerful, imported vehicles very fast and give the security personnel a slip. This caused a lot of confusion and harassment to his security men.

It was certainly very irksome for the youthful Prime Minister to be always surrounded by the gun-toting Protection Group. But this was an occupational nuisance which a mature person would have tolerated with greater patience.

Indira Gandhi used to say that in politics there are no social relations. Rajiv was too good a friend to be either a good politician or a good administrator. His loyalty to his friends like Amitabh Bachchan or Satish Sharma did him much damage, as he could not draw the line between friendship and the public good. The moment the name of the two Bachchan brothers got associated with financial scandals, a more prudent PM would have immediately distanced himself from them. But Rajiv not only resented any allegations levelled at them, he set the CBI hounds after senior Finance mininstry officials in the mistaken belief that they were conducting an enquiry against the Bachchans. He maintained his close relations with the two brothers, and took them or their families out on his holidays.

In defending Satish Sharma's acquisition of real estate and construction of a swimming pool at his farmhouse, he said that a lot of commercial pilots have swimming pools at home.[2] This statement was so patently implausible, that only Rajiv's blind loyalty to Sharma could explain the gaffe.

Nehru and Indira Gandhi mixed with the masses instinctively. Rajiv had problems even when conscious efforts were made to project him as a man of the masses. His image-builders, who were much better informed about the American techniques of packaging and selling the President, but knew little of Mahatma Gandhi as a mass communicator, contrived several gimmicks to sell Rajiv. In a much talked about TV programme the PM was shown as having an informal chat with English-speaking, smartly turned out public school children. Another programme showed a group of prominent lady social workers sitting next to the PM, discussing with him the problems of raising the status of women. Then there was his widely advertised participation in the Doon School Golden Jubilee celebrations for which he got a school blazer specially stitched.

These were all exercises in upper-class snobbery and gave a sense of being left out to the children and women of poorer homes. These forays in public relations actually made the common folk perceive the wide chasm that separated them from their Prime Minister.

Rajiv's much publicized and adversely noticed New Year's Eve parties in Ranthambhor wildlife sanctuary, Andaman Islands and Lakshadweep again showed his lack of appreciation of Indian sensitivities. Ordinarily, it would be cruel and mean to grudge a week's holiday to a head of government who constantly worked for 18 hours a day. But the public censure centred on the style of holidaying and composition of the guest list. Whereas it was in bad taste to carp about invitation to Sonia's relations on the plea that the presence of foreigners compromised the country's security, it was certainly indiscreet of Rajiv to take along Amitabh and the children of Ajitabh Bachchan, while investigations for serious economic offences were pending against the two brothers.

Rajiv did not appreciate that the concept of a holiday is somewhat foreign to the Indian way of life. Nehru's motto was 'Aaram haram hai' (leisure is a sin). Even when he or Indira felt tired and stale, they used to retreat to a quiet Himalayan resort for a few days. But for Rajiv a holiday had to be a binge and an extravaganza. What the people resented was not the amount of money spent on these carnivals, but the splash accompanying them.

Rajiv was as free of communal bias as his grandfather. But he had little appreciation of its deadly nature. For him, it was one of the several counters in the game of politics, and he handled it rather casually. Ghulam Nabi Azad, Indira's Minister of State, once invited him, the two Aruns and Arif Mohammad Khan to dinner. Someone happened to mention the writ filed by some crazy fellow in the Calcutta High Court for banning the holy Koran, as it contained passages offensive to other religions. Rajiv suggested that an agitation should be started against the Jyoti Basu government on this issue. When Arif pointed out that the state government was in no way responsible for this writ, Rajiv replied that, in any case, it will help embarrass Jyoti Basu![3]

The persistence with which Rajiv played up the secessionist role of the Sikh extremists and lambasted the Anandpur Sahib Resolution during his 1984 election campaign deeply hurt the Sikhs, as the entire community was being tarred with the same brush. For Rajiv it was a vote-catching gimmick, and he was unaware of the forces of communal discord he was releasing. His reluctance to initiate action on the Mishra Commission Report on anti-Sikh riots of 1984 was again dictated by a self-defeating expediency.

Rajiv Gandhi's handling of the Shah Bano controversy shows his confused approach to the issues. Shah Bano's plea for grant of maintenance by her ex-husband was granted by the court under section 125 of the Criminal Procedure Code, and the Supreme Court had upheld it in appeal. Rajiv was strongly in favour of the enlightened stand taken by the Supreme Court and wrote on the Home Ministry's file, "There cannot be any compromise with the fundamentalists."[4]

The Assam accord was signed during that period, and the PM had invited the Assamese delegation for a cup of tea. Arif Mohammad Khan, Minister of State for Home, was also there. Rajiv, knowing his progressive views, asked Arif, "why don't you speak on the subject."[5] In his 100-minute intervention in the parliament, Arif put up a brilliant defence of the Supreme Court judgment, quoting chapter and verse from Koran in support of his stand. After the speech Rajiv scribbled, "Congratulations for a wonderful performance" on a slip of paper and passed it to him.[6]

But a few days later Cabinet Minister Z.A. Ansari mounted a virulent attack on the Supreme Court judgment. He could not have done so without clearance from the PM. In a volte-face the government enacted the Muslim (Protection of Rights on Divorce) Act under pressure from the Muslim clergy, amending sections 125 and 127 of the Criminal Procedure Code. The new law laid down that unless both husbannd and wife agree to be governed by the Code, their personal law will prevail. In a refreshing departure from the established Congress culture of sticking to office like a limpet, Arif Mohammad Khan resigned in protest. This episode inevitably put paid to all talk of framing a uniform civil code for all Indian citizens.

Two riots of the Rajiv era deserve special mention. One, the Meerut riots of 1987, in which hundreds of innocent lives were lost and property worth tens of crores destroyed. Particularly reprehensible was the case of Maliana where the Provincial Armed Constabulary (PAC) shot in the back nearly 50 Muslims who were fleeing in panic, and threw their bodies in the nearby canal. When the PM visited Meerut, he was greeted with the slogans of 'PAC zindabad'. Subsequently, when the Cabinet Committee on Political Affairs was discussing this outrage, the concerned officer in attendance recommended deterrent action against the PAC. After some whispering he was gently told to wait outside, as the Committee wanted to discuss a confidential matter.[7]

Then there was the vicious anti-Muslim rioting in Bhagalpur when the 1989 election campaign was in progress. There was good reason for the Muslims to feel that the government had failed to protect them, and this cost the Congress a heavy loss of votes.

Nothing exposes Rajiv Gandhi's opportunistic approach to the communal issue as his handling of the Babri Masjid-Ramjanam-bhoomi dispute. Controversy over the Muslim Women's Bill had not only strengthened Muslim fundamentalism, it also gave a handle to the Hindu chauvinists. Though the Act in no way hurt the Hindus, it was represented as a refusal of the Muslim community to become part of the national mainstream.

During the routine morning briefing one day, Rajiv was informed by his intelligence agencies that the Hindus were much agitated over this issue. Arun Nehru, who was also present, suggested that the Ayodhya issue had been lying dormant for a long time, and it would be a good idea to arrange reopening of the shrine. Then and there the PM rang up Vir Bahadur Singh, CM, UP, to take necessary action. In separate meetings, Muslim leaders were told that as a quid pro quo for the Muslim Women's Bill, the shrine gates will have to be unlocked. This was a deal to which the Muslim spokesmen willingly agreed.[8] Arun Nehru later confirmed to a journalist that Ayodhya "was supposed to be a package deal...a tit for tat for the Muslim Women's Bill."[9] So a petition was arranged to be filed on this issue and the obliging court ordered reopening of the gates, in February 1986.

Little did anybody foresee that this thoughtless act of rank expediency would ultimately lead to the destruction of the Babri Mosque in 1992. Encouraged by this victory, the Vishva Hindu Parishad (VHP) zealots stepped up their campaign to build the Ramjanambhoomi Temple at the disputed site. A move to bring consecrated bricks from all over the country was launched, and nearly 1,50,000 bricks stacked at the site. As the government felt unequal to the task of containing the Hindu communal onslaught, it made a reckless attempt to extract maximum political mileage from this operation.

Buta Singh, Home Minister, lent his good offices to evolve a face-saving device, and the government went so far as to twist a High Court judgment and misrepresented a part of a disputed plot as undisputed. This was the portion where VHP had decided to lay the foundation stone. The modalities for this strategy were worked out in the office of the UP chief minister.[10] Consequently, the Shilanyas was performed on 9 November. Emboldened by this triumph, VHP leader Ashok Singhal boasted, 'If the government thinks it has been bulldozed into allowing the foundation stone laying ceremony, we can bulldoze them further.'

To cap it all, Rajiv started his election campaign from Ayodhya with the declaration that 'main Ram Rajya sthapit karunga' (I will establish Ram Rajya). But the entire strategy boomeranged. On the one hand he lost the Muslim vote and on the other he could not dent the BJP constituency. In fact the BJP score in the new parliament shot up from 2 to 86, and a part of the credit for this spectacular rise must go to Mr Gandhi, who managed to have the worst of both worlds.

38

The Economy

$\mathcal{R}$ajiv's instinctive preference was decidedly for the market economy. If India was to make an impressive entry into the 21st century, she had to industrialize rapidly and go all out to imbibe modern technology. And this, to Rajiv's way of thinking, could not be achieved in a regulated, procedure-ridden economic environment.

When Rajiv came to power the mood was up-beat. And his Government's first budget, presented by V.P. Singh, Finance Minister, gave a clear idea of the shape of things to come. It aimed at overall liberalization of the economy, reducing controls, simplifying the foreign trade regime, relaxing constraints on imports and lowering import duties with the promise of more to follow.

The Government also formulated a Long-Term Fiscal Policy to impart a measure of stability to its economic programmes. This policy was supposed to be coterminous with the Seventh Plan. As annual budgets did not provide a long-term perspective to government's fiscal planning, it aimed at removing this lacuna by providing a much longer time-frame to ensure continuity in this vital area. This was not only supposed to curb adhocism in matters concerning taxation, duties, licencing, etc., but also provide greater confidence to investors about the government's future thinking.

Nani Palkiwala, an eminent tax expert, described the budget as 'epoch making.' The business community felt elated. The stock market, the most sensitive barometer of changes in the economic climate, was exultant. The prices of leading scrips jumped by 3 to 6 times within one year. Hundreds of new issues were floated, and most of them over-subscribed. Investing in shares, earlier confined to the cognoscenti, became a national obsession, and the equity culture spread to millions of new investors. As a result of

liberalization, Indian firms collaborated with foreign manufacturers for the production of a wide range of consumer durables.
Entrepreneuers imported machinery and raw materials more
freely, and boom conditions prevailed in the market. Showrooms
and shops overflowed with colour TV sets, video tape recorders,
a wide range of electrical goods, motor bikes and scooters, with
Maruti cars leading the bandwagon. The middle class, with its
hankering for fancy consumer goods suppressed for long, let itself
go, thus fuelling the boom conditions. Rajiv became the messiah
of the new revolution and a trend-setter for the glitterati with his
designer shoes, T-shirts, watches and sun-glasses.

There is no doubt that Rajiv gingered up the Indian economy and
gave it the much needed push by permitting liberal import of
machinery, technology, spares and raw materials. He also exposed it in a limited way to foreign competition. Industrial production during his period maintained an average yearly growth
rate of 8.5 percent. The economy, which had earlier grown at a
rate of 3.5 percent per year and at 4-4.5 percent in the early
eighties, reached the unprecedented level of 5.6 percent. And
despite the severe droughts of 1987 and increased Defence spending, the price index did not rise above 9 percent.
  But Rajiv Gandhi never framed a coherent, comprehensive
policy of liberalization and deregulation. Moreover, even the
initiatives he took were not followed through with persistence
and determination. His long-term fiscal policy was based on a
sound idea, as it sought to define the limits of such measures as
deficit financing, rates of direct and indirect taxes, and maximum
levels of personal and corporate taxes in a five-year time frame.
But it was never put into practice.

Rajiv's liberalized golden age lasted just two years. A high import
bill, excessive borrowing and mounting budgetary deficits forced
the government to change gear.The down-turn started in 1987
with a steep rise in foreign exchange outgo. Liberal import of
machinery was restricted and this affected the modernization and

expansion plans in the automobile and some other industries. On the other hand, India's capital goods sector was badly hurt owing to indiscriminate import of machinery. The drought had emptied the overflowing granaries. Rapid expansion in some sectors resulted in over-production. The government was forced to hike the prices of several public sector products owing to budgetary compulsions. The first impact of these developments was felt by the over-heated stock market.The prices suddenly started tumbling and soon reached the levels from which they had zoomed in 1985-86.

The budget of 1988-89, instead of coming to grips with the fast deteriorating economic situation, tried to be a 'goodies for all' sort of package with populist undertones. There were reliefs and benefits for the housewife and the farmer, and reduction in import duties for some select industries like textiles and electronics.

But it was the budget of 1989-90 which signalled a retreat from the liberalization programme. Excise duties were raised across the board, railway freight hiked, and an employment surcharge of 8 percent levied. The luxury tax on five-star hotels was doubled and a 10 percent surcharge imposed on all air travel. Duties on luxury items were also raised. Consequently, all consumer durables including cars, scooters and TV sets became more expensive and in some cases the rise was pretty steep.

Thus Rajiv's last budget as PM reversed much of what the first budget had promised.

What was the reason for making such a sharp U-turn? The main compulsion was the imperative of financial stabilization. During Rajiv's first year as Prime Minister, the budgetary deficit stood at Rs. 4,908 crores, and soared to Rs. 17,050 crores when he completed his term, thus registering a rise of 350 percent. The balance of payments deficit climbed from Rs. 5,927 crores to Rs. 9,823 crores in these five years. Comparable figures for total public debt are Rs. 1,59,798 crores and Rs. 3,21,236 crores, marking an increase of 100 percent. As to external debt, inclusive of commercial borrowings and NRI holdings, the amount rose from Rs. 45,341 crores to Rs. 97,966 crores over this period, an escalation of more than

100 percent. Much steeper was the rise in foreign loans obtained by the private borrowers, which jumped fourfold during these five years. This comprised mostly short-term, high-interest debts, the servicing of which resulted in a much heavier drain on foreign exchange.

The second reason for this reversal was political. Rajiv's reputation as the cult figure of the middle class did not fit into the traditional Congress profile of a party of the down-trodden. Alarmed at a series of defeats in the assembly elections, the party was much worried about sprucing up its ideological image. Thus, the budget of 1989-90 was designed to convey the message of 'soaking the rich' and presenting the party leader as a 'man of the masses'.

The Seventh Five Year Plan was coterminus with Rajiv Gandhi's 5-year term as Prime Minister. Gradually planning had lost much of its prestige; Rajiv once called the Planning Commission members as 'a bunch of jokers'. Also, planning stood for an approach to development which relied heavily on state intervention. This obviously went against the PM's ingrained preference for the market economy.

But it needs to be stressed that Rajiv's instinctive aversion to planning was not based on insensitivity to the lot of the poor. In his own way he was a compassionate person and tried his best to improve the living conditions of the impoverished masses. He disfavoured planning, as according to him, it did not offer the most efficient and effective route to development. Whereas there had always been powerful lobbies advocating this view, Rajiv was the first Prime Minister to openly show his preference for the market over planning. But once Rajiv had accepted planning as a necessary evil, he tried to make the best of it. Public investment in the Seventh Plan was pitched at Rs. 1,80,000 crores as against a provision of Rs. 97,500 crores for the Sixth Plan. The highest share of funds went to the energy sector, industry and minerals, and transport. Allocation for rural development was 4.9 percent and agriculture 5.8 percent. Education and Health had to rest content with 2.5 and 0.9 percent.

The poverty alleviation programmes started during Indira Gandhi's time have become the major focus of the planners in tackling rural poverty. "...international experience shows that active public expenditure policies aimed at raising the consumption of the poor are far more effective in promoting equity as compared to tax policies aimed at containing incomes of the rich."[1]

In India a number of such programmes have been launched, and despite all the leakages en route, their impact on lowering the poverty line has been decisive. These programmes fall into two broad categories: one, aiming to promote self-employment and, two, targeted at short-term wage employment. Jawahar Rozgar Yojana, covering the second category of programmes, was launched by the Rajiv Government, and here part of the wages were paid in foodgrains. The scope of Integrated Rural Development Programmes covering the first category was recast during the seventh plan when clusters of target groups, instead of individuals, were given productive assets.

But despite the high potential of these schemes for making a dent in rural poverty, the real per capita expenditure on the total re-distributive package amounted to only Rs. 29 as against Rs. 43 per capita spent on Defence and another Rs. 35 on general administration.[2]

Soon after taking over as PM, Rajiv had warned the public sector executives that they would be held responsibile for the performance of their undertakings, and the loss-making units would be closed. He disapproved of using socialism as a cloak for inefficiency and asked the Congres workers' rally in Madras on 22 December 1987, "Can we afford socialism where the public sector, instead of generating wealth for the people, is robbing and sucking up the wealth of the people." Yet during his entire term of five years, Rajiv Gandhi did not order the closing down of a single loss-making public undertaking, or the shedding of huge labour surpluses that these industries carried.

In crafting his growth strategies, Rajiv placed excessive reliance on the role of pure technology. Import of technology and machinery, and upgradation of the existing production processes were to him the pre-condition to turn India into a modern industrial state. This was a one-dimensional view of technology-driven progress. "The real source of wealth lies no longer in raw materials, the labour force or machines," wrote J.D. Bernal, "but in having a scientific, educated, technological manpower base. Education has become the real wealth of the modern age."[3] Generally known as 'social technology', this vital dimension of technology-linked development hardly received any attention from the Prime Minister.

Rajiv placed a disproportionate emphasis on technology as an engine of development. Whereas it had a crucial role to play in industrial growth, it exercised little influence over other aspects of the economy whose proper management was integral to economic well-being and growth. For instance, unproductive expenditure of the government kept growing without any check, foreign exchange reserves got depleted to an alarming extent, and budgetary deficits kept mounting all the time. Fiscal discipline and proper management of the economy were as essential for development as adoption of modern technology and liberalization.

The prime mover for a regime of self-sustaining industrial growth was a continuously expanding demand. But the government's approach catered to the needs of the upper-middle class only. The much touted estimate of 200-million-strong middle class is pure fiction. It is only the creamy layer of this class which buys cars, luxury items, white goods, computers and other expensive electronic gadgetry. And production plans relying upon the support of this segment are bound to have a narrow base. Even when there prevailed boom conditions during the early phase of Rajiv's 'golden age', the demand for mass consumption goods hardly showed any upward swing. And this could not be otherwise unless strong measures of re-distributive justice were built into the growth design. It was partly owing to the limitations of this narrowly targeted approach that the growth impulse stood exhausted towards the end of the Rajiv era and industrial production started showing a downward trend.

Even if there had been no mid-term turn around in Rajiv Gandhi's programme of deregulation-cum-liberalization, its benefits could not have extended beyond the middle-middle and upper-middle classes. Vast multitudes of his countrymen, who live outside the charmed confines of the market, would have remained blissfully ignorant of the great opportunities unfolding beyond their cramped existence. The chosen few would have, no doubt, triumphantly entered the 21st century, riding the festooned bandwagon of high technology while the rest were still straggling a couple of centuries behind.

39

Accords of Discord

$\mathcal{R}$ajiv Gandhi signed more political accords than any of his predecessors; none of his successors is likely to equal his record.

Punjab Accord

The impact of Operation Blue Star and his mother's assassination had pushed the Punjab problem to the top of his agenda. For too long had it been mismanaged, and Rajiv wanted to apply the overdue corrective at the earliest. His first move was to create a congenial climate by administering the 'healing touch' and sending out conciliatory signals. As most of the Akali leaders had been arrested after Operation Blue Star, a process of their release was started with Sant Harchand Singh Longowal, President of the Party. Simultaneously, Arjun Singh, a shrewd and low-key negotiator, was sent as Governor of Punjab. Many of the detenus were also freed, press censorship removed, ban on the All India Sikh Students Federation lifted, and an enquiry into Delhi riots ordered. On 23 March the PM paid his first visit to Punjab to lay the foundation stone of the martyrs' memorial at Hussainiwala village. He also took this opportunity to announce an economic package.

The signals from Longowal were positive and encouraging. In the begining the tone of his speeches was belligerent, but the government did not react. It realized that after 10 months of incarceration, he needed time to re-establish his equation with his followers by adopting anti-government postures. At his public meetings he made the acceptance of his seven points a pre-condition for talks with the government. But when he visited Delhi at the end of April, he reaffirmed his faith in the unity and integrity of India, and expressed Akali Dal's resolve to seek a Constitutional solution to the Punjab problem.

Rajiv knew how the earlier attempts at accords had been either frustrated by the rivalry of Sikh leaders, or sabotaged by vested interests. So negotiations with the Akalis were conducted in complete secrecy. Giani Zail Singh, Buta Singh and Darbara Singh had no clue as to what was happening. Among the Akalis, except for Sant Longowal and his two close aides, Surjit Singh Barnala and Balwant Singh, nobody, not even Prakash Singh Badal was taken into confidence. The Home Minister, S.B. Chavan, was also kept in the dark.

After Arjun Singh had held a series of meetings with the Akalis, Rajiv invited Sant Longowal to Delhi for direct talks. Despite the reluctance of both Badal and Tohra, the Sant decided to take the plunge. He reached Parliament House on 23 July along with S.S. Barnala and Balwant Singh, and Arjun Singh took them straight to the PM's Office. Rajiv and Longowal were left alone for a one-to-one meeting, and they took little time in establishing a close rapport. The modalities of the agreement had already been worked out and a draft prepared.

The Cabinet sub-committee met Sant Longowal's aides the same afternoon. It was for the first time that the ministers saw the draft agreement. When one to them raised a point about Chandigarh's transfer to Punjab, Barnala told him that "hours were spent on drafting and that Sant Longowal had agreed to come because everything had already been settled." So, it was obvious that the document was not negotiable.[1]

The Cabinet Committee on Political Affairs met on 24 July and cleared the accord. In view of the past record of Bhajan Lal, Rajiv had taken care to get him over to his office for 'consultation'. As Ram Pradhan, the Home Secretary, wrote, "He was capable of disrupting the whole peace process, even while the accord was being worked out..."[2]

The entire country felt elated when the signing of the accord was announced. Rajiv himself was ecstatic; what his great mother could not achieve in years, he had wrapped up in a matter of months. And buoyed up by his newly acquired self-confidence he concluded the Assam accord just three weeks later. And he knew that the Mizoram accord was already under his belt.

The main features of the accord were:

1. The capital project area of Chandigarh would be transferred to Punjab. Haryana would be compensated by the transfer of some Hindi-speaking territories of Punjab. A Commission would determine the Hindi-speaking areas to be thus transferred by following the principle of contiguity and linguistic affinity, with the village as a unit. Both the transfer of Chandigarh to Punjab and Hindi-speaking territories to Haryana would be completed by 26 January 1986.

2. As to the sharing of waters from the Ravi-Beas system, the farmers of Punjab and Haryana would continue to get water not less than what they were using on 1 July 1985. The claims of the two States regarding their shares in the remaining waters would be referred for adjudication to a Tribunal headed by a Supreme Court judge. This Tribunal would give its decision within six months, and it would be binding on both the parties.

3. Regarding the other controversial issues, the Anandpur Sahib Resolution was to be referred to the Sarkaria Commission on Centre-State relations. The government agreed to consider the framing of an All India Gurudwara Bill.

The terms of the accord were not materially different from the "drafts finalised in November 1982 and February 1984, which were initially agreed to by the Akalis but later scuttled by the government itself with last minute changes."[3] This time too the boat was rocked when the Law Ministry added on its own the words "The Commission may also take into consideration such other factors as in its opinion, may be relevant" after the sentence, "The principle of contiguity and linguistic affinity with a village as a unit will be basis of such determination." The addition made by the Law Ministry gave the Commission unfettered freedom to alter this vital provision in any manner it liked.

The Akalis cried foul at this 'tampering' with the agreed draft, and the PM admitted at a Press Club meeting on 11 October that there had been an error in the terms of reference. But he said that as the Commission had already begun its work, it would be difficult to change the terms. He, however, assured that no Congress government would take advantage of this error.

The President's Rule in Punjab was due to expire on 6 October. Rajiv had promised to hold the assembly election before that. The Chief Election Commissioner fixed 22 September as the poll date. This was a wise move, as the pressure of election had curbed the dissidence of leaders like Badal and Tohra. But on 20 August two terrorists shot dead the Sant as he completed his address to a congregation at Sherpur, district Sangrur.

Longowal's death was the first major blow to the Punjab accord. Yet the government acted promptly. The election was postponed by three days only. The Akalis, bewildered and rudderless, quickly came together and cobbled a compromise, choosing Barnala to head the party. The State Government made elaborate arrangements to maintain law and order.

It surpassed everybody's expectations when 66 percent of the electorate turned out to vote, and it happened to be a singularly peaceful election. Winning 73 out of a total 117 seats the Akalis formed the ministry with Surjit Singh Barnala as the Chief Minister, thus bringing to an end two years of Central rule. Successful holding of the assembly election and installation of the Akali ministry showed that the Rajiv-Longowal accord was still in good shape.

Events in Punjab started moving on two separate tracks. One, the process of implementation of the agreement and, two, the development of the political situation on the ground.

The Mathew commission was set up to give an award on the territorial dispute, and the Eradi commission on the sharing of waters between the two states. Justice Mathew was required to submit his report by 31 October 1985 so that all arrangements for the transfer of Chandigarh to Punjab were completed by the stipulated deadline of 26 January 1986. But despite five extensions, the commission could make no specific recommendations and observed, "The irresistible conclusion is that by applying the criterion laid down the commission cannot determine any specific Hindi speaking area in Punjab which should go to Haryana in lieu of Chandigarh."

The problem was that there were no Hindi-speaking areas in Abohar-Fazilka Tehsil which had "contiguity and linguistic affinity with village as a unit" with Haryana. There was a small village, Kandu Kheda, which linked the two areas, and in this village the majority of population spoke Punjabi. The Centre deputed a team of IAS officers to ensure a fair linguistic enumeration of the population of Kandu Kheda, and it turned out that the majority spoke Punjabi. In view of this stalemate, Chandigarh could not be transferred to Punjab on 26 January 1986. Rajiv deferred the date of transfer to 21 June 1987 and a second commission under Justice Venkataramiah was set up on 2 April 1986 to determine and specify other Hindi-speaking areas of Punjab for transfer to Haryana.

Bhajan Lal clearly saw that if the Punjab accord was implemented in letter and spirit, Haryana would be the loser and he would stand discredited. As Ram Pradhan, Home Secretary, who was overseeing the implementation of the accord wrote, "Haryana's intention was clear, not to allow the Commission to proceed with the reference, create a stalemate, delay the transfer of Chandigarh and thus frustrate the accord."[4]

Justice Venkataramiah identified 15,000 acres in Rajpura Tehsil and suggested that the new capital of Haryana should be built there. Barnala accepted the proposal readily. But on 29 May Haryana submitted a list of 483 Hindi-speaking villages of Punjab for transfer to Haryana.

Fed up with Bhajan Lal's antics, Rajiv replaced him by Bansi Lal as CM Haryana on 5 June 1986. But the new CM also could not accept the Commission's proposal to locate the state capital on the 15,000 acres identified by it. Building a new capital is a political decision involving several vested interests, and just any site was not good enough.

Later, in an attempt to somehow settle the issue the Commision recommended the transfer of 70,000 acres to Haryana, ignorimg the contiguity principle. The chairman was also able to quickly spot 45,000 out of the proposed 70,000 acres for transfer.

As the extended term of the Venkataramiah Commission expired on 10 June, he submitted his report on the above lines, and suggested the appointment of a third commission to locate the remaining 25,000 acres for transfer to Haryana. Rajiv made frantic efforts to persuade the two states into accepting some sort of a patchwork solution to save the accord. But the worsening political climate in Punjab had abridged Barnala's options, and Bansi Lal did not have much elbow-room in any case.

Rajiv still felt committed to his promise to transfer Chandigarh to Punjab on 21 June. It was in a desperate hurry that the Desai Commission was appointed on 20 June and asked to submit its report in 24 hours. Later the deadline was extended to 15 July and transfer of Chandigarh to Punjab postponed to 15 August 1986.

But there were serious differences within the Barnala cabinet about the transfer of 70,000 acres from Punjab to Haryana. This was an ad hoc figure, not based on any survey or other parameters. As few Hindi-speaking villages could be identified in the state, this would have meant the transfer of several Punjabi-speaking areas to Haryana. This was not acceptable to the Akali leaders.

The Eradi Commission on the river water dispute gave its report on 30 June 1987. The Prakash Singh Badal group had been threatening agitation on the alleged faulty terms of reference. Its contention was that under international law, and the practice previously followed in India, only riparian states had a claim on the water of rivers flowing through their territory. As neither the Ravi nor Beas rivers flowed through Haryana, that state had no claim on its waters. This agitation gathered force and Barnala also endorsed it.

Thus no settlement could be reached on the major issues of the accord, though the Central government kept saying that 8 out of 10 points had been settled.

Barnala had started with a serious handicap, as both Badal and

Tohra, the two Akali stalwarts, were opposed to him. After the accord, Badal had remarked, '... what the Akalis wanted were firm decisions and not commissions.' Further, the success of the accord meant a death knell for the terrorists and they were bound to go all out to sabotage it.

In such a situation, Barnala needed two things to strengthen his position. One, speedy implementation of the accord and two, a low-key but steady backing by the Centre. When the transfer of Chandigarh to Punjab did not materialize on 26 January 1986 despite high-pitched publicity, it was a big blow to Barnala's prestige and credibility.

During this period there was hardly any let-up in terrorist activity and the militants were again talking about Khalistan. They also started using the Golden Temple as their headquarter. On 29 April 1986, five members of the secessionist Panthic Committee issued the Khalistan Document, proclaiming that Delhi will be their capital. When this news reached the PM, he was furious and told Barnala that punitive action against such elements could no longer be delayed. Even earlier Barnala had been under pressure to act firmly and he realized that if this time he dragged his feet, he may lose his job. So a top secret police operation was mounted and commandos entered the Golden Temple on 30 April. The five militants had already fled and no arms were discovered inside the Temple complex.

The Akali leaders, including some of Barnala's own ministers reacted violently to this desecration of the shrine. They felt that this action amounted to a vindication of Operation Blue Star. Several senior ministers and top Akali leaders resigned. Badal led 26 MLAs to form a new Akali faction.

Barnala now had a massive revolt on his hands. He could survive only with the induction of 21 new ministers and a promise of support from outside by the Congress and other opposition parties in the legislature. This naturally damaged his image among the Sikh masses. He was also ordered by the conclave of head priests to dust shoes of devotees at various Gurudwaras to atone for the sin of sending armed police inside the Temple.

With the Punjab accord lying in shambles, the graph of terrorist violence in Punjab rose steadily. In view of Barnala's loss of mass base, Rajiv was having second thoughts on Punjab. And suddenly, without any provocation or mishap, a Presidential proclamation was issued on 12 May 1987 dismissing the Barnala government and reimposing President's Rule after an interval of 21 months. It was generally believed that this was done to placate the Haryana electorate, where assembly election was due to be held after five weeks.

This was a very ill-advised move. By dismissing an elected government, Rajiv had again removed a useful cushion between the alienated Sikhs and the Centre. The Sikhs were further confirmed in their belief that they could never get justice from 'Delhi Darbar' through direct negotiations, and the Congress would never permit an elected Akali government to complete its term.

Barnala was dismissed owing to the rise in terrorist activity. But the situation worsened steadily. It became a direct confrontation between a Centrally directed police state and the militants. A sizeable moderate segment of the Sikh leadership was just squeezed out.

A flash in the pan was the success of the state government in neatly executing a manoeuvre to flush out militants from the Golden Temple. With the rise in terrorism, extremists had again infiltrated into the Temple with arms and ammunition. With the lesson of Operation Blue Star behind it, this time the government had put through intensive practice a select band of commandos, and made detailed preparations for bottling up the extremists inside the Temple.

At this stage a terrorist lighted the fuse by shooting a senior police officer in the jaw. The Commandos quickly occupied strategic positions around the shrine, picking up all moving objects inside the complex and cutting off all supplies to the militants holed up inside. In view of constant sniping and psychological pressure, nearly 200 militants meekly surrendred in two batches on 15 and 18 May 1988. The entire exercise, code named Operation Black Thunder, was conducted in full view of the world media and had a shattering impact on the morale of the militants.

The precision and neatness of this exercise was in sharp contrast to the bungling of Operation Blue Star. Yet it stands as an isolated event: it was not made a take-off point for a fresh political initiative.

Punjab was bleeding at both ends. At one end was the violence, extortion and rape by the militants, whose ranks had been joined by smugglers, gun-runners and drug-traffickers. At the other end were the police torture and loot, and indiscrimate killings of the youth in fake encounters on the slightest suspicion of complicity.

Not knowing how to get out of this predicament, Rajiv again tried to deliver the healing touch and assembled a new package of conciliatory measures. He told the Lok Sabha on 3rd March 1989 that most of the Jodhpur detenus who were arrested at the time of Operation Blue Star were being released. These 367 prisoners had rotted in Jodhpur jail without trial for 5 years. Further, the Punjab Disturbed Areas Act and the Armed Forces Special Powers Act were withdrawn except in three districts. Restrictions were also removed on the entry of foreigners into Punjab, and special powers under the National Security Act were withdrawn. Non-official committees were also set up to supervise police operations.

By itself the package was a jumble of some overdue measures, and did not amount to a new approach on Punjab. Thus, no headway could be made on the Punjab front during the remaining few months of Rajiv's tenure and the state continued to bleed as before.

Assam Accord

It was a very exuberant Rajiv Gandhi who announced from the ramparts of the Red Fort on 15 August 1985 the signing of the Assam accord. The people went delirious with joy. What an achievement! Just three weeks earlier he had concluded the Punjab accord. The man had the magic touch!

Rajiv wisely discontinued the practice of conducting negotiations through a multiplicity of agencies, and entrusted the job to his

astute and low-key Home Secretary, Ram Pradhan. The progress
of talks itself was deceptively 'smooth. The core issue, as earlier,
was the unending influx of outsiders into Assam. The issue had
been discussed repeately during Indira Gandhi's time, and it was
the accommodative 'give and take of the conference table' which
ultimately produced a mutually acceptable formula.

It was agreed that the infiltrators who entered the state between
1961 and 16 June 1966 should be allowed to stay in Assam, but
only their progeny would enjoy voting rights. Those who came
to Assam between 16 June 1965 and 24 March 1971 (the date on
which a pact was signed between Indira and Mujibur Rehman),
would be allowed to stay, but denied voting rights for 10 years.
And those who arrived after 24 March 1971 were to be identified
and expelled. At the insistence of the AASU delegation, the PM
gave his assurance that the Congress ministry in Assam would
demit office and there would be fresh election to the state assembly. A seperate economic package for Assam was also worked
out under which, among other things, the state was to get a new
oil refinery and a paper mill.

Asam Gana Parishad (AGP), romped home victorious in the assembly election held in December 1985, winning 64 of the 126
seats. Rajiv had acted with courage and sagacity in asking the
Congress ministry to make an exit when it had not even completed half its term. Mahanta was sworn in as Chief Minister.
While walking on cloud nine, little did the AGP know that the
cross carried by the Congress all these years had now been passed
on to it.

One of the first acts of the AGP was to create a Department of
Assam Accord Implementation. But in pursuit of this objective it
came across two hurdles. One, the Centre had shown much
greater drive in signing the agreement than in its execution. Two,
the really important provisions of the accord were almost unim-
plementable.

If the accord had to achieve its objective, lakhs of infiltrators
had to be identified, categorized, served notices, given an opportunity to defend themselves, and to file an appeal against an

adverse decision. All these stages had to be covered under the Illegal Migrants Determination Act.

The state government repeatedly asked the Centre to simplify the Migrants Act so as to expedite the process of detection and expulsion. But there was no response to these pleas. Then, the work on constructing the border road, and erection of the fence between Assam and Bangladesh border was not making much progress. In fact, due to the very difficult nature of the terrain, construction of a fence was almost impossible.

Mauled by various scandals and controversies, and demoralized by an unbroken chain of defeats in assembly elections in various states, the Assam accord ceased to be a priority item for Rajiv. The AGP government itself, with its indifferent record, had lost much of its hold over its followers. So, the stalemate continued.

Mizoram Accord

Rajiv Gandhi performed a hat trick by signing the Mizoram accord in June 1986. It brought to an end more than two decades of insurgency and eleven years of tortuous negotiations.

It was in 1976 that Laldenga, the rebel Mizo leader crusading for an independent state, signed an accord with the Government, accepting Mizoram as an integral part of the Indian Union. Modalities of the process were yet to be worked out when the Emergency and the Janata Party rule intervened. It was only with Mrs. Gandhi's return to power in 1980 that further negotiations with Laldenga were resumed. The draft of an agreement was almost ready when Mrs. Gandhi was killed. As Rajiv differed with some of the provisions of this draft, he entrusted his Home Secretary, Ram Pradhan, to carry on further talks.

The political part of the agreement was negotiated and signed by Arjun Singh with Laldenga on 25 June. It provided that the present Congress government headed by Lal Thanhawla would be replaced by a Congress-Mizo National Front (MNF) coalition, with Laldenga as the Chief Minister. Certain administrative issues were quickly settled owing to Rajiv's accommodative approach.

The most important gain of the accord was that the underground Mizo rebels surrendered their arms and became peaceful citizens of India, and the Congress came back to power defeating the MNF in the 1989 assembly election.

Tripura and GNLF Accords

Rajiv also signed two mini-accords to contain insurgency in the north-eastern state of Tripura and the hill district of Darjeeling, West Bengal.

Tripura presents the extreme case of a local population being reduced to a hopeless minority owing to the large influx of Bangladeshi infiltrators. Thus outnumbered, a group of militant locals formed themselves into a guerrilla outfit, named the Tribal National Volunteers (TNV).

As a result of the accord signed with Hrangkhawl, the TNV leader, the militant organization agreed to lay down arms and surrender within one month. The Centre consented to reserve 20 percent of the seats in the state assembly for the Scheduled Tribes and to rehabilitate 2,500 displaced Jhumia families. It was also agreed to make Hrangkhawl chairman of the Jhumia Rehabilitation Corporation.

Subhash Ghising, an ex-armyman, founder of the Gorkha National Liberation Front (GNLF), demanded the Siliguri subdivision of Darjeeling district of West Bengal be formed into an independent state of Gorkhaland.

After protracted negotiations an accord was reached in 1988 between GNLF and the West Bengal Government for constituting the Nepali majority areas of Siliguri sub-division into a Gorkha Hill Development Council, enjoying considerable devolution of powers. In the Council election held after a few months, GNLF annexed the majority of seats, and thus ended the Gorkhaland agitation.

Kashmir Accord

When the Akalis won the assembly election in Punjab, Rajiv said that though the Congress had lost, the country had won. He adopted even a more statesman-like attitude in signing the Assam accord where the ruling Congress ministry made way for its opponents. A similar approach was adopted for Mizoram.

Within the party Rajiv was much criticized for this 'misplaced' generosity. Thus, when the ministerial crisis arose in Jammu and Kashmir in March 1986, Rajiv asserted that he could not possibly be a party to any agreement that would see his own party wiped out. In fact, this time he went to the other extreme to ensure its survival.

During the 20 months of his misrule, G.M. Shah, the chief minister, had brought the state administration to the verge of a collapse. What brought matters to a head were two weeks of communal riots in which the Kashmiri Pandits were the main victims. In this situation the Congress could no longer afford to associate itself with G.M. Shah, and instructed Mufti Mohammad Syed, the state Congress chief, to pull out of the coalition. As this reduced the CM's following to a minority, Jagmohan, the Governor, dismissed the chief minister on 7 March and himself took over the reins of government. But he did not dissolve the state assembly.

Jagmohan worked with his usual speed and efficiency and effected several improvements. Law and order was brought under control and special attention paid to the redressal of people's grievances. Behind the scenes, a murky scenario of the politics of expediency and survival was unfolding itself in total secrecy. Farooq had realized that he could not remain in power for long without Congress backing. And Congress too was aware that it could not come to power in the state on its own steam. So, after numerous secret meetings stretching over 10 months, both sides cobbled together an accord of convenience. It was agreed that Farooq would be the chief minister under the new dispensation and seats in the next assembly election would be shared in the ratio of 60:40 between the National Conference and Congress.

This accord was signed on 31 October. Then, the two sides formed an alliance, and a caretaker coalition government was sworn in on 6 November 1987. But it was apprehended that disgruntled elements would try to rock the boat if a session of the assembly was convened. The Governor, therefore, dissolved the assembly the very next day on the chief minister's advice. This made it incumbent for the assembly election to be held within the next six months.

The Congress-National Conference alliance swept the poll held after four months. But there were widespread allegations of rigging. Curfew was imposed during the poll to restrict free movement. People were prevented from voting, and counting of votes was undertaken several days after the election.

But increasing disillusionment with a non-performing government led to the rise of extremist forces, violent agitations and anti-India demonstrations. Looking to the disturbed conditions in the state, Pakistan stepped up subversive activities. The Jammu and Kashmir Liberation Front (JKLF) also acquired much greater clout and assumed leadership of the secessionist forces.

Of all the accords signed by Rajiv Gandhi, this one was the most short-sighted. The political reality of Kashmir demanded that the National Conference and Congress remain in a state of mild confrontation. This would have not only given credibility to the former, but also enabled the latter to counterbalance the Conference. Their alliance not only destroyed the prestige of Farooq Abdullah by turning him into a puppet of the Centre, it also removed from the scene a viable opposition party. This created a dangerous vacuum which was gradually filled by extremist and insurgent groups. And what did the Congress get out of this accord? Four measly ministerships which enabled the incumbents to indulge in unbridled corruption.

Though Farooq resigned from chief ministership after Janata Dal came to power, the image of the National Conference as a custodian of Kashmiri interests had suffered irreparable damage. And the loss of the National Conference has been the gain of the secessionists.

It was unfortunate that Rajiv was able to sign the vital Punjab and Assam accords with such ease and speed. This gave him a deceptive sense of confidence and he ended up by signing half a dozen political accords. Most of them backfired with disastrous results.

A basic limitation of these accords was that they were based on an incomplete appreciation of the objective conditions. To some extent, it was implicit in Rajiv's style of conducting negotiations in complete secrecy, involving a limited number of persons. In view of the earlier experience, this caution was quite understandable. But it robbed him of the benefit of having all the necessary information, reactions and feedback to take a comprehensive view of the situation.

Then, Rajiv was so carried away by the euphoric wave of having signed an accord, that he came to treat it as an end in itself. But accords by themselves are only symbolic gestures. They only start a process which may finally lead to the desired goal. The success of an accord lies in its implementation. Here, Rajiv did not show the requisite interest and stamina in attending to the nitty-gritty of the accords he signed with such zest. The chief ministers of Punjab, Assam and Kashmir, all complained that the Centre was not taking much interest in providing the promised funds and implementing various provisions of the agreement.

It was not appreciated by the government that despite the bipartite nature of the accords, the onus of implementation rested on the government. It was the Centre which had to provide funds, activate commissions and tribunals, get their reports in time, and create the instrumentalities for enforcing their provisions. In this sense, these were predominantly one-sided accords and the Centre certainly defaulted in implementing some of their crucial provisions.

This one-sidedness points to another infirmity of these accords. The weakest agreement is signed from a position of strength. Here, on one side there was the full might of a sovereign state and on the other were small regional parties or factions enjoying only discretionary allegiance of their followers. It was, therefore, much harder for them to sell the accord to their people. The Centre should have better appreciated this limitation of the signatories, and given full attention to speedy implementation to shore up their credibility. Barnala, Mahanta, Farooq — all lost the trust of their followers when the promised benefits from the agreements did not accrue.

Rajiv also created unnecessary difficulties for himself by setting deadlines for implementing various provisions of the accords. It is all right for the managing director of a company to prescribe a tight performance schedule, but this approach cannot work in running a country where too many unforeseen variables operate outside your control.

Rajiv's approach to his accords was also too literal and legalistic, whereas their content was primarily political. The Punjab accord could not be implemented as no Hindi-speaking villages in Abohar and Fazilka tehsils were contiguous to Haryana. In view of this constraint, the commissions themselves went outside the ambit of this provision and tried to identify other areas for transfer to Haryana. This was essentially a political exercise, and Rajiv should have exerted his personal influence more forcefully to hammer out a solution through mutual accommodation.

There is little doubt that Rajiv had put his whole heart into concluding these accords. In the initial stages he even sacrificed his party interests to bring peace to the people of the states ravaged by militancy. But none of his major accords could withstand the pressures of realpolitik. Rajiv needed a less complicated world for his worthy intentions to bear fruit.

40

The Smoking Gun

*O*n 1987 three scandals exploded in the face of Rajiv Gandhi, shattering his 'Mr. Clean' image to smithereens. The real damage resulted not so much from the nature of the exposures, as their incredibly inept and unprofessional handling. In fact in two of the three transactions there were no allegations about the PM having received any favours. Yet, owing to political naïvety and misplaced loyalties, Rajiv managed to repeatedly shoot himself in the foot.

Fairfax

The first case to burst in the open pertained to the PM's own direction to V.P. Singh, his Finance Minister, to punish the economic offenders. As a part of this campaign, the Enforcement Directorate of the Ministry of Finance had been investigating some shady deals of Reliance Industries. Dhirubhai Ambani, the Reliance chief, was a no-holds-barred entrepreneur with a genius for cultivating friends in the right places. Finance Ministry had some evidence that he had set up eleven front companies in the tax haven, Isle of Man, for laundering black money. Sometime back he had floated an issue and 15 percent quota of shares reserved for Non-Resident Indians (NRIs), had been bought through Bank of Credit and Commerce International (BCCI). There was some suspicion that this quota had been purchased by Ambani's bogus companies in the Isle of Man to enable Reliance to convert unaccounted foreign exchange into white money.

As luck would have it, Bhure Lal, a crusader-bureaucrat was heading the Enforcement Directorate at that time. During this period, he also came across S. Gurumurthy, who had written a series of damaging articles against Reliance Industries in *The Indian Express*. He told Bhure Lal that he had better engage a foreign detective agency to investigate the affairs of Reliance as it required special expertise. He also suggested the name of Fairfax which had investigated the Watergate case against Nixon. Michael Hershman, the head of this company agreed to meet Bhure Lal in Delhi while on his way to Seoul in connection with another assignment. Hershman was given particulars of cases of suspected fraud against Reliance Industries. As to the payment of fees, the agency was to get remuneration under Finance Ministry's Reward Rules, which could be upto 20 percent of the total value of the unearthed transactions.

Dhirubhai Ambani, who was keeping a close watch on the progress of investigations against him, was not one to passively watch his own ruin. And he launched a counter-offensive in his own style. Suddenly, a letter purported to be written by G. Mckay, vice-president of Fairfax to Gurumurthy, surfaced in the office of Mohan Katre, Director, Central Bureau of Investigation (CBI). This letter stated that Fairfax had been commissioned by the Finance Ministry to investigate the Swiss properties of Amitabh Bachchan and his foreign associates. It also referred to a fee of US $ 5,00,000 to be paid to Fairfax by Nusli Wadia, head of Bombay Dyeing, and R.N. Goenka, owner of *The Indian Express*. A copy of this letter was also given to Amitabh Bachchan.

The letter was obviously a crude forgery. And as Mckay said, "To write such a letter would be a stupid, unprofessional thing to do, like putting a gun to your own head." But stories about investigation against the Bachchan brothers and Rajiv's relations had been circulating for quite some time and after this incident Amitabh became quite jittery. While Katre brought the letter to the PM's notice Amitabh met Rajiv separately.

Another incident that lent credence to this story was the discovery of the draft of Giani Zail Singh's angry letter to the PM on their ongoing controversy. This letter was discovered in a raid on a Delhi guest-house of *The Indian Express* where Gurumurthy normally stayed. In view of the Bhure Lal-Gurumurthy nexus, this was interpreted as further evidence in support of the conspiracy theory against the PM.

As Rajiv's distrust of V.P. Singh mounted, he found Singh's

continuance in Finance Ministry harmful to his interests. On 24 January, 1987 the Raja was shifted from Finance to Defence ministry.

With the departure of his patron, Bhure Lal realized that his days were numbered. As the PM had now taken over the Finance portfolio, he met him to know as to where he stood. Rajiv gave him a pat on the back and said that he should continue the good work he was doing. With a view to clearing the air, Bhure Lal told the PM that some people were spreading the canard that his Italian relations and close friends were being investigated by his Directorate. Bhure Lal affirmed that this was totally false and no investigation was ever started against any of these persons. Rajiv assured him that he need have no apprehensions, and even if his own relations were suspected of any misdeeds he should boldly proceed against them.

On return to his office Bhure Lal prepared a record of his talk with the PM and sent a copy to his boss, the Revenue Secretary, and another one to the Finance secretary. That very evening a senior aide of the PM met Vinod Pande, the Revenue Secretary. He said that in his talk with Bhure Lal, the PM had permitted him to proceed even against his relations and close friends. Pande was asked to advise Bhure Lal to desist from any such move.

A week later, on 10 March 1987, Bhure Lal received his transfer order. Before he handed over charge, all papers pertaining to the Fairfax enquiry were collected from him by the PMO. Simultaneously, the charge of Enforcement Directorate was taken away from Vinod Pande and given to the Finance Secretary, Venkatiramanan. Gurumurthy was arrested in Madras.

Thereafter, both Vinod Pande and Bhure Lal were placed under police surveillance and continuously grilled by CBI in an attempt to extract incriminating evidence in support of the conspiracy theory. Bhure Lal was repeatedly questioned to ascertain whether any enquiry was in progress against the Bachchan brothers.

Meantime, Fairfax became a hot public issue, and the matter was discussed in the parliament. The Rajiv loyalists attacked V.P. Singh for having breached national security by hiring a foreign detective agency and divulging government secrets to it. Singh replied, "I take full responsibility for the Fairfax affair. Anyway, since when has it become anti-national to nab economic offenders?" No Congress MP rose to his defence.

The handling of the Fairfax enquiry is the best illustration of Rajiv's inexperience and gullibility. The case had nothing to do with him or his Italian relations. A business tycoon, just to save his skin, planted a forged letter and killed three birds with one stone. First he shook the Enforcement Directorate off his back. Second, he got rid of the Finance Minister and crusading officers who had become a threat to his survival. Third, he got an opportunity to get close to the Prime Minister. Ambani achieved all this by playing upon the fears of Amitabh Bachchan who, in turn, planted the conspiracy theory in Rajiv's mind. In this manoeuvre he was greatly assisted by Katre, Director, CBI, who was beholden to Ambani for the lucrative business opening he had provided to his son.[1]

HBJ Pipeline

A controversy which rolled into a scandal concerned the award of a contract for the 1760 km-long HBJ gas pipeline. Snam Progetti, a public sector Italian firm which had done business with India for decades, was one of the bidders for its contract. The project attracted attention owing to the pressure tactics of Snam's local representative, Ottavio Quattrocchi, who was a close friend of the Gandhis. As the HBJ pipeline bid by Snam Progetti was found higher by official committees on repeated examinations, the PM himself intervened on Quattrocchi's behalf. In the words of V.P. Singh, the then Finance Minister, "Rajiv told me to re-evaluate the bid. I appointed a committee under the finance secretary. This committee also found the bid expensive. Then the Prime Minister sent me a set of points asking me to assess the Snam Progetti bid on that basis. Strangely enough, the points suggested by him turned out to be those which were earlier sent to the ministry by Quattrocchi. When this didn't work out, pressure was mounted on Finance ministry officials by the Prime Minister's Office who wanted the norms changed and a fresh evaluation."[2]

Though the contract did not go to Snam Progetti owing to V.P. Singh's strong opposition, practically all senior officials dealing with the case had to pay the price.[3]

There never was a hint that Rajiv expected any benefit from this deal. It was fierce loyalty to his friends that obliterated the line dividing personal relations from public morality. This happened repeatedly in the case of the Bachchans.

HDW Submarine Deal

Just one month after V.P. Singh took over as Defence Minister, a telex from the Indian ambassador in Bonn, West Germany, landed on his table. It was a record of the ambassador's meeting with the officials of HDW, a shipyard in Kiel. In 1981 India had placed orders for 4 submarines with that yard and now the ambassador was told to negotiate for two more. He was also asked to obtain a reduction in their price. The shipyard expressed its inability to bring down the price, as HDW was contractually committed to pay seven percent commission on the earlier order, and any repeat orders placed in future.

On 9 April, V.P. Singh set up an official committee to enquire into the whole deal. Whereas he marked the case file to the PM, a press note was simultaneously issued regarding the disclosure made in the telex received from Bonn.

Here, V.P. Singh was obviously playing his own little game. Having fallen foul of the PM and his coterie, he realized that he may have to soon part company with Rajiv. So he wanted to derive the maximum political mileage from the new scandal. As the PM took time to see Singh's note, the press had already splashed the news. Rajiv felt let down and his advisers convinced him that his Defence Minister had stabbed him in the back. The loyalist hounds of the PM were let loose on V.P. Singh. Singh maintained that he was fully within his rights in taking this step and cautioned his colleagues that those who objected to the probe were providing grist to the opposition's mill. In view of the hostility he faced from within the party and the cabinet, V.P. Singh tendered his resignation on 12 April, with Rajiv Gandhi receiving tonnes of flak from the Press and the public.

This was an instance of crass bungling of an issue which Rajiv could have turned to his own advantage. There was never a question of his having received any bribe. In fact the matter attracted notice only because the Government was trying to reduce the price of the submarines. The original deal was perhaps negotiated by Sanjay Gandhi, and the contract signed in 1981 during his mother's prime ministership, when she also held the Defence portfolio. V.P. Singh had been told by the Defence secretary that probably the Hindujas, the wealthiest NRI group, were appointed as the agent. In his note to the PM, V.P. Singh had included this information also.

In view of these facts, there was little provocation for Rajiv to get so upset about V.P. Singh issuing a press note regarding the enquiry ordered into a shady deal. His only motive could have been to prevent any skeletons of his mother's period from tumbling out of the cupboard. But political savvy required that he should turn around V.P. Singh's caper to his own advantage and demand early completion of the enquiry. Instead, by letting loose his pack on the Raja, he only confirmed the general impression that whereas Singh was trying to haul up tax-evaders and middlemen, the PM was shielding them at every step. He took the entire odium of this transaction on himself and turned V.P. Singh into a martyr in the cause of clean politics.

Bofors Scandal

On 16 April 1987, a week after the HDW exposure hit the headlines, Swedish Radio reported that Bofors had paid large bribes through Swiss banks to senior Indian politicians and key defence personnel to win its largest defence contract. Coming as it did on the heels of Fairfax, HDW and V.P. Singh's resignation from the Government, all hell broke loose and Rajiv was faced with the biggest threat to his survival.

It was on 24 March 1987 that India had signed a contract with Bofors, a sister company of Nobel Industries, for the purchase of four hundred 155-mm, FH-77, Howitzers at a cost of US $ 1.3 billion. As Rajiv was very keen to eliminate all middlemen in government contracts, this requirement had been made clear to Bofors before signing the contract. Bofors gave a loosely worded undertaking to the ministry of Defence that no middleman would be engaged for this transaction. Curiously, this condition was not included in the contract.

The government's knee-jerk reaction was to dismiss the allegations as baseless and describe them as part of a conspiracy against the Prime Minister. None bothered to examine the nature of the charges or their implications. It was not realized that the Swedish Radio exposé was only the beginning, and much more was likely to follow. Thus, no long-term strategy of damage control was prepared, nor the nature of the likely damage assessed. Consequently, every fresh revelation caught the government on the wrong foot, and every time a limited response to the specific charge was crafted.

The perspective got further blurred as Rajiv's aides always tried to be more loyal than the king. Immediately after the news broke, the PM convened a meeting of his close advisers to assess the situation. None had any in-depth knowledge of the case, nor did Rajiv brief them in any manner. On 17 April the government categorically denied the allegations, saying, "the news item is false, baseless and mischievous." It was repeatedly stressed that as there were no agents, there could obviously be no pay-off.

Owing to mounting criticism in the parliament India requested the Swedish government to verify charges about the appointment of agents by Bofors. The National Swedish Audit Bureau Report confirmed the main allegations made in the broadcast. Though the Swedes blacked out the names of the parties thus involved, the publication of the censored Report of 4 June 1987 left the government defenceless. It clearly stated that agreements were on record between Bofors and three parties "concerning settlement of commission subsequent to the FH-77 deal and that considerable amounts had been paid to, among others, AB Bofors' previous agents in India."

The opposition accused the government of misleading the House and demanded the PM's resignation. But Bofors tried to make out that the payments in question were in the nature of 'winding up charges' paid after the termination of the agreements with the agents, and not 'commissions' given for services rendered. The government, instead of charging Bofors with breach of contract and threatening punitive action, faithfully parroted Bofor's version, and started plugging this line publicly.

This was a weak defence, and it was blown to bits when *The Hindu*, the most conservative of the English language dailies, published a series of secret Bofors documents on 22 and 23 June, 1988. This was followed by further revelations on 25 and 28 June.

These documents, read with the unexpurgated text of the Swedish Audit Bureau Report published later, established that "Bofors lied when it claimed that no commission was paid to Indians. The company also parted with the truth when it claimed that the last India-related payment was made in December 1986."[4] Actually the payments continued to be made till 30 March 1987.

It clearly emerged that Bofors had made payments to at least four agencies and some individuals in this connection. The agencies were: Pitco of Switzerland, Svenska of Panama, AE Services of England, and Anatronic owned by Win Chaddha and registered in India. Whereas Chaddha's Anatronic was supposed to provide only administrative services in India at a fee of Rs. 2 lakhs per month, it appeared to be closely linked with Svenska, which received over Rs. 30 crores out of the total kickbacks of Rs. 64 crores. The documentary evidence also linked Pitco with the ubiquitous Hindujas, which received the second largest commission. The fourth recipient of commissions was AE Services, which got around Rs. 10 crores.

In view of the serious nature of *The Hindu* disclosures, the government immediately ordered the Enforcement Directorate and CBI to enquire into the matter. At CBI's instance, the Swedish public prosecutor verified the facts at his end and authenticated the documents published by *The Hindu*. But practically no action was taken on receipt of this confirmation. Instead, Rajiv Gandhi offered all sorts of alibis on behalf of Bofors in an interview to a weekly magazine.

It was after more than a year that *The Hindu* published the blacked-out portions of the Swiss National Audit Bureau Report on 9 October 1989, which contained the name of companies which received the commission. Though the paper had promised to reveal fresh evidence in its next issue, it only put out a notice on 11 October that enough had been written "supported by extensive documents," and the subject was being closed. N. Ram, the editor, accused Kasturi, his uncle and the proprietor, of having buckled under government pressure, published further material simultaneously in *The Indian Express* and *The Statesman*. This matter, published on 31 October, contained extracts from the personal diary of Martin Ardbo, former head of Bofors and the person who had negotiated the contract. These entries referred to various dramatis personae by the first letter of their names, and the most damaging entry was supposed to be a reference to a 'Gandhi trustee lawyer'.

This is as far as the known facts can take one regarding the Bofors imbroglio. And how far is that? Not a great distance.

The crux of the story is that the Government of India placed an order on Bofors for the manufacture and supply of 400 155-mm howitzers at a price of about Rs. 1,700 crores. It was stipulated by India that no agents would be involved in this deal. Bofors reneged on this undertaking and paid a commission of Rs 64 crores to at least four agents and some others.

Any shrewd politician would have put Bofors in the dock for breach of faith and forced it to furnish its defence as best as it could. But instead of adopting this straight course, Rajiv put himself in the dock and started justifying Bofor's conduct.

The Indian government tried to follow a dual policy in handling the controversy. On the one hand it wanted to give the impression of striving to unearth the facts. It was at the government's instance that the Swedish authorities asked its National Audit Bureau to investigate the charges. Rajiv assured the parliament, 'Give us the evidence, and we will produce the proof.' S.K. Bhatnagar, Defence Secretary, wrote several letters to Bofors demanding clarifications. But Bofors was subjected to only gentle pressures and the ease with which the company ignored them leads one to infer that much of this correspondence was meant for the record. On the other hand, the government's efforts to absolve the company of all blame are much more noteworthy. The moment the radio story broke, Bofors dismissed it out of hand. India not only accepted Bofor's version at face value, it also asked the Swedish government to repudiate it. But the Swedes expressed their inability to do so, as they had no access to the secret papers of a private concern. Then, owing to all the din raised in India, the government asked the Swedes to conduct an official enquiry. But when the Audit Bureau Report blew the lid off the Bofors version, the PM moved for the constitution of a Joint Parliamentary Committee (JPC) to go into the matter. The committee was packed with loyalist Congressmen and MPs from other friendly parties, and its terms of reference were quite mild. So the opposition boycotted the JPC. When the Bofors team deposed before the committee, its version that the alleged payments were in the nature of 'winding up charges' and no agent was engaged by the company was fully accepted.

All along Bofors was receiving confusing signals from India. On the one hand the Defence ministry and the Indian ambassador to Sweden were mounting pressure to come out clean. On the other, the indications from the PM were not very clear. When a Bofors official visited India and promised to make some revelations "if he was allowed to meet at (the) political level," Rajiv declined the offer on the ground that as the person was not a top-level official, it may create a misleading impression.[5]

The most intriguing aspect in the drama was Rajiv's reaction to the Defence ministry's attempt to put pressure on Bofors to come out with their closely held secret. Arun Singh had personally obtained the PM's clearance to adopt any tactics he chose to force the Company to reveal the full facts about the kickbacks. He had consistently advocated the view that a threat of cancellation of the contract would produce the desired results. By way of abundant caution the Defence ministry obtained Attorney General Parasaran's advice on this issue. He clearly stated that the government was in a very strong position to unilaterally cancel the contract without any adverse repercussions. In reply to another reference to the Army Chief, Sundarji said in his note of 12 June that the cancellation may lead to a delay of 1 to 1 1/2 years in getting a similar weapon from another source, but "it was an acceptable risk from the point of view of totality (of circumstances)." Armed with these expert opinions, on 3 July 1987 the Defence ministry summoned the Vice President of Bofors, who happened to be in Delhi. He was adequately enlightened about the unorthodox techniques employed by the Indian police to extract confessions. The gentleman was deeply shaken and rushed back to Sweden with a promise to return with his colleagues on 6 July to divulge the desired information. A note of this unusual meeting was prepared by the ministry and copies sent to the PM and the Defence minister.

Rajiv returned from the USSR on 4 July and called an informal meeting of the Cabinet Committee on Political Affairs at his residence the same evening. The Defence ministry quickly prepared a note for the CCPA, which was handed over to the members when the proceedings commenced. The PM read the note and flew into a rage. He demanded an explanation for taking this step without obtaining his prior approval. When Arun Singh tried to defend his officers by taking the blame on himself, he also came in for some tongue-lashing. Other CCPA members raised serious objections on the ground that the JPC was already in session, and the meeting of a top-level Bofors team with the Defence ministry officials would be interpreted as the government's attempt to load the dice against a fair investigation. Arun Singh, who was also invited to the meeting, opposed this line of argument. But ultimately it was decided that the Bofors team should be prevented from visiting India.

The PM asked the officials to immediately destroy all copies of CCPA note though he retained his own copy. The office copy of this note remained in the Defence ministry file. The Bofors team in Sweden was contacted immediately and some vague excuse trotted out for postponing its visit.

Around this time, there was another development which had the potential of a major blow-up. In support of his contention that if Bofors was threatened with cancellation of contract it would cough up all the information, Arun Singh had sent a detailed note to the PM. Rajiv took offence at this memo as he thought that it was written for the record. He wrote a long, angry minute in his hand, asking for the full implications of cancelling the contract.' Gopi Arora, Rajiv's most trusted aide, held back this note for his own reasons.[6]

As the PM had received no reply to his note, Sarla Grewal rang up Arun Singh on 14 July to say that her boss had been waiting for comments on the queries raised by him. Arun Singh obviously did not know as to what she was talking about, and asked her to speak to Bhatnagar. But Bhatnagar also had no clue about the matter. So Sarla dictated on the phone the points on which information was required. As the desired material was readily available in the ministry, the Defence Secretary collected it and passed it on to Sarla. Six days later, on 18 July, Arun Singh resigned and the two friends parted company despite Gopi holding back the original hand-written note by Rajiv. Interestingly, Arun Singh never knew about the PM's note having been held back by Gopi till I mentioned this fact to him on 7 November 1995. Of course, a fortnight after Arun Singh's exit, the note was sent to the Defence Ministry.

It was in July 1987 that Rajiv countermanded the tough line pursued by the Defence Ministry. His meeting of 4 July, when he ordered the cancellation of a visit by the Bofors team, was a distinct expression of this change. Later, in his famous interview to *Sunday*, when asked about the payment of commission, Rajiv replied, "...if it was paid for some genuine work that was done for Bofors, then we cannot question it. (This could be) gathering information against the French weapon. That is industrial espionage. You can't grudge them that."[7] This was a plea which even Bofors had not thought of.

As to getting back the sum of Rs. 64 crores paid by Bofors in contravention of their express undertaking, the PM said, "Our first assessment must be: did we get a good price for the gun? We got a good price. To the best of my knowledge money had not been used to influence the decision making process... (and no) money has come to any Indian."[8] Here Rajiv completely skirted the question of Bofors refunding the hefty commission which was obviously included in the price of the gun.

Though it was suggested repeatedly by several persons that Bofors should be threatened with cancellation of the contract to extract the truth, Rajiv always opposed this line. His reply was, "Can we do this?... What is the cost of doing it? If we take some action which is going to cost us some 800 crores, it is hardly worth it."[9] Then he dwelt on the security risk in the delay involved in buying another suitable weapon. In fact, the threat of cancellation was only suggested as a tactical move to put pressure on Bofors, and even this Rajiv was not prepared to entertain.

One result of the interest shown by Defence officials in this matter was that they were specifically told to treat the PMO as the co-ordinating agency for all dealings with Bofors. And Oza, the Indian ambassador to Sweden, who had taken a lively interest in this case, was advised that the JPC was already siezed of the matter, and any queries made by him from Bofors would amount to contempt of the parliament.[10]

Shortly after the scandal broke, it became clear that Win Chaddha and the Hindujas were deeply involved in this affair. Within a week after the Swedish Radio exposé, a respected Swedish daily, *Dagens Nyhetor*, quoting Bofors sources, wrote that commissions had been paid to Hindujas.[11] But after the publication of the *Hindu* documents when reporters sought Rajiv's reaction to Hinduja's involvement, he said that "as they did not hold Indian passports, there was nothing the authorities could do." And this despite the fact that one of the four Hinduja brothers lived mostly in Bombay. Later, in his *Sunday* interview he stated that those *Hindu* documents, "were said by the Swedish Bank to have some defects... There are some doubts about their authenticity."[12]

Though Win Chaddha's role was described as an administrative consultant, he was suspected to be a key player right from the beginning. Yet his premises were raided a month after he had fled the country. While he was in the United States, he visited the Indian Consulate in New York twice on 29 June 1987 to execute a power of attorney. Later, he agreed to return to India to appear before the JPC entirely on his own terms. So he was allowed free movement in India and guaranteed safe return to the USA.

The cleanest chit to Bofors was given by P. Chidambaram, Minister of State for Home, when he stated before the Rajya Sabha that the company had not violated any agreement. Then what was all this pother about? If things were really so above board, where was the need to make all these payments in secret Swiss bank accounts? And what was the reason for the massive cover-up paranoia?

The basic question all along was: did Rajiv Gandhi receive kick-backs in the Bofors deal? No conclusive evidence has ever surfaced to this effect. His name rarely occurs in any record and even when it does, it reveals little. In the earlier stages of negotiations, Arun Nehru seems to have played an important role. In a note recorded in June 1985, Rolf Gauffin, a senior diplomat in the Swedish Embassy in Delhi, wrote to his Foreign Ministry about Nehru's stipulation that "No Indian representative can be informed about what is happening." He also warned that an "absolute condition for further discussions with Bofors and the official Swedish representatives was that neither Rajiv Gandhi's nor Arun Nehru's names should be mentioned in connenction with the coming meeting."[13]

One entry in Ardbo's personal diary reads, "H does not care if Arun Nehru is hurt. He does not mind if even Q is hurt. But G must be saved at all costs." Here H is supposed to refer to Hinduja's, Q to Quattrocchi, and G to Gandhi. Another entry says, "Suggest later meeting with G." The entry that was played up the most, says "Bob (Robert Wilson of AE Services) had talked with Gandhi trustee lawyer."

These references are much too flimsy, scrappy and disjointed to be made the basis of even a biased indictment of Rajiv. The most tell-tale clue to surface so far is the revelation made by the Swiss court regarding the operation of one of the six frozen accounts by Ottavio Quattrocchi. These code-named accounts in Swiss banks pertain to Bofors kickbacks, and were frozen at the instance of the V.P. Singh government on 24 January 1990. Quattrocchi was not even remotely concerned with the Bofors deal, and the question of paying any commission to him for services rendered did not arise. Then how did he come to operate one of the kickback accounts? Moreover, from the beginning of the trial in Geneva, he had been filing appeals against disclosing the names of the account holders to the Indian government. Why was he so nervous about such a revelation? Then, a couple of months after this fact got known, Quattrocchi was quietly transferred out of India. There is some speculation that as Quattrocchi was an old and close family friend of Sonia and Rajiv, this connection may have something to do with his operation (not ownership) of the impugned account.

On 1 September 1995 the magistrate in Geneva closed his investigations and ordered the transfer of documents of blocked Bofors accounts to the government of India. As expected, Hindujas, Quattrocchi, Win Chaddha and others have filed appeals against this order. They can file a second appeal before the Swiss Federal Court. But it is more than likely that before this book is published, the relevant documents may have been already transferred to India. And depending upon the level of indiscretion of the account holders, they may finally settle the issue of Rajiv's innocence or otherwise.

In a rather uncharacteristic outburst, Arun Singh once told General Sundarji, "I know I can bring this government down within 24 hours if I speak." When Sundarji asked him as to why he does not, the General was told that his children were under threat.[14] But this observation, though full of sinister implications, is isolated and uncorroborated to have much evidenciary value.

Yet, the fact remains that a hefty commission of Rs. 64 crores was paid by Bofors to middlemen. And as Adnan Khashoggi, the king of arms agents, said in an interview, "Companies don't offer bribes unless asked for."[15] Moreover, as the Indian government had insisted on the elimination of middlemen, where was the compulsion to pay commissions, and that too in secret Swiss bank accounts ?

There was strong evidence linking Win Chaddha with Svenska, which received a commission of over Rs. 30 crores. But Chaddha was certainly not worth that amount. Was he a front-man for some big gun?

The receipt of commission by AE Services is still more mysterious. This company, incorporated in 1978, had filed no return, had no employees and no business activity between 1979 and 1986. It had actually made a request for dissolution. Then, suddenly, Bofors paid US $7.3 million into its account.[16] Incidentally, it was Bob, the representative of this company, who was supposed to have met the 'Gandhi trustee lawyer' according to an entry in Ardbo's personal diary.

To begin with, Bofors exposures concerned payment of commission to agents in contravention of the explicit instructions of the buyers. But it soon became a major political issue threatening the credibility of the country's Prime Minister. But instead of dealing with it at a political level, Rajiv got entangled in the technical and legal aspects of the case, thus losing sight of its larger political dimensions.

Looking to the potential for mischief of the Swedish Radio's revelations, an astute politician would have met the issue head on, repeatedly accused Bofors of perfidious behaviour, boiled over with holy rage and threatened the company with dire consequences. A commission of enquiry should have been set up, intelligence agencies activated, and the Swedish and Swiss governments bombarded with requests to probe into the scandal.

All this should have been done as political theatrics, even if no action was really intended against Bofors. The company could have been quietly told that this was all meant for public consumption and it would be business as usual under the surface. This approach would have robbed the opposition of its thunder and convinced the Indian people that their Mr. Clean was exploding like a volcano at the first sign of venality.

But whether it was Fairfax, or HDW, or Bofors, Rajiv revealed the locus of his sympathies the moment a scandal surfaced. In one sense he was too simple and too honest to effectively dissimulate. In other words, he was deficient in the basic skills of political survival.

It is instructive to compare the Bofors deal with the purchase of 40 French Mirage fighter planes during Mrs. Gandhi's time in 1983. The value of the French contract was two and a half times the Swedish guns. Yet there was never a ripple about kickbacks. Only the uninitiated would believe that the Mirage deal was any cleaner than the Bofors'. And there lies the difference between a professional and an amateur!

41

Foreign Relations

All members of the Dynasty had a special flair for foreign affairs; none handled them with greater relish and aplomb than Rajiv Gandhi. He started his foreign contacts by a visit to Moscow in May 1985 and to Washington the next month. Both visits were telecast live and his countrymen felt elated to see their telegenic Prime Minister interact with the heads of the two superpowers with such confidence and poise. Rajiv himself thoroughly enjoyed the exposure and publicity that he got, and kept up an average of about twelve foreign visits per annum during his 5-year tenure.

Rajiv loved the big canvas and took part in a large number of summits, conferences and ceremonial gatherings in great style. He addressed three sessions of the UN General Assembly and attended three Commonwealth Conferences, two summits of Non-aligned Movement, three SAARC meetings, and any number of other international get-togethers. He talked loftily of non-alignment, disarmament, co-existence, ecology, anti-racism, problems facing the developing countries, and the like. His extensive travels and personal charm enabled him to establish close equations with a number of world leaders.

An important reason for Rajiv's love of foreign travel was the escape it provided from the pressing problems at home. Prime Ministerial visits have a fairy tale aura about them — red carpet receptions, guards of honour, lavish banquets, laudatory speeches, media exposure — and they have such a tonic effect on the jaded nerves of an overworked head of government.

Crusade against Apartheid

Rajiv's foreign policy covers two distinct areas. First, international issues of common interest to the world community, where India had no direct involvement. Second, issues of direct interest to the country.

The altruistic aspect of Rajiv's foreign policy was a Nehruvian legacy, and Rajiv took a keener interest in it than his mother. His crusade against racialism of South Africa and support for the independence struggle of Namibia are certainly noteworthy.

It was at the Nassau (Bahamas) Conference of Heads of Government of Commonwealth held in October 1985 that it was agreed to put economic pressure on South Africa to abjure apartheid, and five action-points were listed in this behalf. The immediate, unconditional release of Nelson Mandela was also demanded. Britain all along opposed any economic sanctions against South Africa and the USA also supported her stand.

Later, in September 1986, while chairing the Harare NAM summit, Rajiv declared, "The non-aligned should press ahead with sanctions (against South Africa) whether others are prepared to do so or not." It was as a result of this resolve that the 'Africa Fund' was created to support "action for resisting invasion, colonisation and apartheid." In recognition of his initiative Rajiv was made the chairman of the Fund.

Namibian Independence

Rajiv Gandhi vigorously advocated the cause of Namibian independence. Originally, Namibia (South West Asia) was mandated to South Africa by the League of Nations after the First World War. But owing to her rich mineral deposits, South Africa had turned her into a colony, and defied repeated UN resolutions to let the Namibians decide their future. In this intransigence she was fully supported by the United States, which linked the withdrawal of Cuban troops from Angola with Namibian independence.

Under the leadership of Sam Nujoma, the South West African People's Organization (SWAPO) had been agitating against the South African oppression and had attracted worldwide attention. The NAM Declaration of April 1986 had firmly supported the Namibian cause. At the ministerial meeting of the Co-ordination Bureau of the non-aligned countries held in Delhi in April 1985 Rajiv lent strong support to the Namibian struggle, and gave full diplomatic recognition to SWAPO.

As a part of this campaign Rajiv visited the frontline states of Zambia, Zimbabwe, Angola and Tanzania from 14-18 May 1986. India kept supporting the cause of Namibian freedom at all the international forums. Ultimately it was in 1990 that Namibia won independence.

Six-nation disarmament initiative

In continuation of Mrs. Gandhi's six-nation initiative on nuclear disarmament, Rajiv Gandhi convened a meeting of the leaders of Tanzania, Mexico, Greece, Sweden, Argentina and India at Delhi on 28 January, 1985. The focus of discussions was nuclear disarmament to save mankind from extinction. Later, these six nations met at Ixtapa (Mexico) in August 1986. The Mexico Declaration on peace and disarmament called for more vigorous efforts to end the nuclear race. Also, a detailed Action Plan for independent verification of nuclear tests was appended to it. Joint appeals were addressed to the heads of the USA and the USSR to accept the Declaration.

President Reagan rejected the appeal outright as 'nuclear weapons must be tested to counter massive Soviet build-up.' But Gorbachev unilaterally accepted a moratorium on nuclear tests.

While strongly opposing the production of nuclear weapons, Rajiv followed his mother's policy of consistently refusing to sign the nuclear Non-proliferation Treaty. India had always perceived it as an invidious and unequal treaty, as it sought to preserve the hegemony of the nuclear powers, and debarred the entry of newcomers to this exclusive club.

Vietnam and Kampuchea

In January 1987 an Indian delegation led by the Foreign Minister N.D. Tiwari, his minister of state Natwar Singh, and others paid an official visit to Vietnam. There, the Vietnamese Foreign Minister, Cothac, confided to the mission that his country was keen to withdraw from Kampuchea provided a viable arrangement could be worked out. He also suggested that the ASEAN countries may be associated with this exercise.

As a follow-up to the Vietnamese request, Natwar Singh visited all the ASEAN countries to mobilize regional opinion in favour of a settlement. He also had a number of meetings with Prince Sihanouk, the deposed king of Cambodia (Kampuchea), who was living in exile in Paris, and enjoyed wide support in his country. At his instance, Natwar also arranged meetings between him and Heng Samarin, the prime minister of Vietnam. As things moved forward, the United States also got into the act, and both China and America tried to sideline India. Ultimately, a 21-nation conference was convened in Paris to which India was also invited. It was agreed that the Vietnamese forces would withdraw from Kampuchea and election held under the UN auspices. As no single party got a majority, Prince Sihanouk and Heng Samarian formed a coalition. By then the Congress government had been voted out of power.

The settlement of the thorny Kampuchean problem was one of the solid achievements of India diplomacy. The fact that Vietnam approached India to act as an honest broker was also an affirmation of her high standing as a non-aligned nation.

USSR

Rajiv Gandhi and Mikhail Gorbachev struck an excellent equation from the word go. It was the Soviet leader Konstantin Chernenko's death which occasioned Gandhi's first visit to the USSR in March 1985. Two months later he was there again and spent six days in the Soviet Union. Gorbachev paid his first visit to Delhi the same year in November. And during Rajiv's 5-year tenure, the two leaders met eight times.

Rajiv consistently supported Gorbachev's peace initiatives, and became an ardent admirer of his glasnost and perestroika. The most notable event of this period was the signing of the Delhi Declaration in November 1985. It called for complete nuclear disarmament by 2010 AD, dismantling of all military bases outside the national boundaries, and scrapping of military pacts. During this visit the Soviet leader also announced an economic package of 4.2 billion roubles to give a boost to bilateral trade. It also opened the door for Indian firms to deal directly with the Soviet republics and state enterprises.

Obviously, the key to Indo-Soviet friendship was the mutuality of interests. Wherever these interests diverged, differences surfaced. Gorbachev had visions of playing a larger role in the Asia-Pacific region, and outlined the concept of an Asia-Pacific 'Helsinki'. India was not much enthused, and cold-shouldered it. On the other hand, at the end of Gorbachev's visit when India wanted to include a reference to South Africa's apartheid and the negative role of the West on this issue, the Soviets did not agree to it. Embroiled in Afghanistan and facing hostility from China, they were wary to offending the West at that time.

But except for such minor differences, relations between the two states remained cordial, and the close rapport between Rajiv and Gorbachev lent them a warm glow.

The USA

Rajiv's first visit to the United States followed just three weeks after his trip to the Soviet Union. It was a highly gratifying experience for him. The timing was propitious: Ronald Reagan, an affable and avuncular person, was President. There were no immediate irritants. And America was ogling the fast-growing consumer market of India. Rajiv's own image as an admirer of high-tech, his youthfulness and personal charm endeared him instantly to the Americans.

The occasion for the visit was the inauguration of the 'Year of India' cultural festival. At their White House meeting the two leaders, in Reagan's words, "hit it off". Rajiv was invited to address the joint session of the two Houses of the Congress where, echoing Martin Luther King, he said, "I am young and I too have a dream. I dream of an India — strong, independent, self-reliant and in the front rank of nations of the world in the service of mankind." His performance at the National Press Club was superb.

Despite all the build-up he received during this visit, he never failed to project India's genuine interests and concerns. Whereas he told the joint session that "we stand for a political settlement in Afghanistan," he spoke disapprovingly of the American attempt to militarize space and the reduction in contribution to International Development Agency. At the Press Club he objected to the massive supply of arms to Pakistan, as some of these were not defensive.

This visit was essentially a media event, and it was telecast live by Doordarshan in grand style. Neither country broke fresh ground, and the American freeze on arms supply to India was not relaxed. However, Rajiv was able to persuade Reagan to lift the embargo on the sale of a super-computer to India for weather forecasting.

Whereas America had already become India's largest trading partner yet, at the official level, "India did not follow up the initial surge of goodwill to build a more substantial structure of contacts and ties, primarily at the level of the Congress, the media, the intellectual and the academic community."[1]

Indo-American relations could not improve in view of the American supply of Advanced Warning and Control System (AWACS) of air surveillance to Pakistan, and the unloading of heaps of the latest weaponary for use by the Mujahideen against the Russians. India's contention had all along been that these arms would be actually used against her.

China

Both India and China had increasingly come to appreciate the need to live in amity and repair their fractured relations. But the pursuit of conflicting goals and excessive mutual suspicion hampered progress at every step.

India could not ignore the fact of Chinese role in arming Pakistan and helping her to develop her nuclear facilities. China had also assisted Pakistan in upgrading the Karakoram highway which linked Sinkiang with Pak occupied Kashmir. She fully supported Pakistan's claim over the Siachen Glacier.

Then, it was not a very comfortable feeling for India to have a military giant as her neighbour whose might was increasing by the day. China had the largest army in the world, the third largest air force and one of the biggest submarine fleets — including nuclear submarines. This gargantuan war machine, backed up by her spectacular economic growth, had made her a global power, whereas India had graduated to the status of a regional power only.

But there were numerous positive signals also. For years now there had been no evidence of China stoking insurgencies in the Northeastern region of India. She had not supported Pakistan in her efforts to internationalize the Kashmir problem.

Even at the ideological level, there had been a shift towards a more conciliatory approach in her foreign policy. The 13th Congress of the Communist Party of China held in 1987 emphasized the importance of peaceful co-existence with all countries and a final end to the struggle against the Soviet Union.

The Chinese had thrown several hints for the Indian Prime Minister's visit to China. On a trip to India, the Chinese Vice Premier had mentioned that Chou En-lai had come to India four times and Nehru had been to China only once. On another occasion, Li Shuquing, Chinese Vice Foreign minister extended a specific invitation to Rajiv for a state visit. The Indian side was in no hurry to respond. But as the exchange of bilateral visits increased and confidence-building measures got underway, the Indian stand also softened.

In the midst of these developments, there suddenly surfaced the Sumdorang Valley crisis, which brought the troops of the two countries to the brink of a clash. After a long slumber, India's eastern border came alive when Gen. Sundarji launched the exercise Checkerboard in that sector. The Indian army had set up all-weather posts in Sumdorang Valley where the border is not demarcated. When the Chinese discovered this, they also came forward, established a full-fledged post and a helipad overlooking the Valley. Sundarji, the high priest of coercive diplomacy, moved the Indian troops forward, and the rear echelons followed suit. The Chinese took it as an offensive move, and the Indian ambassador at Peking was woken up at midnight to be alerted about this alarming development. Rajiv Gandhi was taken by surprise when he learnt about this episode, and asked the Defence Ministry officials as to what the commotion was all about. They were equally ignorant, as the enterprising General had acted on his own. Immediate troop withdrawal was ordered and the Chinese assured of India's peaceful intentions. The Army's explanation was that it had noticed some forward movement of the Chinese forces and taken defensive action.

Despite opposition from influential sections of the public and party, Rajiv ultimately decided to visit China in December 1988 for five days, and the occasion stands as the high watermark of India-China relations after the 1962 war. This was the first visit by an Indian prime minister to China in 34 years. Undertaken after much trepidation and confabulation, it was a case of better late than never. But in view of the demonology woven around the relations of the two neighbours, Rajiv's initiative was definitely an act of courage and sagacity.

It was the 90-minute meeting between Rajiv and Deng Xiaoping, the 84-year-old Chinese patriarch, that broke the ice. When the two leaders met, Deng, holding Rajiv's hand, addressed him as 'my young friend,' and said, 'Let us forget the past... We have both made mistakes and can learn from each other ... You are young .... You are the future. We are receding into history. There is a new generation of leaders now and a global desire to live in peace, and end conflict and tension. It lies in your hand to shape the destiny of the new world order. Use it wisely.'

The two countries agreed to set up an official level Joint Commission to sort out the border dispute. Also, border issues were separated from other bilateral matters. A Joint Committee was appointed to foster trade and cultural exchanges. India gave full recognition to Chinese sovereignty over Tibet. And a short time after this meeting, China reduced the deployment of troops in Tibet and along the frontier. What this visit achieved was not a breakthrough in the rigid stands of the two countries, but a breakdown of a psychological barrier.

Afghanistan

India had a two-fold interest in the situation developing in Afghanistan. One, it had always been a friendly neighbour, and both Indira Gandhi and Rajiv sincerely tried for the return of peace to that land. Rajiv supported Dr. Najibullah's regime, as his removal was likely to plunge Afghanistan into medieval tribal conflicts. He also kept a dialogue going with Zahir Shah, the deposed king of Afghanistan, in the hope of establishing a government of reconciliation.

The heavy induction of American arms in this area was a cause of considerable concern to India. With the Soviet intervention, Pakistan became a frontline state for the US and received massive arms aid from her. Pakistan exploited the situation fully, and stepped up the export of arms and insurrection to the neighbouring areas of Punjab and Kashmir.

As a part of his peace initiative, Gorbachev announced on 8 February 1988 that the Soviet forces would start pulling out of Afghanistan from May, provided the Geneva talks proved fruitful. The intrepid peacemaker in Rajiv saw an opening for playing a prominent role. He invited President Zia to discuss the modalities of settling the Afghan issue. Zia, who had already been to Delhi twice, is said to have remarked, 'Why? Is there a cricket match going on there?' It was then agreed to hold a secretary-level meeting which, after some foot-dragging, could be convened only on 3 May. "The Indian Foreign Secretary, K.P.S. Menon came back with a clear impression that Pakistan would prevent Indian participation in the solution of the Afghan crisis by all means possible."[2] In fact Pakistan was able to convert even Gorbachev to the view that "Indian involvement would offend Islamic sentiments in Afghanistan."[3]

Maldives

India's quick and decisive action in aborting the coup attempt in Maldives was a minor military operation in her itself, but full of import for the region. At the instance of the former deposed President of the Island, a fortune hunter got together 200 mercenaries from Sri Lanka. He landed them in Maldives on the morning of 3 November 1989 in an attempted coup against Abdul Gayoom, the President. This horde was joined by another 200 men who had earlier sneaked into the Island, and together they occupied the Presidential Palace. Gayoom had already fled, and contacted various world leaders before the invaders could occupy the telecommunication centre. Rajiv, to whom the president spoke personally, promised to help. At around 10 p.m. 300 Indian paratroopers landed at the Maldivian airport, Hulule, and within four hours the mercenaries were on the run. There were no casualties as a result of the Indian army action, though earlier about 20 people were killed when the invaders had attacked the Palace. Britain and the United States praised the Indian government for promoting stability in the region. Countries of South Asia did not miss India's emergence as the gendarme of the region.

Bangladesh

The process of Islamization that the military dictator Zia-ur-Rehman had started was taken further by his successor, Gen. Ershad. Under Zia Bangladesh had become a full-fledged member of the Organization of Islamic Conference, and Ershad had amended the Constitution to make her an Islamic state. Bangladesh had also got much closer to Pakistan and the USA.

The perennially contentious issue of the division of Ganga waters was taken up at the second ASA summit held at Bangalore in December 1986. Here, Gen. Ershad was able to sell the idea of a tripartite approach to Rajiv as Nepal was an equally interested party. Rajiv was taken in by Ershad's glib talk and the Ministry of External Affairs had quite a problem wriggling out of this awkward situation. Ultimately, the Ganga waters continued to be divided on the basis of a Memorandum of Understanding signed in 1986. But this ad hoc arrangement did not last long and from 1988 onwards India drew water on a unilateral basis.

Nepal

India's relations with Nepal have seldom remained on an even keel for long. After hitting a lengthy bald patch, they improved towards the latter part of Mrs. Gandhi's tenure. Then in 1988 a crisis developed when the India-Nepal trade treaties expired and, after two extensions, India informed Nepal that henceforth the bilateral trade would be governed by policies applicable to other nations. This literally meant sealing off the borders between the two countries resulting in an economic blockade. It caused great hardship to the civilian population and attracted adverse notice from the international media.

In 1987-88 Nepal had taken some unnecessarily provocative decisions which upset India. In her 1987 budget she suddenly imposed an additional 55 percent customs duty on Indian goods. And to make matters worse, in December 1988 she granted 60 percent discount in duty on Chinese goods. Nepal also required Indians working in Nepal to obtain work permit.

But the real rub lay in Nepal getting too close to China. The Indian Government learnt in July 1988 that several truckloads of AK-47 assault rifles, ammunition, anti-aircraft guns and other military hardware had crossed over from Tibet into Nepal. India found this much too provocative, especially the acquisition of anti-aircraft guns. This was the last straw and India felt impelled to teach her a lesson, and imposed a virtual economic blockade from 23 March 1989.

Ultimately it was in September 1989 that the King of Nepal and the Indian Prime Minister held four meetings at Belgrade where they had gone for the IX NAM summit. This led to India agreeing to further extension of the expired treaty. And before a new treaty could be signed, Rajiv had lost the 1989 election.

Sri Lanka

In his address to the nation after becoming the Prime Minister, Rajiv Gandhi regretted that the situation in Sri Lanka had rapidly deteriorated. In 1983 Sri Lanka had opted for a military solution when its army launched a violent offensive to subdue the Liberation Tigers of Tamil Eelam (LTTE). Thousands of victims had fled to Tamil Nadu and Indian public opinion was much inflamed.

In 1985, in an attempt to liquidate the LTTE stronghold, Sri Lanka mounted 'Operation Liberation' against Jaffna, and cut off all supplies to the beleaguered areas. In view of the great suffering of the Jaffna Tamils, Rajiv was forced to intervene. On 3 June 1987 India sent a flotilla of 19 fishing boats carrying food supplies, but these had to return on being intercepted by the Sri Lankan navy. Then, five Indian transport planes air dropped 22 tonnes of provisions over Jaffna. India took good care to establish the transparency of this humanitarian mission by taking Indian and foreign journalists in the planes. This came as a shock to Sri Lanka, and resulted in the signing of an agreement permitting unescorted civilian vessels to deliver daily necessities at Jaffna port.

Junius Jayewardene, President of Sri Lanka, had explored possibilities of seeking help from the USA, the UK and other countries to fight the Tamilian insurgency. But none responded as it would have led to a confrontation with India. Only Pakistan and Israel offered assistance, but that was not good enough. This ultimately convinced Jayewardene that there was no escape from directly negotiating with her neighbour for an amicable settlement. And here he was encouraged by Rajiv's positive approach.

The first concrete evidence of the impending India-Sri Lanka accord surfaced when the Tamil Nadu Police raided LTTE hideouts and seized their wireless transmitters on the eve of the SAARC summit in Bangalore in December 1986. During the summit, Rajiv and Jayewardene held secret parleys to evolve a workable package. This ultimately led to India and Sri Lanka signing an accord on 29 July 1987. And with that rose hopes of an end to three decades of ethnic strife in Sri Lanka.

It was an amazing accord. Signed between India and Sri Lanka to settle the LTTE demands, it did not make the militants a signatory to the accord. Prabhakaran was summoned to Delhi for consultations, and the PM talked to him just six hours before he left for Colombo to conclude the agreement. The LTTE leader raised some crucial points for decision before the accord could be accepted. He was told that his views would be duly considered.

The accord provided for the merger of northern and eastern provinces to be governed by an elected provincial council with substantial devolution of powers. This was the area demanded by the LTTE as a homeland. The future of this merger was to be determined by a referendum. Tamil was to become the second official language. India was to ensure that her territory was not used for secessionist activities against Sri Lanka. The onus of ending the LTTE insurgency also lay on India. An annexure provided that Indian observers would monitor the cease-fire, elections to the provincial council and the ensuing referendum. Thus India became the guarantor of the accord.

The agreement was highly unpopular in Sri Lanka. When Rajiv's plane landed at Colombo, there was a huge crowd of Shinhalas protesting against his visit. He and his team had to be flown to the city in helicopters. There were agitations and riots in Colombo. While Rajiv was inspecting a guard of honour, a marine hit him on the shoulder with a rifle butt. Later, an assassination bid was made on Jayewardene inside the Parliament by the JVP, a militant Sinhala group.

Despite all its reservations, the LTTE first agreed to go along with the accord under pressure from the Tamil Nadu CM and the Indian Government. It is really amazing as to how Rajiv took the Tamil Tigers so much for granted. He gave an undertaking that there would be cessation of hostilities within 48 hours of signing the accord and the militants would surrender all arms 72 hours thereafter. The time limit for surrender of arms was later extended by a week and some token surrenders were also made. But LTTE was not prepared to be suddenly disarmed and then play into hands of the wily Sri Lankan President. "... it took us 12 years to build this organisation," said Prabhakaran, "it just can't be dismantled in 72 hours."[4]

The Indian Army was still grappling with this problem when it happened to arrest 17 LTTE militants in October 1987 and, on demand, handed them over to the Sri Lankan Government. Aware of the fate awaiting them, they swallowed cyanide capsules and 12 of them died on the spot. This greatly inflamed the Tamil Tigers and they took it as an act of betrayal. They repudiated the accord and this brought them into direct confrontation with the Indian Peace Keeping Force (IPKF).

The accord clearly provided that the Indian army may be invited by the President of Sri Lanka ... if so required. As Jayewardene was apprehending a coup, he asked for the immediate despatch of Indian troops. On LTTE's repudiation of the accord, the strength of the Peace Keeping Force in Sri Lanka was substantially augmented. And in their effort to disarm the Tamil Tigers, the Indian troops soon got locked in a grim battle with them.

Gradually the number of the Indian troops tied down in Sri

Lanka rose to 45,000, and during the two years of confrontation
with the doughty militants nearly 1100 soldiers lost their lives.
And what was the net gain of this enormously expensive enterprise? India unwittingly assumed the role of the Sri Lankan army
to fight the LTTE for whose protection and rehabilitation the
accord was signed. And so untenable had become India's position
that whether it was the Sri Lankan people, the local Tamils, or
the Indian public, all wanted the IPKF to go home.

The Sri Lankans viewed the accord as an assault on their
national sovereignty, and the Indian troops were seen as an army
of occupation. As opposition to Jayewardene mounted, India was
obliged to give him all assistance to keep him in office. But in the
election held at the end of 1988, he lost to R. Premadasa, who was
known for his strong anti-India stand. He gave a call for the
withdrawal of IPKF from Sri Lanka by 29 July 1989, i.e., on the
completion of its two-year stay in the country.

This created an awkward situation for India. In an election
year, it was embarrassing for Rajiv to swallow this rebuff. But
Premadasa had his own compulsions. The militant Sinhala outfit,
JVP, was acquiring an ever-increasing hold over the people and
indulging in wanton acts of violence. The new President's best
ploy against this onslaught was to himself adopt a stridently
anti-Indian posture. But when he gave a call for the Indian army
to leave, Rajiv refused to comply on the plea that its mission was
not yet finished. This was a weak excuse, as under the accord the
army had come on the Sri Lankan President's invitation and,
consequently, was obliged to leave when he asked it to quit.

Rajiv realized that IPKF's stay in Sri Lanka had become untenable, and a phased pull-out of troops started from April 1989. But
Rajiv wanted a face-saving device for a formal and total withdrawal. This Premadasa was not willing to provide, as the Indian
disgrace was his glory. Talks between the two leaders were held
at Harare and Belgrade NAM meetings for working out an agreement for the withdrawal of IPKF. But it was only after the
Congress defeat in the 1989 general election that the Indian army
fully withdrew from Sri Lanka.

Of all the accords signed by Rajiv, the India-Sri Lanka agreement turned out to be most disastrous. Only its unreserved acceptance by the LTTE could have ensured its success. But the Tamil Tigers were never associated with its formulation, and Prabhakaran had serious reservations about it from the start.

It is also strange as to how anybody familiar with the ground realities in north-eastern Sri Lanka could fix deadlines of 48 and 72 hours for cessation of hostilities and laying down of arms. The LTTE cadres were thinly spread out in dense forests, and quite often they were on the move. It was a time consuming exercise to contact them, and persuade them to give up arms by placing implicit faith in the assurances of a government which they never trusted. Also, Rajiv had not learnt from his Punjab experience that in a fluid political situation when a number of critical factors are not within one's control, it is impractical to prescribe strict time schedules for the completion of specific tasks.

Even if the IPKF landed in Sri Lanka at the invitation of its President, for the Islanders it was a foreign army, and an object of hatred. During its two-year stay in Sri Lanka the Indian Army earned a lot of ill-will, and relations between the two countries soured as never before.

It has been argued that the geo-political situation made it incumbent on Rajiv to send troops to Sri Lanka. If he had not done so, some other country would have stepped in. In fact Jayewardene had tried his best to seek the direct involvement of America and Britain, but failed. Pakistan knew that India was too deeply involved in Sri Lanka to tolerate Pak intrusion, and would not have risked a war over this issue. India's intervention in Sri Lanka also had an adverse South-Asian fallout. It confirmed her image as the 'regional bully' which was not adverse to forcing its will on small neighbours through arms. On the other hand, it was a matter of considerable national humiliation that the IPKF had to quit a neighbouring island in disgrace because it could not overpower a band of a few thousand militants.

Pakistan

Soon after Rajiv Gandhi took over as the Prime Minister, he said, 'For nation-building the first important requisite is peace, peace with its neighbours, peace with the world. And to achieve this objective, 'one cannot remain mired in the past, one must remain flexible.' It would be unfair to think that the Pakistan rulers were not animated by similar feelings. Yet, Indo-Pak relations have remained 'mired in the past,' a hostage to history. Zia-ul-Haq, President of Pakistan, died in an air crash on 17 August 1988. So, the first four years of Rajiv's prime ministership overlapped with Zia's rule in Pakistan. Rajiv met Zia for the first time when he came for Mrs. Gandhi's obsequies. But it was at Chernenko's funeral in Moscow in March 1985 that they could discuss matters of mutual import. Before that, Zia had sent positive signals by ordering the trial of Sikh militants who had hijacked an Indian aircraft in 1981. Subsequently, leaders of the two countries met thrice in New York, Dhaka and Delhi, and agreed to official-level discussions to finalize the draft of a mutual friendship treaty and sort out other differences.

These were all welcome, though symbolic gestures. They did not touch any of the substantive issues of mutual discord. As India-Sri Lanka relation's worsened, and Jayewardene started scouting for military assistance, Pakistan readily offered arms, training facilities and personnel. Zia had never stopped the liberal arms supply to the Sikh extremists in Punjab, or the infiltration of heavily armed saboteurs in the Kashmir Valley. And when India returned the compliment by helping the Sindhi insurgents across the Rajasthan borders, he felt outraged.

The most sterile of all the Indo-Pak conflicts is the confrontation on the Siachen glaciers lying on the Saltoro ridge-Karakoram range. Varying in height from 16,000-19,000 feet, this barren stretch of ice lies in a most inhospitable terrain. Troops of the two countries have clung on to the wilderness since 1983, despite an extremely heavy toll in terms of men, material and machines, and so far all attempts at mutual withdrawal of forces have failed.

Benazir Bhutto's election as Prime Minister of Pakistan on 2 December 1988 raised fresh hopes of an upturn in bilateral relation's between the two neighbours. During the SAARC meeting held in

Islamabad soon after Mrs. Bhutto's election, Rajiv and Benazir had three meetings and established an excellent working equation. During this visit, three bilateral agreements were signed, the best-known being a pledge not to attack each other's nuclear facilities. This was followed by an exchange of several high-level delegations, and agreements were signed to improve trade and cooperate in other fields of common interest.

Rajiv Gandhi paid his first official visit to Pakistan on 16-17 July 1989. This was the first such visit by an Indian prime minister in 30 years. A lot was expected of the Rajiv-Benazir meeting, but neither side had much elbow room for give and take. Benazir was eagerly looking for some gain on the Kashmir front. Rajiv could not go beyond the Simla Agreement.

Both Rajiv and Benazir had impeccable ancestry, had gone abroad for their studies, shared many perceptions and strove sincerely to improve bilateral relations. But so diverse were their national interests and compulsions, that they could hardly make a dent in the objective situation. No amount of atmospherics could cloak the ugly reality of Indo-Pak conflict over Kashmir and Siachen, Pakistan's nuclear programme, her support to the Sikh militants, fuelling of insurgency in Kashmir, and stockpiling of lethal arms with American help. For Pakistan there was the bitter historical legacy of defeat in three wars with India, and loss of half the country owing to India's military intervention in 1971. And then there was always the suspicion of India's hegemonistic designs in South Asia.

It is little wonder then that during the one year interlude of excellent personal relations between the prime ministers of India and Pakistan, very little progress could be made towards normalization.

Operation Brasstacks

In January 1987 India and Pakistan suddenly found themselves hurtling towards a war as a result of a routine military exercise, Brasstacks, undertaken by the Indian army. As this episode exposes the grave risks involved in a domineering General hijacking the democratic decision making process, it deserves to be described separately.

Here, the main actors were: the Prime Minister, who also held charge of the Defence portfolio; Arun Singh, minister of state for Defence, who was de facto Defence Minister; and General K. Sundarji, the Army Chief. Sundarji was a brilliant officer, very articulate and persuasive, with a flair for conceptualizing grand designs. He was also very assertive and ambitious, the type who may lose all sense of proportion if not kept on a tight leash.

The General was able to strike a close personal equation with his minister, Arun Singh, who was himself a very intelligent person of great integrity. But Arun was new to the Government and had insufficient understanding of the fine balance required to be maintained between the military and civilian authorities. And he was dazzled by the glamour of being surrounded and saluted by the three Defence Chiefs.

It was against this backdrop that General Sundarji proposed a large-scale military exercise to test the enhanced mobility of the army through mechanization of Infantry. Rajiv fully endorsed the proposal and phase I of this four-part exercise was staged in May-June 1986. The first two phases were paper exercises and the third phase, slated for November-December 1986, was planned as segmented exercises by different arms and services to support Divisional/Corps level offensive operations in a mobile battle-ground environment.[5] This phase was extended and converted into Operation Trident when troops were moved forward in January 1987 in view of a perceived threat from Pakistan.

Exercise Brasstacks was held in Rajasthan, close to the Pakistan border. Around this time, Pakistan was conducting her own military exercises, Saf-e-Shikan and Flying Horse. The former was scheduled to be completed in November and the latter in December 1986. Not only were these exercises extended, reserves were brought in, and some troops moved to strategic border locations. Pakistan claimed to have done this in view of the perceived threat from the Indian army.

Thus, in the third week of January 1987, a dangerous situation of confrontation between the armed forces of India and Pakistan

had arisen, and any ill-considered or provocative act of brinkman-
ship could have resulted in a full-scale war.

During the critical period of these developments, Rajiv was
holidaying in the Andamans. From there he went to Bangalore
before coming to Delhi. He was not kept informed of the developments on the Indo-Pak front. When he learnt about the
dangerous situation that was developing on the Rajasthan border,
he hit the roof. He told his close aide, Mani Shankar Aiyar,
"You see, these Johnnies had almost pushed us into war with
Pakistan."[6] Next day he repeated the same view to Natwar Singh.
It was his direct telephonic talk with President Zia which led to
the speedy de-escalation of confrontation and the likelihood of a
war was averted.

But even after Rajiv was seized of the matter, events moved in
a zigzag manner. On the one hand, N.D. Tiwari, Defence Minister,
asked the US ambassador to track down Pak troop movements
by satellite and supply six-hourly reports to him. Natwar
Singh, his minister of state, made a similar request to the Soviet
ambassador. Both sources confirmed that there were no war-like
movements by the Pakistani troops.[7] On the other hand, on 18
January, as the crisis was peaking, Gen. Sundarji held a briefing
for some editors where he highlighted the threatening moves by
the Pakistan army across the border. This was done at the direction of the PM. Predictably, next day the press raised a scare about
an impending Indo-Pak war. Two days later, on 20 January the
PM held a press conference at which he drew attention to the
concentration of Pakistani troops along the border. When his
attention was drawn to the statement of his Foreign Secretary,
A.P. Venkateswaran, about his proposed visit to Pakistan, he
sacked him on the spot and asserted that he had no such plans.

On 22 January the Cabinet Committee on Political Affairs was
briefed on the counter-measures being taken, and a massive airlift
of troops was started.[8] Next day there was a hurried round of
discussions at the diplomatic level, and Pakistan proposed urgent
talks for the removal of any misunderstanding. And thus started
the process of systematic de-escalation.

It is rather intriguing as to why India started playing up

Pakistan's aggressive designs when she was aware that this was not the case. The most plausible explanation of this contradictory behaviour is that after being caught on the wrong foot, India adopted a defensive offensive. She tried to show the world that the real provocation came from Pakistan, and India was only reacting to it. This was an inelegant ploy, as the evidence of satellite pictures was too conclusive to permit any fudging.

This is a very bald and superficial narration of facts. But the issues of real concern are some lesser-known developments which have a crucial import for the polity.

Every Monday morning the Defence Minister convened an internal meeting of the Defence Chiefs and top officials where matters of urgent concern to the ministry were discussed. At one of these meetings Gen. Sundarji propounded the thesis that in a situation of direct confrontation the exigencies of war may require that the army commander on the spot takes decisions which should normally be referred to the civilian authorities for clearance. At times such decisions are likely to have political implications.

This was a very dangerous proposition. If it was accepted, and an army commander was aware of the fact, a reckless adventurer could deliberately create such a situation and plunge the country in a war. It is a measure of the hold that the Army Chief had on Arun Singh that he did not object to this view, and the civilian officials also kept quiet.

Earlier, in September 1986, Gen. Sundarji had sketched another scary prospect in the army commanders meeting. He had said that owing to the worsening law and order situation in the country, the Army's involvement in maintaining civil peace had greatly increased. There may arise a situation when almost the whole country may face a breakdown of civil administration and this may require countrywide intervention by the armed forces. Consequently, he told the commanders, it would be necessary to prepare contingency plans for such an eventuality.

The implications of this approach were obvious. The Army Chief was perhaps in an unusually expansive mood when he unfolded this plan. But as luck would have it, the minutes of this

meeting got stolen by Pakistani agents. And when Rajiv met
Benazir Bhutto in Islamabad, she asked him whether he was
aware of his army's plans to stage a coup. She also showed him
a copy of the minutes of his army commanders' meeting. Rajiv
returned a much wiser and sadder man and ordered some secret
enquiries.[9]

Some knowledgeable persons contend that there was a 'hidden
agenda' in Brasstacks. It was not only the biggest exercise ever
staged by the Indian army, some aspects of the mobilization of
forces were awesome. Eleven Divisions and five independent
Brigades were pressed into service. Over a hundred long rakes
were commissioned to haul 2,400 tanks, heavy vehicles and field
guns across the country, from the Eastern Command to Rajasthan.
All this force was lined up along the 350-km long Indo-Pak border
in Rajasthan. All pilots and trainer pilots were withdrawn from
various academies and brought to the border. Live ammunition
was issued to forward formations. At the height of the tension,
the troops were so poised that a concerted forward push could
have separated Sindh from Pakistan and led to a second break up
of the country.

In case this scenario seems too fanciful one may recall
Sundarji's presentation to an extended meeting of the CCPA
towards the end of October 1986. The briefing took place in the
Operations Room and the Army Chief used an array of charts
and maps to make his point. The central issue of his thesis was
that India was then in a position to take on both China and
Pakistan simultaneously. Everybody, including the PM and other
CCPA members listened with rapt attention. K.P.S. Menon, the
Foreign Secretary, voiced mild disagreement. Then Natwar Singh,
who had recently been shifted to External Affairs, said that if India
pursued Sundarji's line and there was a setback on the north-
eastern or western front, the government would not be able to
survive. He further added that in the 1962 debacle of the India-
China war, Krishna Menon was made the sacrificial goat. If something similar happened now, who would be offered as a sacrifice?
This intervention had a salutary effect and the proceedings ended
on a tame note.[10]

It is unlikely that Sundarji ever seriously thought of staging a military coup. But he was certainly itching for a major war, preferably with China, as in his view China and not Pakistan was the real enemy of India. He had sketched several scenarios of 'no loss' and 'low loss' confrontation on the eastern front, and made many video presentations to explain his thesis.

Most dangerously, the General hankered after a war, not because he was convinced of its inevitability, but as it offered him the only path to personal glory and a niche in history. But he did not appreciate that for this to happen, history also must cooperate and provide a suitable opening. This it did in the case of Field Marshal Sam Manekshaw in the shape of the Bangladesh war, but refused to thus oblige Sundarji. In his effort to bend history to his will he hijacked the system and brought the country to the brink of a ruinous conflict.

The most frightening aspect of Brasstacks was the systemic failures that it highlighted. It was unfortunate for the PM to appoint his own friend as the minister of state for Defence and then permit him to function as a de facto Defence Minister. Arun Singh, despite his many fine qualities, was too raw for this sensitive job. And because of his personal equation with the PM, he took decisions on his own that he could not have taken under the rules.

Then, he got too close to the Defence Chiefs for the good of the system. This downgraded the civilian authority. The Defence Secretary used to be sent for by the Minister and was given specific instructions in the presence of Gen. Sundarji, without getting important issues examined from the civilian point of view.

Given the opportunity, everybody likes to lord it over, and the generals more than anybody else. It is a pity that in India it has become taboo to criticize the armed forces even on vital matters of national interest. This has not only distorted the civil-military perspective, but also enabled the defence forces to evade parliamentary scrutiny and get away with colossal waste.

Rajiv's personalized style of governance inevitably lowered the importance of institutions and, at times, resulted in avoidable lapses. When Pakistan's Prime Minister M.K. Junejo met Rajiv Gandhi in November 1986 at Bangalore for the SAARC meet, he referred to the apprehensions raised by the size and location of Exercise Brasstacks. Rajiv assured him that the exercise would be scaled down. But nothing of the sort happened. It is not even known if such instructions were passed on to the concerned authorities.[11]

Important defence matters require extensive consultations and coordination. Constant liaison with ministries of Foreign Affairs and Home is imperative. In this case even the Ministry of Defence hardly knew as to what was happening. When Gen. Sundarji briefed the press of 18th January and there were screaming head-lines in the papers the next day about Pakistan's warlike designs, the Foreign Secretary, A.P. Venkateswaran, was taken by surprise and enquired from Sundarji as to what the hullabaloo was about. Sundarji said that he had himself briefed the press, and that it was done at the PM's instance. But when Venkateswaran asked as to why his ministry was not taken into confidence, Sundarji replied that the External Affairs Minister was present at the meet-ing when the decision was taken. But the Foreign Minister was in Kathmandu at that time, pointed out the Foreign Secretary. Then it transpired that Shiv Shankar, who was earlier the Foreign Minister and was then shifted to Commerce Ministry in October 1986, happened to be present at the meeting. And though he had been replaced by N.D. Tiwari three months back, Sundarji thought that Shiv Shankar was still the Foreign Minister.[12]

The fact is that all the Brasstacks related decisions (were) being taken by the minister of state and the Chiefs of Staff Committee.[13] Again, owing to the perceived clout of Arun Singh, none of the ministers extending logistic support raised questions about the impact of cancelling and diverting hundreds of trains, or disloca-tion of air traffic. Nor did anybody dare question the colossal financial and economic implications of such a huge exercise.

Summing up

Following the example of his grandfather, Rajiv enlarged the vistas on India's foreign policy, took a keen interest in global issues, and introduced an element of moral concern in dealing with international problems. His vigorous advocacy of Namibian freedom, direct involvement in settling the Kampuchean dispute, and strong condemnation of apartheid practised by South Africa produced wholesome results. He gave a fresh impetus to the Non-aligned Movement by making it the champion for nuclear disarmament. His 'Nuclear-free World Plan', presented to the UN in 1988, still ranks as the most comprehensive and constructive document on the subject. In view of the increasing importance of economic issues in international politics, he tried to forge the G-15 — a more compact group of the non-aligned as compared to the unwieldy G-77 — on the lines of the G-7 of industrialized countries.

Though Rajiv Gandhi covered a vast area of international relations, he had no clear-cut foreign policy or world view. He had a flair for the subject, a striking presence, and a strong motivation to achieve concrete results.

Whereas Rajiv was quick to grasp any new opening and wanted speedy processing of the proposal, he spent hours and days on vetting his speeches and drafts. His fastidiousness on this point was a bit misplaced. A head of government's time has to be rationed tightly, and speech writing and drafting has to be left to the staff. This may not produce very satisfying results, but in such matters the top executive has to learn to accept the second best.

Rajiv not only bypassed procedures and cut through red-tape to achieve quick results, he also tended to ignore institutional requirements. During his time the ministry of External Affairs got marginalized, as it was not kept in the picture even about important matters. Both in respect of Brasstacks and Samdurong, confrontation with Pakistan and China reached a crisis point, and the Foreign Ministry was hardly aware of it. Then he deputed his personal aides on sensitive diplomatic assignments, instead of relying on professional diplomats. Gopi Arora was sent to Afghanistan and the USSR on delicate missions. He was an outstanding officer, but he belonged to the IAS. The Foreign Ministry naturally felt downgraded at this approach.

Perhaps Rajiv's greatest regret would have been his inability to mend fences with his immediate neighbours. India's relations with Sri Lanka, Bangladesh, Nepal and Pakistan deteriorated in varying degrees during his tenure. Partly it was due to the big brother's inability to shake hands with the 'small brothers' by descending to their level.

42

Making of a Leader

It was not Rajiv Gandhi's fault that he became Prime Minister of India without serving a proper apprenticeship. In fact his induction into politics had nothing to do with his aptitude for this calling. Nor was he associated with the decision to instal him as the head of government on his mother's assassination.

But when he was sworn in as the PM there was not only a sense of relief, but also of hope and cheer. The known facts about him pointed to a basically well-meaning and decent person, with a keen sense of propriety. It was widely known that he was opposed to the Emergency, objected to Sanjay's cremation close to Nehru's Samadhi, managed to expel Dhirendra Brahmachari from his mother's charmed circle, and disapproved of the likes of Antulay, Gundu Rao and Bhajan Lal. When he removed R.K. Dhawan on assumption of office, a clear message went out that the days of the fixers and manipulators were over.

As if Rajiv's inadequacies for the job were not enough of a handicap, he became the victim of a seductive illusion unwittingly created by the media. It was extensively commented that his unprecedented electoral victory reflected the people's urge for change, for distancing from the old-style politics, and for the freshness of youth. In fact the Indian electorate is not in the least bothered about such fanciful notions. It has been duped often enough by its leaders to expect the moon from them. The voters' concerns are much more mundane and immediate. A modest improvement in their living conditions and a slightly more responsive administration was all that they expected from a new ruler. The desire for change was a projection of the aspirations of the middle class for a greater say in national affairs. But the media appraisal was in full accord with Rajiv's own perceptions, and he accepted it as his basic mandate.

Rajiv's peer group, with its roots in corporate culture, felt greatly excited at the prospect of recreating India after its heart's desire. The phrase that his closest friend, Arun Singh, often used in this connection was 'breaking the mould'.

Being new to the job, the Prime Minister came to rely heavily on the advice and assistance of his two closest friends, Arun Nehru and Arun Singh. Though they too were equally new, Arun Nehru had a much stronger personality, whereas Arun Singh was more cerebral and articulate. Arun Singh attracted public notice much earlier, as he sat with the Prime Minister in most of the meetings. Not unoften he took a leading part in discussions and impressed everybody by his perspicacity and quick grasp. Initially perceived at Rajiv's alter ego, he was seen emerging as the surrogate prime minister. The third person on whom Rajiv relied was V.P. Singh, his Finance Minister, whom he expected to liberalize the economy and clean up the business environment. Singh's first budget was exceedingly well received and the PM got kudos from all quarters. In fact this was the first tangible evidence of Rajiv's desire to change the system.

During the first six months of his term, as Rajiv learned the ropes, he earned a lot of credits in the bargain. And then came his historic visit to the USA in June 1985, his warm reception at the White House by President Reagan, his repeatedly applauded address to the Joint Session of the two Houses, and his scintillating performance at the National Press Club. It had a magical effect on the self-image of the man. These were all solo performances, unprompted by any aide. All these events were televised live by Doordarshan, and some media analysts felt that Rajiv would soon outshine his illustrious grandfather.

The two Aruns were among the first to perceive the difference. Rajiv had started behaving more like a boss and there was a touch of arrogance in his demeanour. Arun Nehru is emphatic that after his American visit, Rajiv was a changed man. He not only felt that he could manage without the advice of his two friends, but also came to believe that "whatever mummy could do, I can do better."[1]

And this newly acquired self-confidence was reinforced by the remarkable Punjab and Assam accords which he signed within two months of his glorious American tour. Mrs. Gandhi had fumbled and faltered for years without making much headway in either case. And here was he, doing the job in a jiffy, and without a flutter. The gods were smiling on him, and he began to perceive himself as an unmatched peace-maker.

Rajiv was obviously growing fast. Both his friends were themselves also growing with the job. It was one thing to be an executive in a medium-sized company, and another to guide the destiny of a nation.The change-over was a heady experience, exceedingly gratifying. As Rajiv Gandhi later said in an interview, "The thing is that authority does all sorts of things (to people)."[2]

Rajiv first gave a definite indication of his desire to discard his crutches when he shifted Arun Singh from the PMO and appointed him as Minister of State for Defence Research and Organization. Sometime later when Nehru got a heart attack and was convalescing in Srinagar, the more sensitive items of his charge were transferred to P. Chidambaram. Later, in the cabinet reshuffle of October 1986 he was dropped from the cabinet.

Arun Singh seemed to be doing well in Defence till Rajiv realized that he was not able to keep a balance between the civilian and the military wings of his ministry. The crunch came when the country almost went to war with Pakistan as a result of the army exercise, Brasstacks, getting almost out of hand. Consequently Rajiv shifted V.P. Singh from Finance to Defence on 24 January 1987 when the Brasstacks crisis reached its peak. With this development, Arun Singh's wings were clipped and the message went home to all concerned. Estrangement between the two friends had actually started around the middle of 1986 when the PM began dealing directly with the ministry's officials. Arun was not always careful to brief the PM, who was also the Defence Minister. No boss would relish such a situation.

But, perhaps, what annoyed the PM the most was his arm-twisting the Bofors management to extract names of kickback beneficiaries. Arun Singh fully realized his friend's sensitivity on this issue only when on 4 July 1987 Rajiv countermanded his decision to summon the Bofors team for interrogation. Estrangement between the two friends had reached a point where Arun Singh could not even get an appointment with Rajiv for weeks. The rebuff of 4 July was a clincher. After several attempts, Arun got to see his friend and submitted his resignation after a longish meeting which failed to clear the air.

The rupture with V.P. Singh was a more direct affair. Rajiv believed that Singh was conspiring to replace him, and Singh realized that it was not in his interest to continue in the government. So he put in his papers on 12 April 1987.

Thus came to an end Rajiv Gandhi's association with his three ace advisers, as also the most productive phase of his regime. Subsequently Rajiv admitted that it was wrong to have key advisers.[3] But these advisers had served him well. And they were the only ones who could tell him unpleasant truths for his own good. Nehru repeatedly advised Rajiv that his honeymoon with the people was over and concrete steps should be taken to redeem the election promises. He warned him against being too rough with the officers and writing sarcastic notes on the files.[4] He opposed Sonia Gandhi's wish to receive the Pope when he alighted at the Delhi airport, as she would have to kneel on the tarmac in full public view to kiss his ring. Arun Singh supported this view, as the Indian people would not have liked it.[5] He also joined V.P. Singh in opposing the award of the HBJ pipeline contract to Snam Progetti, as this act of favouritism would have damaged Rajiv's reputation. As he was in charge of PM's appointments, he kept protesting against his tendency to keep changing the schedule all the time.

This situation partly resulted from Rajiv's inability to control his information channels. When he became the PM, the old guard could not relate to him. To make matters worse, there were the two Aruns who stood as gatekeepers between them and their leader. So, they preferred to wait and watch, and cautiously tried and tested various approach routes to him. And they started their little intrigues, rumour mongering, planting a story here and a canard there. The main thrust of their strategy was that the PM's advisers had become very ambitious, and were creatng their own lobbies and cabals to replace him one day.

Owing to his high visibility and bluster, Arun Nehru became their first target. They tasted blood with his exit. And this was followed in due course by the departure of V.P. Singh and Arun Singh. All the three were fully aware as to what was going on behind their back and they used to joke about it. But there never arose an opportunity to set the record straight.

The exit of the trio was a matter of great satisfaction to the politicians around Rajiv. Now they were assured that their leader was not only gullible but also easily manipulatable. This had a major impact on the course of future events.

This development marks a watershed in Rajiv's political evolution. His horizon started narrowing, and he talked less and less of the transformation he wanted to bring about. Deregulation and liberalization ceased to be major concerns. Glowing references to computers, high technology and the 21st century became a thing of the past. It would be wrong to link these changes directly to the departure of the two Aruns and V.P. Singh. But the fact remains that this episode did lower his zest for change, and seriously cramped his political style and options.

At this stage, two outside events intervened with disastrous effect. One was the Bofors scandal and, two, the PM's confrontation with the President.

Rajiv was wholly a creature of accidents. The first accident pushed him into politics and the second one made him the Prime Minister. The Bofors episode, which irreparably damaged his credibility and plagued him throughout his tenure, was again a pure accident. The Swedish Radio team was actually investigating Bofors' illegal supply of arms to West Asian countries, and the Indian deal turned up just accidentally. But like the earlier accidents, it had a decisive import for Rajiv. Mauled by one revelation after another, it left him a bitter and frustrated man.

The other episode was no accident. The manner in which he provoked a quarrel with Giani Zail Singh, the President, over trivial issues of protocol and prestige, not only underlined his political immaturity, but also that streak of obstinacy and arrogance which surfaced ever so often in his career.

It had been a convention for the prime ministers to regularly brief the President on weighty affairs of state and the outcome of important foreign visits. Rajiv not only discontinued this practice but publicly claimed credit for having broken several conventions. The Giani was not consulted before signing the Punjab, Assam and Mizoram accords. The government also did not clear most of the proposals for the President's foreign visits. One Congress minister openly charged him with harbouring terrorists in Rashtrapati Bhawan. Cabinet ministers stopped calling on the Giani and the Congress-ruled states were discouraged from inviting him. I was specifically told that he was getting excessive exposure on Doordarshan.

The President ignored these pinpricks for some time, and then started showing his annoyance openly. He refused to sign the Indian Post Office (Amendment) Bill 1986 and raised several queries. He objected to various clauses of the Mizoram agreement. He pulled up Kumudben Joshi, Governor Andhra Pradesh, and Ram Dulari Sinha, Governor Kerala, for taking undue interest in state politics.

As differences between Rajiv and the Giani became public knowledge, Madhu Dandavate, MP, charged the PM of violating article 78 of the Consititution by not furnishing information asked for by the President. Rajiv refuted this charge. As this was factually incorrect, Zail Singh rebutted Rajiv's claim in a letter written the very next day. As this letter was also leaked to a national daily, it raised a storm and there were demands to discuss it in the parliament.

The opposition parties saw a great opportunity in this confrontation, and started advising the Giani to dismiss Rajiv on charges of corruption. The fact that the President's term was expiring in July 1987, gave a sharper edge to this controversy. The bait of a second term was dangled before Zail Singh as a quid pro quo.

This was a bizarre scenario, and the President was careful not to indulge in adventurism. He stipulated that as V.P. Singh was the only credible alternative to Rajiv Gandhi, he must agree to become the new PM. Singh refused to accept this proposition. Secondly, the CPI(M) also dissociated itself from such a murky plot. In view of these developments, Zail Singh, the shrewd politician that he was, advised his supporters that the legitimate arena for this battle was the floor of the House. Rajiv also adopted a more conciliatory approach, and the storm soon blew over with the election of R. Venkataraman as the new President on 15 July 1987.

Having burnt his fingers once, Rajiv was careful to have no 'key' advisers. But advisers are a necessary evil for a head of government, and their number multiplied after the exit of the three principal counsellors.

Rajiv Gandhi's new advisers, coming from diverse backgrounds, may be bunched into three or four categories. First, there was a small group of elders like Uma Shankar Dixit, P.V. Narasimha Rao and N.D. Tiwari, who had vast experience of the party and government and gave sober, dependable counsel. Owing to the generational gap, the PM had no emotional affinity with them, and none of them got very close to him. Then, there was a sizeable group of new entrants, both politicians and professionals. Chidambaram, Rajesh Pilot, Sam Pitroda, Ghulam Nabi Azad, Natwar Singh, Mani Shanker Aiyer — all belonged to this category. Whereas Pilot and Azad were earthy, grass roots level politicians, the others had a much greater cultural rapport with the PM. Natwar and Mani played a major role in shaping Rajiv's foreign policy, and Pitroda had a decisive influence in matters concerning technology.

The third group comprised the practitioners of realpolitik. They were: Arjun Singh, Buta Singh, Shiv Shankar, Fotedar and Sitaram Kesri. The first two were masters of the art of political manipulation, and the third one was treated as a legal wizard by the PM. Fotedar and Kesri, despite the initial setback, were political jugglers and master fixers. Their stock steadily rose as the PM came to rely more and more on their resourcefulness.

Satish Sharma and Amitabh Bachchan were the only two

friends of Rajiv who survived all vicissitudes and retained his full trust. They were often used as sounding boards on a variety of issues, and Satish resigned his airlines job to become his friend's full-time aide.

Naturally, Rajiv's estimation of his advisers kept changing in view of their performance, and there were frequent exits and entries. Political management and disaster control were areas of greatest concern to the PM, and here he relied the most on Buta Singh, Arjun Singh, Shiv Shankar and Fotedar. These politicians placed a high premium on manipulation, guile and chicanery. This not only lowered the level of political discourse, it inevitably got them into trouble once in a while. What is worse, it hurt the moral standing of the Prime Minister.

For instance Shiv Shankar was Rajiv's main legal adviser on Fairfax and the Bofors scandals. He relied excessively on legal quibbling and technical ploys to refute the charges. This confirmed the general impression that the PM was trying to hide the truth and shield the guilty by weaving a web of lies. Then he overreached himself in sponsoring the Defamation Bill, bringing odium on himself and his master. Again it was he who managed to set up the pliable Thakkar Commission to fix R.K. Dhawan, and the Thakkar-Natarajan Commission to give adverse findings against V.P. Singh and his officers in the Fairfax case.

Buta Singh played a crucial role in preventing Giani Zail Singh from taking any rash action against Rajiv. He turned one of Giani's most trusted advisers into a mole and worked through him to brainwash the President. He was also instrumental in recommending the dismissal of the Barnala government in Punjab, which greatly intensified the terrorist activity in the state. He played a major role in arranging *shilanyas* of Ramjanambhoomi temple which alienated the Muslim community on the eve of the general election.

In the beginning Rajiv had impressed everybody with his openness and transparency. After some time he started his own little games of intrigue and deception. Arun Nehru said in an interview that "Rajiv told Sharad Pawar, 'Arun did not want you, I wanted you...' He told newspaper editors that Arun Singh is inefficient.

He told me, 'Be careful of Arun Singh' (in Hindi). He told Farooq that he is removing Mufti Mohammad Sayeed. He told Mufti that he is removing Farooq."[6] Whereas Arun Nehru's charges against his estranged cousin should be normally taken with a pinch of salt, this interview was published when Rajiv was still the PM, and he could have very well refuted the accusations if they were untrue.

After the exit of his three principal advisers, Rajiv was ringed around by sycophants and yes men. This was particularly dangerous in the case of a person who himself did not have a strong political instinct. Indira Gandhi too had plenty of advisers, and she changed them faster than he did. But after consulting them, she quietly pondered over their advice and then exercised her own independent judgement. By comparison, Rajiv suffered from two handicaps. His knowledge base about the country's problems and the party organization was much smaller. And he was always in a great hurry. Lacking his mother's critical faculties, he was prone to accept in toto the advice he received. At the same time there was also the tendency to change his mind too readily.

As Arun Nehru observed, "He changes his mind every day. One thing today another tomorrow (in Hindi)... at nine he says something, at 12 he says something, at 3 he says something and at 6 he says something else."[7] This is a trait to which most people who worked with him can bear witness.

These two seemingly contrary tendencies of taking quick decisions on the advice of his counsellors and changing his mind all the time are, in fact, two sides of the same coin: they reveal a flabby mind whose opinions and beliefs had no firm anchorage.

Only in a revolutionary struggle can a leader uphold his ideals untarnished. But the harsh realities of politics and governance can force even the most intrepid of visionaries to make compromises and forsake cherished goals. The tragedy of Rajiv Gandhi is not that he failed to redeem his earlier promises, but that he ended up by aligning with the same forces that he had vowed to fight against.

The main items on his original agenda were: liberalization and deregulation of the economy; streamlining the public sector; liberating the Congress party from the clutches of power brokers; holding organizational elections; injecting a heavy dose of technology into the system so that India marches proudly into the 21st century; giving the people a cleaner government that 'works faster'; replacing the politics of confrontation by a policy of accommodation, and bringing about "a new atmosphere of cooperation and friendship in South Asia."

These were not very radical concepts. Practically all his predecessors had expressed more or less similar sentiments. What made these promises catch the nation's imagination was the refreshing air of candour, emphasis and earnestness with which they were made.

And what does one find at the end of Mr. Gandhi's term? The budget of 1988-89 had put paid to the liberalization drive; public sector continued to be as sluggish as ever; Congress organizational elections were never held; import of technology slackened when the liberalization policy got a setback; the PM stopped talking about the 21st century altogether; the government did not work faster and, instead of a cleaner administration, corruption got a further boost owing to the kickback scandals; the politics of accommodation did not flourish and confrontation with the opposition parties frequently paralysed the parliamentry proceedings; and in South Asia India's relations with Pakistan, Sri Lanka, Bangladesh and Nepal worsened in varying degrees.

When he became Prime Minister, he threw out R.K. Dhawan, did not let Pranab Mukherjee come near him, treated A.R. Antulay and Gundu Rao as lepers, and kept Jagannath Mishra and Bhajan Lal at arm's length. But gradually, one after the other, all these 'undesirables' trooped back to his camp, and some of them got quite close to him. The most symptomatic of this turn-around was the re-appointment of R.K. Dhawan as officer on special duty in early 1989. The irony of the situation was that Dhawan, in his new avatar, wielded much greater power than he ever did under Indira Gandhi. During her time he was a server; now he came as a saviour.

After Rajiv joined politics in 1981, he had a long and intimate chat with Rajiv Desai, a US-based columnist and a friend. When Desai asked him about his vision of India, he replied that they had to keep their party together. On being prodded, Gandhi was quick to admit "he did not know or had not thought of things." Desai told him, "You cannot be a great-grandson of Motilal and the grandson of Jawaharlal and the son of Indira ... if you had not thought about India. Your entire family had practically given itself to India, so how can you not have a vision?" When pushed further, Rajiv Gandhi stated that "... the whole issue was the passivity of our people. Our people are very content. He said what we have to attack is the passivity of the people who do not realise they have to generate something for others. They are satisfied with themselves." Desai's laconic reaction was, "I was so completely bowled over."[8] In fairness to Gandhi it must be said that at the time of this interview he had hardly any exposure to politics. But for a person of 37 who grew up in the house of the person who wrote *The Discovery of India*, and whose grandfather and mother lived and breathed India, this level of innocence and naïvety was breathtaking.

It is this absence of a coherent world-view and ideological orientation that explains the composition of Rajiv's package of reforms which he unfolded on becoming Prime Minister. It was an assortment of well-meaning, forward-looking and beneficial measures which did not fit into a cohesive policy frame. But even these measures would have done the country a lot of good if they had been firmly implemented in a systematic manner.

Here Rajiv suffered from three handicaps. First, he failed to create the instrumentalities for the realization of his programme. The institutions he inherited were thoroughly discredited. Instead of restoring these to health, he turned them into tools for fulfilling his own designs. The CBI was completely disgraced in the process of covering up the kickback seandals. Judiciary was harmed when commissions headed by pliant Supreme Court Judges were used to fix opponents.

Secondly, he not only failed to establish linkages with the groups likely to gain from his reforms, he even alienated the traditional Congress vote banks like the minorities, Scheduled

Castes and Scheduled Tribes.

Thirdly, he did not have the perseverance and grit of a successful national leader who could produce results even in the face of heavy odds. His liberalization programme, the most ambitious item on his agenda, he gave up at the first sign of opposition from within his party. The next Congress government under P.V. Narasimha Rao managed to push it through despite a precarious majority in the parliament.

Paradoxical though it may seem, Rajiv was seriously handicapped by his advantages. He became PM because of his lineage. But that also exposed him to continuous comparison with his grandfather and mother. He had the advantage of starting with a clean slate, but that implied lack of experience. He was young and people expected a new style of politics from him. But this led him to alienate the old guard. He was forward-looking and talked of the 21st century. This laid him open to the charge of being cut off from the Indian reality. He assiduously cultivated the image of Mr. Clean; this made every little spot of dirt on his spotless *khadi kurta* stand out as an ugly blot.

Also, most of the forces that plagued his tenure were released during his mother's time. Institutional decay, emasculation of the Congress party, confrontationist politics — all materialized during Indira's regime.

Rajiv was also exceptionally unlucky in the number of stinking kickback scandals he had to face. Commissions on large foreign deals had been gathered earlier also, but the skeletons did not tumble out the way they did during his time. What is really tragic is that although there was no proof of his direct involvement in a single case, his exceedingly inept handling needlessly made him their focal point. These scandals hit him really hard. His self-assured bounce was soon gone, his clean image badly soiled, and his credibility impaired even in the eyes of his partymen.

If we move away from the specifics and view the Rajiv era in the larger historical context, two issues merit attention. One, the Congress defeat in a series of assembly elections which greatly dampened the PM's spirits and lowered his standing within the party. But actually, this was the unfolding of a process long delayed by some exceptional circumstances. India was too vast and diverse a country to have a single-party rule both at the centre and the states. But the towering personalities of Jawaharlal Nehru and Indira Gandhi just froze this process, as they felt that this trend would imperil national unity. The first tremors of change were felt in 1967 when the Congress lost the assembly elections in a number of major states, and ill-assorted coalitions formed ministries. This happened as Mrs. Gandhi's position became shaky within her own party.

The next phase of this process of federalization was resumed during Rajiv Gandhi's tenure and has continued unabated since then. There are two reasons for this phenomenon. One, after Indira Gandhi, no charismatic leader of high stature emerged to hold back the regional forces. Two, with the spread of democratic culture and decline of the Congress, various national and state-level parties had acquired sufficient clout to assert themselves against the ruling party at the Centre. Thus, the main reason for the Congress defeat in assembly elections was not so much Rajiv's incompetence as the unfreezing of a long delayed political process.

The second issue concerns the steady decline in the quality of national leadership. If one compares the forties to the eighties, you have Rajiv Gandhi in place of Mahatma Gandhi, Sardar Buta Singh in the seat of Sardar Vallabhbhai Patel, and Ghulam Nabi Azad instead of Maulana Abul Kalam Azad as the tallest Congress Muslim leader. But this decline has not resulted from a sudden plunge. Nehru of the forties had considerably shrunk in size by the time he left the scene. Indira Gandhi not only lacked her father's stature and vision; after 1971 hers was a continuous downhill slide.

The diminution in the stature of leaders was accompanied by exponential aggravation of the rapidly mounting national problems. India's greatest achievements, that is, economic development and empowerment of the people, released forces of self-assertion, conflict and discord which have made governance of the country an almost impossible task.

The problem with tracing the trajectory of Rajiv Gandhi's growth as a leader is that after the initial surge, resulting mainly from his first budget and the two fragile accords, one hits a plateau as troubles suddenly start pouring in one after the other. The last three years of Rajiv's term show practically no signs of growth. Actually there is retreat on several important fronts. As time passed, his original élan and optimism ebbed away; he became peevish, bitter and cynical, and lost his capacity to trust and inspire trust. He ended up wooing the power brokers he once so despised, and insincerely mouthed tired cliches about his commitment to socialism and the growth of the public sector.

So oppressive and debilitating is the ambience of Indian politics that it diminished Nehru, it diminished Indira Gandhi, and it diminished Rajiv Gandhi the most. But whereas Nehru and Indira diminished with advancing years, Rajiv did so in mid-life.

43

Political Management

As Congress president, Rajiv Gandhi had his agenda clearly defined: to cleanse the party, and to democratise it. His speech at the Congress Centenary Celebrations at Bombay on 28 December 1985 contains the most scathing expose of the ills afflicting the party. Adopting a Savonarolian posture, he exhorted:

> Millions of ordinary Congress workers throughout the country are full of enthusiasm for the Congress policies and programmes. But they are handicapped, for on their backs ride the brokers of power and influence, who dispense patronage to convert a mass movement into a feudal oligarchy ... they are reducing the Congress organisation to a shell from which spirit of service and sacrifice has been emptied... We talk of high principles and lofty ideals needed to build a strong and prosperous India. But we obey no discipline, no rule, follow no principle of public morality, display no sense of social awareness, show no concern for public weal. Corruption is not only tolerated but considered a hallmark of leadership.

This speech was an instant hit with the media, and the middle-class intelligentsia lapped up every word of it. Rajiv's stock as Mr. Clean shot up a dozen notches. But only a non-political leader could have delivered such a speech. It was the right speech by the right person on the wrong occasion. The Indian National Congress had been a great organization with a glorious past. Its centenary celebrations were a time of coming together, of nostalgically recalling its magnificent deeds, of sober stock-taking and making resolves to 'revive the old spirit of service and sacrifice.' But this searing indictment left the traditional leadership floundering. They felt that the new generation had no use for them; that their leader spoke the language of an outsider.

A break from the past was evident everywhere. The Gandhi cap was nowhere in evidence, *khadi* was no longer the 'livery of freedom,' the leaders stayed in air-conditioned comfort of five-star hotels, away from the sweating and grubby delegates who created mayhem owing to the lack of basic facilities.

Rajiv was convinced that the Congress could be revived at the grass roots only if organizational elections were held. And he made sincere efforts to do this. When he was the Congress general secretary his colleague, G.K. Moopanar declared on 6 October 1982, "party elections will be completed by 20 January 1983." After becoming the Congress president he announced on 5 May 1985, "We have taken steps to complete elections before the AICC(I) session in December, 1985." At the centenary session in Bombay the CWC Resolution desired "Elections to be held by July 1986." Then, after another postponement on 28 September, Moopanar stated, "Organisational elections due in October 1986 have been put off by a few months." Advisedly, no specific date was mentioned this time.

Rajiv continued his efforts to hold elections during this period. On 19 January 1986 he declared at a specially convened press meeting that he proposed to make the party supreme vis-a-vis the government. He said that he was appointing Arjun Singh as Congress vice-president to perform such duties as "assigned by me." Actually his brief was to hold party elections.

As the membership drive prior to elections picked up and party leaders at various levels became active, Rajiv started receiving reports that a large number of bogus members were being enrolled. The senior party bosses were masters of the manipulation game. Rajiv apprehended that if elections were held under these conditions, the old guard sidelined by him may come to control the party machine and ultimately pose a challenge to his authority.

Reports had also been pouring in that the cadres were not happy with his style of working. A Congressman hangs on to his leader's coat-tails only so long as he wins the elections for him. But a string of reverses in the assembly polls had tarnished the leader's image. Rajiv's fears of a simmering revolt against him were further confirmed when the mild-tempered Kamalapati Tripathi, working president of the party, wrote him a letter in

May 1986 stating, "Congressmen are puzzled and bewildered at the rapid disintegration of the party at all levels and shocked at the casual, ad hoc and inept handling of party matters by you and your so-called operators." This letter was duly leaked to the press and caused much embarrassment to Rajiv.

Assailed by all these misgivings, Rajiv Gandhi reluctantly · threw in the sponge and stopped talking about the organizational elections. In fairness to him it should be conceded that holding of party polls is a very complex and difficult enterprise. A situation where anybody may enrol anybody as a member, the threat of bogus members becomes formidable. After all, Indira Gandhi had also tried to hold such elections in 1972, but abandoned the attempt half-way through. And never again did she make another effort. But, on the other hand, the gains from having elected bodies at all levels were so colossal that Rajiv should have persisted with his resolve and gone through the ordeal. The entire leadership of the party was so thoroughly discredited that none could have mustered courage to challenge him openly.

Even if organizational elections had been held, it is not certain that they would have led to party democracy. After all, there are elected parliament and elected state legislatures and yet the system is highly centralized. Rajiv's style of working was very individualistic. He seldom processed major policy issues and decisions through the normal channels and had a penchant for springing surprises. Though he was the Congress president, he seldom visited the party headquarters. Interaction between him and his general secretaries was minimal. On an average, he changed four to five general secretaries every year.

In the much more serious matter of nominating candidates for the state and parliamentary elections, Rajiv bypassed the party apparatus. In the selection of candidates for various by-elections in 1985, the Congress Parliamentary Board was asked to recommend candidates. But the actual selection was made by the two Aruns. To add insult to injury, the Board was not even intimated about the final outcome.

Then, out of the blue, Rajiv's telecom adviser Sam Pitroda

prepared a grand 'Bharat Bachao' plan which the PM accepted without discussion in any party forum. As a follow up, workshops and seminars were held to indoctrinate the party workers. The exercise was organized on the pattern of a reorientation course for middle-level corporate managers. The plan was killed by ridicule.

Nothing beats the suddenness of Rajiv's decision to go in for an early general election. Just back from a tour of the south, he convened a meeting of the 5-member Cabinet Committee on Political Affairs on the morning of 17 October 1989, and made the cryptic announcement, 'I am ready for the polls.' None demurred; only some procedural issues were discussed. Then, he walked into the adjoining room where his cabinet was waiting and declared, 'We have decided to go to the polls.' Just like that! There were no prior consultations with cabinet colleagues, or the CWC, or the party leaders.

Rajiv Gandhi's authority within his party was weakened by two factors. First, a chain of electoral defeats, starting from assembly polls in early 1985 to the disastrous debacle in the Tamil Nadu state election in early 1989. Second, his style of party management which was not designed to win friends. He kept aloof from the party workers, made even CMs wait for days and weeks before granting an appointment, and could not establish a rapport with the senior leaders. Despite all the promises to reform the party, he did not have much to show by way of results. Organizational elections were not held, and except for lowering the voting age from 21 to 18 years, no electoral reforms were introduced. The much talked of code of conduct for Congressmen could not be framed and the 'one man one post' principle was not enforced. Not only did he himself continue to hold two top posts, the PCC chiefs of such important non-Congress-ruled states as Karnataka, Andhra Pradesh and West Bengal simultaneously held ministerial posts at the Centre.

This weakening of the supremo's hold encouraged internal dissidence and factionalism in the states. It was by no means a new phenomenon. Indira used to promote it herself to discourage the emergence of strong regional leaders. But Rajiv lacked both her adroitness and clout. Thus, whereas during Indira's time dissidence was a controlled and well-directed activity, with Rajiv it tended to get out of hand. As early as mid-1986 a number of Congress CMs and state party chiefs were facing strong dissidence from within. The UP CM, Bir Bahadur Singh, a protégé of Arun Nehru, was battling his patron's opponents. In Madhya Pradesh, the two old rivals, V.C. Shukla and P.C. Sethi, had come together and launched a joint campaign against Arjun Singh, the CM. In Rajasthan the former CM, S.C. Mathur was gunning for Hardeo Joshi, the current incumbent. In Bihar, the former CM Jagannath Mishra was scheming to depose Chief Minister Bindeshwari Dubey. In Karnataka, Kerala and West Bengal, the so-called 'Indira loyalists' were fighting the 'Rajiv loyalists'. And in all these battles there was no evidence of any effective intervention by the Congress president.

There were several cases of party bosses openly disapproving of Rajiv's management of party affairs. A letter written by 10 MPs on 20 July 1988 went so far as to suggest some form of collective leadership to mend matters. But it was the open revolt by the MLAs of Madhya Pradesh and Bihar assemblies in the beginning of 1988 which marked the nadir of the PM's prestige. Rajiv asked Arjun Singh to step down from office as a result of an adverse High Court judgement, and wanted Madhav Rao Scindia to be elected in his place. Although Arjun Singh agreed to resign, he also fomented a revolt by the Congress MLAs against the High Command's orders. Central observers, including Buta Singh, were sent to oversee the election. They were abused, booed and manhandled, and ultimately Madhav Rao, PM's nominee, had to retreat and Moti Lal Vora was installed as the compromise chief minister.

Around the same time, the Governor of Bihar and the assembly speaker were asked to resign for promoting dissidence against the CM. The Governor stepped down but the speaker defied the High Command's order. More serious was the revolt by the Congress MLAs against their Chief Minister, Bhagvad Jha Azad, whom Rajiv had hand-picked for the job. Again, the Central

mediators were roughed up and not allowed to address the
MLAs. Things calmed down only when Fotedar intervened and
Bindeshwari Dubey, the former chief minister, assured the MLAs
of Azad's early exit without authorisation from above.

This sort of dissidence, at times verging on open defiance of
the party president's authority, was a new and ominous development. Rajiv Gandhi initiated several measures to curb this
menace, but his approach remained essentially piecemeal. His
mother had faced much bigger threats to her authority in her
earlier years as PM. But she had devised a definite strategy and
pursued it for over three years. At the end of the day the Syndicate
was completely routed and she was able to fashion the sort of
party she wanted. Her son had neither the talent nor the perseverance for this sort of campaign.

A fresh initiative to re-activate the party was taken when it was
decided in April 1987 to aggresively counter the opposition
onslaught about corruption and kickbacks in Defence deals.
Demonstrations were to be organized and public meetings and
rallies held to inform the people that all this campaign of calumny
was part of a well-laid conspiracy by the imperialist powers to
destablize the government. Party men were also advised to 'talk
freely about V.P. Singh.' The Youth Congress was revamped to
spearhead field campaigns, and its newly appointed president
dutifully proclaimed, "My top priority is to liquidate V.P. Singh."

The follow-up action included holding of numerous seminars
in different states and the preparation of a report covering various
developmental and populist measures, ranging from Panchayati
Raj to the 20-Point Programme. This report was discussed by the
National Seminar on Party Building held in Delhi in September
1988. Various action plans were prepared and strict time-limits
laid down for implementation.

In a hard-hitting speech at the Boat Club, Rajiv Gandhi declared
on 16 May 1987, "Inside the soft glove, there is an iron hand. And
if the grip is not proper with the glove, it has to be removed."
Actually the glove had already been removed in the government's no holds barred vendetta against *The Indian Express*. The

newspaper had been relentlessly exposing various scandals against the PM, and Ram Jethmalani's daily dose of 'Ten Questions' hit him where it hurt most. Scores of cases were registered against the publishers, tax hounds let loose, lease of the *Express* building at Delhi cancelled and its office raided. Yet the doughty Ram Nath Goenka, the proprietor, refused to bend.

Then, Rajiv vent his spleen against the non-Congress (I) state governments. While inaugurating the Farakka Barrage he threatened to start an enquiry into the misuse of flood-relief funds by the West Bengal government. In Andhra Pradesh, Congress leaders tried to spread dissidence against N.T. Rama Rao. Governors Kumudben Joshi of Andhra and Ram Dulari Sinha of Kerala, both former politicians, were directed to pay frequent visits to districts and praise the performance of the Central government.

Rajiv also had a tendency to add fresh steps to the existing hierarchies, thus offending the old guard. Uttar Pradesh and Rajasthan were placed under central co-ordination committees to be presided over by the young minister of state, Ghulam Nabi Azad. He appointed old rivals of the chief ministers on these two committees, who only aggravated the existing problems. In Madhya Pradesh things were made more difficult for Arjun Singh, the chief minister, by the re-admission of his old rival, S.C. Shukla. These were self-defeating moves and only made his task of party management more intractable.

Owing to his keenness to do things himself, Rajiv unnecessarily got into the firing line. Indira Gandhi had her hatchet men, and took good care to create buffers to insulate herself from trouble-prone areas. Also, she never openly showed her preference for one faction over the other. Rajiv followed no such strategy. In fact, to some extent, dissidence in the states resulted from his inability to remaim aloof from various factions, and to design a mechanism for conflict management. R.K. Dhawan was re-inducted to strengthen his hands. But it was perceived as an act of desperation and admission of failure to manage political affairs with the help of the available resources.

Electoral reverses always hurt a leader. His skill lies in minimizing their adverse impact on the party and public opinion. But the way Rajiv conducted some of the election campaigns showed not only a lack of political finesse, but also an inability to read the people's mood. When he started campaigning for the West Bengal assembly election in March 1987, he overrated his popularity with the masses and believed that he would be able to get the better of Jyoti Basu. His campaigning was aggressive and he had unpleasant things to say about the highly respected CM. When the results came, CPI(M) had further improved its position. Three months later, at the end of a vigorous campaign in Haryana, the Congress got a real drubbing and its strength was reduced from 90 to 5 seats in a house of 146. But his biggest miscalculation in this matter was to go it alone in the Tamil Nadu assembly poll in the beginning of 1989. The Congress had a weak base in the state and prudence required that it forge an alliance with either the DMK or AIADMK. But the large crowds at his meetings again led him to overestimate his clout. Consequently, owing to a division of votes, the DMK won absolute majority and the Congress got only 26 seats in a house of 234.

After having started as a very affable and accommodating leader, Rajiv suddenly changed gear and opted for his mother's style of confrontationist politics. But Indira Gandhi was never rude even to her worst opponents, and refused to indulge in personal invective. Rajiv had no such qualms.

Initially, Rajiv launched his verbal missiles not with a malicious intent but out of boyish fascination for repartee and a clever turn of phrase. In his Boat Club meeting in November 1984 he said, "When a giant tree falls, the earth shakes." This was in reference to the carnage following Indira's murder. He did not realize how much offence he was causing to the Sikhs by this wisecrack. In another speech in October 1985 he said, "Conspiracies are being hatched and they have their godfathers abroad." And then the punch line, 'Hum unko nani yaad dila denge.' (We will make them remember their grandmother). It was a coarse one-liner, typical of the Bombay film culture and the listeners were shocked to hear such a crude jibe from so refined a person. Even during the most serious discussions one could see him scribbling some funny comments on the proceedings and pass the slips to someone sitting some distance away.

One can take an indulgent view of Rajiv trying to amuse himself by these his juvenile witticisms, but for the fact that every word that a Prime Minister utters carries weight, or should carry weight. In such a high office it is better to be dull but discreet than smart but flippant.

Unfortunately for Rajiv, it was in dealing with his political opponents that he committed his most damaging verbal excesses. While campaigning in West Bengal, he called the venerable Jyoti Basu, 'an old man who should retire.' In the Tamil Nadu campaign he said that Karunanidhi, the DMK leader, wore dark glasses as he was scared to face the people. On 27 February 1989 the opposition walked out in protest when Rajiv accused it of being sympathetic to the demand for Khalistan. When Rajiv called the opposition members 'liars', there was a big furore. The PM had to apologize and his remarks were expunged. At one point he said that if lies had to be avoided, the opposition would have to leave. He made fun of MPs who were not proficient in English and more than once remarked, 'perhaps he should take lessons in English.' When this advice was tendered to Madhu Dandvate, he shot back, 'I have learnt my English from my teacher, not an air hostess.'

The level of the parliamentary debate and the dignity of the House largely depend upon the example set by its leader. The opposition in the eighth Lok Sabha became very aggressive and critical after various kickback scandals surfaced. It went all out to defame the Prime Minister in the hope of dislodging the Congress from office in the next general election. Even otherwise, the level of political morality had been declining over these years and hit the bottom when S. Thangaraju, an MP from Tamil Nadu, dramatically opened his large briefcase in the Parliament to show currency notes worth rupees five lakhs offered to him for changing his party. Then, after a bout of fisticuffs in the House, a Telugu Desam

MP had to be carried out on a stretcher. And there was a junior minister who accused the President of India in the parliament of harbouring secessionists.

In this sort of atmosphere it was all the more incumbent on the leader of the House to show restraint when provoked, and exercise a sobering influence on the MPs from both sides, so that leaders of the opposition parties felt encouraged to follow suit. But when the leader himself adopted belligerent postures and used abrasive language, things did repeatedly get out of hand.

Rajiv had scant respect for established parliamentary conventions. It is always a prominent opposition leader who is appointed as chairman of the Public Accounts Committee. But under Rajiv an MP from a non-Congress party which had supported the Congress was appointed as the chairman. As a mark of protest, all the opposition MPs withdrew from all three financial committees of the House. And the entire opposition walked out in mid-1989 over the government's refusal to allow a parliamentary debate on the Comptroller and Auditor General's report on Bofors.

The Congress centenary session of December 1985 and the AICC session held at Maraimalainagar, Madras, in April 1988 mark the opposite poles of Rajiv's ambitious resolve to regenerate the party and change its character. At Bombay he went hammer and tongs for the brokers of power. At Madras he claimed, "The Congress is the only party which identifies with the poor and the oppressed, which fights for the cause of the deprived and the depressed.The Congress is the only party of principle."

At Maraimalainagar the cult of sycophancy had made a triumphant come-back and tired cliches about socialism and the public sector were flogged in various resolutions. A senior leader like Arjun Singh described Rajiv as 'the only key to India's success in every field.' Sitaram Kesri, mimicking D.K. Barooah, claimed, 'With Rajiv is linked the country's fortune. If he is demoralized the country gets demoralized. We must eliminate all those who dare to malign the youngest prime minister.'

There were two reasons for this U-turn. One, after all their tall claims, the opposition parties had failed to establish any charge of corruption against Rajiv Gandhi. Moreover, no viable alternative to him had emerged from within the party. Thus a Congressman felt that he was still the surest vote-catcher and could best ensure the party's survival. Secondly, Rajiv himself was demoralized, as his efforts to change the party only weakened his position. This was particularly so after he got involved in various financial scandals.

At Madras it appeared that Rajiv had again got on top of the party, as there was not a single note of dissidence against him. In reality, it marked a complete retreat of Rajiv and the truimph of the old Congress culture. The system had tamed an intrepid reformer into a docile conformist.

The party machine that Rajiv rigged up for the 1989 general election was no different from the earlier outfit. The 'brokers of power' like A.R. Antulay, Gundu Rao, and Pranab Mukherjee, who were earlier thrown out in the cleansing process, had been readmitted. So was Indira's arch fixer, R.K. Dhawan. Among the other important leaders associated with the exercise were Buta Singh, Shiv Shankar and P.V. Narasimha Rao. None of these worthies could be accused of youth, idealism or dynamism. They were typical old-style operators, grooved in the manipulative Congress culture. Even in the selection of candidates, all except 50 of the sitting MPs were re-nominated.

The election was scheduled to be held on 22, 24 and 26 November 1989. Rajiv's election strategy focussed on robbing the opposition of its thunder by co-opting its main demands in the Congress manifesto. Thus emphasis was laid on decentralization of the polity, electoral reforms and eradication of corruption. The opposition was severely lambasted for defeating the Nagar Palika and Panchayati Bill in the Rajya Sabha. It was mostly a negative campaign. There were no glowing accounts of the government's achievements, or glimpses of a brighter future. Rajiv's most persistent appeal was to save the country from disintegrating by voting the Congress back to power. The spectres of communalism and foreign conspiracies were frequently raised. No wonder the campaign enthused neither the crowds nor the party.

Stung by the charge of inaccessibility, Rajiv made special efforts to reach out to the masses. He had already started meeting the Congress MPs on a regular basis. Rajiv's Home Minister facilitated the performance of *shilanyas* at Ayodhya to win over the Hindu vote. Rajiv even went to Deoraha Baba, a godman, to seek his blessings.

The opposition soon recovered from the initial shock of the sudden announcement of the polls, and various parties forged electoral alliances or reached agreements on seat adjustment. The Janata Dal, headed by V.P. Singh, formed the National Front in alliance with some regional parties. The BJP and CPI(M) were the other major partners in this patch-work.

V.P. Singh fully exploited the fallout from corruption charges against the government. In his typical folksy, rural idiom he accused Rajiv of having bartered the country's honour and sold out national security through foreign agents. He promised clean administration, and settlement of the Punjab and Ayodhya issues by mutual consultations.

Whereas the opposition mood was upbeat, Rajiv was mostly on the defensive. The Congress party was also demoralized and did not see a winner in their leader. In fact posters carrying his picture were not in great demand, and some candidates were not keen on Rajiv's visit to their constituencies. Towards the end of electioneering, some scheduled meetings for him had to be cancelled as the organizers were uncertain about the public response.

The election results did not come as much of a surprise. The Congress remained the single largest party with 193 seats. The National Front came out next with 141 and the left alliance with 51 seats. The BJP was the biggest gainer, having raised its tally from 2 in the previous parliament to 86 in this election. The Congress, which lost its majority in the parliament, had its strength reduced to less than half as compared to its 1984 score. Except in the south, the Congress fared poorly in the rest of the country, where it could win only 90 seats. The four southern states not only gave it 103 MPs, but the party was also able to win the assembly polls in Andhra Pradesh and Karnataka.

Besides his lacklustre performance, Rajiv made some costly tactical mistakes in the election. After leaving the Congress, V.P. Singh had started building up his own constituency in a systematic manner. The Congress grossly underestimated the danger posed by this development and crafted no strategy to counter Singh's rising influence. It had somehow convinced itself that owing to the opposition's failure to prove any charges of kickbacks against Rajiv Gandhi, corruption had become a non-issue. In fact the opposition played it up vigorously and this led to considerable erosion of the Congress vote. Above all, by associating itself with the Ayodhya *shilanyas*, the Congress fell between two stools. It alienated the Muslims completely and the BJP walked away with the orthodox Hindu vote.

As the Congress was reduced to a minority, Rajiv declined to make a bid to form the government in the absence of a clear mandate. The Left Alliance and BJP promised to support the National Front from outside, and V.P. Singh was sworn in as Prime Minister with the backing of over 280 MPs on 5 December 1989.

Post-election developments made two things clear about Rajiv. First, contrary to what many people had predicted, there was not the slightest sign of revolt against his leadership. He was elected as leader of the Congress Parliamentry Party without a single dissenting voice. Second, like his mother after the 1977 defeat, he was just not prepared to tone down his imperious style. On 7 October, 1990 he sacked the Chief Minister of Karnataka publicly at a press conference, just as he had removed his Foreign Secretary in 1987. And he was restrained with difficulty from meeting out the same treatment to Sharad Pawar, Chief Minister, Maharashtra. The fault of these two CMs was that they had dared to display signs of independence.

Though the Congress was demoralized after the defeat, Rajiv hardly took any steps to revitalize the party by introducing a measure of inner democracy. In the run up to the mid-term poll in 1991 when he set up a committee to determine the party's overall strategy, it comprised General Krishna Rao, Professor

A.M. Khusro, former bureaucrats R.D. Pradhan and M.S. Rasgotra, and Sam Pitroda. Another Committee set up to raise funds included Captain Satish Sharma, R.K. Dhawan and a Delhi businessman, Lalit Suri. Rajiv was not unduly concerned as to what the senior Congress leaders would feel about following the election strategy devised by a group of bureauucrats and professionals who did not have a day's experience of running party affairs.

V.P. Singh's National Front Government was even more brittle than the Janata Party regime, as here BJP had agreed to lend support only from outside. Besieged by intractable problems, V.P. Singh played his trump card in August 1990 by accepting the Mandal Commission's recommendation to reserve 27 percent of government jobs and seats in educational institutions for the Other Backward Classes. This not only led to violent agitations in some parts of the country; it undermined the BJP's ambition to be the sole custodian of Hindu interests. Separate reservation for the backwards threatened to split its constituency. As a counterblast, the BJP gave a sort of ultimatum to the government to settle the Ayodhya dispute by 30 October.

L.K. Advani, the president of BJP, had decided to lead a *rath yatra*, (chariot-pilgrimage) from Somnath to Ayodhya to rouse Hindu consciousness for building the Ramjanambhoomi Mandir. What Advani did was to drive a chariot of fire, setting the countryside aflame with communal hatred. The government was determined to prevent his chariot reaching Ayodhya on the stipulated 30th of October, and he was arrested in Samastipur, Bihar, while he was heading towards his destination.

In retaliation, the BJP and VHP storm-troopers assaulted Babri Masjid, and twelve of them were killed when the police opened fire. Though the Masjid was saved, the National Front government fell, owing to withdrawal of support by the BJP. This led to frantic horse-trading by various parties and Chandra Shekhar split the National Front by walking away with 54 MPs. He struck a deal with Rajiv Gandhi who promised to support his candidature for prime ministership. This was a replay of the Janata Party split with Chandra Shekhar taking on the role of Charan Singh.

V.P. Singh resigned on 7 November after holding office for 11 months. Chandra Shekhar was installed as the PM on 20 November and lasted just for four months. The Congress withdrew its support when Rajiv Gandhi charged the government of breach of trust. The provocation was the detailing of two policemen to keep a tab on his activities.

Chandra Shekhar submitted his resignation on 6 March 1991. The President asked him to continue as a caretaker PM and the mid-term poll was scheduled for 20, 23 and 26 May. So, Rajiv was again in the electoral arena, sooner than he expected.

Frantic preparations were started by the Congress with several committees working round the clock. Rajiv again undertook his gruelling electioneering, criss-crossing the country by the fastest available means of transport. This time Rajiv was very particular to bridge the communication gap with the people and repeatedly ignored security precautions to mingle with the masses. Moreover, in an unwise move the government had downgraded his security cover as an economy measure by replacing the Special Protection Group by a smaller National Security Guard. This naturally exposed Rajiv to greater security hazards.

This was an election without waves. But it was the most communal and violent poll so far. The first phase covering 200 constituencies in north India was over on 20 May. In the afternoon, Rajiv stopped over in Delhi to spend a few moments with the family before rushing off to the south for the concluding phase of electioneering. This was the last time he saw his wife, and the poignancy of this meeting has been captured by Sonia in a masterpiece of restrained narrative:

"We bade each other a tender goodbye — and he was off. I watched him, peeping from behind the curtain, till he disappeared from view...

"This time forever."[1]

After fifteen hours of a punishing round of election meetings, Rajiv reached Sri Perambudur at 10 p.m. for his last engagement. As he was wending his way through the milling crowds, Dhanu, a human bomb, approached him unobtrusively, bent to touch his feet, and Rajiv was blown to bits in a flash.

Thus came to a tragic end the most illustrious dynasty in the annals of democracy. Nowhere else in the modern age a family saw so much glory, was associated with such momentous events, left such a deep imprint on the history of its country. But it was also a dynasty marked by fate: two of its three members were brutally assassinated, and both the deaths resulted from their greatest errors of judgement: Indira Gandhi for Operation Blue Star, and Rajiv for his misadventure in Sri Lanka. Seldom has nemesis been so stern and unsparing.

An Overview

44

An Overview

$\mathcal{I}$ would like to open the last chapter of my book with a justification of its title, especially as two of Indira Gandhi's closest aides disapproved of it. When I met P.N. Haksar for an interview, he was visibly annoyed on learning that I was writing a political biography of Nehru-Gandhi family entitled *The Dynasty*. He was emphatic that Nehru never tried to groom Indira as his heir,[1] and then gave me a lecture on E.H. Carr's *What is History?* Later, when I met G. Parthasarathy, he suggested in his own gentle way that *The Dynasty* was not an appropriate title for my book. And at a press briefing on 14 February 1996, Arjun Singh stated that it would be a 'distortion of history' to apply the term "dynasty" to the Nehru-Gandhi family.

Jawaharlal Nehru-Indira Gandhi-Rajiv Gandhi form a dynasty not because three generations of a family succeeded one another as prime ministers of India, but owing to the institutionalization of the dynastic principle by cultivating the image of charismatic leadership. It was the Nehruvian charisma that Indira inherited, and despite her unimpressive performance in the beginning, she carried the day as she was wearing her father's mantle.

It may be argued that after all Mrs. Gandhi succeeded Nehru 19 months after his death, and Rajiv succeeded his mother after her assassination. So neither Nehru nor Indira could have manoeuvred the installation of an heir. But this is where the legitimizing role of charisma comes in.

In his general theory of 'authority' Max Weber distinguishes between three types of legitimacy — and 'charismatic' is one of them. Nehru's charisma was built up as a result of his dominant role during the freedom movement. And his succession as Gandhi's heir was legitimized by the Mahatma himself when he specifically nominated him to that position.

Though it offends the republican spirit, dynastic rule is not necessarily evil. It answers some deep-rooted, primeval craving of a feudal society for adulation and deification. Not only India, but other countries of South Asia like Sri Lanka, Pakistan and Bangladesh seem to love dynasties. And in India the dynastic rule has served a useful purpose. After Independence there was urgent need for stability, continuity and institutional legitimization. Nehruvian charisma not only provided the necessary support and ensured smooth successions, the process of dynasty formation itself acquired a legitimizing role. The dynasty became a focal point of aura and myth, and served as a political centre.

Secondly, it was owing to the dynastic element that charisma was inherited. Nehru assiduously cultivated his charisma and became its rightful beneficiary. But to begin with, Indira Gandhi had nothing charismatic about her. She was cold, detached, uncommunicative, and a poor speaker. Though later she showed remarkable qualities of leadership, it was the dynastic charisma which gave her the initial push. And though Rajiv had neither an opportunity to cultivate a public persona, nor had he his mother's leadership qualities, he completely dominated the political scene owing to his dynastic charisma.

But the Nehru-Gandhi family, sustained by personal charisma as it was, lacked the self assurance and sense of security of a monarchic, hereditary dynasty. Therefore, each member had not only to make special efforts to reinforce the dynastic charisma, but also capture, centralize and hold as much power as possible. That is where the dynastic ambition clashed with the national good. According to Weber, after a charismatic leader has played his historical role "he has to set about creating rational administrative rules; secondary individuals have to be endowed with the authority of the leader, symbols replace the person, and there ensues the 'routinization of charisma.'"[2]

This vital development did not and, could not, take place in India as here personal charisma was used to build dynastic rule instead of a decentralized polity. Symbols never replaced the leader and charisma, instead of being routinized, was sedulously personalized. Consequently not only secondary individuals were never endorsed with the authority of the leader, secondary leadership structures were systematically dismantled to remove all possible threats to dynastic rule. In fact so completely was the Congress party stripped of leadership talent that even after P.V. Narasimha Rao had completed his full five-year term as Prime Minister, many Congressmen could think only of appealing to Rajiv Gandhi's widow to lead the party in the 1996 general election.

Thus, whereas Jawaharlal Nehru, Indira Gandhi and Rajiv Gandhi made invaluable contributions to the making of modern India, they also inhibited the polity from realizing its full democratic potential in consonance with the country's federalist ethos. And the fact that these three illustrious members of a family belonged to a self-conscious charismatic dynasty is central to their style and performance.

In their perceptions and styles Jawaharlal Nehru, Indira Gandhi and Rajiv Gandhi were three very different individuals, and they left a deep impress of their personalities on their times. Yet, some common trends run through the four decades of the Nehru-Gandhi era which may be usefully reviewed. Of no less interest would be a broad appraisal of the impact of this period on the future of the Indian polity.

For half a century now India has survived as a full-fledged, vibrant democracy. Though Nehru was the main architect of this institution, Indira and Rajiv also never wavered in their commitment to it. Even after Mrs. Gandhi imposed the Emergency, she was all the time anxious to restore the normal rule of law — and did it as soon as she could. So firmly has democracy become rooted in India that no political party, of whatever hue, has ever espoused an alternative system.

The Dynasty's second greatest contribution has been the promotion of the secular culture. Indira and Rajiv did occasionally use the communal card to derive political advantage, but their allegiance to secularism was unquestioned. Though the secular ideal has been under attack from various quarters, the vast majority of Indians subscribe to it. Even the most communal of outfits dare not openly preach their creed, and try to couch their rhetoric in the secular idiom.

Democracy and secularism are the two pillars of Indian polity: all other institutions rest on them. It is owing to these two factors that a highly divided, unequal and conflict-ridden country like India has held together. Not only that. Gradually the feeling of national identity has seeped deep down to the remotest parts of the country. Whatever other differences people may have, few feel that they are not Indians.

Despite all the setbacks, hurdles and false starts, the country has been on the move. Before Independence, famines were endemic. Though the population increased two-and-a-half times during the four decades under review, India has managed to feed her people without ever facing serious famines. No less creditable is the fact that the life expectancy of Indians has nearly doubled over this period.

During the first half of the 20th century the trend rate of growth averaged around one percent per annum. During the next three decades the comparable figure stood at 3.7 percent, and then climbed to five to six percent. Of course, too much should not be read into this performance, as Independence released productive forces which were bound to push up growth. Moreover, the other two Asian giants, Japan and China, registered growth rates which were two to three times higher.

Introduction of planning and creation of a massive public sector are other milestones of this era. Among other things, planning did curb further aggravation of regional disparities and ensured a fair allocation of resources to the states. The public sector, despite all its failings created a vast infrastructure and provided a solid base of heavy industry, thus making available the basic wherewithals for industrial growth.

Then, Nehru's initiative in fleshing out the concept of Non-alignment in a world sharply divided into two hostile camps gave a voice to the Third World countries and enabled them to exercise a restraining influence in international affairs.

The country defaulted seriously in regard to mass literacy and the educational system had an elitist bias. Yet, this system produced highly skilled scientific and technical manpower which has enabled India to make a mark in several frontier areas of science like nuclear power, space, oceanography and defence production. She has made notable advances in missile technology and designed her own satellites. In the fast-growing field of computer software, Indian expertise has won international recognition.

These achievements, by no means spectacular, are not insignificant either. But seen in the global context, India's performance has been disappointing. India was the one great hope of the third world. Its leadership was widely acknowledged. Given the advantages of a highly educated manpower, a fair degree of entrepreneurial skills and vast natural resources, she was expected to rapidly emerge as a model of development for the newly liberated colonies. But these hopes were belied. Actually, in terms of economic growth India slipped all along the line. Whereas she was the tenth industrial nation in the world in 1950, three decades later she occupied the twenty-seventh position. And her share of world trade declined from 2 percent to 0.42 percent over this period. According to the Human Development Report (1993) of UNDP, India occupied 134th place among 173 nations, and Pakistan, Vietnam, Myanmar, Thailand, Zambia and Botswana ranked above her. The degree of deprivation at the lower levels of the population is surpassed nowhere in the world except the sub-Saharan region of Africa. And the country would enter the 21st century with the largest number of illiterates in the world.

This is not the place to explore the socio-historical reasons for this uninspiring record. But very briefly, we may enumerate some of the objective factors which prevented India from doing as well as Japan or China. Very importantly, these two countries enjoy a large measure of cultural, ethnic and linguistic homogeneity. Both have a tradition of a high degree of civic discipline and respect for authority. It is, therefore, easier to mobilize their people for common nation-building tasks. In India the position is just the reverse. Its highly heterogeneous society is riven by all sorts of linguistic, regional, religious, ethnic and caste cleavages; the Indian ethos inculcates individualism and not social cohesion. The freedom movement was all along subversive of the established authority, and this habit has persisted even after Independence.

The entropy — the measure of manifest disorder — of such a system is bound to be pretty high. In this context, the introduction of liberal democracy was not an unmixed blessing. It gave free play to various centrifugal forces and restricted the state's authority to enforce social discipline. Nehru had hoped that with industrialization and modernization, divisive forces would weaken and secular issues come to occupy the centre stage. But experience has shown that sectarian concerns have a much greater hold over the minds of the people, and regional, communal and caste loyalties arouse passions much more readily than unemployment or injustice.

All these were given factors, implicit in the Indian situation at the time of Independence. The second group of factors which inhibited progress pertain to the quality of Indian leadership during these four decades. Owing to the height from which Jawaharlal Nehru and Indira Gandhi dominated the Indian political scene, one normally thinks of these individuals only when talking of the calibre of leadership. But a vast country with two dozen states cannot be governed by just one person. Below the prime minister, ranging from the Central cabinet ministers to the village panchayat *pradhans*, there are thousands of leaders who determine the political culture of the country. But this enormous area of multilayered leadership, overshadowed by the banyan trees of the Nehru-Gandhi family, remained stunted. Thus, Nehru, Indira or Rajiv — none had the support of mature and strong leadership at the lower rungs, nor could their failings and deficiencies be made up by the strengths of the regional and local leaders. Consequently, lacking the back-up of a corrective mechanism, the inadequacies of the three prime ministers got embedded in the system, leading to various distortions.

The Congress had become a truly national party by fostering the culture of consensus. Nehru was keenly aware that after Independence this consensus would have to be strengthened further if the highly diverse and fragmented Indian society had to be held together. And he succeeded in this attempt to a remarkable degree.

But with the Congress split of 1969, the tradition of consensus was destroyed for good. A party with a fine record at conflict-resolution itself became a victim of inner strife. The opposition parties came to be treated as enemies, and the lively cut and thrust of parliamentary debates was replaced by violence of language and stridency of tone.

Nehru greatly underestimated the impact of population explosion, communalism and corruption on the future course of events. Actually, population was not a very hot issue during the Nehru era, though the unanticipated spurt in the fifties and sixties invalidated several plan projections of growth. It was the steep drop in the death rate from 27.4 per thousand in 1951 to 12.5 in 1981 that resulted in this explosion. By the time full realization of its implications had dawned, Sanjay Gandhi came up with his mass sterilization programme which not only gave a serious setback to family planning, but also put paid to any energetic future initiatives.

As to communalism, Nehru had hoped that India's composite culture, modernization and growth would weaken and dissolve sectarian divisions. The composite culture was partly a product of the feudal milieu which was given a body-blow by the land reforms. Modernization and growth did churn up the society, but very unevenly. Also their impact was rather feeble and secular forces could not derive much sustenance from an environment of mass poverty and backwardness.

Still, Nehru was able to keep the communal elements in check owing to his firm and unwavering commitment to secularism. But Indira Gandhi and Rajiv were not averse to wooing communal forces to gain electoral advantage. This was a disastrous policy and turned secularism into a negotiable counter in the game of political expediency. Thus the fight against communalism ceased to be a moral crusade.

It is in respect of corruption that the Dynasty's record is least satisfying. Whereas Nehru only tolerated it, Indira turned it into a national institution. With her amoral approach to statecraft, she used money to strengthen her hold over both state power and politics. Little did she realize that both would lose their legitimacy in the process. Rajiv was too naïve to handle the deadly monster of corruption with any degree of skill. Irrespective of the extent of his involvement in various kickback scandals, the shadow of corruption not only marred his political future, but also gave the country a very odious reputation for graft.

In certain ways Indira Gandhi's statecraft has left a deeper mark on the Indian polity than Nehru's. And naturally so; as hers was a stronger personality, she had a better grasp of the ground reality, and possessed an unmatched talent as a practitioner of realpolitik. Her driving force was the pursuit of power. Thus, though she was undoubtedly a democrat, she strengthened only the state and herself, not the citizen or democracy. It was this very trait which led her to devalue institutions, favour greater centralization, weaken the Congress party and the state governments, personally control party funds, and become the sole dispenser of privilege and patronage. This led to the paradox of the emergence of a court culture and personality cult within a democratic setup.

Another basic trait of Mrs. Gandhi which got ingrained in the country's political life was distrust. Born out of her childhood experiences, it was reinforced when she blundered into devaluing the rupee in the very first year of her rule. Having burnt her fingers so early in office, she never again trusted any aide or minister implicitly. And gradually she developed distrust into a powerful weapon of self-defence.

This was a most unfortunate development for the Indian polity. Such a gigantic enterprise as India, multi-layered and diverse, could not be run effectively without trusting a whole lot of people, and without inspiring trust. As Indira did not trust anybody, nobody could trust her either. This robbed the system of its self-assurance and initiative, and for every small decision people used to run to the PM for 'guidance'. Though Rajiv started as a person of generous impulses, his early reverses converted him to his mother's philosophy of distrust.

The profession of politics, relying heavily on opportunism and expediency, has a fair degree of distrust built into it. But by placing this corrosive emotion at the core of their politics, both Indira Gandhi and Rajiv deprived the system of much of its vigour and synergy.

As a result of her divisive heterogeneities, the question of national unity and stability would remain central to Indian polity. The all-embracing alliance structure devised by the Congress during the freedom movement provided the best insurance against disruptive forces.

After Independence the base of this alliance-structure was considerably broadened. During the freedom struggle, the majority of Muslims were not with the Congress. But after Partition, they first looked upon the Congress for security and then for jobs and economic opportunities. Thus excluding the communists and the communal parties, the Congress embraced a very vast constituency.

But this alliance was too nebulous and contained too many contradictions to last. The first major group to leave it was the newly empowered land-owning peasantry. Millions of tenants had become proprietors with the abolition of Zamindari, and they emerged as a powerful demand group. They wanted parity of treatment with the urban middle-classes, and concessions on par with the industrial sector. But the state just did not have the resources to satisfy these aspirations. So this led to their alienation from the Congress and, except in the 1984 general election, the farmers have never voted *en bloc* for it.

This development forced Indira Gandhi to re-work the Congress alliance structure by concentrating on a coalition of the minorities, upper castes and the depressed classes.

Another important factor which forced her hand was the Congress split of 1969. Whereas the split itself was the outcome of a fierce power struggle, Indira gave it an ideological slant by projecting it as an assertion of progressive elements against the old-style bossism of the Congress. But to give credence to this proposition, Mrs. Gandhi promoted a second split. She argued that the omnibus character of the Congress diffused the ideological focus and made it difficult to mobilize radical forces for specific nation-building tasks. Narrowing of income disparities, and programmes of poverty eradication and social justice required well-targeted initiatives and well-defined goal objectives. This was a well-meant, plausible standpoint. But it implied readiness to hit entrenched vested interests and thus risk a split within the existing social configurations. So the launching of her *garibi hatao* programme was accompanied by a drive at nationalization of certain important sectors of industry and regulation of economic activity.

Despite a large element of populism in her radicalism, Mrs. Gandhi earnestly tried to give a pro-poor orientation to her policies in her effort to hammer out a new alliance structure for the Congress. But her programme suffered from several snags. For one, her approach was ad-hocish; it lacked consistency and strong commitment. More importantly, instead of revamping the party apparatus to provide the necessary impetus for change, she came to rely increasingly on the state machinery to implement her radical agenda. This only led to the progressive narrowing of the pluralist space within Indian politics, and further strengthening of the centralizing and homogenizing tendencies of Indira's statism.

Thirdly, "the basic contradiction in Indira Gandhi's brand of populism ... lay in the fact that whereas her appeal was to the rural masses and the poorer strata, the power structure at the Centre on which she relied so much was essentially urban, upper middle class bureaucratic and to not a small extent capitalist."[3]

This dichotomy between Indira's populist politics and power structure made her specially vulnerable to movements of mass discontent. Developments of the early and mid-seventies which led to the declaration of the Emergency, resulted basically from her failure to politically manage the economy and satisfactorily solve problems of food shortages and unemployment. And thereafter all attempts to evolve a stable alternative alliance structure have failed. In fact it was the desperate quest for a viable coalition of demand groups which led Indira to flirt with Hindu communalism, and thereby alienate the Muslim vote-bank as never before.

Decline of the mighty Congress and the breakdown of its culture of concensus naturally produced voids and discontinuities in the Indian political system. But this also offered opportunities to regional parties to assert themselves. Simultaneously, various sectarian and parochial identities also became more vocal and demanded due recognition. Consequently, towards the close of the Rajiv era, most of the larger states were ruled by the regional or non-Congress national parties, and when the next Congress government came to power in 1991, caste politics had become a major force.

It is plausible to argue that these developments have weakened the forces of national cohesion and exposed the polity to fissiparous trends. But two factors should be noted in this connection. The growth of the regional parties has come about as a result of the interplay of democratic forces. The same may be said of the rise of caste politics. These phenomena represent a reaction to the over centralization of the polity in an essentially federal milieu, and the appropriation of state's resources by the miniscule upper-caste elite. This was an arrangement wholly repugnant to the republican ethos, and its continuance would have further aggravated social conflicts and fostered political instability. Thus these seemingly centrifugal trends have only provided safety-valves in an overcharged system.

Secondly, these regional and sectarian identities do not weaken national unity. Practically all the groups proclaim implicit allegiance to the nation state and look up to it for funds, resolution of inter-state disputes, succour during natural calamities, siting of industrial projects, and such other favours. The quarrel of these groups and parties is not against the Centre, but against one another. And all of them compete for winning the favour of the Centre. Thus the potential of regionalism and sectariansim as a threat to national unity is an overblown bogy.

Then, there are the powerful pan-Indian cohesive forces which promote national integration. The greatest of them all is democracy. Its checks and balances and conflict-resolving mechanisms ensure that discontents of large groups do not remain bottled up for long. The ever expanding market and the middle class, with their secular concerns, are powerful agents of national consolidation. Infrastructure promotes pan-Indian commerce by welding regional resources and facilities into national grids. In the Indian context, even the armed forces, which have played a destabilizing role elsewhere, act as a unifying agent owing to their composite character and diverse composition.

This account may create the impression that any talk of threat to national unity is only motivated rhetoric, lacking any basis in reality. That certainly is not the case. The only reasonable inference that the ground reality in India warrants is that the prevailing conditions contain a number of positive factors which nurture national integration, and there exists no imminent threat to the country's stability. But this does not eliminate forces which may reverse the process. Perhaps the greatest threat to India's political cohesion stems from the political class itself. This not only refers to the reckless destruction of institutions and spread of unbridled corruption, but also to increasing resort to opportunism and expediency in gaining power and pelf. As sectorial interests and sectarian agendas have a sort of visceral appeal for the masses, their excessive exploitation can aggravate social conflicts. No less dangerous is the attempt to get political advantage out of sensitive ethnic and regional issues. The situation in the north-eastern states, Punjab and Kashmir would have remained quite manageable if the Congress government had not tried to serve party interests in handling deep-rooted, genuine grievances of the people.

Thus, manipulative and unprincipled politics poses a greater threat to national unity than the inner contradictions and conflicts of a developing, multi-ethnic society.

It is interesting to note that in a sense India's political stability rested on two props: the Dynasty, and an elaborate network of relations with the USSR. But neither of these supports was integral to the Indian situation. It was fortunate that Nehru was there to head the government when India became independent. And it was a matter of vital importance that the Nehru-Gandhi dynasty ruled the country for four decades, thus giving a high degree of stability and continuity to the fledgling polity. But Nehru may well not have been there in 1947 to become the prime minister. There is not the least doubt that India would have been a very different country in that case.

The growth of Indo-Soviet relationship was again a fortuitous development. Stalin never bothered to befriend India. Nehru was totally averse to Radhakrishnan's proposal for an Indo-Soviet friendship treaty. It was only Khruschev's initiative and his generous responses which started the process of Indo-Soviet amity. It may have never happened. And yet, this relationship had a decisive impact on the way the Indian polity shaped.

Whether it was national security, or economy or foreign affairs, India's Soviet connection was of crucial importance. Actually, India never had an autonomous doctrine of security, and mostly crafted her approach in response to external events. Indian armed forces relied heavily on Soviet arms supplies. Her navy and air force were particularly dependent on Soviet armament, and indigenous manufacture under licence.

India's public sector was again built up by the import of heavy machinery and transfer of technology from the USSR. The rupee trade and buy-back arrangements gave a boost to Indian trade, especially as poor quality and shoddy goods could be exported to the communist bloc without any threat of competition from rival manufacturers.

In her foreign relations, India was largely dependent on the Soviet Union for defending her stand on Kashmir, and it was the Soviet veto in the Security Council which repeatedly came to her rescue. Again, it was the assurance of the Soviet backing which enabled India to confidently face the Chinese and American pressures. In the absence of the Indo-Soviet Friendship Treaty, it would have been very difficult for India to defy the menace from the US Seventh Fleet during the Bangladesh war, and it was this shield which prevented China from intervening on behalf of Pakistan.

The Nehru-Gandhi dynasty and Indo-Soviet friendship have been the two most decisive influences in shaping post-Independence India. What an unholy thought to think that neither of these props may have been there!

During the four decades of the Dynasty's rule the world underwent three revolutionary changes which altered the rules of every political and economic game. The first was the blossoming of what Eric Hobsbawm calls the Golden Age of Capitalism. "World output of manufactures quadrupled between the early 1950s and the early 1970s, and what is even more impressive, world trade in manufactured products grew tenfold."[4]

The second was the technology revolution which accorded primacy to the service sector in the advanced countries and enabled them to relegate the smoke-stack industries to the third world. Great advances in computer and communication technologies integrated the globe through information highways and gave awesome reach to the operations of transnational corporations.

The third revolution resulted from the breakup of the USSR and the consequent end of the Cold War. This was, perhaps, the most important event of the 20th century.

These three revolutions made globalization of the economy a much more immediate and pervasive phenomenon. Among other things it forced India to urgently reconsider her approach to economic growth and make some hard choices.

Indira Gandhi, and more so Rajiv, had already initiated the process of liberalization of the Indian economy. When the Congress returned to power in 1991 the country had just enough foreign exchange to pay 15 days' import bill. As a result of sharply escalating budgetary deficits, mounting foreign debt and balance of payments shortfalls, the economy was in a really bad shape. Thus cornered P.V. Narasimha Rao opted for a policy of systematic liberalization.

Since the introduction of Planning this is the most significant economic reform that the country has undertaken, and its success or failure will have a far-reaching impact on Indian polity. This programme definitely integrates India with the global capitalist system and marks a clear break with the socialist-pattern-of-society plank. It has thus aroused strong emotions on both sides of the ideological divide. But one fact is irrefutable. Not only has the socialist economic agenda collapsed across the board, the only important communist power left in the arena, that is, China, has also gone in for extensive liberalization and laid out the red carpet for the multinational corporations. Even in India, no critic of liberalization has been able to suggest a viable alternative, and Jyoti Basu, the eminent communist Chief Minister of West Bengal, is openly wooing global capital.

This does not mean that the Indian programme of structural adjustment has been a success. On the one hand foreign exchange reserves steadily improved and stood at US $ 25 billion in April 1995. Foreign investments rose steadily and exceeded US $ 9 billion in March 1995. On the other hand, revenue decificit could be contained within the budgeted limits for 1991-92 only and then got out of hand. The consumer price index remained above 10 percent during 1991-96. Industrial production slumped in 1991-92, and gradually reached the level achieved during Rajiv's tenure. Then, 76 percent of the foreign capital inflow went to portfolio investments, which added nothing to the country's productive capacity.

More importantly, the effect of the reforms on the life of the common man has not been very wholesome. The capital expenditure of the government as a percentage of GDP indicates the level of funds allocated to welfare and growth. This has steadily declined from 5.9 percent in 1990-91 to 3.6 percent in 1994-95, indicating continuous withdrawal of the government from long-term development commitments. Moreover, to ease the pressure on rising revenue deficits, net transfers to the states have decreased from 6.1 percent of the GDP in 1990-91 to 4.6 percent in 1994-95. This reduction directly hits allocations for agriculture, education, health and other welfare activities.

As a reaction to decades of regulation of the Indian economy and with increasing emphasis on its marketization there is a danger of going to the other extreme, and treating the state and the market as antagonistic to each other. In fact even in the most highly marketized economies their roles are complementary. "The framework within which the market operates is politically defined."[5] In fact "The great post-war economic success stories of capitalist countries," says Hobsbawn, "... are stories of industrialization based, backed, supervised, steered, and sometimes planned and managed by governments from France and Spain in Europe to Japan, Singapore and South Korea."[6] The fierceness with which the USA and Japan protect their economies and the extent to which Amercia goes to extract concessions for her multinationals should temper the hostility of Indian free-marketeers to state intervention.

It is premature to judge the merits of Manmohan Singh's structural adjustment programme and much will depend on how the new government after the 1996 general election responds to the situation. But it can be safely predicted that now the process of reforms cannot be reversed. Secondly, compared to most other countries, India has fared much better in controlling the side-effects of adjustment. And thirdly, in the Indian situation it will be disastrous to ignore social distribution in pursuit of growth.

Nehru's land reforms were the most important measure for changing property relations in rural India. Various development schemes were also launched to create more employment opportunities for the landless. Central to most of the growth programmes was the hope that they would lead to shifting of the unemployed and under employed labour from agriculture to industry. However, these plans did not produce any significant impression on rural poverty.

But after a couple of decades things started moving and the change gradually acquired the dimensions of a silent revolution. This process has transformed the countryside in a more basic manner than any reform introduced by the government. Equally important is the fact that this shift is occurring owing to the inner dynamics of the rural society and government initiative has little to do with it.

One may examine this phenomenon by first enumerating the factors which have brought about this change. While examining Nehru's land reforms (Chapter 7) it was noted that failure to enforce land ceilings had considerably diluted their usefulness. Since then partitions of holdings through two generations of heirs have appreciably reduced their size, thus rendering land ceilings a side issue. Secondly, abolition of Zamindari had led to the elimination of formal tenancy also, as recorded tenants could acquire ownership rights. This pushed tenancy underground, depriving even regular tenants of any rights. Thirdly, the spread of the Green Revolution has brought a sea change in the situation by rendering self-cultivation quite profitable. Thus a large number of landowners started cultivating their fields, even if they had to hire tractors and harvesters. More importantly, the Green Revolution made the retention of a large labour force unnecessary. Workers were now required for short spells at a time for various agricultural operations. Thus, it was cheaper to hire migrant contract labour when required, instead of employing a regular work force. These casual workers got higher wages, but one could get rid of them at a moment's notice and without the hassle of traditional claims. For the same reason, even bonded labour became less attractive. And as wage-rates of short-term cash labour were higher,this also made the Minimum Wages Act almost redundant.

The aggregate effect of these developments was that the earnings of farmers went up considerably. Secondly, a sizeable segment of landless labour did not find employment in agriculture; but those who did, earned higher wages. Consequently, on the one hand the proportion of net consumers whose demand was not confined to wage goods increased substantially. On the other, the Green Revolution and the introduction of capitalist agriculture further reduced employment opportunities for the landless.

Simultaneously, there has been a diversification of rural economy in the unorganized, non-formal and non-agricultural sector. There has mushroomed a large crop of first-generation, small entrepreneurs, specially in the service sector and small-scale manufacture. This welcome opening not only provides employment to displaced landless labour, it also enables them to get higher wages.

The second phase of this silent revolution is unfolding in the towns. Many urban areas are now abuzz with industrial activity and self-employed small entrepreneurs are changing their character. Although it is the metropolitan conglomerates which attract all the limelight, it is the urban areas at a lower level which throb with productive activity. The following examples will help to highlight this point.

Dewas[7] is a fastest-growing industrial town in India, and the nearby Pitampura has the largest industrial estate in Asia. Gurgaon produces one-third of the country's sanitaryware and one-fourth of its bicycles. Nearly 70 percent of the Indian mixies are manufactured in Ambala, 80 percent of the truck and bus bodies are built in Namakkal and the neighbouring Thiruchengudda. Seventy-five percent of the clock-work is made in Morvi. Various public sector enterprises have turned the sleepy, pilgrim town of Haridwar into a bustling industrial complex, and the historical township of Panipat has become a major exporter of a wide range of consumer goods. The ancient port of Bharuch has developed into a major industrial and commercial centre and a prominent container terminal.

This is only an illustrative list; there are hundreds of other towns which are pulsating with similar entrepreneurial activity.

This development has produced two far-reaching results. One, it exercises a pull effect on the rural areas and lakhs of villagers have migrated to these places in search of employment or higher wages. They send a part of their earnings back home and this is leading to the much awaited transfer of capital to the countryside. Secondly, when these migrant workers return to their homes, they take with them the aspirations, appetites and outlook of these towns. Perhaps 40 percent of the village households have at least one family member working in some nearby town. The cumulative effect of this level of social mobility and its consequent impact on the financial status and attitudes of the village folk can be well imagined.

But this churning up of urban India is entirely unplanned, chaotic and directionless. The number of villagers drifting to the towns is far in excess of the available jobs. Also, the rapid urban growth is wholly haphazard. Many of these growth centres do not have even rudimentary civic amenities. This has led to extensive degradation of environment, and hordes of migrants virtually live in pigsties. Secondly, this has led to a sharp rise in crime rate and proliferation of mini mafias.

All in all, this multi-pronged silent revolution has not only resulted in social mobility of massive dimensions, it is also leading to the restructuring of the economy and re-working of the rural-urban equation on a gigantic scale. And all this is happening without much intervention by the state.

A great movement like the freedom struggle could not have been sustained without projecting a credible vision of a golden future. And after Independence it was necessary to create another vision or myth to foster hope in India's destiny as a great nation. Nehru did hold out the promise of a 'socialist pattern of society', and devised several strategies to realize it. But the promise was not backed up by performance. Even a couple of months before his death, Nehru was still talking of ushering socialist pattern of society at the Bhubaneshwar Congress session.

Once Indira Gandhi's radical phase was over, she systematically dismantled institutions in pursuit of personal power and dynastic ambitions. And the kickback scandals about Rajiv eroded the very credibility of the prime minister's office.

"Every society must teach itself and its young," writes M.J. Robinson, "that its basic values are good and its institutions are appropriate for achieving these values. In other words, each society ... must peddle legitimacy."[8] But even during Nehru's time this process of teaching the young never really got going. Despite all the populist rhetoric, the bulk of the people did not acquire much of a stake in the system. A progressive decline in the norms of public life and neglect of the common weal robbed the political class of its credibility, and cynicism became the most pervasive national sentiment.

All these developments have damaged the morale of the people and deprived them of the solace of hope in an assured future. No nation can aspire to greatness without cultivating an exalted vision of its destiny. Indians are an uncertain nation today, in search of a new identity. Even the intelligentsia does not know where it belongs. There is no leader who inspires people's respect and no political agenda which they endorse. Given to excessive self-deprecation, they lament too much.

Assailed by doubt, peering into a hazy future, with little pride in its achievements, this is hardly the state in which the world's largest democracy should be entering the 21st century.

References

Note: The following abbreviations have been used in these notes:
1. In referring to Jawaharlal Nehru's two famous books, *An Autobiography* and *Discovery of India*, the names of the author and publisher have been omitted. The publisher of these books is Oxford University Press (OUP), India.
2. SW — Selected Works of Jawaharlal Nehru, Sangam Books.
3. SW (Second Series) — Selected Works of Jawaharlal Nehru, Second Series, Jawaharlal Nehru Memorial Trust.
4. Speeches — Jawaharlal Nehru's Speeeches, Publications Division, Ministry of Information and Broadcasting, Government of India.
5. Letters — Jawaharlal Nehru's Letters to Chief Ministers, Publications Division, Ministry of Information and Broadcasting, Government of India.

1 THE GREY DAWN

1. Maulana Abul Kalam Azad, *India Wins Freedom*, Orient Longman, p. 203.
2. Maulana Azad, op. cit. p. 225.
3. Ibid, p. 210.
4. Bipan Chandra, *The Rise and Growth of Economic Nationalism in India*, Peoples Publishing House, p. 55.

2 NEHRU ON NEHRU

1. Jawaharlal Nehru, *Discovery of India*, Preface, OUP, p. 10.
2. Ibid, p. 68.
3. Ibid, *Discovery of India*, p. 50.
4. Jawaharlal Nehru, *An Autobiography*, OUP, p. 596.
5. Ibid, p. 599.
6. SW, Vol.12, p. 686 (Letter to his wife Kamala, 19 July 1935)
7. Letter dated 9 April 1944, Mrs. V.L. Pandit's Papers.
8. *Discovery of India*, p. 24.
9. *An Autobiography*, p. 597.

10. Letter to Bharati Sarabhai, 6 July 1931, SW-Vol.V, p. 317.
11. *Discovery of India*, p. 22.
12. Nehru: Letters to his Sister, Hutheesingh, dated 22 March 1944, Ed., Faber and Faber, p. 149.
13. Letter to Kamala Nehru, op. cit.
14. *An Autobiography*, pp. 207-08.
15. B.R. Nanda, *The Nehrus*, OUP, 1962, p. 180.
16. *Discovery of India*, p. 58.
17. Letter to Bernard Hollowood, 22 May 1959.
18. SW, Vol. 13, p. 658, Letter to Padmaja Naidu, 12 Nov. 1936.
19. *An Autobiography*, pp. 77-78.
20. Ibid, p. 77.
21. Ibid, p. 207.
22. Ibid, p. 27.
23. Ibid, p. 48.
24. Tibor Mendes, *Conversations With Nehru*, Secker and Warburg, p. 30.
25. Bipan Chandra et al, *India's Struggle for Independence*, Penguin Books, 1988, p. 266.
26. *An Autobiography*, pp. 194-95.
27. Ibid, p. 606.
28. Nehru, *An Anthology*, Ed. S. Gopal, OUP, 1980, pp. 566-67.

3 NEHRU ON GANDHI

1. *An Autobiography*, p. 73.
2. Ibid, p. 370.
3. Ibid, p. 372-73.
4. Ibid, p. 260.
5. Ibid, p. 76.
6. Ibid, p. 509.
7. Ibid, p. 526.
8. Jawaharlal Nehru, *Whither India*, Kitabistan, Allahabad, 1933, pp. 19 and 34.
9. D.G. Tendulkar, *Mahatma*, Vol.VII, Times of India Press, Bombay, p. 14.
10. *An Autobiography*, p. 516.
11. Ibid, p. 515.
12. Ibid, p. 84.
13. Jawaharlal Nehru, *India and the World*, George Allen and Unwin, p. 33.
14. *An Autobiography*, p. 540.
15. Ibid, p. 543.
16. Ibid, p. 549.

17. Ibid, p. 580-81.
18. *Selected Writings of Jawaharlal Nehru*, 1916-1950, Ed. J.S. Bright, Indian Printing Works, New Delhi, p. 37.
19. Letter to Mahatma Gandhi, SW Vol. III. p. 14.
20. Jawaharlal Nehru, *A Bunch of Old Letters*, Asia Publishing House, 1928, p. 57.
21. SW, Vol. V, p. 489.
22. Jawaharlal Nehru, *A Bunch of Old Letters*, Gandhi's letter to Agatha Harrison, 30 April 1936, op. cit.
23. Tendulkar's *Mahatma*, op. cit., Vol. VI, p. 43.
24. SW, Vol. III, p. 19.
25. Tibor Mende, *Conversations with Mr. Nehru*, Secker and Warburg, p. 36.
26. Ibid, p. 23.
27. *Discovery of India*, p. 473.
28. Tibor Mende, op. cit., p. 23.
29. *An Autobiography*, p. 255.
30. Ibid, p. 509.
31. Tendulkar's *Mahatma*, op. cit. Vol.VI, p. 43.
32. Tibor Mende, op. cit. p. 22.
33. Ibid, p. 29.
34. Ibid, p. 30.
35. Ibid, p. 31.

4 ROOTING OF DEMOCRACY

1. *An Autobiography*, p. 52.
2. *Speeches*, Vol. I, p. 232-33, (8 March 1949).
3. *Discovery of India*, p. 65.
4. Llyod and Susanne H. Rudolph, *The Modernity of Tradition*, Orient Longman, p. 256.
5. Paul R. Brass, *Ethnicity and Nationalism*, Sage Publications, p. 251.
6. Llyod and Susanne H. Rudolph, *In Pursuit of Lakshmi*, Orient Longman, pp. 21-25.
7. R.K. Karanjia, *The Philosophy of Nehru*, Allen and Unwin, p. 139.
8. Quoted by Inder Malhotra, *Indira Gandhi*, Hodder and Stoughton, pp. 61-2.
9. Quoted by Zareer Masani, *Indira Gandhi*, OUP, p. 106.
10. SW (Second Series), Vol. 16-I, p. 340.

5 SOCIALISM: SCIENTIFIC AND OTHERWISE

1. Tibor Mende, *Conversations with Mr. Nehru*, Secker and Warburg, p. 14.
2. *An Autobiography*, p. 163.

3. SW, Vol. II, Report of Brussels Congress, p. 289.
4. SW, Vol. IV, p. 192.
5. SW, Vol. VII, pp. 80-1.
6. Ibid, p. 181-82.
7. *An Autobiography*, p. 302.
8. *An Autobiography*, p. 588.
9. Ibid, p. 552.
10. Ibid, p. 589.
11. Ibid, p. 362-63.
12. Ibid, p. 587.
13. Ibid, p. 591.
14. Ibid, p. 366-67.
15. SW, Vol. VIII, p. 182-83.
16. Sumit Sarkar, *Modern India*, Macmillan, pp. 345-46.
17. Constituent Assembly Debates, Vol.I, p. 97-8.
18. Ibid, p. 60.
19. *Speeches*, Vol. III, p. 17-18.
20. R.K. Karanjia, *The Mind of Nehru*, George Allen and Unwin, p. 100
21. Lok Sabha Debates, 23 May 1956, Vol.V, Part II.
22. Jawaharlal Nehru, *Bunch of Old Letters*, Asia Publishing House. pp. 113-15.
23. Ibid, p. 184.
24. Ibid, p. 197.
25. Michael Brecher, *Nehru — A Political Biography*, OUP, pp. 513-14.
26. Stanley A. Kochenak, *The Congress Party of India*, Princeton University Press, p. 139.
27. Tandon Papers, Quoted by S. Gopal, op. cit. Vol. II, p. 94, Note 126.
28. Stanley A. Kochenak, op. cit. p. 21.
29. S. Gopal, op. cit. Vol. II, p. 94.
30. Ibid, p. 155.
31. Francine R. Frankel, *India's Political Economy*, OUP, p. 5.
32. Letter to Deputy Chairman, Planning Commission, 12 Nov. 1958.
33. Jawaharlal Nehru, *The Basic Approach*, AICC Economic Review, 15 Aug. 1958.
34. Ibid,

6 NEGLECT OF MASS EDUCATION

1. Seven Commandments for South, *Mainstream*, 24 Oct. 1992.
2. A Message to Hindustani Talimi Sangh, 28 Nov. 1957.
3. Tibor Mende, *Conversations with Mr. Nehru*, Secker Warburg, p. 114.
4. pp. 35-36.

5. p. 89.
6. pp. 16 and 18.
7. Directorate of Adult Education, Literacy Digest, Table 8.
8. Ibid.
9. Work, Wages and Well-being in an Indian Metropolis.
10. Ministry of Human Resources, *Challenge of Education*, 1985, p. 5.
11. Myron Weiner, *Compulsory Education and Child Labour*, RGICS, p. 28.
12. Ibid, pp. 23-24.
13. J.P. Naik, op. cit., pp. 13-14.
14. *Seminar*, No. 158 (1972), "Tomorrow Began Yesterday".
15. Ibid, "Breakdown of Schools".
16. *Pedagogy of the Oppressed*, Penguin Books, p. 14.
17. *Economic and Political Weekly*, 21 Nov. 1992.
18. Ibid.
19. Usha Rai, *The Indian Express*, 9 Sept. 1992.
20. N.D. Sharma, *The Indian Express*, 9 Sept. 1992.
21. R.K. Karanjia, *The Philosophy of Nehru*, Allen and Unwin, p. 27.
22. Letter to Bernard Hollowood, 22 May 1959.
23. P. Jarvis et al, *"International Journal of Lifelong Education"*, Jan.-Feb. 1994, p. 39.
24. D.P. Nayar, *Education as Investment*, Ed. Baljit Singh, Meenakshi Prakashan, p. 62
25. Para 2.12(2).
26. Para 2.11.

7 LAND REFORMS DERAILED

1. Daniel Thorner, "Land Reforms", in AR Desai, Ed., *Rural Sociology in India*, Popular Prakashan, Bombay, p. 479.
2. First Five Year Plan, Planning Commission, p. 184.
3. A.M. Khusro, *The Economy of Land Reforms and Farm Size in India*, Macmillan and Co., p. 13.
4. Report of National Commission on Agriculture, Vol. XV, p. 51.
5. The Selected Papers of Wolf Ladejinsky, *Agrarian Reforms an Unfinished Business*, Ed. Louis J Wallinsky, OUP, p. 378.
6. Pranab Bardhan, *The Political Economy of Development in India*, OUP, p. 59 (note).
7. Grigory Kotosky, *Agrarian Reforms in India*, Peoples Publishing House, p. 104.
8. Paul A. Baran, "The Political Economy of Backwardness", in A.R. Desai, Ed., op. cit. p. 904.
9. Letter to H.K. Mahtab, 20 Dec. 1959.

8 COLONIAL BUREAUCRACY PRESERVED

1. *An Autobiography*, p. 445.
2. Letter of 30 May 1948, SW (Second Series), Vol. VI, p. 230.
3. Vishnu Sahai, Jawaharlal Nehru's Impact on Public Administration, *Nehru Centenary Volume*, OUP, p. 554.
4. Letter to Krishna Hutheesingh, 1 Nov. 1947, SW, Vol. IV, (Second Series) p. 585.
5. Letter of 12 Oct. 1947, SW, Vol. IV (Second Series) p. 584.
6. *Speeches*, 21 Dec. 1954, Vol. III, p. 7.
7. Edwin S. Montagu to Lord Chelmsford, Viceroy of India, 15 May 1917.
8. *Letters*, Vol. II, p. 609.
9. Vattachi, *Brown Sahib Revisited*, Penguin Books, pp. 22-23.

9 PLANNING FOR ECONOMIC JUSTICE

1. *The First Five Year Plan*, pp. 31-32.
2. S. Gopal, *Jawaharlal Nehru, A Biography*, Vol. II, p. 159.
3. R.K. Karanjia, *The Philosophy of Nehru*, Allen and Unwin, p. 84.
4. R.K. Karanjia, *The Mind of Mr. Nehru*, Allen and Unwin, p. 50.
5. *Speeches*, Vol. III, p. 53.
6. Lok Sabha Debates, 23 May 1956, Vol. V, Part-III.
7. *Jawaharlal Nehru*, Ministy of Education, p. 20.
8. Meghanad Desai, India: Emerging Contradictions of Slow Capilist Development, Robin Blackburn, Ed., *"Explosion in a Subcontinent"*, Penguin Books, p. 17.
9. Manmohan Singh, quoted by Ishar J. Ahluwalia, *Productivity and Growth in India Manufacturing*, OUP, p. 9.
10. Mabboob-ul-Haq, *The Poverty Curtain*, OUP, p. 19.
11. Ibid, p. 14.
12. Sukhamoy Chakravarty, *Development Planning*, OUP, p. 18.

10 PUBLIC SECTOR'S COMMANDING HEIGHTS

1. S.S. Khera, *Government in Business*, Asia Publishing House, p. 9.
2. K.N. Kabra in Ed. Malcolm A. Adiseshiah, *The Why, What and Whither of Public Sector Enterprises*, Lancer International, p. 85.
3. Pranab Bardhan, *The Political Economy of Development in India*, OUP, p. 72.
4. Malcolm A. Adiseshiah, op. cit. p. 13.
5. S. Gopal, *Jawaharlal Nehru*, Vol. III, p. 111.

11 COMMUNITY DEVELOPMENT AND PANCHAYATI RAJ

1. Jawaharlal Nehru on Community Development, Publications Division, Government of India, p. 22.
2. Bhaskra Rao et al, *Nehru and Administration*, Ajanta Publications, p. 249.
3. Abstracted from Kurukshetra, 2 Oct. 1973, p. 27.
4. *Speeches*, Vol. III, p. 6.

12 NATION IN THE MAKING

1. *Discovery of India*, pp. 562-63.
2. Ibid, p. 67.
3. Ibid, p. 191.
4. Llyod and Susanne Rudolph, *In Pursuit of Lakshmi*, Orient Longman, p. 60.
5. Rashiduddin Khan, *Bewildered India*, Har Anand, New Delhi, p. 294
6. Rajni Kothari, *Seminar 357*, p. 14.
7. K.M. Panikkar, *The Foundations of New India*, op. cit., p. 242. Allied Publishers, p. 49.
8. Paul R. Brass, *Ethnicity and Nationalism*, Sage Publications, p. 157.
9. Address delivered at Scheduled Castes and Scheduled Areas Conference, New Delhi, on 7 June 1952.

13 COMMUNALISM

1. D.F. Karaka, *Nehru — the Lotus Eater of Kashmir*, Derek Verschoyle, p. 104.
2. S. Gopal, *Jawaharlal Nehru*, Vol. II, p. 206
3. *An Autobiography*, p. 374.
4. SW, Vol. VII, p. 69.
5. Ibid, p. 66.
6. *Discovery of India*, p. 246.
7. Llyod and Susanne Rudolph, *In Pursuit of Lakshmi*, Orient Longman, p. 48.
8. Rashiduddin Khan, *Bewildered India*, Har Anand, New Delhi, p. 288.
9. Hamid Dalwai, *Muslim Politics in India*, Nichiketa Publications, Bombay, p. 11.
10. Ibid, p. 18.
11. Ibid, p. 32.
12. Ibid, p. 58.

13. *We or Our Nationalism Defined*, Bharat Prakashan, Delhi, p. 27.
14. SW, Vol. VI, p. 165.
15. *An Autobiography*, p. 136.
16. Bipin Chandra, op. cit. p. 77.
17. Collins Dictionary of Sociology, p. 557.
18. *Discovery of India*, p. 382.
19. Bipin Chandra, op. cit. p. 79.
20. Paper in Socialism on the Threshold of 21st Century, in Milos Nicolic, Ed., Verso p. 66.
21. SW, Vol. IV, p. 573.
22. Llyod and Susanne Rudolph, op. cit. p. 40.
23. Ibid, p. 39-40.
24. Quoted by Bipin Chandra, op. cit. p. 66.
25. I have relied on his *Communalism in Modern India*, and 31st Chapter of *India's Struggle for Independence* for a summary of his views.
26. Randhir Singh, *Theorising Communalism*, EPW, 23 July 1988.
27. Address by M.K. Gandhi to a Missionary Conference in Madras, 2 Feb, 1916.
28. Rashiduddin Khan, op. cit. p. 288.
29. V.S. Narvane,1964, quoted by P.C. Joshi in his paper on "Some Reflections on Indian Secularism and the Gandhi Nehru Tradition".
30. Ibid.
31. Ibid.

14 GOVERNANCE AND INSTITUTIONS

1. S. Gopal, *Jawaharlal Nehru*, Vol. II, p. 214.
2. Ibid, p. 198.
3. Ibid, p. 198.
4. Tibor Mendes, *Conversations with Nehru, Secker and Warburg*, p. 40.
5. S. Gopal, op. cit. p. 309-11.
6. *Speeches*, Vol. III, p. 55.
7. Tibor Mende, op. cit. p. 94.
8. S. Gopal, op. cit., p. 121.
9. Earlier the chief minister of J and K was called prime minister.
10. *Speeches*, Vol. I, p. 197.
11. Letter to B.G. Kher, 26 July 1949, SW (Second Series), Vol. XII, p. 458.
12. S. Gopal, op. cit. Vol. II p. 99. (Letter to Rajagopalachari, 15 April 1951.)
13. Michael Edwards, *Nehru — A Political Biography*, OUP, p. 250.

15 SCIENCE AND CULTURE

1. SW, Vol. IX, p. 616.
2. *Speeches*, Vol.III, p. 164.
3. Motilal Nehru, *Selected Works*, Vol. I, Vikas Publishing House, pp. 94-95.
4. SW, Vol. I, pp. 51-52.
5. Baldev Singh, *Jawaharlal Nehru on Science and Culture*, Nehru Memorial Museum and Library, p. v.
6. Ibid,
7. SW, Vol. VIII, p. 811.
8. Message to Indian Science Congress on its Silver Jubilee, 26 Dec. 1937.
9. SW, Vol.6, p. 265. (Letter to Indira Gandhi from Dehra Doon Jail, 12 July 1934.)
10. Message to Indian Science Congress, op. cit.
11. *Nehru Centenary Volume*, OUP, p. 363.
12. S. Gopal, *Jawaharlal Nehru*, Vol. II, p. 306.
13. Speech at the inauguration of Indian Rare Earths Ltd., 1952.
14. D.S. Kothari, "Science in Universities", in A Chakravarty, Ed., *India Since 1947*, Allied Publishers, p. 309.
15. A. Rahman, "R and D, Economy and Industry", an unpublished paper made available to the author by Dr. A. Rahman.
16. Narrated to the author by Dr. A. Rahman.
17. Prison Diary, SW, Vol. V, p. 461.
18. K.K. Hebar, *Nehru Centenary Volume*, OUP, p. 264.
19. S. Gopal, op. cit. p. 315.

16 FOREIGN AFFAIRS

1. *An Autobiography*, p. 166.
2. Speech at the Asian Congress, *Speeches*, Vol. I, p. 300.
3. *Speeches*, Vol. I, p. 281.
4. *Speeches*, Vol. I, p. 285.
5. Jawaharlal Nehru, *India's Foreign Policy*, Publications Division, Government of India, p. 80.
6. Ibid, p. 79.
7. Ibid, p. 32
8. Nehru's telegram to Nasser, 31 Oct. 1956.
9. Letter to S. Radhakrishnan, 6 Feb. 1950, SW (Second Series),Vol. XIV, p. 543.
10. S. Gopal, op. cit. pp. 254-55.
11. *Speeches*, Vol. I, p. 217.

12. *Letters*, Vol. I, 2 Oct. 1949, p. 471.
13. Nand Lal, *Jawaharlal Nehru*, in V. Grover Ed. ,Deep and Deep Publications, New Delhi, p. 586.

17 PAKISTAN AND KASHMIR

1. S. Gopal, *Jawaharlal Nehru*, Vol. II, p. 20.
2. Sisir Gupta, *Kashmir: Study in India and Pakistan*, Asia Publishing House, p. 101.
3. Ibid, p. 103.
4. Rajindar Sareen, *Pakistan — the India Factor*, Allied Publishers, p. 218.
5. Ibid, p. 432.
6. V.P. Menon, *The Story of Integration of States*, Orient Longman, p. 394.
7. Constituent Assembly Debates, 2 Nov. 1947.
8. Sisir Gupta, op. cit., p. 330.
9. Ibid, p. 330.
10. Nehru's letter to Maharaja of Kashmir, 13 Nov. 1947, in S. Gopal, op. cit., p. 117.
11. S. Gopal, op. cit., p. 118.
12. Quoted by S. Gopal, op. cit. p. 130.
13. Y.D. Gundevia, *Outside the Archives*, Sangam Books, Pune, p. 318.
14. Based on a letter written by Nehru to Patel from Paris on 27 Oct. 1946, S. Gopal, op. cit., p. 33.

18 INDIA-CHINA SHOWDOWN

1. *Bunch of Old Letters*, 26 Nov. Asia Publishing House, p. 276.
2. S. Gopal, *Jawaharlal Nehru*, Vol.III, p. 237.
3. Neville Maxwell, *India's China War*, Jaico Publishing House, p. 108.
4. Sudhakar Bhat, *India and China*, Popular Book Service, p. 141.
5. Ibid, p. 142.
6. Neville Maxwell, op. cit. p. 118-19.
7. S. Gopal, op. cit. p. 134.
8. T. Karki Hussain, *Sino Indian Conflict*, Thomson Press (India), p. 13.
9. N. Maxwell, op. cit. p. 82.
10. Brig. J.P. Dalvi, op. cit. p. 38
11. Ram Gopal, *India-China-Tibet Triangle*, Pustak Kendra, Lucknow, p. 105.
12. Frank Moraes, *Witness to an Era*, Vikas Publishing House, p. 220-21.
13. D.R. Mankekar, *The Guilty Men of 1962*, The Tulsi Shah Enterprises, Bombay, p. 110.
14. S. Gopal, op. cit. Vol. II., p. 190.
15. Ibid, pp. 181 and 197.

16. Ibid, Vol. III, pp. 36-37.
17. B.R. Nanda, Ed., *India's Foreign Policy*, Vikas Publishing House, p. 125.
18. N. Maxwell, op. cit. p. 202.
19. S. Gopal, op. cit. p. 204.
20. Ibid, p. 218.
21. Brig. J.P. Dalvi, op. cit. p. 86.
22. N. Maxwell, op. cit. p. 354.
23. S. Gopal, op. cit. Vol. II, pp. 108-09.
24. S. Gopal, op. cit. Vol. III, p. 220.
25. *Letters*, 28 Oct. 1962.

19 NEHRU — THE MAN

1. *Discovery of India*, p. 24.
2. Ibid, p. 566.
3. SW, Vol. I, p. 338, (Letter to Father, 1 Sept.1922).
4. Letter, 30 June 1955, in S. Gopal, *Jawaharlal Nehru*, Vol.II, p. 236.
5. *Nehru Centenary Volume*, OUP, p. 438.
   Unwin, p. 133 and 23.
6. Ibid, p. 19.
7. *Nehru Centenary Volume*, OUP, p. 605.
8. Ibid, p. 442.
9. S. Gopal, *Jawaharlal Nehru*, Vol. I, p. 87.
10. *An Autobiography*, p. 40.
11. Ibid, p. 479.
12. Ibid, p. 562-63.
13. Ibid, p. 561.
14. Ibid, pp. 40-41.
15. Ibid, p. 42.
16. Ibid, p. 43.
17. *An Autobiography*, p. 20
18. M.J. Akbar, *Nehru*, Viking, p. 569; D.Y. Gundevia, *Outside the Archives*, Sangam Books, p. 157.
19. Pupul Jayakar, *Indira Gandhi*, Viking, pp. 91-92.
20. M.O. Mathai, *Reminiscences of Nehru Age*, Vikas Publishing House, pp. 204-07.
21. S. Gopal, op. cit. Vol. III, p. 108.
22. R. Zakaria, Ed., *A Study of Nehru*, Times of India Publication, p. 177.
23. Amiya and B.G. Rao, *Six Thousand Days*, Sterling Publications, p. 369
24. Ibid, p. 370.
25. S Gopal, op. cit. Vol. III, p. 300.
26. Ibid, p. 270.

27. *India Wins Freedom*, Revised Edition (1988), Orient Longman, p. 180.
28. Rafiq Zakaria, op. cit. p. 155.
29. R.K. Karanjia, *The Mind of Nehru*, George Allen and Unwin, p. 79.
30. *An Autobiography*, p. 173.
31. Michael Edwards, *Nehru — A Political Biography*, Allen Lane, p. 259.
32. Ibid, p. 250.
33. Rajkumari Amrit Kaur Ed., in *Nehru Abhinandan Granth*, Granth Committee, New Delhi, p. 140.
34. *An Autobiography*, p. 377.
35. *Discovery of India*, p. 513.
36. *An Autobiography*, p. 377.
37. *Discovery of India*, p. 131.
38. *An Autobiogrphy*, p. 377.
39. SW, Vol. V, p. 459, (Letter to Bapu from prison, 7 March 1933).
40. *Discovery of India*, p. 26.
41. *An Autobiography*, p. 377.
42. *Discovery of India*, p. 27.
43. Ibid, p. 445.
44. Ibid, p. 532.
45. *Discovery of India*, p. 512.
46. *Speeches*, Vol. III, p. 433.
47. R.K. Karanjia, op. cit. p. 32.
48. *Discovery of India*, p. 32.
49. Ibid.
50. Ibid, p. 31.
51. Ibid, p. 87.
52. SW, Vol. Letter, 4 Sept. 1948, p. 501.
53. Swarajya, 6 June 1964.
54. *Nehru Centenary Volume*, OUP, p. 719.

21 BORN TO RULE

1. Inder Malhotra, *Indira Gandhi*, Hodder and Stoughton, p. 83.
2. Ibid, p. 84.
3. Kuldip Nayar, Interview, 11 Nov. 1965.
4. Pupal Jayakar, *Indira Gandhi*, Viking, pp. 176-77.
5. Michael Brecher, *Succession in India*, OUP, p194.
6. Ibid, p. 193.
7. Ibid, p. 202.
8. Pupul Jayakar, op. cit., p. 187.

22 SHAKY START

1. Indira Gandhi, *My Truth*, Vision Books, p. 116.
2. Uma Vasudeva, *Indira Gandhi*, Publishing House, p. 44.

23 THE MASTER STRATEGIST

1. Pupul Jayakar, *Indira Gandhi*, Viking, p. 196.
2. Ibid, p. 199.
3. *The Times of India*, 24 Dec. 1966.
4. I.K. Gujral in an interview with the author. Gujral was with Indira Gandhi at Bangalore and personally witnessed this drama.
5. Ibid, pp. 35-36.

26 EMERGENCY: PHASE-I

1. Narrated to the author by Chandrajit Yadav.
2. Narrated to the author by N.K. Mukarji.
3. Pupul Jayakar, *Indira Gandhi*, Viking, p. 272.
4. Narrated to the author by Subhadra Joshi.
5. Ibid.
6. Narrated to the author by I.K. Gujral.
7. Narrated to the author by Nikhil Chakravartty.
8. D.R. and Kamla Mankekar, *Decline and Fall of Indira Gandhi*, Vision Books, p. 5.
9. Kuldip Nayar, *The Judgement*, Vikas Publishing House, p. 24.
10. Narrated to the author by N.K. Mukarji.
11. J.B. Kriplani, *The Nightmare and After*, Popular Prakashan, p. 32.
12. Pupul Jayakar, op. cit., p. 278.
13. Narrated to the author by I.K. Gujral.
14. Ibid.

27 EMERGENCY: PHASE-II

1. Pupul Jayakar, *Indira Gandhi*, Viking, pp. 304-07.
2. Ibid.
3. J.B. Kriplani, *The Nightmare and After*, Popular Prakashan, p. 29.
4. David Selbourne, *An Eye on India*, Penguin Books, p. 29
5. Narrated to the author by Subhadra Joshi.
6. Pupul Jayakar, op. cit. p. 296.
7. Narrated to the author by Chandrajit Yadav.
8. Narrated to the author by Mohd. Yunus.
9. Pupul Jayakar, op. cit., pp. 252-53.

28 INTERREGNUM-II

1. Pupul Jayakar, *Indira Gandhi*, Viking, p. 321.
2. Ibid, p. 333.
3. Ibid, p. 337.

29 THE COME-BACK

1. Pupul Jayakar, *Indira Gandhi*, Viking, p. 412.
2. A.G. Noorani, "Indira Gandhi and Indian Muslims"; *EPW*, 3 Nov. 1990.
3. Ibid.
4. Ibid.
5. Pupul Jayakar, op. cit. p. 445.
6. P.C. Alexander, *My Years With Indira Gandhi*, Vision Books, p. 35.
7. Inder Malhotra, *Indira Gandhi*, Hodder and Stoughton, p. 297.

30 OPERATION BLUE STAR AND AFTER

1. Hindu-Sikh population ratio in Punjab is genereally reported as 48:52. As per 1981 census the population of Punjab was 1,67,88,915, out of which 62,00,195 were Hindus and 1,01,99,141 Sikhs. This gives a ratio of 36.9 percent Hindus and 60.75 percent Sikhs. (The balance is made up of Jains, Christians and others.)
2. Indira Gandhi, *My Truth*, Vision Books, pp. 117-18.
3. Mark Tully and Satish Jacob, *Amritsar*, Rupa and Co., p. 62.
4. Kuldip Nayar and Khushwant Singh, *Tragedy of Punjab*, Vision Books, p. 43.
5. Ibid, p. 72.
6. Mark Tully et al, op. cit. pp. 134-35.
7. pp. 69-78.
8. Kuldip Nayar et al, op. cit., p. 44.
9. op. cit. p. 79.
10. Kuldip nayar et al, op. cit., p. 61-63.
11. op. cit. p. 91.
12. Mark Tully et al, op. cit., p. 117.
13. Mark Tully et al, op. cit., p. 134.
14. Ibid, p. 172.
15. op. cit., p. 440.
16. Ibid.
17. Ibid, p. 441
18. Ibid, p. 481.

31 ECONOMY AND DEVELOPMENT

1. Ishar J. Ahluwalia, "Contribution of Planning to Indian Industrialisation", in Terence Byre, Ed., *The State and Development Planning in India*, OUP, p. 360.
2. Zareer Masani, *Indira Gandhi*, OUP, p. 282.
3. Ishar J. Ahluwalia, op. cit., p. 373.
4. Rakesh Mohan, "Industrial Policy and Controls", in Bimal Jalan Ed., *The Indian Economy*, Viking, p. 108.
5. Second Five Year Plan, pp. 96-99.
6. Rakesh Mohan, op. cit., p. 89.
7. B.S. Minhas et al, "Declining Incidence of Poverty in 1980s: Evidence Vs Artifacts", *EPW*, 6-13 July, 1991.
8. *The Hindustan Times*, 21 Dec. 1991.
9. T.S. Papola, "The Question of Unemployment", in Bimal Jalan Ed., op. cit. p. 308.
10. T.S. Papola, op. cit. p. 307.

32 FOREIGN POLICY

1. *The Times of India*, 4 April 1975.
2. D.P. Dhar's version was later contested by Abdul Sattar in a four-part article published in *Dawn* in July 1995. Sattar was Director General in the Pakistan Foreign Office when the Simla Agreement was signed. He claims that the Agreement was signed under conditions of 'coercion and blackmail', and hints that it may be repudiated one day. He refutes Dhar's claim of an oral understanding reached with Bhutto. But as Sattar was not present at the meeting and Dhar was, it is likely that Dhar's version is based on greater access to inside information.
3. Quoted by Abdul Sattar in the above article.
4. *The Hindustan Times*, 22 June 1984.
5. Inder Malhotra, *Indira Gandhi*, Hodder and Stoughton, pp. 218-19.
6. Ibid, p. 96.
7. Uma Vasudeva, *Indira Gandhi*, Vikas Publishing House, p. 360.
8. Pupul Jayakar, *Indira Gandhi*, Viking, p. 191.

33 STATECRAFT AND STYLE

1. Narrated to the author by I.K. Gujral.
2. Both these incidents were narrated to the author by I.K. Gujral.
3. Ibid.
4. Narrated to the author.

5. P.C. Alexander, *My Years with Indira Gandhi*, Vision Books, p. 59.
6. Narrated to the author.
7. Mary Carras, *Indira Gandhi*, Beacon Press, Boston, p. 239.
8. Ibid.
9. Ibid, pp. 243-44.
10. Ibid, p. 250.
11. Pupul Jayakar, *Indira Gandhi*, Viking, p. 158.
12. Cited with the permissiom of Admiral S.M. Nanda.
13. Narrated to the author by I.K. Gujral.
14. Janardan Thakar, *All the Prime Minister's Men*, Vikas Publishing House, p. 169.
15. op. cit., p. 154
16. Zareer Masani, *Indira Gandhi*, OUP, p. 155.
17. Llyod I. and Susanne H. Rudolph, *In Pursuit of Lakshmi*, Orient Longman, p. 84.

34 THE PERSON

1. Pupul Jayakar, *Indira Gandhi*, Viking, p. 479.
2. Dorothy Norman, *Indira Gandhi: Letters to a Friend*, Weidenfeld and Nicholson, p. 29.
3. Ibid, p. 57.
4. Pupul Jayakar, op. cit., p. 187.
5. Ibid, p. 479.
6. Nayantara Sehgal, *Indira Gandhi: Emergence and Style*, Vikas Publishing House, pp. 24-25.
7. Pupul Jayakar, op. cit., p. 190.
8. Ibid, pp. 203-04.
9. Inder Malhotra, *Indira Gandhi*, Hodder and Stoughton, p. 289.
10. Zareer Masani, *Indira Gandhi*, OUP, p. 262.
11. Narrated to the author by H.Y. Sharada Prasad, Information Adviser to Mrs. Gandhi.
12. Narrated to the author by N.K. Mukarji.
13. Pupul Jayakar, op. cit., p. 189.
14. Indira Gandhi, *My Truth*, Vision Books, p. 55.
15. B.R. Nanda, *The Nehrus*, OUP, p. 329.
16. Ibid, p. 273-74.
17. Ibid, p. 312-13.
18. *The Philosophy of Mr. Nehru*, Allen and Unwin, p. 42.
19. *The Illustrated Weekly of India*, 14-20 Nov. 1976.
20. Durga Das, *India From Curzon to Nehru and After*, Collins, pp. 370-71.

21. In an interview to Francine Frankel, *India's Political Economy — 1947-1977*, OUP, p. 242.
22. Kuldip Nayar, *Between the Lines*, Allied Publishers, p. 17.
23. Ibid, p. 9.
24. H.D. Malviya in an interview to Janardan Thakar, *All the Prime Minister's Men*, Vikas Publishing House, p. 18.
25. *After Nehru Who?*, Rupert Hart-Davis, p. 159.
26. Pupul Jayakar, op. cit., pp. 291 and 403.
27. Ibid, p. 404.

35 TRAGIC ACCESSION

1. P.C. Alexander, *My Years With Indira Gandhi*, Vision Books, p. 154.
2. Rahul Kuldip Bedi, "Politics of a Pogram", a report, in Arun Shourie Ed., *The Assassination and After*, Roli Books International, p. 52-55.
3. Ibid, p. 58.
4. Arun Shourie, *Them and Us*, op. cit. p. 83.
5. Ibid, p. 83.
6. Dharma Kumar, *The Times of India*, 15 Nov. 1984.
7. Pupul Jayakar, *Indira Gandhi*, Viking, p. 417.
8. Nicholas Nugent, *Rajiv Gandhi*, Universal Book Stall, p. 48.
9. Ibid, p. 54.

37 ADMINISTRATION

1. Rajiv Gandhi, "Responsive Administration", inaugural speech delivered at the Workshop of district collectors at Hyderabad on 13 Feb. 1988.
2. *Sunday*, Interview, 13-19 Nov. 1988.
3. Narrated to the author by Arif Mohd. Khan.
4. Ibid.
5. Ibid.
6. Ibid.
7. Narrated to the author by the concerned officer.
8. Narrated to the author by Arif Mohd. Khan.
9. Nicholas Nugent, *Rajiv Gandhi*, Universal Book Stall, p. 187.
10. Narrated to the author by Arif Mohd. Khan.

38 THE ECONOMY

1. Sudipto Munde and Govinda Rao, "Issues in Fiscal Policy", in Bimal Jalan Ed., *The Indian Economy*, p. 238.
2. Ibid, pp. 231-32.
3. *Science in History*, Penguin Books, Vol. I. p. 15.

39 ACCORDS OF DISCORDS

1. Ram Pradhan, *Working With Rajiv Gandhi*, HarperCollins, pp. 51-52. (As Home Secretary, Pradhan was present at this meeting.)
2. Ibid, p. 53.
3. *India Today*, 15 August 1985.
4. op. cit., p. 81.

40 THE SMOKING GUN

1. *Sunday*, 3-9 Sept. 1989.
2. *India Today*, Interview, 1-15 March 1988.
3. Ibid.
4. Chitra Subramaniam, *Bofors: The Story Behind the News*, Viking, p. 124.
5. *Sunday*, Rajiv Gandhi's Interview, 13-19 Nov. 1988.
6. Narrated to the author by Mani Shankar Aiyar.
7. *Sunday*, 13-19 Nov. 1988.
8. Ibid.
9. Ibid.
10. Narrated to the author by B.M. Oza, the ambassador.
11. Chitra Subramaniam, op. cit. p. 9.
12. Ibid, p. 55.
13. Ibid, p. 191.
14. Ibid, p. 243-44.
15. *India Today*, 15 May, 1987.
16. Chitra Subramaniam, op. cit., pp. 142 and 233.

41 FOREIGN RELATIONS

1. *Sunday*, 3 Jan. 1987.
2. J.N. Dixit, *Anatomy of a Flawed Inheritance*, Konark Publishers, p. 104.
3. Ibid.
4. *India Today*, Interview, 15 Aug. 1987.
5. P.R. Chari, Stephen P. Cohen, et al, *Brasstacks and After:, an ACDIS Study*, p. 21.
6. Narrated to the author by Mani Shankar Aiyar.
7. Narrated to the author by Natwar Singh.
8. P.R. Chari et al, op. cit., p. 25.
9. The two incidents cited here have been narrated to the author by primary sources on condition of anonimity.
10. Narrated to the author by Natwar Singh.
11. P.R. Chari et al, op. cit., p. 23.

12. Narrated to the author by A.P. Venkateswaran.
13. P.R. Chari et al. op. cit., p. 32.

42 MAKING OF A LEADER

1. Narrated to the author by Arun Nehru.
2. *Sunday,* 13-19 Nov. 1988.
3. *Sunday,* 27 Nov.-3 Dec. 1988.
4. Narrated to the author by Arun Nehru.
5. Ibid.
6. *Sunday,* 1-7 May 1988.
7. Ibid.
8. Rajiv Desai, Interview, in Harish Chandra, Ed., *Rajiv Gandhi: Many Faces*, Noida News Pvt. Ltd., Delhi, p. 126.

43 POLITICAL MANAGEMENT

1. Sonia Gandhi, *Rajiv*, Viking, p. 15.

44 AN OVERVIEW

1. I have already dealt with the matter in Chapter 34, pp. 376-78.
2. *The Fontana Dictionary of Modern Thought*, Second Edition, p. 77.
3. Rajni Kothari, *Politics and the People*, Vol. II, Aspects Publications Ltd., p. 500.
4. Eric Hobswan, *Age of Extremes*, Viking, p. 261.
5. F.H. Cordoso, *Social Consequences of Globalisation*, India International Centre, 1996.
6. Eric Hobswan. op. cit., p. 269.
7. (1) Percentages given here are opproximate. They have been collected from various reports and research workers, as no systematic, official survey is available on this subject.
   (2) Some of these outstanding examples of industrial growth are hardly known to the common person, and to highlight this point I have deliberately not mentioned the states where these towns are located.
8. R.P. Adler, Ed., *Understanding Television*, Praeger Publishers, p. 197.

Index